Individual Income Taxation

Individual Income Taxation

An Application Approach

Joni Larson

PROFESSOR AND ASSISTANT DIRECTOR OF THE
GRADUATE TAX PROGRAM
THOMAS M. COOLEY LAW SCHOOL

CAROLINA ACADEMIC PRESS

Durham, North Carolina

Library of Congress Cataloging-in-Publication Data

Larson, Joni.
 Individual income taxation : an application approach / Joni Larson.
     pages cm
 Includes bibliographical references and index.
 ISBN 978-1-61163-154-8 (alk. paper)
 1. Income tax--Law and legislation--United States. I. Title.

 KF6369.L37 2013
 343.7305'2--dc23

                        2012051082

Carolina Academic Press
700 Kent Street
Durham, North Carolina 27701
Telephone (919) 489-7486
Fax (919) 493-5668
www.cap-press.com

Printed in the United States of America

Contents

V · BUSINESSES

VII • Timing Methodologies

VIII · CHARACTERIZATION

IX · Non-Recognition Provisions

X · Assignment of Income

I

Introduction to
Federal Income Tax

Chapter 1

Introduction to Federal Income Tax

The Internal Revenue Code is the collection of statutes that make up our Federal taxing system. It is a system based on income, with its objective to impose tax each year on a taxpayer's accession to wealth.

Unless otherwise permitted, each taxpayer must report all gross income. Income can be derived from many sources, such as salary, investment activities (e.g., interest, dividends), and business profits. To this end, the Code has several provisions defining what is included in gross income. It also has several Code provisions specifically allowing the taxpayer to exclude (not report) certain types of income.

> Accessions to wealth
> – <u>Excludable income</u>
> = Gross income

Each taxpayer must report his gross income from investment activities. However, the taxpayer's accession to wealth is income from the investment activity, less the costs he incurred to generate the investment income. The Code specifically identifies deductions related to generating investment income; the taxpayer can claim these deductions to determine his net investment income.

Each taxpayer must report his gross income from business activities. To tax only the taxpayer's accession to wealth, he is allowed to deduct costs he incurred to generate the business income. The Code specifically identifies deductions the taxpayer can claim to determine his net business income.

Even though the tax is to be imposed on the taxpayer's accession to wealth, he is not entitled to claim a deduction unless it is specifically allowed by the Code. In general, no deductions are allowed for personal expenses. That having been said, there are many such deductions authorized, such as for home mortgage interest, charitable contributions, and medical expenses. Given their personal nature, in most instances while some deductions are allowed, the amount that may be deducted is limited.

The Code provides the framework for identifying these different sources of income, identifying allowable deductions, and combining the amounts to determine taxable income. It provides the tax rates that apply to different types of income and to different layers of taxable income. In general, the taxpayer determines his tax liability as follows:

First: Determine the taxpayer's gross income. It includes his net income from business activities, his net income from investment activities, and any other sources of gross income. It does not include any items specifically permitted to be excluded.

Second: Determine adjusted gross income. The taxpayer's gross income is reduced by specifically-identified deductions. Because there is no percentage limitation applicable to these deductions, they often are referred to as "above the line" deductions.

>   Gross income
>   – <u>Above the line deductions</u>
>   = Adjusted gross income

Third: Determine taxable income. The taxpayer's adjusted gross income is reduce by the personal exemption and either the standard deduction or itemized deductions (whichever is greater). Itemized deductions often are referred to as "below the line" deductions because some are allowed only to the extent they exceed a percentage of adjusted gross income.

>   Adjusted gross income
>   – Personal exemption
>   – <u>Standard deduction or itemized deductions</u>
>   = Taxable income

Fourth: Determine the tax liability. The taxpayer's tax liability is determined by multiplying taxable income by the applicable tax rate. The tax rates are graduated, meaning that as the amount of income increases, the tax rate on additional amounts or layers of income increases. In addition, some types of income are taxed at lower, preferential, rates. If the taxpayer is entitled to a credit, he can reduce his tax liability by the amount of the credit.

It may seem the computation of a taxpayer's tax liability is nothing more than filling in the blanks on a tax return. However, the amounts that are reported on the tax return are based on an understanding and interpretation of the Code. As with any other statutory system, controversy can arise as to correct interpretation. To avoid possible imposition of penalties, the attorney advising his client generally must be able to establish that his interpretation is supported by substantial authority.

Moreover, an attorney knowledgeable about tax law can assist his client in structuring his business, investment, and personal activities so that they result in the least amount of tax liability. The legal minimization of tax liability has long been recognized as acceptable tax planning.

> "The legal right of a taxpayer to decrease the amount of what otherwise would be his taxes, or altogether avoid them, by means which the law permits, cannot be doubted." As a general rule a tax avoidance motive is not to be considered in determining the tax liability resulting from the transaction.[1]

Finally, individuals (meeting a minimum income requirement), partnerships, corporations, trusts, etc. are required to file a tax return. Accordingly, any client may have a tax issue and that issue can arise in any area of legal practice, from divorce law to criminal matters to environmental concerns. Accordingly, every attorney, even those who do not practice tax law, must be able to identify a tax issue to properly assist his client. It may be helpful to understand that tax issues can be grouped into the following broad categories:

- What is gross income? What can be excluded from gross income?

- When there is gross income, who must report it?

---

1. Cowden v. Commissioner, 289 F.2d 20, 23 (5th Cir. 1961), quoting Gregory v. Helvering, 293 U.S. 465 (1935).

- What deductions, whether personal, related to an investment activity, or arising from a business, is the taxpayer permitted to deduct?
- What tax rate applies to income and gains? Are there any limits on the amount of loss that can be claimed?
- In what year must the taxpayer report income? In what year must the taxpayer report deductions?

Take a moment and review the Form 1040, U.S. Individual Income Tax Return, and Schedule A, Itemized Deductions. Consider the following:

- Where is gross income reported?
- What gross income items are represented on this part of the return?
- What deductions are allowed in determining adjusted gross income? Are the deductions business related, investment related, or personal in nature?
- Where is "adjusted gross income" reflected?
- Where is the taxpayer asked to choose between the standard deduction and itemized deductions?
- If the taxpayer elects to itemize, where are those deductions listed?
- What itemized deductions are allowed? Are the deductions business related, investment related, or personal in nature?
- Which itemized deductions are limited by the amount of adjusted gross income?
- Where is "taxable income" reflected?
- Where is the total tax liability reflected?
- Having determined total tax liability, how does the taxpayer determine how much he still owes or whether he is entitled to a refund?

Exhibit: Form 1040

Form 1040 — Department of the Treasury—Internal Revenue Service (99) — U.S. Individual Income Tax Return — **2012** — OMB No. 1545-0074 — IRS Use Only—Do not write or staple in this space.

For the year Jan. 1–Dec. 31, 2012, or other tax year beginning , 2012, ending , 20 — See separate instructions.

Your first name and initial — Last name — Your social security number

If a joint return, spouse's first name and initial — Last name — Spouse's social security number

Home address (number and street). If you have a P.O. box, see instructions. — Apt. no. — ☒ Make sure the SSN(s) above and on line 6c are correct.

City, town or post office, state, and ZIP code. If you have a foreign address, also complete spaces below (see instructions).

Foreign country name — Foreign province/state/county — Foreign postal code

Presidential Election Campaign — Check here if you, or your spouse if filing jointly, want $3 to go to this fund. Checking a box below will not change your tax or refund. ☐ You ☐ Spouse

Filing Status — Check only one box.
1 ☐ Single
2 ☐ Married filing jointly (even if only one had income)
3 ☐ Married filing separately. Enter spouse's SSN above and full name here. ☒
4 ☐ Head of household (with qualifying person). (See instructions.) If the qualifying person is a child but not your dependent, enter this child's name here. ☒
5 ☐ Qualifying widow(er) with dependent child

Exemptions
6a ☐ Yourself. If someone can claim you as a dependent, do not check box 6a
b ☐ Spouse
c Dependents:
(1) First name Last name | (2) Dependent's social security number | (3) Dependent's relationship to you | (4) ☒ if child under age 17 qualifying for child tax credit (see instructions)

If more than four dependents, see instructions and check here ☒ ☐

d Total number of exemptions claimed

Boxes checked on 6a and 6b — No. of children on 6c who: • lived with you • did not live with you due to divorce or separation (see instructions) — Dependents on 6c not entered above — Add numbers on lines above ☒

Income

Attach Form(s) W-2 here. Also attach Forms W-2G and 1099-R if tax was withheld.

If you did not get a W-2, see instructions.

Enclose, but do not attach, any payment. Also, please use Form 1040-V.

7 Wages, salaries, tips, etc. Attach Form(s) W-2 — 7
8a Taxable interest. Attach Schedule B if required — 8a
b Tax-exempt interest. Do not include on line 8a — 8b
9a Ordinary dividends. Attach Schedule B if required — 9a
b Qualified dividends — 9b
10 Taxable refunds, credits, or offsets of state and local income taxes — 10
11 Alimony received — 11
12 Business income or (loss). Attach Schedule C or C-EZ — 12
13 Capital gain or (loss). Attach Schedule D if required. If not required, check here ☒ ☐ — 13
14 Other gains or (losses). Attach Form 4797 — 14
15a IRA distributions 15a b Taxable amount — 15b
16a Pensions and annuities 16a b Taxable amount — 16b
17 Rental real estate, royalties, partnerships, S corporations, trusts, etc. Attach Schedule E — 17
18 Farm income or (loss). Attach Schedule F — 18
19 Unemployment compensation — 19
20a Social security benefits 20a b Taxable amount — 20b
21 Other income. List type and amount — 21
22 Combine the amounts in the far right column for lines 7 through 21. This is your total income ☒ — 22

Adjusted Gross Income

23 Educator expenses — 23
24 Certain business expenses of reservists, performing artists, and fee-basis government officials. Attach Form 2106 or 2106-EZ — 24
25 Health savings account deduction. Attach Form 8889 — 25
26 Moving expenses. Attach Form 3903 — 26
27 Deductible part of self-employment tax. Attach Schedule SE — 27
28 Self-employed SEP, SIMPLE, and qualified plans — 28
29 Self-employed health insurance deduction — 29
30 Penalty on early withdrawal of savings — 30
31a Alimony paid b Recipient's SSN ☒ — 31a
32 IRA deduction — 32
33 Student loan interest deduction — 33
34 Tuition and fees. Attach Form 8917 — 34
35 Domestic production activities deduction. Attach Form 8903 — 35
36 Add lines 23 through 35 — 36
37 Subtract line 36 from line 22. This is your adjusted gross income ☒ — 37

For Disclosure, Privacy Act, and Paperwork Reduction Act Notice, see separate instructions. — Cat. No. 11320B — Form **1040** (2012)

Exhibit: U.S. Individual Income Tax Return

Form 1040 (2012)   Page **2**

Tax and Credits	38	Amount from line 37 (adjusted gross income)	38
	39a	Check { ☐ You were born before January 2, 1948, ☐ Blind. } Total boxes	
		if: { ☐ Spouse was born before January 2, 1948, ☐ Blind. } checked ▷ 39a	
Standard Deduction for—	b	If your spouse itemizes on a separate return or you were a dual-status alien, check here ▷ 39b☐	
• People who check any box on line 39a or 39b or who can be claimed as a dependent, see instructions.	40	Itemized deductions (from Schedule A) or your standard deduction (see left margin) . .	40
	41	Subtract line 40 from line 38	41
	42	Exemptions. Multiply $3,800 by the number on line 6d	42
	43	Taxable income. Subtract line 42 from line 41. If line 42 is more than line 41, enter -0- . .	43
	44	Tax (see instructions). Check if any from: a ☐ Form(s) 8814 b ☐ Form 4972 c ☐ 962 election	44
• All others:	45	Alternative minimum tax (see instructions). Attach Form 6251	45
Single or Married filing separately, $5,950	46	Add lines 44 and 45 . . . . ▷	46
	47	Foreign tax credit. Attach Form 1116 if required	47	
Married filing jointly or Qualifying widow(er), $11,900	48	Credit for child and dependent care expenses. Attach Form 2441	48	
	49	Education credits from Form 8863, line 19	49	
	50	Retirement savings contributions credit. Attach Form 8880	50	
Head of household, $8,700	51	Child tax credit. Attach Schedule 8812, if required . . .	51	
	52	Residential energy credits. Attach Form 5695	52	
	53	Other credits from Form: a ☐ 3800 b ☐ 8801 c ☐ ___	53	
	54	Add lines 47 through 53. These are your total credits	54
	55	Subtract line 54 from line 46. If line 54 is more than line 46, enter -0- . . . . . ▷	55
Other Taxes	56	Self-employment tax. Attach Schedule SE	56
	57	Unreported social security and Medicare tax from Form: a ☐ 4137 b ☐ 8919 . .	57
	58	Additional tax on IRAs, other qualified retirement plans, etc. Attach Form 5329 if required . . .	58
	59a	Household employment taxes from Schedule H	59a
	b	First-time homebuyer credit repayment. Attach Form 5405 if required	59b
	60	Other taxes. Enter code(s) from instructions	60
	61	Add lines 55 through 60. This is your total tax . . . . ▷	61
Payments	62	Federal income tax withheld from Forms W-2 and 1099 . .	62	
	63	2012 estimated tax payments and amount applied from 2011 return	63	
If you have a qualifying child, attach Schedule EIC.	64a	Earned income credit (EIC)	64a	
	b	Nontaxable combat pay election 64b		
	65	Additional child tax credit. Attach Schedule 8812	65	
	66	American opportunity credit from Form 8863, line 8	66	
	67	Reserved	67	
	68	Amount paid with request for extension to file	68	
	69	Excess social security and tier 1 RRTA tax withheld . . .	69	
	70	Credit for federal tax on fuels. Attach Form 4136 . . .	70	
	71	Credits from Form: a ☐ 2439 b ☐ Reserved c ☐ 8801 d ☐ 8885	71	
	72	Add lines 62, 63, 64a, and 65 through 71. These are your total payments . . . . . ▷	72
Refund	73	If line 72 is more than line 61, subtract line 61 from line 72. This is the amount you overpaid	73
	74a	Amount of line 73 you want refunded to you. If Form 8888 is attached, check here . ▷ ☐	74a
Direct deposit? See instructions.	▷ b	Routing number ||||||||| ▷ c Type: ☐ Checking ☐ Savings	
	▷ d	Account number |||||||||	
	75	Amount of line 73 you want applied to your 2013 estimated tax ▷ 75	
Amount You Owe	76	Amount you owe. Subtract line 72 from line 61. For details on how to pay, see instructions . ▷	76
	77	Estimated tax penalty (see instructions) 77	

Third Party Designee	Do you want to allow another person to discuss this return with the IRS (see instructions)? ☐ Yes. Complete below. ☐ No		
	Designee's name ▷	Phone no. ▷	Personal identification number (PIN) ▷

Sign Here	Under penalties of perjury, I declare that I have examined this return and accompanying schedules and statements, and to the best of my knowledge and belief, they are true, correct, and complete. Declaration of preparer (other than taxpayer) is based on all information of which preparer has any knowledge.		
Joint return? See instructions. Keep a copy for your records.	Your signature	Date	Your occupation	Daytime phone number
	Spouse's signature. If a joint return, both must sign.	Date	Spouse's occupation	If the IRS sent you an Identity Protection PIN, enter it here (see inst.)

Paid Preparer Use Only	Print/Type preparer's name	Preparer's signature	Date	Check ☐ self-employed	PTIN
	Firm's name ▷			Firm's EIN ▷	
	Firm's address ▷			Phone no.	

Form **1040** (2012)

Exhibit: Schedule A, Itemized Deductions

SCHEDULE A (Form 1040)	Itemized Deductions	OMB No. 1545-0074
Department of the Treasury Internal Revenue Service (99)	☒ Information about Schedule A and its separate instructions is at www.irs.gov/form1040 .	**2012**
	☒ Attach to Form 1040.	Attachment Sequence No. 07

Name(s) shown on Form 1040		Your social security number

Medical and Dental Expenses	Caution. Do not include expenses reimbursed or paid by others.	
	1 Medical and dental expenses (see instructions)	1
	2 Enter amount from Form 1040, line 38 [2]	
	3 Multiply line 2 by 7.5% (.075)	3
	4 Subtract line 3 from line 1. If line 3 is more than line 1, enter -0-	4
Taxes You Paid	5 State and local (check only one box):	
	a ☐ Income taxes, or ⎫	5
	b ☐ General sales taxes ⎭	
	6 Real estate taxes (see instructions)	6
	7 Personal property taxes	7
	8 Other taxes. List type and amount ☒ _____	
		8
	9 Add lines 5 through 8	9
Interest You Paid **Note.** Your mortgage interest deduction may be limited (see instructions).	10 Home mortgage interest and points reported to you on Form 1098	10
	11 Home mortgage interest not reported to you on Form 1098. If paid to the person from whom you bought the home, see instructions and show that person's name, identifying no., and address ☒ _____	
		11
	12 Points not reported to you on Form 1098. See instructions for special rules	12
	13 Mortgage insurance premiums (see instructions)	13
	14 Investment interest. Attach Form 4952 if required. (See instructions.)	14
	15 Add lines 10 through 14	15
Gifts to Charity If you made a gift and got a benefit for it, see instructions.	16 Gifts by cash or check. If you made any gift of $250 or more, see instructions	16
	17 Other than by cash or check. If any gift of $250 or more, see instructions. You must attach Form 8283 if over $500 . . .	17
	18 Carryover from prior year	18
	19 Add lines 16 through 18	19
Casualty and Theft Losses	20 Casualty or theft loss(es). Attach Form 4684. (See instructions.)	20
Job Expenses and Certain Miscellaneous Deductions	21 Unreimbursed employee expenses—job travel, union dues, job education, etc. Attach Form 2106 or 2106-EZ if required. (See instructions.) ☒ _____	21
	22 Tax preparation fees	22
	23 Other expenses—investment, safe deposit box, etc. List type and amount ☒ _____	
		23
	24 Add lines 21 through 23	24
	25 Enter amount from Form 1040, line 38 [25]	
	26 Multiply line 25 by 2% (.02)	26
	27 Subtract line 26 from line 24. If line 26 is more than line 24, enter -0-	27
Other Miscellaneous Deductions	28 Other—from list in instructions. List type and amount ☒ _____	
		28
Total Itemized Deductions	29 Add the amounts in the far right column for lines 4 through 28. Also, enter this amount on Form 1040, line 40	29
	30 If you elect to itemize deductions even though they are less than your standard deduction, check here . . . . ☒ ☐	

For Paperwork Reduction Act Notice, see Form 1040 instructions.	Cat. No. 17145C	Schedule A (Form 1040) 2012

II

Gross Income

Includes all accessions to wealth, such as:	Excludes:
• Compensation for services • Business profits • Profit from the sale of property • Interest • Rents • Royalties • Dividends • Alimony • Cancellation of debt	• Loans and deposits • Gifts and inheritances • Life insurance • Certain prizes and awards • Qualified scholarships • Personal injury damages • Fringe benefits • Health insurance • Workers' compensation

Chapter 2

Gross Income — Overview

Gross Income

Includes all accessions to wealth, such as:	Excludes:
• Compensation for services • Business profits • Profit from the sale of property • Interest • Rents • Royalties • Dividends • Alimony • Cancellation of debt	• Loans and deposits • Gifts and inheritances • Life insurance • Certain prizes and awards • Qualified scholarships • Personal injury damages • Fringe benefits • Health insurance • Workers' compensation

Read

Code Section 61

Treas. Reg. §§ 1.61-1(a)

A. Tax Liability

Congress might have chosen any number of methods for assessing and collecting tax, such as a tax on the value of real property (subject to the apportionment requirement), a tax on the value of tangible personal property (subject to the apportionment requirement), a tax on sales, a value-added tax, or a consumption tax. The method Congress selected was to impose a tax on each taxpayer's accession to wealth, measuring the accession over a 12-month timeframe. Accordingly, the overall objective of the Internal Revenue Code is to set forth the rules needed to measure this annual accession to wealth.

The Code measures a taxpayer's accession to wealth by first considering the amount of gross income the taxpayer had during the year. The definition of gross income is one of the most fundamental rules found in the Code. The total of all the taxpayer's accessions to wealth during the year often is referred to as gross income.

Section 61. Gross Income Defined

(a) General Definition.—Except as otherwise provided in this subtitle, gross income means all income from whatever source derived, including (but not limited to) the following items:

(1) Compensation for services, including fees, commissions, fringe benefits, and similar items;
(2) Gross income derived from business;
(3) Gains derived from dealings in property;
(4) Interest;
(5) Rents;
(6) Royalties;
(7) Dividends;
(8) Alimony and separate maintenance payments;
(9) Annuities;
(10) Income from life insurance and endowment contracts;
(11) Pensions;
(12) Income from discharge of indebtedness;

* * *

Next, the taxpayer subtracts amounts permitted by the Code (commonly referred to as deductions). Deductions are discussed in detail later in this textbook.[1] The difference between gross income and the allowable deductions is the taxable income.[2]

Summary—Formula for Taxable Income

Gross income
– Deductions
Taxable income

Taxable income is subject to tax.[3] The taxpayer multiples the taxable income by the applicable tax rate. The tax rates are graduated, meaning that as the amount of income increases, the tax rate on additional amounts, or layers, of income increases.[4]

Example. Georgia, a single individual, has $40,000 of taxable income for the taxable year. Assume the tax rates for a single individual are as follows:

---

1. See Parts IV, V, and VI of this textbook.
2. Section 63(a).
3. Section 1.
4. Id.

If taxable income is:	The tax is:
Not over $8,500	10% of the taxable income
Over $8,500 but not over $34,500	$850 plus 15% of the excess of $8,500
Over $34,500 but not over $83,600	$4,750 plus 25% of the excess of $34,500
Over $83,600 but not over $174,400	$17,025 plus 28% of the excess over $83,600
Over $174,400 but not over $379,150	$42,449 plus 33% of the excess over $174,400
Over $379,150	$110,016.50 plus 35% of the excess over $379,150

Her tax liability is determined as follows:

$8,500 × 10%
+ $26,000 × 15%
+ $ 5,500 × 25%

Or

$850*
+ $3,900*
+ $1,375
= $6,125

* Note that the chart already computes the tax liability for the first two brackets. ($850 + $3,900 = $4,750)

Finally, if the taxpayer is entitled to a credit, his tax liability is reduced by the amount of the credit.[5]

Distinction between a Deduction and a Credit

A deduction reduces the amount of taxable income the taxpayer must report. To the extent his taxable income is reduced, his tax liability will be less.

A credit reduces the amount of the taxpayer's tax liability.

Example. Marcus, a single individual, has $80,000 of gross income for the taxable year. Consider the following alternative scenarios.

Deduction: Marcus is entitled to claim a $10,000 deduction. Accordingly, his taxable income is $70,000 ($80,000 gross income, less $10,000 deduction) and his tax liability is $13,625 ($4,750 plus 25% of the excess over $34,500).

Credit: Marcus is entitled to a $10,000 credit. His taxable income is $80,000 and his tax liability is $16,125 ($4,750 plus 25% of the excess over $34,500). He can reduce this tax liability by the amount of the credit, or by $10,000, making his tax liability $6,125 ($16,125, less $10,000).

---

5. See Part IV, Credits Against Tax, of the Code.

B. Definition of Gross Income

While Section 61 states that gross income includes income from all sources, over the years what accessions to wealth come within Section 61 has been subject to controversy, with the Supreme Court being called on to provide guidance several times. In *Eisner v. Macomber*,[6] the taxpayer owned stock. Rather than pay cash dividends, the corporation declared a stock dividend. When a corporation declares a stock dividend, the shareholder receives additional shares of stock, rather than cash, as the dividend. The taxpayer and the Commissioner disagreed as to whether the stock dividend represented an accession to wealth the taxpayer was required to include in gross income.[7]

At issues was the gross income provision from the 1913 Tax Act. While the language from that provision is not the same as the language in Section 61, the earlier provision also defined income broadly and inclusively. The Supreme Court interpreted the provision as including "gain derived from capital, from labor, or from both combined."[8] Because the stock dividend was not gain derived from capital, from labor, or from both combined, it was not gross income.

In subsequent cases, the Supreme Court struggled with the definition of gross income it had created in *Eisner v. Macomber* as the definition proved too narrow to encompass many items that readily appeared to constitute gross income. Over the years, the court has relegated the *Eisner v. Macomber* definition of gross income to the facts in that case. It also provided a more powerful and useful definition of gross income in *Commissioner v. Glenshaw Glass Co.*[9] In *Glenshaw Glass Co.*, the taxpayer received an award of punitive damages that it believed was not includable in gross income under Section 22(a) (the precursor to Section 61). In disagreeing with the taxpayer (respondent), the Supreme Court said:

> Nor can we accept respondent's contention that a narrower reading of Section 22(a) is required by the Court's characterization of income in *Eisner v. Macomber*, 252 U.S. 198, 207, as "the gain derived from capital, from labor, or from both combined." The Court was there endeavoring to determine whether the distribution of a corporate stock dividend constituted a realized gain to the shareholder, or changed "only the form, not the essence," of his capital investment....
>
> Here we have instances of undeniable accessions to wealth, clearly realized, and over which the taxpayers have complete dominion. The mere fact that the payments were extracted from the wrongdoers as punishment for unlawful conduct cannot detract from their character as taxable income to the recipients.[10]

---

6. 252 U.S. 189 (1920).

7. It may be useful to note that a stock dividend merely increases the number of shares of stock outstanding, but does not change the value of the corporation. For example, assume there are 1,000,000 shares of stock outstanding held by 10,000 different shareholders. The corporation declares a stock dividend, giving each shareholder one additional share of stock for each share owned. Thus, if the shareholder owned five shares, he would receive five additional shares, so that he would own a total of 10 shares. If the shareholder owned 100 shares, he would receive 100 additional shares, so that he would own a total of 200 shares. After the dividend distribution there would be 2,000,000 shares of stock outstanding, all held by the same 10,000 shareholders, and held in the same relative proportions.

8. Eisner Macomber, 252 U.S. 189, 207 (1920), *citing* Doyle v. Mitchell Bros. Co., 247 U.S. 179, 185 (1918).

9. 348 U.S. 426 (1955).

10. Commissioner v. Glenshaw Glass Co., 348 U.S. 426, 430-31 (1955).

Thus, gross income is an accession to wealth, clearly realized, over which the taxpayer has control. All accessions to wealth are includable in gross income unless the taxpayer can provide authority to exclude the amount.[11]

Rule—Gross Income

Gross income is an accession to wealth, clearly realized, over which the taxpayer has control. All accessions to wealth are included in gross income unless the taxpayer can provide authority to exclude the amount.

C. Application of Rules

Example 1. Hannah is the manager of a fast food franchise. For the year, her taxable income is $50,000. Assuming the same tax rates as in the example in the text, her tax liability is $4,750 plus 25% of the excess over $34,500 per year, or

= $4,750 plus 25% of the excess over $34,500
= $4,750 + 25% ($50,000 − $34,500)
= $4,750 + $3,875
= $8,625

Example 2. Terrill is the manager of a chain shoe store. For the year, his taxable income is $50,000. In addition, he is entitled to a $2,000 credit. His tax liability is $8,625 (tax owed on the $50,000 of taxable income), less the $2,000 credit, or $6,625.

Example 3. Alex has a savings account at BankCo. This year, he received $50 in interest. Alex has $50 of interest income that he must include in his gross income.

Example 4. Joanne filed a lawsuit against Super Cars, Inc. She won a judgment against the corporation, including an award of $10,000 in punitive damages. Joanne must include the $10,000 of punitive damages in her gross income.

D. Problems

1. Jason, a single individual, owns and operates a car wash. For the year, his taxable income is $20,000. Assuming the same tax rates as in the example in the text, what is his tax liability for the year?

2. Callie, a single individual, owns and operates an auto supply store. For the year, her taxable income is $20,000. In addition, she is entitled to a $1,000 tax credit. What is her tax liability for the year?

---

11. Section 61.

E. Analysis and Application

1. Your client has asked you to explain to her what is included in "gross income" for tax purposes. What do you tell her?

2. Your client has asked you to explain to her what marginal tax rates are. What do you tell her?

3. Identify three items from everyday life that represent gross income (an accession to wealth).

4. Must the taxpayer receive cash (as opposed to property, an intangible asset, etc.) to have gross income?

5. Wesley is the owner of a small convenience store. He sells gasoline, pantry items, a small assortment of auto repair items, and magazines.

    a. Identify how he receives an accession to wealth (gross income).

    b. Should he be taxed on this gross income? Why or why not?

    c. Can you explain what amount his tax liability should be based on?

6. Your client asks you about the most current tax rate schedule for a married individual filing a joint return. Where can you find the tax rate schedules?

Chapter 3

Common Sources of Gross Income

Gross Income

Includes all accessions to wealth, such as:	Excludes:
• **Compensation for services** • Business profits • Profit from the sale of property • **Interest** • **Rents** • **Royalties** • Dividends • Alimony • Cancellation of debt	• Loans and deposits • Gifts and inheritances • Life insurance • Certain prizes and awards • Qualified scholarships • Personal injury damages • Fringe benefits • Health insurance • Workers' compensation

Read

Code Section 61

Treas. Reg. §§ 1.61-1(a), -2(a)(1), -2(d)(1), -14(a)

A. Gross Income

Gross income includes income (accessions to wealth) derived from any and all sources.

1. Compensation for Services

When a taxpayer is paid compensation for his services he has an accession to wealth he must include in his income.[12] While most often wages are paid in cash, the form of the payment is irrelevant. Nor is compensation limited to traditional wages. Compensation also includes bonuses and tips. For example, compensation may be paid through an all-expense paid (bonus) trip provided by the employer to the employee.[13]

---

12. Section 61(a)(1).
13. See, e.g., McCann v. United States, 81-2 U.S.T.C. ¶ 9689 (Ct.Cl. 1981), *aff'd*, 696 F.2d 1386 (Fed. Cir. 1983).

In some cases, a close look at the facts may be needed to see that the payment represents compensation for services. For example, in *Goodwin v. United States*,[14] a reverend received a small, fixed salary. The congregation developed a regular procedure for taking up collections specifically to supplement his salary. Because the collections were taken by the congregation as a whole and the collections were routinized and structured, the collections represented compensation for services. "Regular, sizable payments made by persons to whom the taxpayer provides services are customarily regarded as a form of compensation and may therefore be treated as taxable income."[15]

Barter transactions. Payment for services can be made with services or property. These types of transactions, those in which payment is made with something other than cash, are called barter transactions. The form of the payment is irrelevant. What is important is that the taxpayer has been compensated for his services and, therefore, has received gross income.[16]

Example. Mary drafts Max's will. She would normally charge $500. Rather than pay in cash, Max agrees to paint Mary's house. He would normally charge $500 to paint her house.

Mary was compensated with a payment composed of services rather than cash. Nevertheless, she has received $500 as compensation for her legal services. She must include this amount in her gross income. (Note that Max also was compensated with a payment composed of services rather than cash. He has received $500 as compensation for his painting services. He must include this amount in his gross income.)

2. Treasure Trove

Treasure trove is an item that the taxpayer finds, claims possession of, and is entitled to keep. For example, when a taxpayer finds a ten dollar bill and no potential owner is around, he has treasure trove. When a taxpayer finds treasure trove, he has an accession to wealth and must include the value of the treasure trove in his gross income. The most famous opinion involving treasure trove is a district court case, *Cesarini v. United States*.[17] In 1957, Mr. Cesarini purchased a used piano. In 1964, he found cash tucked away inside the piano. When Mr. Cesarini objected to reporting this cash as a taxable accession to wealth, the court held that the cash, as treasure trove, must be included in his income for 1964, the year he found it.[18]

3. Payment of Debt by a Third Party

When a third party pays an obligation of the taxpayer, the taxpayer has an accession to wealth that he must include in his gross income.[19] In *Old Colony Trust Co. v. Commissioner*[20] Mr. Wood was employed by American Woolen Company and received a

---

14. 67 F.3d 149 (8th Cir. 1995).
15. Goodwin v. United States, 67 F.3d 149,152–53 (8th Cir. 1995).
16. Rev. Rul. 79-24, 1979-1 C.B. 60.
17. 296 F, Supp. 3 (1969).
18. Cesarini v. United States, 296 F. Supp. 3 (N.D. Ohio 1969), *aff'd*, 428 F.2d 812 (6th Cir. 1970).
19. The taxpayer may be able to exclude the amount from gross income. See the discussion of exclusions in Part III.
20. 279 U.S. 716 (1929).

salary of $978,725. The company's board adopted a resolution in which it agreed to pay Mr. Wood's income taxes and thereafter paid the IRS $681,170 on behalf of Mr. Wood.[21]

Before the board resolution		After the board resolution	
Salary:	$978,725	Salary:	$978,725
Tax liability:	<$681,170>	Tax liability:	-0-
Net:	$297,555	Net:	$978,725

Mr. Wood was better off by the amount of $681,170 (his tax liability) when his employer paid his income taxes for him. The Supreme Court stated —

> The payment of the tax by the employers was in consideration of the services rendered by the employee and was a gain derived by the employee from his labor. The form of the payment is expressly declared to make no difference. It is therefore immaterial that the taxes were directly paid over to the Government. The discharge by a third person of an obligation to him is equivalent to receipt by the person taxed.[22]

As the court notes, Mr. Wood realized income through the discharge of the obligation, even though he did not directly receive cash or other property. In the end, his compensation was composed of wages ($978,725), plus the obligation paid on his behalf by his employer ($681,170), or $1,659,895.[23]

While *Old Colony* involved the issue of an employer paying a debt on behalf of its employee, the accession to wealth that arises when a third party pays a taxpayer's debt is not limited to employer/employee relationships. In *Dean v. Commissioner*[24] the taxpayers were the sole shareholders of a corporation. The corporation owned the taxpayer's residence and allowed the taxpayers to live there rent free. The taxpayers were required to include in their gross income the fair rental value of the residence.

Practical Note

In determining the tax consequences of the discharge of an obligation by a third party, it may be helpful to ask why the third party would agree to pay the taxpayer's debt.

What is the relationship between the taxpayer and the third party?
Is the third party an employer?
Is the third party a related party?

---

21. The case involved more than one year. For simplicity's sake, only one year will be discussed.
22. Old Colony Trust Co. v. Commissioner, 279 U.S. 716, 729 (1929).
23. The taxpayer's tax liability was computed based on his income of $1,659,895. Once he determined the total amount of tax he owed, he received credit for the $681,170 already paid on his behalf by his employer. He was liable for the remainder.
24. 187 F.2d 1019 (3d Cir. 1951).

4. Interest, Rents, Royalties, Etc.

Other payments that represent an accession to wealth must be included in gross income. For example, payments to the taxpayer of interest, rents, royalties, and dividends are includable in income.[25]

5. Illegally Obtained Income

Income obtained from illegal sources represents an accession to wealth. It would be an unexpected windfall to allow criminals not only the fruits of their illegal activities, but also a tax-free accession to wealth.[26]

Tell Me More

A taxpayer may be criminally liable when he fails to properly report his income. For example, see the following statutory provisions:

Section 7201: Attempt to Evade or Defeat Tax
Section 7202: Willful Failure to Collect or Pay Over Tax
Section 7206: Fraud and False Statements

The Fifth Amendment protects an accused taxpayer, or a taxpayer facing possible criminal prosecution, from being compelled to testify against himself or provide evidence needed to prosecute the taxpayer for a crime. The protection may be invoked whenever a taxpayer reasonably believes his testimony could furnish a link in the chain of evidence needed to prosecute him for a crime. Because an income tax return requests information necessary to compute the tax liability, and not facts needed to pursue a criminal prosecution, courts have uniformly held that an argument based on the Fifth Amendment will not support the taxpayer's position that he is not required to prepare and file a tax return.

---

6. Imputed Income

There are endless examples of when a taxpayer performs services from which he or his family benefits. For example, when he cleans the house, mows the lawn, changes the oil in the car, or paints his house, he (and his family) is better off than before he completed the tasks. Nevertheless, when a taxpayer provides services for himself or his family (this benefit is called imputed income), he is not required to include the value of the services in his gross income. This rule holds true as long as only the taxpayer or his family are benefiting from these services and no third party is involved. For example, if the taxpayer grows his own vegetables which he and his family enjoy, the taxpayer does not have to include the value of the vegetables in his gross income. However, if he sold the vegetables

---

25. Section 61(a).
26. James v. United States, 366 U.S. 213 (1961).

at the farmers' market, because a third party is involved, he would have to include the accession to wealth from the sales in his gross income.

Summary of Rules

Gross income includes an accession to wealth from any source, including:

- Compensation for services (wages, bonuses, tips, etc.)
- Payment of a debt by a third party
- Treasure trove (found items)
- Interest
- Rents
- Royalties
- Dividends
- Illegally obtained funds

It does not include imputed income.

B. Application of Rules

Example 1. Hannah is the manager of a fast food franchise. She earns a salary of $50,000 per year. In addition, for being one of the top ten managers in the country, she won an all-expense-paid five-day cruise to the Bahamas. Hannah has income equal to $50,000 plus the fair market value of the five-day cruise.

Example 2. Terrill is the manager of a chain shoe store. He earns a salary of $50,000 per year. This year, there was a manager's meeting in New Orleans and Terrill was required to attend. At the meeting, the managers discussed trends in footwear, marketing opportunities, and methods for reducing costs.

Terrill has $50,000 of income. He is not required to include the value of the New Orleans trip as it was not a bonus; it was a trip he was required to take to carry out his duties as manager of the store.

Example 3. Jerry works at Gramdma's Cookhouse as a waiter. He earns $10 per hour, plus tips. During the year he was paid $20,000 and received $10,000 in tips. Jerry has $30,000 of income for the year.

Example 4. Nancy is a C.P.A. and belongs to a barter club. Through the organization she made arrangements for Tom to fix her car. In exchange, she agreed to prepare his tax return.

Nancy has gross income equal to the value of the car repair services she received from Tom. (Note that Tom also has gross income equal to the value of the tax return preparation services he received from Nancy.)

Example 5. Sheyoto provides consulting services to Candy. Candy does not have the cash to pay for the services, so instead gives Sheyoto a painting worth $2,000. Sheyoto has gross income equal to the fair market value of the painting, or $2,000.

Example 6. Clarence bought a painting at an estate sale. Several years later, he decided to replace the frame. When he removed the backing he discovered an original copy of the Declaration of Independence. Clarence has treasure trove; he must include the fair market value of the Declaration of Independence in his gross income.

Example 7. Alex has a savings account at BankCo. This year he received $50 in interest. Alex has $50 of interest income that he must include in his gross income.

Example 8. Tony owns a duplex. This year he received $20,000 in rental payments. Tony has $20,000 of rental income that he must include in his gross income.

Example 9. Tim wrote a how-to manual that was published by a local publishing company. For the year he earned $5,000 in royalties. Tim has $5,000 of income from royalties that he must include in his gross income.

Example 10. Sally worked at the local bank. Over several months she was able to embezzle $50,000 and remain undetected. Sally has $50,000 of illegally obtained income that she must include in her gross income.

Example 11. Bob and Silvia have four children. At 15, Tanya is the oldest. When Bob and Silvia go out for the evening, Tanya is often called upon to baby-sit her three younger siblings. Even though Bob and Silvia save money by not having to pay a babysitter, they are not required to include in their gross income the value of Tanya's babysitting services.

C. Problems

1. Charlie, an accountant, worked for an accounting firm. This year his salary was $70,000. He saved $10,000 of his salary by placing it into a savings account. By the end of the year, the savings account had earned $100 of interest. In January, he traveled to Orlando to represent his firm at the annual meeting of accountants. The organizers of the event had several evening activities planned, including a trip to one of the local theme parks. He also prepared and filed his own tax return for the previous year. From what sources does Charlie have gross income?

2. Over coffee one day, Don and his friends, Amy and Ned, realize they have very different abilities and assets, but abilities and assets that would benefit each other. Don agrees to draft Amy's will. Amy agrees to prepare Ned's tax return. Ned agrees to give Don a painting he had purchased earlier that year and that Don had always admired (its value at the time of the exchange was the same as what Ned had paid for the painting). Are there any tax consequences from this round-robin exchange? If so, what are they?

3. Janice designs and produces women's handbags. The business is lucrative and she often can sell each bag for over $100. Twice a year she designs and produces a bag for herself. Does Janice have gross income from the two bags that she otherwise would have had to purchase at a cost of over $100 each?

4. Kaylie works as a cashier at the general store. On occasion, she is running short of cash and will take a $20 bill from the cash register and use it to buy gas. She does this about once a month. Because she likes her job and her boss, she usually works overtime, without telling her boss and without logging the time, when she takes money from the cash register. What are the tax consequences to Kaylie as a result of this arrangement?

D. Analysis and Application

1. Is it fair to say the taxpayer has an accession to wealth when he is paid for his labor? Didn't he have to expend his labor to receive the compensation? Isn't the payment simply making him "whole," rather than providing any accession?

2. You are an associate with Finley and Maxwell, LLC, a very successful law firm. The managing partner has assigned to you the responsibility of organizing the firm's annual week-long retreat. All he told you was, "we will be staying at Luau Resorts in Maui. Oh, yes—when you are putting together the agendas, don't forget how much the partners enjoy taking in the sights!"

    a. What tax concerns do you have?

    b. How might you address those concerns?

3. Carol lives in New York and travels frequently to see her daughter in California. She signs up for all frequent-flyer programs offered by the airlines and always registers her miles for each trip to California. This year she has accumulated enough frequent flyer miles for a free trip. She turns in some of her miles and, in exchange, receives a free ticket to California.

    a. Are there any tax consequences to Carol when she receives the frequent flyer miles? If so, what are they?

    b. Are there any tax consequences to Carol when she receives the ticket? If so what are they?

    In formulating your analysis and response, you may want to consider:

    *   Charley v. Commissioner, 91 F.3d 72 (9th Cir. 1996)
    *   Commissioner v. Glenshaw Glass Co., 348 U.S. 426 (1955)
    *   Announcement 2002-18, 2002-1 C.B. 621

4. Frank is a scuba diving fanatic. In the past he has located and explored sunken ships as they rested on the ocean floor. Lately, he has been able to expand on his passion by raising these ships to the surface and claiming any items of value found on the ships as his own. His "salvage" operation has been very successful. This past year he raised two ships from the ocean floor. On these ships he found three chests with gold and silver coins, a relatively in-tact china set, and various odds and ends used by the crew. Are there any tax consequences from Frank's salvaging of the ships?

    In formulating your analysis and response, you may want to consider:

    *   Commissioner v. Glenshaw Glass Co., 348 U.S. 426 (1955)
    *   Cesarini v. United States, 296 F. Supp. 3 (N.D. Ohio 1969), aff'd 428 F.2d 812 (6th Cir. 1970)

5. Dora Robertson lives on a ranch in Texas. She met James Acres through a dating service. After several dates, James revealed to Dora that he had knowledge about a map located in Mexico that would reveal the location of buried gold on her ranch. Dora agreed to pay James $10,000 so he could travel to Mexico and obtain the map. When he returned, he used the map to locate the place indicated on her ranch and, after a fair amount of digging, unearthed a box containing metal bars resembling gold. Dora and James agreed to store the gold on her property until James could determine whether Dora would have the right to keep the bars.

Several months later, James had moved in with Dora. Eventually, James told Dora that he learned of a second map located in Mexico that also revealed the location of buried gold on her ranch. Dora agreed to pay James $50,000 so he could travel to Mexico and obtain the second map. Again, the map proved accurate and James was able to unearth another box that held more gold bars. He convinced Dora to allow him to take the gold bars into town to be converted to cash. "If there is any problem with explaining where these bars came from, I don't want you involved. Let me handle it." She agreed. When James returned, he explained that he had been robbed of all the gold bars on his way into town.

Dora did some investigating and eventually discovered that James had deceived her. She immediately broke off her relationship with him and kicked him out of her house. She was embarrassed by how easily she had been deceived and refused to report the incident to law enforcement or demand that James return the money. Eventually, the statute of limitations barred her from taking any action against James.

What are the tax consequences, if any, to James? In formulating your analysis and response, you may want to consider:

- Commissioner v. Glenshaw Glass Co., 348 U.S. 426 (1955)
- James v. United States, 366 U.S. 213 (1961)
- Kreimer v. Commissioner, T.C. Memo. 1983-672

6. Research project: Research the different types of tips an employee might receive and the tax consequences from receiving them. Prepare a presentation.

7. Research project: Research the various types of illegally-obtained income a taxpayer might receive and the tax consequence from receiving them. Prepare a presentation.

8. Prepare a concept map to explain gross income.

A concept map is a visual diagram showing links between and among important related concepts. The process of creating a concept map requires the integration of new information with prior knowledge. A concept map can be used to clarify what has been read and heard by creating a visual representation of key terms around a central idea or concept. It is not intended to establish a hierarchy between concepts (as an outline would), only the existence of a relationship between concepts.

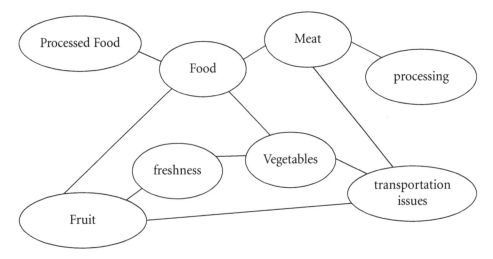

Chapter 4

Gains Involving Property

Gross Income

Includes all accessions to wealth, such as:	Excludes:
• Compensation for services • Business profits • **Profit from the sale of property** • Interest • Rents • Royalties • Dividends • Alimony • Cancellation of debt	• Loans and deposits • Gifts and Inheritances • Life insurance • Certain prizes and awards • Qualified scholarships • Personal injury damages • Fringe benefits • Health insurance • Workers' compensation

Read

Code Sections 61(a)(3); 1001(a), (b), (c); 1012(a)

Treas. Reg. §§ 1.61-2(d)(2)(i); 1.61-6(a); 1.1001-1(a); 1.1001-2(a)(1)

A. Gain from the Disposition of Property

Gross income includes income (accessions to wealth) derived from any and all sources.[27] Once a taxpayer acquires property, the property can increase in value. However, the Code does not require the taxpayer to report that increase in wealth until he has disposed of the property. In general the accession to wealth is the amount of profit the taxpayer has in the property, or the difference between the amount the taxpayer sold the property for and the amount he paid for it. To measure this profit, the Code provides specific terminology.

1. Basis

The basis of property is the amount the taxpayer originally paid for the property.[28] In general a taxpayer will purchase an item for its fair market value. Note that the focus is

---

27. Section 61.
28. Section 1012(a).

on the amount paid for the property; the source of the payment is not relevant. For example, the fact that the taxpayer borrowed money to purchase property is not relevant in determining how much he paid for the property.

Section 1012. Basis of Property — Cost

(a) In General. — The basis of property shall be the cost of such property ...

Example. Billy purchased five shares of stock for $100 each and each share had a fair market value of $100. His basis in each share of stock is $100. The source of the money Billy used to purchase the stock is irrelevant.

In the famous case of *Philadelphia Park Amusement Co. v. United States*[29] the taxpayer owned a 50-year franchise to operate a railroad that provided transportation to an amusement park. It obtained a 10-year extension of the franchise in exchange for a bridge. Later, a tax issue arose involving the tax consequences of the transaction and Philadelphia Park was required to establish the value of the 10-year franchise extension at the time of purchase. While the taxpayer was unable to effectively value the franchise extension, the court suggested the taxpayer might be able to value the bridge. Since the bridge was used as payment for the franchise extension, the two properties should have been worth the same amount at the time of the exchange. The court did note that, while the amount paid for the property should be the fair market value of the property, if there is some inequality, the basis is equal to the fair market value of the property received.

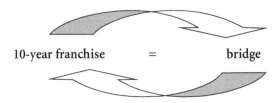

10-year franchise   =   bridge

Tell Me More

In certain circumstances, the basis of an asset will be adjusted. It will be increased for capital expenditures and decreased for depreciation. This basis is called the adjusted basis. These concepts are discussed in Chapters 22, 25, and 29.

    cost
  + capital expenditures
  − <u>depreciation</u>
    adjusted basis

---

29. 126 F. Supp. 184 (Ct. Cl. 1954).

2. Amount Realized

The amount realized is the amount the taxpayer sold the property for.[30] In general a taxpayer will sell an item for its fair market value. What types of assets the taxpayer receives as payment for the item he is selling is irrelevant; the focus is on the value of the payment.

Section 1001. Determination of Amount of and Recognition of Gain or Loss

(b) Amount Realized. — The amount realized from the sale or other disposition of property shall be the sum of any money received plus the fair market value of the property (other than money) received ...

While the statutory provision refers to payments in the form of cash or other property, case law requires also including the receipt of services and debt relief in amount realized.[31] In sum, the total value of what the taxpayer receives in exchange for his property is the amount realized. This equality can be seen by comparing the following:

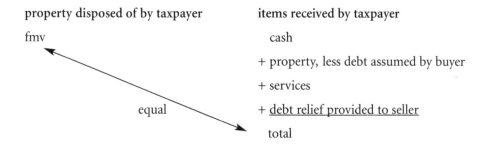

property disposed of by taxpayer	items received by taxpayer
fmv	cash
	+ property, less debt assumed by buyer
	+ services
equal	+ <u>debt relief provided to seller</u>
	total

Example. Emily owns Blackacre and Blackacre has a fair market value of $10,000. She decides to sell Blackacre to Rose. Rose has offered to purchase Blackacre by giving Emily any one of the following combinations:

- $10,000 cash
- $4,000 cash and stock worth $6,000
- $10,000 of legal services
- Paying Emily's $3,000 Visa bill and providing her $7,000 of legal services

---

30. Section 1001(b).
31. Tufts v. Commissioner, 461 U.S. 300 (1983) (amount realized includes, at a minimum, the amount of non-recourse debt); Crane v. Commissioner, 331 U.S. 1 (1947) (amount realized includes recourse debt); International Freighting Corp., Inc. v. Commissioner, 135 F.2d 310 (2d Cir. 1943) (amount realized includes services).

Any one of these combinations would result in Emily receiving $10,000 in exchange for Blackacre.

Debt can be included in the computation in two separate places, but they do not refer to the same debt. First, if the property used as payment is subject to a debt, the amount of the payment is the net value of the property (the fair market value of the property, less the debt it is being taken subject to). Second, if the purchaser takes the taxpayer's property subject to the debt, the taxpayer's debt relief is part of the purchase price.

Example. Christina owns Whiteacre and Whiteacre has a fair market value of $10,000. She decides to sell Whiteacre to Jack. Jack agrees to transfer Yellowacre to Christina as payment for Whiteacre. Yellowacre has a fair market value of $12,000 and is subject to a $2,000 mortgage. Christina has agreed to assume the mortgage on Yellowacre.

Christina is receiving $10,000 in exchange for Whiteacre— $12,000 worth of property, less the $2,000 debt she is taking the property subject to.

3. Gain Realized and Recognized

The difference between the amount realized and the basis of the property sold is the gain realized.[32] This formula permits the taxpayer to recover the amount he paid for the property tax free. This recovery is sometimes called a return of capital.

Amount realized
– Basis
Gain realized

Section 1001. Determination of Amount of and Recognition of Gain or Loss

(a) Computation of Gain or Loss. — The gain from the sale or other disposition of property shall be the excess of the amount realized therefrom over the adjusted basis provided in section 1011 for determining gain ...

Unless the code provides otherwise, any gain realized must be recognized.[33] To recognize gain means to report it on the taxpayer's income tax return.

Gain Realized and Gain Recognized

Gain realized is the difference between the amount realized and the adjusted basis of the property.

Gain recognized is the amount of gain realized the taxpayer must report on his income tax return.

---

32. Section 1001(a).
33. Section 1001(c).

> **Tell Me More**
>
> The Code provides that, in specific situations, the taxpayer is relieved of reporting the gain realized (i.e., no gain is recognized) or will defer recognizing a portion of the gain realized until a later time. These provisions are addressed in Chapters 42, 43, 44, and 47.

B. Barter Transactions

Payment for property can be made with services or other property. These types of transactions, those in which payment is made with something other than cash, are called barter transactions. The form of the payment is irrelevant. What is important is that the taxpayer has been paid for his property and must compute the gain (or loss) realized on disposition.

C. Tax Cost Basis

If the taxpayer receives property as compensation for services, he has not paid for the property. But, he has reported the value of the property as compensation for services. Accordingly, for tax purposes, the taxpayer has made a tax investment in the property. In these situations, his basis in the property is the amount of compensation he reported. (If he also has paid some portion of the purchase price, the payment is included in the basis computation.)

Example. Justin provided $500 in consulting services to Cynthia. Cynthia did not have any cash. Instead, she paid Justin by giving him a painting worth $500. Several years before, she had purchased the painting for $100. Note that this transaction is a barter transaction, as no cash is involved.

Justin has received $500 worth of property as compensation for services; he must include the $500 in his gross income. His basis (a tax cost basis) in the painting is the amount of gross income he reported, or $500.

Cynthia has disposed of property. Her amount realized is $500 (the value of the services she received in exchange), and her basis is $100. Accordingly, Cynthia has $400 of gain realized from disposition of property. She must recognize (report) the gain.

D. Bargain Purchases

The basis of property is the amount the taxpayer originally paid for the property. In general, a taxpayer will purchase an item for its fair market value.

There are, however, a few situations when the taxpayer will pay less than the fair market value for the property. How such a transaction is treated depends on the reason why the taxpayer paid less than fair market value.

If the taxpayer simply received a "good deal" on the purchase of the property, there are no tax consequences at the time he purchases the property.[34] Instead, any gain in the property will be recognized when he sells the property.

In contrast, if the reduced price is a disguised payment to the taxpayer, the payment must be characterized and treated accordingly. In these situations, the basis in the property is the sum of the basis and the tax cost basis. Note that the tax consequences of any transaction are based on its substance, not the form in which it is cast.

Example. Chad works for a computer software company. At the end of each year, the company allows the employees to purchase select used computers for $20. Chad purchased a computer. The company could have sold the computers for $100 (the fair market value of the computers was $100). The offer is only open to employees and the company is aware it could sell the computers for more to the public. The reduction in price of the computer from its fair market value, $80, is a form of compensation for services. Chad must include $80 of compensation for services in his income. Chad's basis in the computer is the $20 he paid for the computer (basis) plus the $80 of compensation income he reported (tax cost basis), for a total basis of $100.

Substance versus Form

There may be times when the form of a transaction does not match the substance of the transaction. For tax purposes, in almost all cases, the tax consequences will be based on the substance of the transaction (and not its form). Accordingly, the substance of the transaction must be determined.

Example: Karen provided $500 in consulting services to Lori, but Lori did not pay her any money. A few weeks later Lori gave Karen a painting worth $500. While Karen may argue that Lori's giving her the painting was unrelated to the services Karen had provided, if the substance of the transaction was that the painting was payment for services, Karen must include $500 in her income as compensation for services.

Summary of Definitions

Basis: Basis of property is the amount paid for the property, generally the fair market value of the property.

Tax cost basis: Basis of property is equal to the amount of income the taxpayer reported upon receipt of the property when property has been received in exchange for services.

Amount realized: The amount a taxpayer receives when he sells the property. It usually is composed of any combination of cash, property, services, and debt relief.

---

34. See, e.g., Pellar v. Commissioner, 25 T.C. 299 (1955), *acq.* 1956-2 C.B. 7.

Gain realized: The difference between the amount realized and the basis.

Gain recognized: The amount of gain realized the taxpayer must report on his tax return.

E. Application of Rules

Example 1. Basis. George purchased Whiteacre for $100,000. He used $10,000 of his own funds and $90,000 he had borrowed from BankCo. His basis in Whiteacre is $100,000.

Example 2. Tax Cost Basis. Eileen purchased Greenacre. The fair market value of Greenacre at the time of the purchase was $10,000. Eileen paid for the property by performing $10,000 worth of legal services for the seller. She must include $10,000 in her gross income as compensation for services. Eileen's (tax cost) basis in Greenacre is $10,000.

Example 3. Tax Cost Basis. Phil performed $1,000 in legal services for Ray. In exchange for the services, Ray gave Phil a watch worth $1,000. Phil must include $1,000 in gross income as compensation for services. Phil's (tax cost) basis in the watch is $1,000.

Example 4. Tax Cost Basis. Ortho prepared a contract for Paul. Ordinarily, Ortho would charge about $1,200 for his services. In payment for Ortho's services, Paul gave Ortho Redacre, which was worth $1,000.

Ortho must include $1,000 in his gross income as compensation for services. His (tax cost) basis in Redacre is $1,000.

Example 5. Amount realized. Constance owned Blackacre and Blackacre had a fair market value of $50,000. She decided to sell Blackacre to Tony. In exchange, Tony gave Constance $10,000 and stock worth $40,000. Constance's amount realized is $50,000.

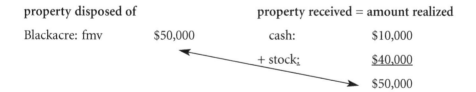

property disposed of		property received = amount realized	
Blackacre: fmv	$50,000	cash:	$10,000
		+ stock:	$40,000
			$50,000

Example 6. Amount realized. Tim owned Whiteacre. He decided to sell Whiteacre to Bill. In exchange, Bill gave Tim $20,000 and stock worth $40,000. Tim's amount realized is $60,000 (and the fair market value of Whiteacre must have been $60,000).

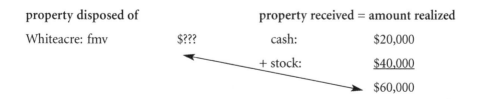

property disposed of		property received = amount realized	
Whiteacre: fmv	$???	cash:	$20,000
		+ stock:	$40,000
			$60,000

Example 7. Amount realized. Nancy owned Greenacre, which was worth $70,000. She decided to sell Greenacre to Abby. In exchange, Abby gave Nancy $30,000 and Redacre. Redacre was worth $50,000 and was subject to a $10,000 liability. Nancy took Redacre subject to the liability. Nancy's amount realized is $70,000.

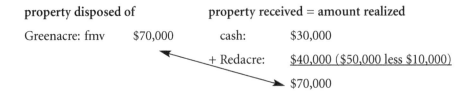

property disposed of   **property received = amount realized**

Greenacre: fmv $70,000   cash: $30,000

                                    + Redacre: $40,000 ($50,000 less $10,000)

                                                 $70,000

Example 8. Amount realized. Kimber owned Roseacre, which was worth $70,000 and was subject to a $10,000 liability. She decided to sell Roseacre to Jeff. In exchange, Jeff gave Kimber $60,000. He took Roseacre subject to the liability. Kimber's amount realized is $70,000.

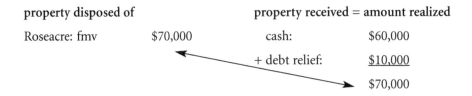

property disposed of   **property received = amount realized**

Roseacre: fmv $70,000   cash: $60,000

                                         + debt relief: $10,000

                                                        $70,000

Example 9. Gain realized. Constance owned Blackacre. She had purchased Blackacre for $10,000. She decided to sell Blackacre to Tony for $50,000, its current fair market value. In exchange, Tony gave Constance $10,000 and stock worth $40,000. Constance has $40,000 of gain realized. She must recognize (report) the gain on her tax return.

Amount realized: $50,000
Basis: <10,000>
Gain realized: $40,000

Example 10. Gain realized. Kimber owned Roseacre. She had purchased Roseacre for $60,000. Its current fair market value was $70,000 and it was subject to a $10,000 liability. She decided to sell Roseacre to Jeff. In exchange, Jeff gave Kimber $60,000. He took Roseacre subject to the liability. Kimber's gain realized is $10,000. She must recognize (report) the gain on her tax return.

Amount realized: $70,000
Basis: <60,000>
Gain realized: $10,000

Example 11. Bargain purchase. While at a garage sale, Taylor spotted a vase that was an antique worth $10,000. It was marked at $5. She quickly purchased the vase and left the garage sale.

Taylor has simply received a "good deal" on the purchase of the vase; there are no tax consequences at the time of purchase. Her basis in the vase is $5, the amount she paid for it.

F. Problems

1. Francie purchased Whiteacre for $20,000. Consider the tax consequences to Francie under the following alternative scenarios.

   30K is Amount Realized

   a. Three years later, she sold the property for $50,000.

   b. When she bought the property she took out a $5,000 mortgage. She sold the property three years later for $55,000 cash. In addition to the cash payment the buyer also assumed the mortgage, which was still $5,000.

   50K

   c. Three years later, she sold the property for a painting. The painting was worth $70,000. What is her basis in the painting? *20K*

   d. Three years later, she sold the property for legal services. The legal services otherwise would have cost her $25,000. *5K in Amount Realized*

2. Sam is an architect. This year, one of his clients was unable to pay him in cash. Instead, the client gave him a piano worth $20,000. Sam accepted the piano in full satisfaction of the outstanding bill.

   the 20K Amount Realize

   a. What are the tax consequences to Sam upon receipt of the piano?

   b. What are the tax consequences to Sam if he sells the piano five years later for $25,000? *5K Amount Realized*

3. Deb works for an accounting firm. Every year the firm replaces the three oldest desks with three new desks. The accounting firm allows the employees to purchase the old desks. This year Deb purchased one of the desks. What are the tax consequences to her from the purchase under the following alternative scenarios:

   a. The accounting firm sells the old desks for $100 each. The firm is unaware that each desk is actually worth $1,000.

   b. The accounting firm sells the old desks for $100. The firm is aware that each desk is actually worth $1,000.

   c. The accounting firm sells the old desks for $100. The firm believes each desk is worth $300, but each is actually worth $1,000.

4. Over coffee one day, Don and his friends, Amy and Ned, realize they have very different abilities and assets, but abilities and assets that would benefit each other. Don agrees to prepare all Amy's estate planning documents, including a complicated will and trust. Amy agrees to transfer Greenacre to Ned. She had purchased Greenacre three years earlier for $5,000 and it was currently worth $7,000. Ned agrees to give Don a painting. He had purchased the painting five years earlier for $1,000 and it was currently worth $7,000. Are there any tax consequences from this round-robin exchange? If so, what are they? *No, they are all gifts*

5. Cathy works for Trucks Express, a delivery service. At the end of each year, her employer removes the trucks that are 10 years old from the fleet and offers them for sale to the employees. Even though the trucks are generally worth $5,000, the employer allows them to be purchased by an employee for $500. This year, Cathy purchased one of the trucks. What are the tax consequences to Cathy? What is her basis in the truck?

6. Sally loves to frequent antique shops, hoping to expand on her collection of plates. During the summer she purchased a pink plate with flowers etched into the glass. She paid $15. This fall, when a friend was visiting, the friend noticed the plate and

(good deal)

commented on how rare and expensive it was. The friend estimated that the plate was worth $15,000. What are the tax consequences to Sally? *$15.00 until she sells it then her Amount Realized* [handwritten annotation]

G. Analysis and Application

1. How will your client be able to establish his basis in property he is selling? What documentation should he have? What complications will arise if he cannot find the necessary documentation?

2. Jim owns a landscape painting. He bought it five years ago for $5,000 and it is currently worth $50,000. Sandy owns Greenacre. She purchased the undeveloped land ten years ago for $30,000 and it is currently worth $50,000. Jim and Sandy agree to exchange properties, with Jim getting Greenacre and Sandy getting the landscape painting. Since both are giving up property worth $50,000 and getting property worth $50,000 they believe neither has an accession to wealth he or she must report. Are they correct?

3. Tim purchased his first home five years ago. After having watched numerous home-improvement shows, he decided to do some remodeling. As part of the remodeling project, he removed the plaster board in the living room, exposing the inside of the wall. Tim discovered that, rather than using traditional insulation, someone had used layers of posters advertising movies from the 1960s. Tim carefully removed the posters and had them appraised. Because of how rare the posters are, they were valued at $100,000.

    Does Tim have any income tax consequences based on his discovery? In formulating your analysis and response, you may want to consider:

    -   Commissioner v. Glenshaw Glass Co., 348 U.S. 426 (1955)
    -   Cesarini v. United States, 296 F. Supp. 3 (N.D. Ohio 1969), *aff'd* 428 F.2d 812 (6th Cir. 1970)
    -   Pellar v. Commissioner, 25 T.C. 299 (1955)

Chapter 5

Interest Received

Gross Income

Includes all accessions to wealth, such as:	Excludes:
• Compensation for services • Business profits • Profit from the sale of property • Interest • Rents • Royalties • Dividends • Alimony • Cancellation of debt	• Loans and deposits • Gifts and inheritances • Life insurance • Certain prizes and awards • Qualified scholarships • Personal injury damages • Fringe benefits • Health insurance • Workers' compensation

Read

Code Sections 61(a)(4); 72(a)(1), (b), (c)

Treas. Reg. § 1.72-9

A. Interest Received

Gross income includes income (accessions to wealth) derived from any and all sources. When a taxpayer loans money to a third party, he expects the third party to not only repay him the amount borrowed, but also pay him interest. When the third party returns the amount borrowed, the taxpayer does not have gross income; it is merely a return of capital—there is no accession to wealth. However, the interest the third party pays to the taxpayer does represent an accession to wealth; the taxpayer must include the interest in his gross income.[35]

---

35. Section 61(a)(4).

B. Annuities

1. Receipt of Taxable Interest

An annuity is a type of financial investment. The taxpayer provides funds to the company selling the annuity. In return, the company will return the funds, plus interest, over a number of years.

The return of the taxpayer's original funds is merely a return of capital and not a taxable event. The interest paid by the annuity company is an accession to wealth, and the taxpayer must include the interest in income.[36]

2. Computation of Portion of Payment Allocable to Interest

Each year that the annuity company makes a payment to the taxpayer, the payment must be allocated between the non-taxable return of capital and the interest payment. Congress had at least three options in determining what portion of each payment represented interest. It could have required the initial payments to be interest, with all the remaining payments a return of capital. Or it could have allowed the taxpayer to receive a return of capital first, with interest payments coming last. Or, it could have required a portion of each payment to be part return of capital and part interest. It selected the last option, with the interest portion being a ratable portion of the payment each year.[37]

Example. Kip purchases an annuity from InvestmentCo. Under the terms of the annuity, Kip pays InvestmentCo $50,000 and InvestmentCo will pay Kip $55,000 over five years ($11,000 each year). The difference between what Kip paid InvestmentCo and what InvestmentCo will pay Kip, $5,000, represents interest. The interest is reported ratably, or $1,000 each year.

Year	Return of Capital	Interest	Total Payment
1	$10,000	$1,000	$11,000
2	10,000	1,000	11,000
3	10,000	1,000	11,000
4	10,000	1,000	11,000
5	10,000	1,000	11,000
Totals:	$50,000	$5,000	$55,000

---

36. Id.
37. Section 72(a)(1), (b)(1).

Rather than pay the taxpayer a fixed amount for a set number of years, the annuity company may agree to pay the taxpayer a fixed amount for the remainder of the taxpayer's life. In this situation, the taxpayer's life expectancy must be determined before the allocation between return of capital and interest can be ascertained. The regulations under Section 72 have life expectancy tables and these tables are used to estimate how long the taxpayer will live.[38]

Example. Dexter purchases an annuity from InvestmentCo. Under the terms of the annuity, Dexter pays InvestmentCo $35,000 and InvestmentCo will pay Dexter $5,000 each year for the rest of his life. Based on the life expectancy tables, Dexter's life expectancy is 8 years. Thus, we expect that InvestmentCo will pay Dexter $5,000 for 8 years for a total amount paid of $40,000. The difference between what Dexter paid InvestmentCo, $35,000, and what InvestmentCo will pay Dexter, $40,000, represents interest. The $5,000 of interest is reported ratably, or $625 each year.

Year	Return of Capital	Interest	Total Payment
1	$4,375	$625	$5,000
2	4,375	625	5,000
3	4,375	625	5,000
4	4,375	625	5,000
5	4,375	625	5,000
6	4,375	625	5,000
7	4,375	625	5,000
8	4,375	625	5,000
Totals:	$35,000	$5,000	$40,000

Annuity formulas. While the amount of taxable income can be determined by considering the ratable portion of each payment, the Code provides a formula for determining the amount of each payment that may be excluded from gross income. The remainder of each payment must be included. The formula for the amount that can be excluded is as follows:

$$\frac{\text{investment in the contract}}{\text{expected return}} \times \text{yearly payment} = \text{excludable amount}$$

investment in the contract = the amount the taxpayer has paid to the annuity company

expected return = the total amount the annuity company is expected to pay the taxpayer

---

38. Treas. Reg. § 1.72-9.

Summary — Annuity Formulas

To determine how much of each annuity payment a taxpayer can *exclude* from gross income, utilize the following formula:

$$\frac{\text{investment in the contract}}{\text{expected return}} \times \text{yearly payment} = \text{excludable amount}$$

To determine how much of each annuity payment a taxpayer must *include* in income, utilize the following formula:

$$\text{yearly payment} - \text{excludable amount} = \text{taxable amount}$$

Example. Kip purchases an annuity from InvestmentCo. Under the terms of the annuity, Kip pays InvestmentCo $50,000 and InvestmentCo will pay Kip $55,000 over five years ($11,000 each year).

Applying the annuity formulas:

$$\frac{\$50,000}{\$55,000} \times \$11,000 = \$10,000 \text{ excludable amount}$$

$11,000 – $10,000 = $1,000 taxable amount

Payments when taxpayer outlives his life expectancy. If the taxpayer has purchased an annuity where he will be paid a sum every year for his life, what portion of the payment represents interest is determined based on his life expectancy. Of course, it is possible he will outlive his life expectancy. When this occurs, he has recovered the entire amount of his original investment and any additional payments represent interest. Accordingly, the full amount of such payments must be included in his income as interest.[39]

Example. Kip purchases an annuity from InvestmentCo. Under the terms of the annuity, Kip pays InvestmentCo $50,000 and InvestmentCo will pay Kip $11,000 each year for the rest of Kip's life. Based on the life expectancy tables, Kip's life expectancy is 5 years. Thus, we expect that InvestmentCo will pay Kip $11,000 for 5 years for a total amount paid of $55,000, as follows:

Year	Return of Capital	Interest	Total Payment
1	$10,000	$1,000	$11,000
2	10,000	1,000	11,000
3	10,000	1,000	11,000
4	10,000	1,000	11,000
5	10,000	1,000	11,000
Totals:	$50,000	$5,000	$55,000

Assume Kip lives for an addition two years. We can see from the chart above that at the end of year 5 he has completely recovered his original $50,000 investment. The entire

---

39. Section 72(a), (b)(2).

amount of the payments in year 6 and 7 represents interest and must be included in his gross income.

Year	Return of Capital	Interest	Total Payment
6	-0-	$11,000	$11,000
7	-0-	11,000	11,000
Totals:	$-0-	$22,000	$22,000

Result when taxpayer dies before his life expectancy. If the taxpayer has purchased an annuity where he will be paid a sum every year for his life, what portion of the payment represents interest is determined based on his life expectancy. Of course, it is possible he will not live as long as his life expectancy. When this occurs, he has not recovered the entire amount of his original investment. This failure to recover his investment is a loss, reportable on his final income tax return.[40]

Example. Kip purchases an annuity from InvestmentCo. Under the terms of the annuity, Kip pays InvestmentCo $50,000 and InvestmentCo will pay Kip $11,000 each year for the rest of Kip's life. Based on the life expectancy tables, Kip's life expectancy is 5 years. Thus, we expect that InvestmentCo will pay Kip $11,000 for 5 years for a total amount paid of $55,000.

If Kip passes away after three years and the annuity payments stop, he will not recover his entire investment.

Year	Return of Capital	Interest	Total Payment
1	$10,000	$1,000	$11,000
2	10,000	1,000	11,000
3	10,000	1,000	11,000
Totals:	$30,000	$3,000	$33,000

Of his $50,000 investment, he will recover $30,000. Kip can claim a loss for the remaining $20,000 he will not recover.

C. Examples

Example 1. Liz purchased an annuity from Insurance Co. Under the terms of the annuity, Liz paid Insurance Co $100,000 and Insurance Co will pay Liz $150,000 over ten years ($15,000 each year). The difference between what Liz paid Insurance Co and what Insurance Co will pay Liz, $50,000, represents interest. The interest is reported ratably, or $15,000 each year.

Applying the annuity formulas:

---

40. Section 72(b)(3).

$\dfrac{\$100,000}{\$150,000} \times \$15,000 = \$10,000$ excludable amount

$\$15,000 - \$10,000 = \$5,000$ taxable amount

Year	Return of Capital	Interest	Total Payment
1	$10,000	$5,000	$15,000
2	10,000	5,000	15,000
3	10,000	5,000	15,000
4	10,000	5,000	15,000
5	10,000	5,000	15,000
6	10,000	5,000	15,000
7	10,000	5,000	15,000
8	10,000	5,000	15,000
9	10,000	5,000	15,000
10	10,000	5,000	15,000
Totals:	$100,000	$50,000	$150,000

Example 2. Samantha purchased an annuity from Annuity Co. Under the terms of the annuity, Samantha paid Annuity Co $40,000 and Annuity Co will pay Samantha $10,500 each year for the rest of her life. Based on the life expectancy tables, Samantha's life expectancy is 4 years. Thus, we expect that Annuity Co to pay Samantha a total of $42,000. The difference between what Samantha paid Annuity Co and what Annuity Co will pay Samantha, $2,000, represents interest.

Year	Return of Capital	Interest	Total Payment
1	$10,000	$500	10,500
2	10,000	500	10,500
3	10,000	500	10,500
4	10,000	500	10,500
Totals:	$40,000	$2,000	$42,000

Example 3. Samantha purchased an annuity from Annuity Co. Under the terms of the annuity, Samantha paid Annuity Co $40,000 and Annuity Co will pay Samantha $10,500 each year for the rest of her life. Based on the life expectancy tables, Samantha's life expectancy is 4 years.

Samantha lived for three years beyond her life expectancy. At the end of the fourth year, Samantha has completely recovered her original $40,000 investment. The entire amount of the payments in year 5, 6, and 7 represents interest and must be included in her gross income. Samantha must report $10,500 of interest in years 5, 6, and 7.

Example 4. Samantha purchased an annuity from Annuity Co. Under the terms of the annuity, Samantha paid Annuity Co $40,000 and Annuity Co will pay Samantha $10,500 each year for the rest of her life. Based on the life expectancy tables, Samantha's life expectancy is 4 years.

Samantha passed away after the second year and the annuity payments stopped. She will not recover her entire investment.

Year	Return of Capital	Interest	Total Payment
1	$10,000	$500	10,500
2	10,000	500	10,500
Totals:	$20,000	$1,000	$21,000

Of her $40,000 investment, she recovered $20,000. Samantha can claim a loss for the remaining $20,000 she will not recover.

D. Problems

1. Last year Jeremy loaned $10,000 to his friend. This year his friend repaid the $10,000 and paid him an additional $1,000 for use of the money.

    a. What are the tax consequences to Jeremy in the year he made the loan to his friend?

    b. What are the tax consequences to Jeremy this year when he receives the $11,000?

2. Mack purchased an annuity for $45,000. Under the terms of the annuity, the annuity company will pay Mack a total of $55,000 over the next six years. How much of the $55,000 the company pays Mack must he include in his gross income?

3. George purchased an annuity for $45,000. Under the terms of the annuity, the annuity company will pay George $10,000 a year for six years. What are the tax consequences to George in each of the next six years?

4. Juan purchased an annuity for $100,000. Under the terms of the annuity, the annuity company will pay Juan $25,000 each year for the remainder of his life. Juan's life expectancy is five years.

    a. What are the tax consequences to Juan in each of the next five years?

    b. Alternatively, what are the tax consequences to Juan if he lived for eight years?

    c. Alternatively, what are the tax consequences to Juan if he passed away after receiving the payment in the second year and the annuity payments stopped?

E. Analysis and Application

1. If a taxpayer has an annuity to be paid during his life do you agree that the total amount of each payment received after he has lived for his life expectancy should be taxable? Could you explain this tax result to a client?

2.   Marcus is 55 years old.

   a.   Based on the life expectancy tables, what is his life expectancy?

   b.   If he purchased an annuity for $100,000 and the annuity company agreed to pay
        him $5,000 each year for the remainder of his life, what are the tax consequences
        to Marcus?

3.   If you had to locate the life expectancy tables, where might you find them?

Chapter 6

Loans and Cancellation of Debt

Gross Income

Includes all accessions to wealth, such as:	Excludes:
• Compensation for services • Business profits • Profit from the sale of property • Interest • Rents • Royalties • Dividends • Alimony • **Cancellation of debt**	• Loans and deposits • Gifts and inheritances • Life insurance • Certain prizes and awards • Qualified scholarships • Personal injury damages • Fringe benefits • Health insurance • Workers' compensation

Read

Code Sections 61(a)(12); 108(a)(1), (3), (d)(1)-(3), (f)(1)

Treas. Reg. §§ 1.61-12(a)

A. Loans

Gross income includes income (accessions to wealth) derived from any and all sources.[41] When a taxpayer borrows money, he does not have an accession to wealth. Even if he has complete control over the money, does not have to segregate the funds or otherwise account for the money, and can use the money however he chooses, he does not have gross income. The reason why there is no gross income is because of the offsetting obligation to repay the amount borrowed; the taxpayer does not have an accession to wealth.

Example. Nadine had a savings account with $10,000 and a $1,000 debt owed to Visa, giving her a net worth of $9,000.

Nadine borrowed $3,000 from BankCo and deposited the funds into her bank account. Even though her bank account has increased to $13,000, her net worth has not increased

---

41. Section 61(a).

because she has an additional obligation of $3,000; her net worth is still $9,000. Because there has been no accession to Nadine's wealth, she does not realize any gross income from the transaction.

Before loan from BankCo		After loan from BankCo	
Savings account	$10,000	Savings account	$13,000
Visa	<1,000>	Visa	<1,000>
		BankCo loan	<3,000>
Net worth:	$9,000	Net worth:	$9,000

If a taxpayer is repaid an amount owed to him, he does not have an accession to wealth. He has simply received a return of his capital.

Example. Miryoung had a savings account with $10,000 and had loaned $4,000 to Linda. Three years later Linda repaid the $4,000 and Miryoung deposited the money into her savings account. There are no tax consequences to Miryoung either from loaning the money or upon receiving repayment.

Before repayment of loan		After repayment of loan	
Savings account	$10,000	Savings account	$14,000
Loan	4,000		
Net worth:	$14,000	Net worth:	$14,000

B. Income from Discharge of a Debt

When the obligation to repay is discharged in whole or in part, the taxpayer has cancellation of indebtedness income.[42] The amount of the income generally is the difference between the amount of debt outstanding and the amount paid in satisfaction of the debt.

In *Kirby Lumber Co. v. United States*[43] the taxpayer borrowed funds and later discharged the debt by paying less than the outstanding amount of debt. The court held that Kirby Lumber had gross income equal to the difference between the amount owed and the amount paid to discharge the debt.

Let's take an example reflective of *Kirby Lumber*, but simpler. Kirby had a bank account containing $100,000 and no liabilities. He borrowed $10,000 from Lendco, signing a note in which he agreed to repay the funds at the end of three years. He deposited the borrowed funds into his bank account. If we consider his financial situation before and after the transaction it would appear as follows:

---

42. Section 61(a)(12).
43. 284 U.S. 1 (1931).

Before the loan		After the loan	
Bank account:	$100,000	Bank account:	$110,000
Liability:	-0-	Note:	<10,000>
Net:	$100,000	Net:	$100,000

Because there has been no change to Kirby's net worth on account of the loan, he does not have gross income.

In year two, Kirby believes he will not be able to repay the debt. He enters into negotiations with Lendco and eventually Lendco agrees to accept $2,000 in full satisfaction of the debt. Assuming all other items have remained the same (while certainly an artificial assumption, it keeps all other items the same, allowing us to see just the impact of the settlement of the debt on Kirby's net worth), the transaction could be viewed as follows:

Before the settlement		After the settlement	
Bank account:	$110,000	Bank account:	$108,000
Liability:	<10,000>	Note:	-0-
Net:	$100,000	Net:	$108,000

Because there has been an $8,000 increase in Kirby's net worth due to discharge of $8,000 of the debt, Kirby has $8,000 accession to wealth, or $8,000 of gross income from cancellation of indebtedness.[44]

Summary

Tax consequences of obtaining a loan: To the extent the taxpayer has borrowed money that he has an obligation to repay, he does not have gross income.

Tax consequences from cancellation of debt: If:

- A taxpayer has borrowed money that he has an obligation to repay; and
- Part of the obligation to repay is later forgiven;

He has gross income to the extent he no longer is required to repay the borrowed amount.

Contingent or contested liabilities. Until the amount of the outstanding debt is determined, there can be no forgiveness of that debt. Accordingly, under the contested liability doctrine, there is no cancellation of indebtedness income upon settlement of a *disputed* debt. For this provision to be applicable, the taxpayer must dispute the original amount of the debt in good faith.

There is a split among the circuits when dealing with debts that are, or might be considered, disputed or unliquidated. The Third Circuit held that the contested liability

---

44. Section 61(a)(12); Kirby Lumber Co. v. United States, 284 U.S. 1 (1931).

doctrine can be used if the original amount of the debt was liquidated (i.e., determinable), but unenforceable. In *Zarin v. Commissioner*[45] the taxpayer borrowed over $3 million from a casino. When he could not repay the borrowed amount, the taxpayer and the casino agreed to a settle the debt with a payment of $500,000. The taxpayer agreed to the payment even though the underlying debt was a gambling debt that was not enforceable under state law.

The Commissioner argued that the taxpayer could not contend it was a contested liability because the amount of the debt was not unliquidated (i.e., undeterminable). The Commissioner argued that rather than being unliquidated, the debt was unenforceable. The Third Circuit disagreed with the Commissioner and held that when the enforceability of the debt is at issue the amount of the debt is in dispute, making the contested liability doctrine applicable. Accordingly, the court found there was no discharge of indebtedness income when the taxpayer paid just $500,000.

In *Preslar v. Commissioner*[46] the Tenth Circuit held that the contested liability doctrine can be used only if the original amount of the debt is unliquidated. The taxpayer agreed to purchase a ranch for $1 million, financed by a loan. When $800,000 of the loan amount remained outstanding, a dispute arose as to what was an acceptable method of payment. The taxpayers filed an action for breach of contract and the suit was eventually settled with the taxpayers agreeing to pay $300,000 and lender agreeing to forgive the remaining $500,000 of debt. The taxpayer argued that the $500,000 of extinguished debt was not cancellation of indebtedness income because the debt was not enforceable.

In reaching its decision, the Tenth Circuit disagreed with the position of the taxpayer and the holding of the Third Circuit in *Zarin*. For a liability to be contested, the original amount of the debt must be unliquidated; if the parties treated the transaction as a loan when the proceeds were received, then the transaction should be treated consistently when the loan is discharged. In *Preslar*, because no legitimate dispute arose regarding the nature or amount of the loan at issue, it was not a contested liability and the contested liability doctrine was, therefore, inapplicable. When $500,000 of the debt was discharged, the taxpayers had $500,000 in cancellation of indebtedness income.

Liability would have given rise to a deduction. No cancellation of indebtedness income is realized if the payment of the liability would have given rise to a deduction that has not yet been deducted.[47] The exclusion makes economic sense: if the taxpayer had been required to include the amount in gross income and would have been entitled to a deduction in the same amount, the net result would be a wash.

Example. Felix owns and operates a car dealership on rented property. He is entitled to a deduction for the rent he pays. Because business has slowed down considerably, Felix is unable to pay the rent. The landlord forgives three months worth of unpaid rent. Felix is not required to include the forgiven rent in his gross income. If he had done so, he would have been entitled to a deduction for a rental payment. The income and the deduction would be in the same amount.

Purchase Money Debt Reduction. A seller may sell property to a buyer-taxpayer and finance the sale. Later, the buyer and seller may agree to reduce the outstanding amount of debt owed with respect to the property. If the seller does so, the reduction is treated

---

45. 916 F.2d 110 (3d Cir. 1990), *rev'g* 92 T.C. 1084 (1989).
46. 167 F.3d 1323, 1328 (10th Cir. 1999), *rev'g and remanding* T.C. Memo. 1996-543.
47. Section 108(e)(2).

as a reduction in purchase price and not cancellation of indebtedness income. The property's basis is reduced by the same amount the debt was reduced.[48]

C. Exclusion of Cancellation of Indebtedness Income

Section 108 provides an exclusion for income from cancellation of indebtedness income. Note, however, that the exclusion may apply only if the income at issue is cancellation of indebtedness income (as opposed to any other type of income).

1. Discharge Occurs While the Taxpayer Is in Bankruptcy

Discharge of indebtedness income can be excluded if the discharge occurs as part of a bankruptcy proceeding.[49]

Section 108. Income From Discharge of Indebtedness

(a) Exclusion From Gross Income. —

(1) In General. — Gross income does not include any amount which (but for this subsection) would be includible in gross income by reason of the discharge (in whole or in part) of indebtedness of the taxpayer if —

(A) the discharge occurs in a title 11 case . . .

Example. Marika filed a Chapter 7 bankruptcy. As part of the bankruptcy proceedings her $10,000 debt owed to BankCo was discharged. Marika has $10,000 of income from cancellation of the debt. However, she can exclude this amount from her income because the debt was discharged as part of a bankruptcy proceeding.

Tell Me More

If the taxpayer has debt discharged through a bankruptcy proceeding, it is not entirely without tax consequences. He is required to reduce certain tax attributes to the extent of the excluded income. The reduction is made to the following tax attributes, in the order listed:

The taxpayer may elect to reduce the basis of depreciable property. Then, the taxpayer must reduce:

---

48. Section 108(e)(5). For this provision to apply, the buyer-taxpayer cannot be in bankruptcy or be insolvent.

49. Section 108(a)(1)(A).

First: Any net operating loss

Second: Any general business credits

Third: Minimum tax credit

Fourth: Any net capital loss

Fifth: The basis of property

Sixth: Passive activity losses or credits

Seventh: Foreign tax credit carryovers

Any remaining excluded cancellation of indebtedness income is disregarded.[50]

Steps for Determining Cancellation of Indebtedness Income When the Taxpayer Has Filed for Bankruptcy

1. Determine the amount of income the taxpayer has from the cancellation of a debt.

2. To the extent discharge of the debt occurred as part of a bankruptcy, exclude the amount from the taxpayer's income.

2. Discharge Occurs While the Taxpayer Is Insolvent

Discharge of indebtedness income can be excluded if the taxpayer is insolvent at the time of the discharge.[51] But the exclusion extends only to the extent of the taxpayer's insolvency.[52] A debtor is insolvent if his liabilities exceed the fair market value of his assets. The determination of solvency is made immediately before any debt has been discharged.[53]

Section 108. Income from Discharge of Indebtedness

(a) Exclusion From Gross Income. —

(1) In General. — Gross income does not include any amount which (but for this subsection) would be includible in gross income by reason of the discharge (in whole or in part) of indebtedness of the taxpayer if— ...

(B) the discharge occurs when the taxpayer is insolvent ...

(3) Insolvency Exclusion Limited to Amount of Insolvency. — In the case of a discharge to which paragraph (1)(B) applies, the amount excluded under paragraph (1)(B) shall not exceed the amount by which the taxpayer is insolvent.

---

50. Section 108(b).
51. Section 108(a)(1)(B).
52. Section 108(a)(3).
53. Section 108(d)(3).

Note that this results in the taxpayer reporting the cancellation of indebtedness income only to the extent the taxpayer becomes solvent.

Example. Nick owns assets with a fair market value of $230,000. He owes $150,000 to BankCo and $150,000 to Visa. Because his liabilities ($150,000 + $150,000 = $300,000) exceed his assets by $70,000, Nick is insolvent.

Assets: $230,000
Liabilities: 300,000
              <$70,000>

BankCo enters into an agreement with Nick where Nick will pay BankCo $70,000 and BankCo will forgive the remaining $80,000 of the debt. Nick has $80,000 of cancellation of indebtedness income. He can exclude the indebtedness income to the extent he is insolvent. Thus, he can exclude $70,000 and must report the remaining $10,000 as cancellation of indebtedness income.

$80,000 of debt relief:

$10,000 – amount of debt relief recognized

$70,000 – amount of debt relief excluded from income

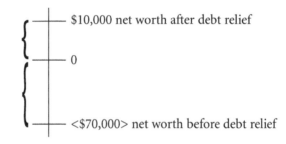

$10,000 net worth after debt relief

0

<$70,000> net worth before debt relief

$80,000 cancellation of indebtedness income
– 70,000 extent to which Nick was insolvent
$10,000 recognized income

Tell Me More

If the taxpayer has excluded cancellation of indebtedness income from gross income to the extent the taxpayer was insolvent, the exclusion is not entirely without tax consequences. He is required to reduce certain tax attributes to the extent of the excluded income. The reduction is made to the tax attributes in the same manner as a taxpayer who has had a debt discharged in bankruptcy.[54]

Steps for Determining Cancellation of Indebtedness Income When the Taxpayer Is Insolvent

1. Determine the amount of income the taxpayer has from the cancellation of a debt.

2. Determine the extent to which the taxpayer was insolvent before the debt was discharged.

----

54. Section 108(b).

3. Subtract the amount by which the taxpayer was insolvent (determined in step 2) from the amount of income from cancellation of the debt (determined in step 1). The remainder, if any, is the amount of income from cancellation of the debt the taxpayer must report.

3. Discharge of Certain Student Loans

The discharge of a student loan, whether in whole or in part, constitutes discharge of indebtedness income.[55] That income may be excludable from gross income if the discharge is pursuant to a provision that the individual work for a certain period of time in a certain profession.[56]

To qualify for the exclusion, the loan must be to an individual to assist in attending an educational organization and made by specifically identified types of entities.[57] In addition, the student must work for a certain period of time in a certain profession for a broad class of employers. The work must be in an occupation or area with unmet needs and the work must be performed for or under the direction of a tax-exempt charitable organization or a governmental entity.[58]

4. Qualified Principal Residence Indebtedness

The downturn in the economy has left many taxpayers unable to make their mortgage payments. Moreover, the value of the house often is insufficient to cover the outstanding mortgage. Thus, if the taxpayer simply walks away from the home, to the extent the debt exceeds the value of the house, the taxpayer still has an outstanding liability. In many cases the bank forgives this remaining outstanding amount. The forgiveness of an outstanding mortgage is discharge of indebtedness income. This income can be excluded if it qualifies as "qualified principal residence indebtedness."[59]

Qualified principal residence indebtedness is debt incurred in acquiring, constructing, or substantially improving any qualified residence of the taxpayer and secured by the residence.[60] The aggregate amount that can be treated as acquisition indebtedness cannot exceed $2,000,000 ($1,000,000 in the case of a married individual filing a separate return).[61] Principal residence is defined the same as in Section 121.[62] The discharge must be related to a decline in the value of the residence or to the financial condition of the taxpayer.[63] When the exclusion applies, the taxpayer must reduce the basis in his residence by the amount excluded (but not below zero).[64]

---

55. Section 61(a)(12).
56. Section 108(f)(1).
57. Section 108(f)(2).
58. Rev. Rul. 2008-34, 2008-2 C.B. 76.
59. Section 108(a)(1)(E).
60. Sections 108(h)(2); 163(h)(3)(B)(i).
61. Sections 108(h)(2); 163(h)(3)(B)(ii).
62. Section 108(h)(5). Section 121 is discussed in Chapter 42. See also Treas. Reg. 1.121-1(b).
63. Section 108(h)(3).
64. Section 108(h)(1). The exclusion does not apply to a discharge in bankruptcy. It is applied before the insolvency exclusion, unless the taxpayer elects otherwise. Section 108(a)(2)(A), (C).

D. Substance Over Form

The tax consequences resulting from the cancellation of indebtedness are based on the substance of the transaction and not the form or the taxpayer's characterization of the transaction. More specifically, in some situations a transaction must be broken down into it component parts, with the correct tax consequences applied to each separate part.

For example, when the taxpayer already owed the bank $400,000 he borrowed an additional $500,000. He used the borrowed funds to purchase Blackacre for $500,000. Five years later Blackacre had increased in value to $600,000 and the taxpayer owed the bank a total of $800,000 (considering both loans). However, the taxpayer was insolvent and unable to repay the $800,000 debt (and would continue to be insolvent even if the $800,000 debt were forgiven). The taxpayer and the bank entered into an agreement whereby the taxpayer would transfer Blackacre to the bank and the bank would forgive the debt.

The agreement between the taxpayer and the bank must be broken down into its component parts. First, the taxpayer has disposed of property, Blackacre. The bank would pay no more than the fair market value for the property, or $600,000. The amount realized from the disposition of Blackacre is $600,000. The taxpayer's basis was $500,000. Accordingly, the taxpayer has $100,000 of income from the disposition of property; he must include this $100,000 in his income.[65]

Because the bank paid for Blackacre with $600,000 of debt relief, the taxpayer's debt to the bank has decreased by $600,000, from $800,000 to $200,000. Then the bank forgave the $200,000 debt. Forgiveness of debt is an accession to wealth that must be included in income.[66] However, the taxpayer can exclude the $200,000 accession to wealth because he is insolvent both before and after the debt relief.[67]

In sum, based on the agreement entered into between the taxpayer and the bank, the taxpayer must report $100,000 (from the disposition of property).

E. Application of Rules

Example 1. Tigran borrowed $5,000 from BankCo. Three years later, he repaid the funds. There are no tax consequences to Tigran, either in the year he obtained the loan or in the year he repaid the loan.

Example 2. Roman was a shareholder in StockCo. This year StockCo paid him $5,000. There is no evidence the transaction was a loan, such as a promissory note or other evidence of an obligation to repay. The $5,000 payment is a dividend which Roman must include in his gross income.

Example 3. Deborah borrowed $15,000 from BankCo. Five years later, when she owed $10,000 on the loan, she lost her job and was unable to continue making payments. BankCo forgave the debt. Deborah has $10,000 of income from cancellation of the debt.

---

65. Section 61(a)(3).
66. Section 61(a)(12).
67. Section 108(a)(1)(B).

Example 4. A local charity was conducting a fund drive. When they called Allison, she pledged to contribute $1,000. However, when it came time to mail in her pledge, she only sent $600. She was unable to afford the remaining $400 of the pledge.

Because Allison was not in the situation described in *Kirby Lumber* (borrowed funds with an offsetting obligation to repay) there can be no cancellation of indebtedness income.

Example 5. Susan hired Al to landscape her yard. Susan agreed to pay Al $10,000. When Al had finished his work, Susan was very unhappy. Several shrubs and flowering trees she had requested be incorporated into the landscaping plan had not been planted. Susan believed this substantially diminished the value of the landscaping and that Al's work did not merit a payment of $10,000. After lengthy negotiations, Al agreed to accept $7,000 as payment in full.

Because the $10,000 debt to Al was disputed, it is not a debt for tax purposes. Accordingly, there can be no cancellation of indebtedness income when the parties agree to a payment of $7,000.

Example 6. Stephanie owns and operates a beauty salon. She rents the building in which her shop is located and is entitled to a deduction for the rent that she pays. Because business has slowed down considerably, Stephanie has been unable to pay the last six months of rent. She contacts the landlord and the landlord agrees to forgive four months worth of unpaid rent.

Stephanie is not required to include the forgiven rent in her gross income. If she had done so, she also would have been entitled to a deduction for a rental payment. (Note that the income and the deduction would be in the same amount—a wash.)

Example 7. Evan purchased a tractor from FarmCo, agreeing to pay FarmCo a total of $15,000 over the next five years. However, Evan's business fell on hard times and he was unable to make all the scheduled payments. He contacted FarmCo and negotiated a reduced purchase price for the tractor. FarmCo agreed Evan would be required to pay only a total of $13,000 for the tractor. The reduction is treated as an adjustment of the purchase price; Evan does not have to report any cancellation of indebtedness income. (Evan's basis in the tractor also is reduced to $13,000.)

Example 8. Blair filed a Chapter 7 bankruptcy. As part of the bankruptcy proceedings his $15,000 debt to SupplierCo was reduced to $10,000. Blair has $5,000 of income from the cancellation of debt. However, he can exclude this amount from his income because the debt was discharged as part of a bankruptcy proceeding.

Example 9. David owns assets with a fair market value of $80. He owes $200 to BankCo. Because his liabilities ($200) exceed his assets ($80) by $120, David is insolvent.

BankCo enters into an agreement with David where David will pay BankCo $80 and BankCo will forgive the remaining $120 of the debt. David has $120 of cancellation of indebtedness income. He can exclude the indebtedness income to the extent he is insolvent. Because he was insolvent by $120, he can exclude all $120 of cancellation of indebtedness income.

Example 10. Tony owns assets with a fair market value of $130. He owes $100 to BankCo and $100 to Visa. Because his liabilities ($100 + $100 = $200) exceed his assets ($130) by $70, Tony is insolvent.

BankCo enters into an agreement with Tony where Tony will pay BankCo $20 and BankCo will forgive the remaining $80 of the debt. Tony has $80 of cancellation of indebtedness income. He can exclude the indebtedness income to the extent he is insolvent.

Because he is insolvent by $70, he can exclude $70 and must report the remaining $10 as cancellation of indebtedness income.

F. Problems

1. Janice borrows $10,000 from her employer. She signed a promissory note agreeing to repay the amount over five years. Three years later, when she had reduced the out-standing amount of the note to $7,000, she found herself unable to make the remaining payments. What are the tax consequences to Janice under the following alternative scenarios.

   a. Her employer agrees to forgive the remaining $7,000 balance of the loan.

   b. Her employer agrees to forgive the remaining $7,000 balance of the loan if she agrees to work every Saturday for the next six months.

2. When Beth was in need of money she borrowed $5,000 from her sister. Beth agreed to repay her sister as soon as she could. Is this transaction a loan? If not, what else might it be?

3. Otto is large-scale land developer. He hired an architect to prepare blueprints for a large condominium complex he was going to build later in the year, agreeing to pay the architect $10,000. Even though the architect said he had spent a considerable amount of time preparing the plans and prepared them to Otto's specifications, Otto was unhappy with the end product. After lengthy and often heated negotiations, Otto and the architect agreed to a payment of $8,000. What are the tax consequences to Otto?

4. Bob filed a Chapter 11 bankruptcy. As part of the bankruptcy workout proceedings, his $25,000 debt to FarmCo was reduced to $15,000 and his $50,000 debt to AgriTec was reduced to $10,000. What are the tax consequences to Bob?

5. Paul owns assets with a fair market value of $300,000. He owes $500,000 to BankCo and $200,000 to LendCo. BankCo enters into an agreement with Paul where Paul will pay BankCo $200,000 and BankCo will forgive the remaining $300,000 of the debt. What are the tax consequences to Paul?

6. Christian owns assets with a fair market value of $400,000. He owes $500,000 to BankCo. BankCo enters into an agreement with Christian where Christian will pay BankCo $200,000 and BankCo will forgive the remaining $300,000 of the debt. What are the tax consequences to Christian?

G. Analysis and Application

1. What documents would you ask your client to provide to you to establish that a transaction was a loan? What provisions would you hope to find included in the documents?

2. Create a list of questions to ask a client to obtain information necessary to determine if the client has income from the cancellation of indebtedness and if that income can be excluded.

3. Tim is your client. For the past three years he has been trying to pay off his credit card debt. This year, unable to substantially reduce the balance, he negotiated with the credit card company for a reduction in the amount owed.

   a. Are there any tax consequences to Tim from the reduction? To answer this question, do you need any additional information?

   b. Given that your answer may seem counter-intuitive to Tim, how could you most effectively explain your conclusion to him?

4. In 2005 Thomas purchased land in Florida with the intention of developing the property into a resort destination with multiple gated communities. In 2006, he contacted a developer who specialized in land development. To finance the development, Thomas borrowed $1,000,000 from First Bank. The project was substantially completed by mid-2007, with the land subdivided into plats, electricity and power available at each site, and the entire development connected to the city sewer.

   In late 2007, a series of murders and robberies in the area substantially hurt tourism and impacted Thomas's ability to sell the lots. The lack of sales impacted his cash flow and he was unable to continue making payments on the loan from First Bank. Furthermore, because of ensuing financial pressures, Thomas was unable to market the lots on a consistent or productive basis.

   Even though he worked with the bank for several months to bring payments on the loan current, in 2009 he defaulted on the loan. He deeded the land with the improvements to First Bank. At the time of the transfer, the outstanding amount of the debt was $800,000. His basis in the property and the improvements was $500,000 and the fair market value was $600,000. In exchange, First Bank forgave the remaining outstanding debt. Even so, Thomas was still insolvent.

   What are the tax consequences to Thomas of the transactions? In formulating your analysis and response, you may want to consider:

   • United States v. Kirby Lumber Co., 284 U.S. 1 (1931)

   • Bressi v. Commissioner, T.C. Memo. 1991-651

   • Gehl v. Commissioner, 50 F.3d 12 (8th Cir. 1995)

5. Mr. and Mrs. Pratt entered into an agreement with their bank to reduce the outstanding amount owed on their credit card. Cancellation of the debt resulted in cancellation of indebtedness income. The taxpayers argued that the reduction was a retroactive reduction of the rate of interest, resulting in a reduction in the purchase price of the loans from the bank, and, therefore, not cancellation of indebtedness income.

   Do you agree with Mr. and Mrs. Pratt? In formulating your analysis and response, you may want to consider:

   • United States v. Kirby Lumber Co., 284 U.S. 1 (1931)

   • Estate of Smith v. Commissioner, 198 F.3d 515 (5th Cir. 1999), *rev'g and remanding* 108 T.C. 412 (1997)

   • Earnshaw v. Commissioner, T.C. Memo. 2002-191.

III

Items Excluded from Gross Income

Includes all accessions to wealth, such as:	Excludes:
• Compensation for services • Business profits • Profit from the sale of property • Interest • Rents • Royalties • Dividends • Alimony • Cancellation of debt	• Loans and deposits • Gifts and inheritances • Life insurance • Certain prizes and awards • Qualified scholarships • Personal injury damages • Fringe benefits • Health insurance • Workers' compensation

Chapter 7

Deposits and Prepayments

Gross Income

Includes all accessions to wealth, such as:	Excludes:
• Compensation for services	• **Loans and deposits**
• Business profits	• Gifts and inheritances
• Profit from the sale of property	• Life insurance
• Interest	• Certain prizes and awards
• Rents	• Qualified scholarships
• Royalties	• Personal injury damages
• Dividends	• Fringe benefits
• Alimony	• Health insurance
• Cancellation of debt	• Workers' compensation

Read

Code Sections 61(a)

Treas. Reg. §§ 1.61-8(b)

A. Background

Gross income. Gross income includes income (accessions to wealth) derived from any and all sources.[1] It includes every accession to wealth, unless there is an exception. Receiving a prepayment is an accession to wealth. Receiving a loan or security deposit is not.

B. Deposits

If the taxpayer receives a deposit, the taxpayer has an obligation to return the funds if the required conditions underlying the transfer of money have been met. This result holds true even though the taxpayer has full use of the funds, does not need to segregate them,

---

1. Section 61(a).

or otherwise account for the funds. Any increase in his assets is offset by his obligation to repay the deposit, as agreed by the parties.

Example. Lou owns an apartment building. Lou enters into a lease with Emily, agreeing to lease an apartment to her for $1,500 a month. He also requires her to pay a $1,000 security deposit. If at the end of the lease she leaves the apartment in good condition he will return the security deposit to her.

At the time Lou enters into the lease and receives the $1,000 security deposit, he does not have an accession to wealth because he has an obligation to return the funds to Emily if she complies with the terms of the lease agreement.

C. Prepayment

When a taxpayer receives a prepayment of income, the taxpayer does not have a corollary obligation to return the funds. Accordingly, the taxpayer has an accession to wealth (gross income).[2]

Example. PhoneCo sells cell phones. Celeste purchased a phone from PhoneCo and paid $500 for 900 minutes of use on the phone. Celeste cannot receive a refund for the prepaid minutes if she decides she does not want to use them. PhoneCo has received a $500 prepayment and must include this amount in its gross income.

Rules

- Because of the offsetting obligation to repay the funds, neither a loan nor a security deposit is gross income.
- Because there is no offsetting obligation to repay a prepayment, a prepayment is gross income.

D. Distinguishing a Deposit from a Prepayment

In some situations, it may be not be readily apparent whether a transaction is a deposit or prepayment. The characterization of the transaction depends on who has control over the funds. This determination is made at the time the transaction is entered into and is based on the terms of the contract.[3]

In *Commissioner v. Indianapolis Power & Light Co.*[4] certain customers were required to pay a deposit to the electric company before an account would be established. The deposit was to assure the payment of future electric bills.

---

2. Section 61(a).
3. Commissioner v. Indianapolis Power & Light, 493 U.S. 203 (1990).
4. 493 U.S. 203 (1990).

The customers required to make the deposit were those with poor credit. The deposits were not physically segregated and could be used by the electric company for any purpose. However, the electric company paid interest on deposits held for a specified length of time. If a customer established a history of timely payments, he could request a refund of the deposit either through a cash payment or by having the deposit applied to a future bill. If a customer terminated service he could receive a refund of the deposit.

The Supreme Court looked at the rights and obligations of the electric company and the customer at the time the deposit was made. The factual issue before the court was whether the electric company had some guarantee it would be allowed to keep the funds. The court found that, having made a deposit, a customer was not required to purchase any amount of electricity. In addition, when the customer established a good payment history, the customer could ask for a refund of the deposit or direct that it be credited against future bills.

Based on these facts and circumstances, the electric company did not have the control over the funds it would have had if it had been a prepayment. Rather, the deposits were subject to an obligation of the electric company to repay the funds when the account was terminated or when the customer established a good payment history. Because the timing and method of the refund were largely within the control of the customer, the customer controlled the funds, qualifying them as deposits.[5]

Determination — Deposit or Prepayment

- Based on who has control of the funds.
- The determination of who has control is made at the time the parties enter into the contract based on the terms of the contract.

Commissioner v. Indianapolis Power & Light Co., 493 US 203 (1990)

E. Application of Rules

Example 1. Lou owns an apartment building. Lou enters into a lease with Emily, agreeing to lease an apartment to her for $1,500 a month. He also requires her to pay a $1,000 security deposit. If, at the end of the lease, she leaves the apartment in good condition he will return the security deposit to her.

At the time Lou enters into the lease and receives the $1,000 security deposit, he does not have an accession to wealth. He has an obligation to return the funds to Emily if she complies with the terms of the lease agreement.

Five years later, Emily gave Lou notice that she would not be renewing the lease. She asked Lou to apply the security deposit to her last month's rent. She left the apartment in good condition. At the time Lou converts the funds from a security deposit to a lease payment he has gross income (rental income).

---

5. *Indianapolis Power & Light, Co., supra.*

Example 2. Trevor owns an apartment building. Trevor enters into a lease with Katie, agreeing to lease an apartment to her for $1,500 a month. Under the lease agreement, Katie must pay the last month's rent when she signs the lease. At the time Trevor enters into the lease he receives a prepayment of rent which is includible in his income.

F. Problems

1. Joshua decided to vacation at Lake Tahoe for a week in January. In November of the prior year he located a house to rent. The owner of the home required Joshua to make a $1,000 deposit to hold the reservation. Joshua sent the deposit in late November. After Joshua had completed his stay in January the owner calculated how much Joshua owed, taking into consideration the $1,000 deposit. What were the tax consequences to the owner in November when he received the deposit? Do you need any additional information to make the determination? *Not Taxable until it is make a determination* [handwritten]

2. Madeleine owns and operates a dance studio. If a client wants to take dance lessons, he must agree to take a minimum of ten lessons. While the ten lessons must be paid for in advance, the client can schedule each lesson based on his own schedule.

    In December Hasid paid for ten lessons but was able to take only one before the end of the year. He will take the remaining nine lessons the following year. Has Madeleine received a prepayment when Hasid paid for the ten lessons?

3. Isabella performs magic tricks. She was hired by Renaissance Festival to perform at the festival every Saturday from May through August. On May 1 the Renaissance Festival paid her a $10,000 lump sum as payment for all the performances. What were the tax consequences to Isabella when she received the payment on May 1?

G. Analysis and Application

1   Draft language for a rental agreement establishing a payment as a security deposit.

2   Draft language for a rental agreement establishing the payment of the last month's rent as a prepayment.

3   The local gas company wants to require new customers to pay a deposit before the gas to the house or apartment is turned on. The company does not want the payments characterized as prepayments. Draft language for the gas company to include in the contact that will allow the payments to be characterized as deposits.

Chapter 8

Gifts and Inheritances

Gross Income

Includes all accessions to wealth, such as:	Excludes:
• Compensation for services	• Loans and deposits
• Business profits	• **Gifts and inheritances**
• Profit from the sale of property	• Life insurance
• Interest	• Certain prizes and awards
• Rents	• Qualified scholarships
• Royalties	• Personal injury damages
• Dividends	• Fringe benefits
• Alimony	• Health insurance
• Cancellation of debt	• Workers' compensation

Read

Code Sections 102; 1014(a)(1); 1015(a)

Treas. Reg. §§ 1.102-1(a), (b); Prop. Reg. 1.102-1(f); 1.1001-1(e); 1.1001-2(a)(1), (4)(iii); 1.1015-1(a); 1.1015-4

A. Background

Gross income. Gross income includes income (accessions to wealth) derived from any and all sources.[6] It includes every accession to wealth, unless there is an exception. Receiving a gift or inheritance is an accession to wealth.

Basis. A taxpayer's basis in property is the amount the taxpayer paid for the property.[7] In general, when a taxpayer purchases property, he pays fair market value for the property. Thus, normally a taxpayer's basis in property is the fair market value of property at the time of purchase.

---

6. Section 61(a).
7. Section 1012(a).

B. Gifts

1. Rule and Definition of Gift for Federal Income Tax Purposes

A gift represents an accession to wealth — the taxpayer is better off after receiving the gift than before the gift. However, Congress decided it would be too intrusive and administratively difficult to measure the value of every gift that a taxpayer received during a taxable year. Thus, as a matter of policy, Congress decided to exclude the receipt of a gift from gross income. Under Section 102, gifts are excluded from gross income.

Section 102. Gifts and Inheritances

(a) General Rule. — Gross income does not include the value of property acquired by gift, bequest, devise, or inheritance.

(b) Income. Subsection (a) shall not exclude from gross income —

    (1) the income from any property referred to in subsection (a); or

    (2) where the gift, bequest, devise, or inheritance is of income from property, the amount of such income....

(c) Employee gifts.

    (1) In general. Subsection (a) shall not exclude from gross income any amount transferred by or for an employer to, or for the benefit of, an employee....

There is no ambiguity in the Code as far as providing an exclusion from gross income for gifts. However, there has been some uncertainty about what constitutes a gift for purposes of coming within the exclusion because the Code does not define "gift." The Supreme Court in *Commissioner v. Duberstein*[8] addressed this issue.

Mr. Duberstein was the president of Duberstein Iron & Metal Company. Mr. Berman was the president of Mohawk Metal Corporation. Both companies were in the business of buying and selling metals. For many years, the two companies and two presidents had done business together. Occasionally Mr. Berman would ask Mr. Duberstein if he knew of potential customers for his company's products, and, if Mr. Duberstein knew of any, he would supply the information to Mr. Berman.

On one occasion, the information Mr. Duberstein provided to Mr. Berman was so beneficial, Mr. Berman gave Mr. Duberstein a Cadillac. Mr. Duberstein stated that he had not been expecting anything in exchange for the information he had provided and, moreover, did not believe he needed an additional car. Mohawk deducted the value of the Cadillac as a business expense on its corporate income tax return. Mr. Duberstein excluded the value of the car from his gross income, claiming it was a gift.

---

8. 363 U.S. 278 (1960).

In determining whether the car was a gift from Mr. Berman to Mr. Duberstein, the court began by noting that the definition of gift for tax purposes was not the same as the colloquial or common-law definition of gift. It is not sufficient that the transferor have no moral or legal obligation to transfer the property. The Supreme Court, instead, focused on the intent of the transferor. The transfer must proceed from a "detached and disinterested generosity,"[9] in the sense that the transferor expects nothing in return. The transfer must be made out of affection, respect, admiration, or charity. Whether this intent is present is made on an objective basis, based on the facts and circumstances.[10]

Based on the facts before it, the Supreme Court concluded that Mr. Berman transferred the Cadillac to Mr. Duberstein as compensation for Mr. Duberstein's past services or as an inducement to be of service in the future. Because the Cadillac was not transferred out of affection, etc., the Cadillac was not a gift. Mr. Duberstein could not exclude the value of the car from his gross income.

Definition of Gift

A gift proceeds from a detached and disinterested generosity out of affection, respect, admiration, charity, or like impulses.

- The most critical consideration is the transferor's intent.
- The transferor's intent is determined objectively by "application of the fact-finding tribunal's experience with the mainsprings of human conduct to the totality of the facts of each case" (i.e., based on the facts and circumstances).

Commissioner v. Duberstein, 363 US 278 (1960)

Note that whether a transfer qualifies as a gift is highly dependent upon the relationship between the parties. If a transfer is made in a business context, it is unlikely the transfer will qualify as a gift. In contrast, if there is no business relationship between the parties, it is more likely the transfer will qualify as a gift.

2. Limitations on Gift Exclusion

While the value of property received by a taxpayer as a gift can be excluded from gross income, income from that property cannot be excluded.[11] For example, if the taxpayer receives stock as a gift, he can exclude the value of the stock (the gift) but not any dividends (income) paid with respect to the stock.

Similarly, a transfer of income cannot be excluded as a gift.[12] For example, if the taxpayer receives the right to receive dividends paid with respect to stock as a gift, he cannot exclude the dividends (income) from his gross income as a gift.

---

9. Commissioner v. Duberstein, 363 U.S. 278, 285 (1960).
10. *Duberstein*, 363 U.S. at 289.
11. Section 102(b)(1).
12. Section 102(b)(2).

Finally, property that is transferred from an employer to or for the benefit of an employee cannot be a gift.[13] In general, such transfers must be treated by the employee as compensation for services.

Summary of Items That Cannot Be Excluded from Gross Income as a Gift

The following items cannot be excluded from income as a gift:

- Income generated from property received as a gift.
- A gift of income.
- Transfers of cash or property by an employer to an employee.

---

3. Part Gift, Part Sale

A taxpayer may sell property for less than its fair market value, intending the transfer to be partly a gift[14] and partly a sale. The taxpayer-seller realizes gain to the extent the amount realized exceeds his basis in the property. If the taxpayer-seller sells the property for less than his basis, he cannot recognize (report) a loss on the disposition.[15]

Example. Patsy owned Whiteacre. Her basis in the property was $10,000 and its fair market value was $50,000. Patsy sold Whiteacre to Quinn, her niece, for $40,000.

The transaction is partly a gift and partly a sale. Patsy realizes gain to the extent the amount realized ($40,000) exceeds her basis in the property ($10,000). Thus, Patsy has a $30,000 gain. Patsy has made a gift to Quinn of $10,000 ($50,000 fair market value of the property, less $40,000 paid).

If Patsy had sold Whiteacre to Quinn for $7,000, Patsy realizes a $3,000 loss ($7,000 amount realized less $10,000 basis). Patsy cannot recognize (report) the loss. Patsy has made a gift to Quinn of $43,000 ($50,000 fair market value of the property, less $7,000 paid).

4. Transferee's Basis in the Gifted Property

The general rule is that the basis of property is the amount paid for the property.[16] However, when a taxpayer receives a gift, he has not paid for the property. Thus, the general rule can have no applicability to property received as a gift. Aware of this problem,

---

13. Section 102(c)(1).

14. For the transfer to be in part a gift, the transferor must have the intent identified in Commissioner v. Duberstein, 363 U.S. 278 (1960), of detached and disinterested generosity. If there is a different intent, such as an intent to provide compensation, the part-gift, part sale rules will not apply.

15. Treas. Reg. § 1.1001-1(e)(1).

16. Section 1012(a). Chapters 22, 25, and 29 discuss adjustments to basis. If the basis has been so adjusted, the analysis is performed with the adjusted basis used in place of the cost basis of the property.

Congress enacted rules for determining the basis of property received as a gift. Within these rules, there is a general rule and a special rule.[17]

Section 1015. Basis of Property Acquired by Gifts and Transfers in Trust

(a) Gifts after December 31, 1920. If the property was acquired by gift after December 31, 1920, the basis shall be the same as it would be in the hands of the donor ... except that if such basis ... is greater than the fair market value of the property at the time of the gift, then for the purpose of determining loss the basis shall be such fair market value....

General rule. Under the general rule, the donee takes the donor's basis in the property.[18] Sometimes this basis is called a carry-over basis.

Example. Stan purchased Pinkacre for $10,000. Five years later, when the value of Pinkacre had increased to $25,000, he gifted the property to Marie. Under the general rule, Marie would take Stan's basis in the property so that her basis in Pinkacre is $10,000.

Special rule. Congress did not want the donor to be able to transfer a loss to a donee through a gift of depreciated property. Accordingly, to the extent of the decrease in value of the property in the hands of the donor, the donee is not allowed to claim a loss when the donee subsequently sells the property. Congress achieves this result by giving the donee a basis in the property equal to the fair market value of the property as of the date of the gift.[19]

When property has decreased in value as of the date of the gift, for purposes of determining gain or loss when the donee disposes of the property, the donee's basis in the gifted property will depend on whether the value of the property in the hands of the donee: stayed the same or increased but to not more than what the donor paid for the property (all the property's decrease in value occurred in the hands of the donor); continued to decrease in value (part of the property's decrease in value occurred in the hands of the donor and part in the hands of the donee); or increased to such an extent it eliminated any prior decrease in value (all the property's decrease in value that had occurred in the hands of the donor has evaporated and the property is now worth more than what the donor paid for it). These three possibilities and the related basis are further described below:

- **Donee sells the property for any amount between what the donor paid for the property and the fair market value of the property at the time of the gift**: using the donor's basis to measure loss on disposition, the loss represents the loss that occurred while the property was owned by the donor. The donee is not permitted to claim this loss. Accordingly, the donee reports none of the loss (reports nothing).

- **Donee sells the property for an amount less than the fair market value of the property as of the time of the gift**: the property has decreased in value while owned by the donee. The donee is permitted to realize the loss that occurred while he owned the property. In other words, the special rule applies and the donee's basis in the property is its fair market value as of the date of the gift.

---

17. Section 1015(a).
18. Section 1015(a).
19. Section 1015(a); Treas. Reg. § 1.1015-1(a).

- **Donee sells the property for an amount greater than what the donor paid for the property:** the property has increase in value while owned by the donee. The donee is required to recognize only the profit in the property based on the donor's purchase price. In other words, the general rule applies and the donee takes over the donor's basis in the property.

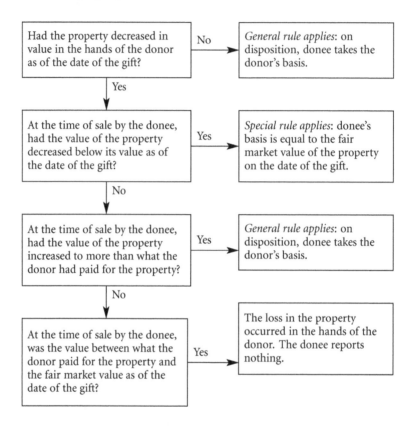

Pictorial Example of Basis Rules for Gifts of Depreciated Property

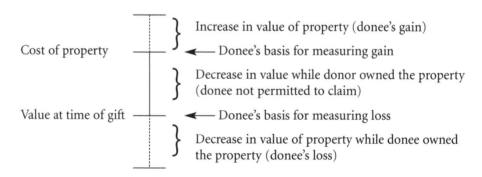

Rules for property received in a part gift, part sale transaction. If property was sold to the donee at less than its fair market value, the transaction was partly a gift and partly a sale. In such situations, the donee's basis is the greater of the amount paid for the property or the donor's basis in the property. If the result of the application of the above rule is that the basis is the donor's basis in the property, the basis is subject to the general and special rules described above.[20]

C. Inheritances

1. General Rule — Inheritances

An inheritance represents an accession to wealth — the taxpayer is better off after receiving the inheritance than before the inheritance. However, Congress decided it would be too intrusive and administratively difficult to measure the value of every inheritance a taxpayer received during a taxable year. Thus, as a matter of policy, Congress decided to exclude receipt of an inheritance from gross income.[21]

Under Code Section 102, an inheritance (whether a bequest, devise, or inheritance) is excluded from gross income. This rule holds true regardless of whether the beneficiary received cash or property under the decedent's will or through intestacy. It is also true regardless of whether the beneficiary received cash or property under the terms of the will or based on resolution of a will contest. For example, in *Lyeth v. Hoey*[22] an heir who had not been included in the will brought an action to contest the will. As part of the settlement agreement a portion of the estate was paid to the heir. The heir was allowed to exclude from gross income as an inheritance the amount he received under the settlement agreement.

2. Beneficiary's Basis in Inherited Property

The general rule is that the basis of property is the amount paid for the property.[23] However, when a taxpayer receives an inheritance, he has not paid for the property. Thus, the general rule can have no applicability to property received as an inheritance. Aware of this problem, Congress enacted a rule for determining the basis of property received as an inheritance. The beneficiary takes a basis equal to the fair market value of the property as of the date of the decedent's death.[24] Sometimes this basis is called a stepped-up or stepped-down basis.

Section 1014. Basis of Property Acquired From a Decedent

(a) In General. — Except as otherwise provided in this section, the basis of property in the hands of a person acquiring the property from a decedent or to

---

20. Treas. Reg. § 1.1015-4(a).
21. Section 102(a).
22. 305 U.S. 188 (1938).
23. Section 1012(a). Chapters 22, 25, and 29 discuss adjustments to basis. If the basis has been so adjusted, the analysis is performed with the adjusted basis used in place of the cost basis of the property.
24. Section 1014(a)(1).

whom the property passed from a decedent shall, if not sold, exchanged, or otherwise disposed of before the decedent's death by such person, be—

(1) the fair market value of the property at the date of the decedent's death....

Tell Me More

The executor of an estate may elect to value the estate's property at a time after the date of the decedent's death. If this election is made, the beneficiary's basis in the property is equal to the fair market value of the property as of the alternate valuation date.[25]

Summary — Basis Rules

Donee's basis in property received as a gift:

- **Appreciated property**: If the value of the property at the time of the gift is greater than what the donor paid for the property, donee takes the donor's basis in the property.

- **Depreciated property**: If the value of the property at the time of the gift is less than what donor paid for the property, donee's basis depends on what happens to the value of the property while he owns it.

  ○ *Decreases below the fair market value of the property at the time of the gift.* Donee takes the fair market value of the property as of the time of the gift as donee's basis in the property. Donee will have a loss equal to the decrease in value while donee owned the property.

  ○ *Increases in excess of the donor's purchase price.* Donee takes the donor's basis in the property. Donee will have a gain on disposition of the property.

  ○ *Increases in value, but not in excess of the donor's purchase price.* The decrease in value of the property represents the loss in the property while the donor owned it. Donee reports nothing.

Basis in Property Received as an Inheritance:

The beneficiary takes a basis in the property equal to the fair market value of the property as of the date of the decedent's death.

Tell Me More

The income tax should not be confused with the estate and gift (excise) tax. The Internal Revenue Code imposes a gift and estate tax on gifts made during lifetime and on assets owned at the time of death. This tax is in addition to—and separate from—the income tax that must be paid by a taxpayer each year.

---

25. Section 2032(a).

Estate Tax: An estate tax is imposed on the total net value of the decedent's estate as of the date of death.[26] In general, the net value is the total of the fair market value of all the assets of the estate, less liabilities, charitable contributions, expenses of the estate, and the marital deduction. The estate is entitled to the unified credit, which can be used to offset the amount of tax due.

Gift Tax: Generally the estate tax cannot be avoided by giving away assets prior to death. The estate and gift tax is a "unified" tax. This means that, in addition to being applicable to assets held at death, it is applicable to gifts made during lifetime.[27] The gift tax is based on the fair market value of the gift on the day the gift is made. However, the tax is only applicable to the extent the value of the gift exceeds $12,000. This exclusion is available to the donor each year and for each separate recipient. The annual exclusion for gifts is indexed annually for inflation.

D. Application of Rules

Example 1 — Gift of income-generating property. Andy transferred an apartment building to his son, Bill. Because the transfer is a gift, Bill can exclude the value of the apartment building from his gross income. However, the exclusion of gifts from gross income does not extend to the income generated from the property (to rent). Thus, Bill cannot exclude the rents received from the tenants from his gross income.

Example 2 — Gift of income. Charlie transferred to Dave, his son, the right to receive all rents from tenants living in an apartment building Charlie owned. Charlie retained ownership of the apartment building.

The exclusion of gifts from gross income does not extend to a gift of income. Thus, Dave cannot exclude the rents received from the tenants from his gross income.

Example 3 — Part gift, part sale. Ellen owned Blackacre. Her basis in the property was $30,000 and its fair market value was $50,000. Ellen sold Blackacre to Francie, her niece, for $40,000, intending the sale to be in part a gift.

The transaction is partly a gift and partly a sale. Ellen realizes gain to the extent the amount realized ($40,000) exceeds her basis in the property ($30,000). Thus, Ellen has a $10,000 gain. Ellen has made a gift to Francie of $10,000 ($50,000 fair market value of the property, less $40,000 paid).

Francie's basis in Blackacre is the greater of the amount paid for the property ($40,000) or Ellen's basis in the property ($30,000). Francie's basis in the property is $40,000.

Example 4 — Part gift, part sale. Grace owned Whiteacre. Her basis in the property was $30,000 and its fair market value was $50,000. Grace sold Whiteacre to Hannah, her niece, for $20,000, intending the sale to be in part a gift.

---

26. See Section 2001, et. seq.
27. See Section 2501, et. seq.

The transaction is partly a gift and partly a sale. Grace realizes a $10,000 loss ($20,000 amount realized, less $30,000 basis). Grace cannot recognize the loss. Grace has made a gift to Hannah of $30,000 ($50,000 fair market value of the property, less $20,000 paid).

Hannah's basis in Whiteacre is the greater of the amount paid for the property ($20,000) or Grace's basis in the property ($30,000). Hannah basis in the property is $30,000.

Example 5 — Gift of appreciated property. Inez owned Greenacre. Her basis in the property was $50,000 and its fair market value was $75,000. Inez gave Greenacre to Jenny, her aunt. Because the transfer is a gift, Jenny can exclude the value of Greenacre from her gross income.

Five years later, Jenny sold Greenacre for $40,000. Because the property had increased in value at the time Inez gifted it to Jenny, the general rule applies and Jenny takes Inez's basis in the property, $50,000. Jenny realizes a $10,000 loss on sale (amount realized of $40,000, less basis of $50,000).

AR =	$40,000
AB =	50,000
Loss	<$10,000>

Example 6 — Gift of depreciated property. Kyle purchased Blueacre for $10,000. Five years later, when the value of Blueacre had decreased to $6,000, he gifted the property to Lennie, his son. Three years later, Lennie sold Blueacre for $12,000.

Because Lennie is selling Blueacre for an amount greater than what Kyle purchased it for, the general rule applies and Lennie uses Kyle's basis to measure gain in the property. Because Blueacre has increased in value $2,000 from the time Kyle purchased it, on sale Lennie realizes a $2,000 gain.

AR =	$12,000
AB =	10,000
Gain	$2,000

Example 7 — Gift of depreciated property. Marie purchased Redacre for $10,000. Five years later, when the value of Redacre had decreased to $6,000, she gifted the property to Natalie, her daughter. Three years later, Natalie sold Redacre for $3,000.

Because the property had decreased in value at the time Marie gifted the property to Natalie and Natalie sold the property for an amount less than the fair market value at the time of the gift, the special rule applies. Natalie uses the fair market value of the property to measure the loss in the property. Because Redacre decreased in value $3,000 while Natalie owned the property, on sale Natalie realizes a $3,000 loss.

AR =	$3,000
AB =	6,000
Loss	<$3,000>

Example 8 — Gift of depreciated property. Owen purchased Greenacre for $10,000. Five years later, when the value of Greenacre had decreased to $6,000, he gifted the property to Paula, his niece. Three years later, Paula sold Greenacre for $9,000.

Because Paula sold the property for an amount less than what Owen paid for the property (even though greater than the fair market value of the property at the time of the gift), upon the sale Paula does not realize any loss. All the loss in the property occurred while Owen owned it (decrease from $10,000 at the time of purchase to $9,000 at the time of sale). Paula is not allowed to claim the loss.

Example 9—Inherited property. Russ purchased Yellowacre for $50,000. In his will he provided that Yellowacre would be devised to Sam. Russ passed away this year. At the time of his death, Yellowacre was worth $30,000.

Because the transfer is an inheritance, Sam can exclude the value of Yellowacre from his gross income. His basis in Yellowacre is the fair market value of the property as of the date of Russ's death, or $30,000.

E. Problems

1. Tom owned Pinkacare. His basis in the property was $20,000 and its fair market value was $50,000. Tom sold Pinkacre to his niece for $10,000.

    a. What must Tom report?

    b. What basis does his niece take in Pinkacre?

2. On January 1, Evelyn transferred a bank account containing $100,000 to Julie, her daughter. During the year the bank account earned $5,000 in interest. How much must Julie report?

3. Jan purchased Whiteacre for $50,000. Five years later, when the value of Whiteacre had decreased to $40,000, she gifted the property to Bonnie. Three years later, Bonnie sold Whiteacre for $60,000.

    a. What are the tax consequences to Jan?

    b. How much gain or loss must Bonnie report from the sale of Whiteacre?

4. Victoria purchased Greenacre for $50,000. Five years later, when the value of Greenacre had decreased to $40,000, she gifted the property to Laurie. Three years later, Laurie sold Greenacre for $25,000. How much gain or loss must Laurie report from the sale of Greenacre?

5. Sara purchased Redacre for $100,000. Five years later, when the value of Redacre had decreased to $85,000, she gifted the property to Tamara. Three years later, Tamara sold Redacre for $90,000. How much gain or loss should Tamara report from the sale of Redacre?

6. Nick purchased Blackacre for $100,000. Nick did not prepare a will, but died intestate. Based on the state's intestacy provisions, Blackacre was transferred to his son, Marty. At the time of Nick's death, Blackacre was worth $120,000.

    a. Must Marty include the value of Blackacre in his gross income?

    b. What is his basis in Blackacre?

7. Francine owned Whiteacre. Her basis in the property was $50,000 and its fair market value was $75,000. Francine sold Whiteacre to Sam, her nephew, for $60,000.

    a. How much gain or loss must Francine report?

    b. What basis does Sam take in Whiteacre?

8. Loretta works at the local diner. Each night she collects approximately $50 in tips. Must Loretta include the tips in her gross income? Why or why not?

9. Beth works at the local casino. Each night she collects approximately $50 in "tokes." Must Beth include the tokes in her gross income? Why or why not?

F. Analysis and Application

1. Carmen is in your office. She tells you she received Whiteacre from her father (now deceased) five years ago. She is planning on selling the property and that, based on comparable sales in the area, she thinks it is worth $50,000. She asks you to explain to her what the tax consequences of the sale will be to her.

    a. Make a list of the questions will you need to have answered before you can give her an answer.

    b. What problems do you foresee if she is not able to answer your questions? How will you go about getting the information you need to provide her an answer?

2. Fernando is a solo practitioner. He practices in a small town where most of the residents know each other. Fernando has performed a substantial amount of work for Mr. Alexander, a local farmer. Because of several poor seasons of soy bean crops Mr. Alexander does not have a lot of cash. However, the land he farms and his farm equipment is worth a substantial amount of money. Fernando and Mr. Alexander agree that Mr. Alexander need not pay for the legal services now. Rather, the legal fees will be paid out of Mr. Alexander's estate. Mr. Alexander's will provides for this payment.

    What are the tax consequences when Mr. Alexander passes away and Fernando receives a distribution from the estate? Does it matter if Fernando prepared the will? Does it matter if Fernando handles the probate proceeding? In formulating your analysis and response, you may want to consider:

    • Commissioner v. Glenshaw Glass, 348 U.S. 426 (1995)

    • Commissioner v. Duberstein, 363 U.S. 278 (1960)

3. Tom works for his father's business. At the end of the year, his father gave all of his employees a box of imported Belgian chocolates. In addition, his father gave Tom three tins of imported Greek coffee beans. Must Tom include the value of the chocolates and coffee beans in his gross income? Why or why not? In formulating your analysis and response, you may want to consider:

    • Commissioner v. Glenshaw Glass, 348 U.S. 426 (1995)

    • Commissioner v. Duberstein, 363 U.S. 278 (1960)

    • Wolder v. Commissioner, 493 F.2d 608 (2d Cir. 1974)

    • Prop. Treas. Reg. § 1.102-1(f)(2)

4. Irving's father passed away and Irving was named as the personal representative of the estate. As part of his duties, Irving constructed an inventory of the estate assets, paid his father's outstanding liabilities, paid the liabilities incurred by the estate, distributed the estate assets consistent with the terms of the will, and eventually closed the estate. As personal representative, Irving was entitled to be paid by the estate for his services.

    The amount distributed to Irving was $50,000. Irving wants to know if he has to include the $50,000 in his gross income.

    a. What are the possible answers you might give Irving?

b.   Make a list of the questions will you need to have answered before you can give him your best answer.

In formulating your analysis and response, you may want to consider:

- Commissioner v. Glenshaw Glass, 348 U.S. 426 (1995)
- Commissioner v. Duberstein, 363 U.S. 278 (1960)
- Wolder v. Commissioner, 493 F.2d 608 (2d Cir. 1974)
- Rev. Rul. 57-398, 1957-2 C.B. 93

5.   Sally, Terri, and Julie are sisters. When their mother passed away, she left her entire estate to Sally. Terri and Julie were very upset. They had several long discussions with Sally in which they made it clear they thought Sally had exercised undue influence over their mother, given that she lived closer to their mother and had more opportunities during the years before her death to spend time with their mother. The three sisters entered into a settlement agreement that they filed with the probate court. The agreement required the estate to divide their mother's property equally between the three sisters.

What are the income tax consequences to each of the three sisters? In formulating your analysis and response, you may want to consider:

- Commissioner v. Glenshaw Glass, 348 U.S. 426 (1995)
- Commissioner v. Duberstein, 363 U.S. 278 (1960)
- Lyeth v. Hoey, 305 U.S. 188 (1938)
- Marcus v. Commissioner, T.C. Memo. 1996-190

6.   When Nora's mother (Maxine) turned 80, Nora agreed to have her mother move in with her and she would take care of Maxine. Nora took care of Maxine until Maxine died five years later.

When a probate estate was opened and Maxine's will filed with the probate court, Nora discovered that her mother had left everything to Maxine's friend Brian. Maxine and Brian had fallen out of touch over the years and during that same time frame Nora had reestablished her relationship with her mother. Maxine had repeatedly promised Nora that she would leave Nora her entire estate. Based on her mother's representations to her, Nora filed a claim against the estate for breach of contract. When the claim was settled, Nora was entitled to receive two-thirds of her mother's estate.

What are the tax consequences to Nora upon receipt of two-thirds of her mother's estate? In formulating your analysis and response, you may want to consider:

- Commissioner v. Glenshaw Glass, 348 U.S. 426 (1995)
- Commissioner v. Duberstein, 363 U.S. 278 (1960)
- Lyeth v. Hoey, 305 U.S. 188 (1938)
- Braddock v. United States, 434 F.2d 631 (9th Cir. 1970)
- Miller v. Commissioner, T.C. Memo. 1987-271

Chapter 9

Life Insurance

Gross Income

Includes all accessions to wealth, such as:	Excludes:
• Compensation for services	• Loans and deposits
• Business profits	• Gifts and inheritances
• Profit from the sale of property	• **Life insurance**
• Interest	• Certain prizes and awards
• Rents	• Qualified scholarships
• Royalties	• Personal injury damages
• Dividends	• Fringe benefits
• Alimony	• Health insurance
• Cancellation of debt	• Workers' compensation

Read

Code Sections 61(a)(4), (10); 101(a), (c), (d), (g)(3)

A. Background

Gross income includes income (accessions to wealth) derived from any and all sources. It includes every accession to wealth, unless there is an exception. Receiving the proceeds of a life insurance policy is an accession to wealth.[28]

B. Life Insurance

1. Background

There are three different roles related to a life insurance policy (in addition to the life insurance company itself): the policy holder, the insured, and the beneficiary. The policy holder agrees to make payments to the insurance company and in return the insurance

---

28. Section 61(a)(10).

company agrees to pay an agreed-upon amount (often referred to as the "face amount" of the policy) to the beneficiary upon the death of the insured. For example, Mike purchases a life insurance policy from Insurance Company. The policy provides that it will pay $100,000 to Jeff when Tom passes away. Mike is the policy holder, Tom is the insured, and Jeff is the beneficiary. This text is concerned only with the tax consequences to the beneficiary upon receipt of the policy proceeds.

There are many different kinds of life insurance, with the cost of the insurance and the benefits available to the beneficiary differing depending on the type of policy. It is not necessary to learn the differences between these types of policies — the tax consequences to the beneficiary are the same regardless of the type of policy.

Tell Me More

Section 101 applies to life insurance contracts. "Life insurance contract" is defined in Section 7702. To come within the definition, the contract must not be predominately an investment vehicle and must shift risk from the policy holder to the life insurance company and there must be a distribution of risk among policy holders.

There are a variety of types of life insurance.

Term insurance: As its name suggests, it provides insurance for a specified term. The amount paid for the policy (the premium) reflects solely the amount needed to pay for protection in the event of death. When the term expires, the policy holder owns nothing.

Whole life insurance: The policy remains active until it matures or the policy holder fails to make premium payments. The premium payments remain the same from year to year. Because the risk of death increases each year, the cost of insurance coverage increases each year. To keep premium payments level, the insurance company must collect more than the amount needed to pay for protection in the event of death in the early years, and will collect less than is needed in later years. The excess amounts collected in the earlier years are invested on behalf of the policyholder and may represent an untaxed accession to wealth. To the extent of these excess payments and investment earnings, the policy will have a cash surrender value or funds that can otherwise be accessed through a policy loan.

---

2. Tax Consequences of Receipt of Policy Proceeds

When the insured passes away, the life insurance contract provides that the policy proceeds are to be paid to the beneficiary. Without a doubt, upon receipt of the policy proceeds, the beneficiary has an accession to wealth. However, Congress believed it was an inopportune time to impose tax. Accordingly, the Code permits the beneficiary to exclude the policy proceeds from his gross income.[29]

---

29. Section 101(a)(1).

Section 101. Certain Death Benefits

(a) Proceeds of Life Insurance Contracts Payable by Reason of Death —

> (1) General Rule. — Except as otherwise provided … gross income does not include amounts received (whether in a single sum or otherwise) under a life insurance contract, if such amounts are paid by reason of the death of the insured. …

Paid upon the death of the insured. For the statutory exclusion of receipt of policy proceeds from gross income to apply, the policy proceeds must be paid upon the death of the insured and not for a different reason.[30] In the following examples, the payments are not paid by reason of the death of the insured and, therefore, would not be excludable from income.

- When policy proceeds are paid to extinguish a debt they are treated as paid due to the existence of the obligation and not the death of the insured.

  Example. Carter purchased a life insurance policy. Upon his death, the policy proceeds were required to be paid to the holder of his mortgage to extinguish the debt. Because the amount was paid to extinguish the debt, the proceeds were not paid upon the death of the insured.

- If the insured surrenders the policy in exchange for its cash value the payment is not paid upon the death of the insured and the insured must recognize gain to the extent the cash value exceeds the premiums previously paid.

Exception for transfer of the policy. If the owner of the policy transfers the policy for consideration (during his life), the statutorily-provided exclusion is modified. The amount excluded from gross income cannot exceed the total of the consideration plus any premiums and other amounts paid by the transferee.[31]

This exception is not applicable (and the general exclusionary rule applies) if:[32]

- the contract's basis is determined in whole or in part by reference to the basis in the hands of the transferor (e.g., the policy was transferred by gift);

- the transfer is to the insured; or

- the transfer is to a partner of the insured, to a partnership in which the insured is a partner, or to a corporation in which the insured is a shareholder or officer.

3. Receipt of Interest

If there is a delay in payment of the policy proceeds such that the beneficiary also receives an interest payment, the exclusion from income does not extend to the interest.[33]

---

30. Id.
31. Section 101(a)(2).
32. Id.
33. Section 101(c).

Section 101. Certain Death Benefits

(c) Interest—If any amount excluded from gross income by subsection (a) is held under an agreement to pay interest thereon, the interest payments shall be included in gross income.

Example. The beneficiary of a life insurance policy is to receive $100,000. However, because the life insurance company does not make the payment until the following year, the beneficiary receives $110,000; the payment of the additional $10,000 represents interest. The beneficiary can exclude the $100,000 of life insurance proceeds, but must include the $10,000 of interest.

Payments over time. If the policy proceeds are paid to the beneficiary over a period of time, such as for a term of years or the beneficiary's life, the beneficiary will be paid interest in addition to the policy proceeds. To determine the tax-free and taxable portion of each payment, the payment must be prorated.[34]

Section 101. Certain Death Benefits

(d) Payment of Life Insurance Proceeds At a Date Later Than Death—

(1) General Rule.—The amounts held by an insurer with respect to any beneficiary shall be prorated (in accordance with such regulations as may be prescribed by the Secretary) over the period or periods with respect to which such payments are to be made. There shall be excluded from the gross income of such beneficiary in the taxable year received any amount determined by such proration.

Gross income includes, to the extent not excluded by the preceding sentence, amounts received under agreements to which this subsection applies.

(2) Amount Held By An Insurer.—An amount held by an insurer with respect to any beneficiary shall mean an amount to which subsection (a) applies which is—

(A) held by any insurer under an agreement provided for in the life insurance contract, whether as an option or otherwise, to pay such amount on a date or dates later than the death of the insured, and

(B) is equal to the value of such agreement to such beneficiary

(i) as of the date of death of the insured (as if any option exercised under the life insurance contract were exercised at such time), and

(ii) as discounted on the basis of the interest rate used by the insurer in calculating payments under the agreement and mortality tables prescribed by the Secretary....

---

34. Section 101(d).

With respect to each payment, the excludable portion is the prorata amount of the policy proceeds. The taxable portion is the prorata amount of interest.[35]

Example. The beneficiary of a life insurance policy is to receive $100,000. The beneficiary agrees to have the life insurance company pay him $30,000 a year for the next five years. At the end of five years, the beneficiary will have received a total of $150,000 ($30,000 × 5).

Portion of payment allocable to policy proceeds   100,000/$150,000 = 2/3

Portion of payment allocable to interest   50,000/150,000 = 1/3

Thus, 2/3 of each payment represents tax-free policy proceeds and 1/3 represents taxable interest.

Year	Policy Proceeds	Interest	Total Payment
1	$20,000	$10,000	$30,000
2	20,000	10,000	30,000
3	20,000	10,000	30,000
4	20,000	10,000	30,000
5	20,000	10,000	30,000
Total	$100,000	$50,000	$150,000

Summary of Rules — Life Insurance

- Life insurance policy proceeds paid upon the death of the insured are excludable from gross income.
- Interest received on policy proceeds is not excludable from gross income.
- If the beneficiary receives the proceeds over time, the tax-free policy proceeds and the taxable interest must be prorated with respect to each yearly payment.

---

4. Exception for Chronically Ill Insured

The Code provides an exception to the requirement that the policy proceeds are excludable only if paid upon the death of the insured.[36] If the insured is terminally ill or chronically ill and cashes out the policy, the amounts received will be treated as if received on account of the death of the insured. The insured is terminally ill if he has been certified by a physician as having an illness or physical condition that can reasonably be expected to result in death in 24 months or less after the date of the certification.[37] The insured is

---

35. Id.
36. Section 101(g)(1).
37. Section 101(g)(4)(A).

chronically ill when he has been certified within the preceding 12-month period by a licensed health care practitioner as being either of the following:[38]

- unable to perform at least two activities of daily living for a period of at least 90 days due to a loss of functional capacity, or

- having severe cognitive impairment requiring substantial supervision to protect the individual from threats to health and safety.

The exception also is applicable if the proceeds are obtained from a third party who is a viatical settlement provider.[39] A viatical settlement provider is a person in the business of purchasing or receiving assignments of life insurance policies on the life of a terminally ill or chronically ill person.[40]

Dollar limitations. If the person is terminally ill, the exception applies to all amounts paid with respect to that person's life. If the person is chronically ill, the exclusion applies only to the cost of qualified long-term care or payments of $175 per day or $63,875 per year (the amount is adjusted for inflation).[41] The exclusion applies only to the extent the person has not been reimbursed by medical insurance proceeds.[42] (If the person would qualify as terminally ill and chronically ill, the person is treated as terminally ill.[43])

C. Application of Rules

Example 1 — Policy proceeds. Rachel purchased a life insurance policy insuring the life of Char. Madeline was the named beneficiary of the policy. Pursuant to the terms of the policy, when Char passed away, Madeline received $100,000. Madeline can exclude the policy proceeds from her gross income.

Example 2 — Policy proceeds and interest. Liz purchased a life insurance policy insuring her own life. Sam was the named beneficiary of the policy. Pursuant to the terms of the policy, one year following when Liz passed away, Sam was to receive $200,000 plus interest from the date of Liz's death to the date of payment. The year following the year Liz passed away, the life insurance company paid Sam $225,000. Sam can exclude $200,000 as proceeds of the life insurance policy, but must include the $25,000 of interest.

Example 3 — Policy proceeds paid over time. Macy purchased a life insurance policy insuring her own life in the amount of $50,000. She named Charles as the beneficiary of the policy. Pursuant to the terms of the policy, the policy proceeds, plus interest, are to be paid out over ten years. Macy passed away and the life insurance company paid Charles $6,000 a year for the next ten years.

Charles will receive a total of $60,000 ($6,000 × 10 years). With respect to each payment 5/6 ($50,000 policy proceeds/$60,000 total payments) represents payment of the policy

---

38. Sections 101(g)(4)(B); 7702B(c)(2).
39. Section 101(g)(2)(A).
40. Section 101(g)(2)(B)(i). The statutory provision includes additional requirements the provider must meet.
41. Sections 101(g)(3)(D); 7702B(d)(2)-(6).
42. Sections 101(g)(3)(A)(i); 7702B(d)(2)(B).
43. Section 101(g)(4)(B).

proceeds and 1/6 ($10,000 interest/$60,000 total payments) represents interest. Thus, for each $6,000 payment, $5,000 represent tax-free policy proceeds and $1,000 represents taxable interest.

Example 4—Transfer for value. Raphael pays $500 for a life insurance policy insuring Miguel's life with a face amount of $10,000. Subsequently, Raphael transfers the policy to Muriel for $700 and Muriel becomes the beneficiary. When Miguel passes away, Muriel receives $10,000. Instead of excluding the entire $10,000 of policy proceeds, Muriel can exclude $700, plus any additional premium payments Muriel has made.

D. Problems

1. Rocky paid $1,000 for a term policy on his life with a face amount of $50,000. He named Betsy as the beneficiary. Unfortunately, Rocky died during the year. What are the tax consequences to Betsy upon receipt of the $50,000?

2. Each year, Albert pays $500 in premiums for a whole-life insurance policy on his life with a face amount of $500,000. He has named Carl as the beneficiary. After having paid the premiums for three years, Albert died. What are the tax consequences to Carl upon receipt of the $500,000?

3. Erin purchased a life insurance policy on her life in the amount of $100,000. She named Cesar as the beneficiary. Erin passed away. Pursuant to the terms of the policy, one year following the year Erin passed away, the life insurance company paid Cesar $103,000. What are the tax consequences to Cesar?

4. Tory purchased a life insurance policy on her life in the amount of $200,000. She named Scott as the beneficiary. Tory passed away and Scott elected to receive the policy proceeds over the next ten years. The insurance company will pay Scott $25,000 each year. What are the tax consequences to Scott each year for the next ten years upon receipt of the $25,000?

5. Kevin is diagnosed with pancreatic cancer and is not expected to live more than six months. He sells his life insurance policy to a viatical settlement provider for $50,000. What are the tax consequences to Kevin upon receipt of the $50,000?

E. Analysis and Application

1. Cindy, one of your estate planning clients, is 45 years old, married and has three children. Two of the children are in grade school and the third is in junior high. Cindy works as a chef at the local bakery. Her husband owns and operates his own auto repair shop. Cindy asks you about whether she or her husband or both should obtain a life insurance policy. Specifically, she would like to know what role a life insurance policy would play in their estate plan.

   a. What do you tell her?

   b. If you believe she, her husband, or both should obtain life insurance policies, who should be the named beneficiaries? Why?

2.   Clark operates a high-end art gallery as a sole proprietorship. Robyn had worked for him for several years before Clark discovered she was embezzling money from the gallery. She would countersign checks made out to the gallery and deposit them into an account she had opened and had sole control over. Until he discovered the embezzlement, Clark had not been aware the funds had been received by the gallery and, accordingly, the embezzled amounts were never reported as part of the gallery's income.

When Clark discovered the embezzlement, he confronted Robyn with his evidence. She refused to either acknowledge her wrongful acts or reimburse the gallery. Clark fired Robyn and initiated a lawsuit against her for recovery of the embezzled funds. Before the litigation concluded, Robyn fell ill and passed away. Robyn's husband eventually entered into a settlement with Clark, assigning to Clark the proceeds of her life insurance policy.

What are the tax consequences to Clark? In formulating your analysis and response, you may want to consider:

- Commissioner v. Glenshaw Glass, 348 U.S. 426 (1955)

- Rev. Rul. 72-164, 1972-1 C.B. 28

- Estate of Rath v. Commissioner, 608 F.2d 254 (6th Cir. 1979)

Chapter 10

Prizes and Awards

Gross Income

Includes all accessions to wealth, such as:	Excludes:
• Compensation for services	• Loans and deposits
• Business profits	• Gifts and inheritances
• Profit from the sale of property	• Life insurance
• Interest	• **Certain prizes and awards**
• Rents	• Qualified scholarships
• Royalties	• Personal injury damages
• Dividends	• Fringe benefits
• Alimony	• Health insurance
• Cancellation of debt	• Workers' compensation

Read

Code Sections 74; 274(j)(1)-(4)

Treas. Reg. § 1.74-1(a)

A. Background

Gross income includes income (accessions to wealth) derived from any and all sources.[44] It includes every accession to wealth, unless there is an exception. Receiving a prize or award is an accession to wealth.

B. Prize or Award

When a taxpayer receives a prize or award, the taxpayer has an accession to wealth and must include the fair market of the prize or award in his gross income.[45] The taxpayer is

---

44. Section 61(a).
45. Section 74(a).

responsible for determining the fair market value of the prize or award.[46] In general, the fair market value is the value at which a willing buyer would pay a willing seller for an item when neither party is under a compulsion to buy or sell and both parties have access to all relevant information.[47]

C. Exceptions

In two situations the taxpayer can exclude the value of a prize or award from his gross income. Under Section 74(b) the taxpayer can exclude the value of a prize or award from his gross income if the following conditions are met:

1. The amount was received primarily in recognition of religious, charitable, scientific, educational, artistic, literary, or civic achievement;

2. The recipient was selected without any action on his part to enter the contest or proceeding;

3. The recipient is not required to render substantial future services as a condition to receiving the prize or award; and

4. The prize or award is transferred by the recipient to a governmental unit or charitable organization[48] pursuant to a designation made by the recipient.

To satisfy the criteria that the prize or award is given away, the recipient may reject the award.[49]

Tell Me More

If the taxpayer excludes the value of the prize or award from gross income, he may not claim a charitable contribution deduction for giving away the prize or award.[50]

Under the second exception, the taxpayer can exclude the value of a prize or award from his gross income if it is an employee achievement award and meets certain criteria. To be an employee achievement award, the payment must not be a disguised form of compensation. In addition, to be excludable it must be:

• From an employer to an employee;

• Tangible personal property;

• Awarded for length of service or safety; and

• Awarded as part of a meaningful presentation.

---

46. See, e.g., McCoy v. Commissioner, 38 T.C. 841 (1962), acq. 1963-2 C.B. 5.
47. See Treas. Reg. §20.2031-1(b); Treas. Reg. §25.2512-1.
48. See Section 170(c)(1) or (2).
49. See Rev. Rul. 57-374, 1957-2 C.B. 69.
50. The deduction for a charitable contribution is discussed in Chapter 18.

To be awarded for length of service, the employee must have been employed for five years or more and not have received a length of service award for any of the five years preceding receipt of the award. To be a safety award, it must be awarded to someone who is not a manager, administrator, clerical employee, or other professional employee. In addition, such an award cannot be made to more than 10 percent of the employer's qualified employees.

If the prize or award meets the above criteria it is then subject to a dollar limitation that is tied to the deduction allowed the employer. In turn, the deductibility by the employer depends on whether the award is a "qualified plan award." Finally, to be an employee plan award, the award must be awarded as part of a written plan that does not favor highly compensation employees.

The employer can deduct up to $400 for each employee for the cost of the employee achievement award. If the award is a "qualified plan award," the employer can deduct up to $1,600 for each employee.

If the entire cost is deductible by the employer, the employee can exclude the award from his gross income. If the cost of the award is greater than the amount allowed as a deduction, the employee must include the greater of:

- The portion of the cost of the award that is not allowable as a deduction to the employer, or
- The excess of the value of the award over the employer's deduction.

The remainder of the value of the award is excluded from the employee's gross income. However, the employee is never required to include an amount greater than the value of the award.

Summary of Rules — Awards

- A prize or award is an accession to wealth that must be included in the taxpayer's gross income.
- The taxpayer can exclude the prize or award if either:
    - He can satisfy the requirements of Section 74(b)
        - The amount was received primarily in recognition of religious, charitable, scientific, educational, artistic, literary, or civic achievement;
        - The recipient was selected without any action on his part to enter the contest or proceeding;
        - The recipient is not required to render substantial future services as a condition to receiving the prize or award; and
        - The prize or award is transferred by the recipient to a governmental unit or charitable organization pursuant to a designation made by the recipient.
    - The award is an employee achievement award (subject to the applicable dollar limitations)
        - The award is from an employer to an employee;
        - Of tangible personal property;

∘ Awarded for length of service or safety; and

∘ Awarded as part of a meaningful presentation.

D. Application of Rules

Example 1. Mark is selected to be a contestant on a daytime television game show. He wins a side-by-side washer and dryer. Mark has received a prize and he must include the fair market value of the washer and dryer in his gross income.

Example 2. Amanda has been employed by Company for 15 years. In December at the Company Holiday Party, Company awarded her a gold watch to commemorate her length of service. Company paid $600 for the watch and in its hands has a fair market value of $500. Company does not have a written plan (i.e., the watch was not a qualified plan award).

Because the award is not a qualified plan award, the maximum Company may deduct is $400. Because the cost of the watch was greater than the amount Company was allowed to deduct, Amanda must include the greater of the portion of the cost of the award not deductible by Company ($200) or the excess of the value of the award over Company's deduction ($100). Amanda can exclude $400 as a qualified employee achievement award and must report $200.

E. Problems

1. Dr. Manja recently won a Noble Prize. He received a check in the amount of $1 million at a special reception for Nobel Prize winners in Oslo, Norway. What are the tax consequences to Dr. Manja?

2. Leonard has been employed by EventCo for two years. In the past year, he worked tirelessly on a proposal to make the EventCo building safer for the employees if a fire starts in one of the offices. When he finished, he presented his proposal to the board of directors. The board unanimously voted to adopt the proposal. In addition, at the following staff meeting they gave Leonard an expensive engraved pen set. EventCo paid $400 for the set and in its hands it had a fair market value of $350. EventCo does not have a written qualified award plan. What are the tax consequences to Leonard?

3. Mary was a contestant on an evening television show. The premise of the show was that a bachelor would consider a number of different women to ask to be his wife. During each weekly episode, the bachelor would eliminate one contestant. The following week, each contestant who remained would receive a prize. Mary remained on the show for two weeks before she was eliminated. She received two prizes: a necklace and a bracelet. What are the tax consequences to Mary?

4. In January of each year, journalists who cover the fashion world come together to select the best dressed actor or actress of the previous year. The winner is awarded $10,000 and must permit his or her picture to be used in an article about the award. In addition, the winner must provide fashion-related quotes that can be used in the article. This year, Maria, a rising movie star, was awarded the prize of best dressed actress. What are the tax consequences to Maria?

F. Analysis and Application

1. If Section 74(a) where not included in the Code would you still conclude that prizes and awards were included in income?

2. Anita is a sales person for a local car dealership. Each year her employer gives the top three sales people and his or her spouse an all-expense-paid cruise through the Caribbean. This year Anita had the third highest sales, so she and her husband were awarded the trip.

   a. What are the tax consequences to Anita?

   b. What are the tax consequences to her husband?

   c. If they have gross income, how will they know what amount to include on their tax return?

   In formulating your analysis and response, you may want to consider:

   - Commissioner v. Glenshaw Glass, 348 U.S. 426 (1955)

   - McCann v. United States, 81-2 USTC ¶ 9689 (Ct. Cl. 1981, aff'd, 696 F.2d 1386 (Fed. Cir. 1983)

   - McCoy v. Commissioner, 38 T.C. 841 (1962)

3. President Obama was awarded the Nobel Peace Prize in 2009. The award included a medal, a diploma, and $1.4 million. What were the tax consequences from receiving the award?

4. Fred worked for Fashion Express Corp. as an assistant to a home interior fashion consultant. Last year Fashion Express created a contest for its fashion consultants. Each consultant who brought in ten new clients would win a week long trip (with his or her wife/husband) to the Bahamas. Five consultants brought in ten or more new clients. Of the five, four decided to take the trip.

   Given the "difficult nature" of highly creative people such as fashion consultants, Fashion Express decided to also send five assistants on the trip to help out as needed. The assistants were selected through a random drawing. An assistant who won was expected to take his spouse. Each assistant selected for the trip was told the reason he was going was to "help manage the consultants." Accordingly, he was expected to be with the consultant as much of the time as possible. It was made clear to him that part of his responsibilities was to protect the image of Fashions Express as created (or damaged) by the actions of the consultants. Fred was selected for the trip. He attended with his wife Alicia. No sales activity occurred during the trip.

   What are the tax consequences to Fred and Alicia from the trip to the Bahamas? Are there additional facts you would like to know?

   In formulating your analysis and response, you may want to consider:

   - Commissioner v. Glenshaw Glass, 348 U.S. 426 (1955)

   - McCann v. Commissioner, 81-2 U.S.T.C. ¶ 9689 (Ct. Cl. 1981), aff'd, 696 F.2d 1386 (Fed. Cir. 1983)

   - Patterson v. Thomas, 289 F.2d 108 (5th Cir. 1961)

   - McCoy v. Commissioner, 38 T.C. 841 (1962)

Chapter 11

Qualified Scholarships and Educational Assistance Programs

Gross Income

Includes all accessions to wealth, such as:	Excludes:
• Compensation for services • Business profits • Profit from the sale of property • Interest • Rents • Royalties • Dividends • Alimony • Cancellation of debt	• Loans and deposits • Gifts and inheritances • Life insurance • Certain prizes and awards • **Qualified scholarships** • Personal injury damages • Fringe benefits • Health insurance • Workers' compensation

Read

Code Sections 25A(a)-(d); 117; 127(a), (b)

Prop. Reg. § 1.117-6(b), (c)(1)-(3)(i), (d)(1)-(2)

A. Background

Gross income includes income (accessions to wealth) derived from any and all sources.[51] It includes every accession to wealth, unless there is an exception. Receiving a scholarship is an accession to wealth.

---

51. Section 61(a).

B. Qualified Scholarships

When a taxpayer receives a scholarship the taxpayer has an accession to wealth. He can exclude the value of the scholarship to the extent it is a "qualified scholarship."[52] To be a "qualified scholarship," the scholarship must be:[53]

- used for qualified tuition and related expenses such as fees, books, supplies, and equipment required for courses;
- by a degree-seeking student; and
- at a qualifying educational institution.

A degree-seeking student is:[54]

- a student attending a primary or secondary school;
- an undergraduate or graduate student pursuing an academic or professional degree at a college or university; or
- students at educational institutions who are pursuing certain qualifying employment-training programs or programs acceptable for full credit towards a bachelor or higher degree.

The exclusion does not apply to amounts paid for room and board.[55] Nor does it apply to amounts paid for teaching, research, or other services required as a condition for receiving the scholarship.[56] Similarly, it does not include payments made as compensation for services. Medical interns and residents and graduate teaching and research assistants who receive a payment (whether direct or indirect) as compensation for their services cannot exclude the payment as a qualified scholarship.[57]

Bingler v. Johnson[58] involved a scholarship that, in substance, was compensation for services. The employees could participate in a two-phase program that offered subsidized postgraduate study. Under the first phase, the employee would be paid for a 40-hour week but could use up to eight of those hours to attend classes. The employee was reimbursed for the cost of tuition. Under the second phase, when an employee had completed the preliminary requirements for a doctorate, he could apply for an educational leave of absence. His proposed dissertation topic had to be approved by his employer and the approval was based on whether the topic had some relevance to the employee's work. If the leave was approved, the employee would work full time on fulfilling his dissertation requirements. During this time he would receive a percentage of his salary and continue to receive all employee benefits. The employee was required to submit progress reports and, upon completion of the leave, return to work for the employer for at least two years.

The issue before the court was whether the payments each program participant received were a qualified scholarship, excludable under Section 117. In holding that the amounts paid to the employees did not constitute a qualified scholarship the Supreme Court stated—

---

52. Section 117(a).
53. Section 117(a), (b).
54. Prop. Reg. § 1.117-6(c)(4).
55. Prop. Reg. § 1.117-6(c)(2).
56. Section 117(c).
57. Section 117(c); Bingler v. Johnson, 394 U.S. 741 (1969); Burstein v. United States, 622 F.2d 529 (Ct. Cl. 1980); Ellenwood v. Commissioner, T.C. Memo. 1984-606.
58. 394 U.S. 741 (1969).

The employer-employee relationship involved is immediately suggestive, of course, as is the close relation between the respondents' prior salaries and the amount of their "stipends." In addition, employee benefits were continued. Topics were required to relate at least generally to the work of the Bettis Laboratory. Periodic work reports were to be submitted. And, most importantly, Westinghouse unquestionably extracted a *quid pro quo*. The respondents not only were required to hold positions with Westinghouse throughout the "work-study" phase of the program, but also were obligated to return to Westinghouse's employ for a substantial period of time after completion of their leave.[59]

The theme of compensation for services has also arisen in connection with athletic scholarships. In Revenue Ruling 77-263[60] the Service considered whether athletic scholarships would qualify for the exclusion. It concluded that they would, but only if the university does not require the student to participate in a particular sport, does not require a particular activity in lieu of participation, and cannot terminate the scholarship in the event the student cannot participate.

Even though the exclusion for a qualified scholarship does not cover all costs associated with obtaining an education, there is no tracing requirement. The student can exclude an amount up to the total of qualifying costs, with any remainder not being excludable.

Tell Me More

The impact of educational expenses also may arise when considering deductions. For example, Section 162 and Treas. Reg. § 1.162-5 address whether a taxpayer is entitled to a deduction for educational expenses he pays.

This issue is discussed in Chapter 17.

C. Employment-Related Exclusions of Educational Benefits

Qualified Tuition Reduction Program. If an educational organization[61] has a qualified tuition reduction program, the employee can exclude a qualified tuition reduction for education below the graduate level.[62] If the student is a graduate student, he must be engaged in teaching or research activities.[63]

A qualified tuition reduction program can be available not only to the employer's employees, but also to employees of some other educational organizations.[64] Moreover, "employee" is broadly defined and includes the employee, the employee's spouse, the employee's

---

59. Bingler v. Johnson, 394 U.S. 741, 756–57 (1969).
60. 1977-2 C.B. 47.
61. As described in Section 170(b)(1)(A)(ii).
62. Section 117(d)(1), (2).
63. Section 117(d)(5).
64. Section 117(d)(2).

dependents, and the surviving spouse of a deceased employee.[65] However, the exclusion does not extend to payments for research, teaching, or other services required of the student to receive the qualified tuition reduction.[66]

Educational assistance program. An employee can exclude up to $5,250 of amounts paid by the employer for educational assistance.[67] The educational assistance program must meet certain requirements.[68] The exclusion extends to payment for tuition, fees, books, supplies, and equipment but does not extend to payments for courses involving sports, games, or hobbies.[69]

D. Education Tax Credit

A qualifying taxpayer may claim one of two available education-related credits.[70] The individual must have qualified tuition expenses for pursuing college or graduate degrees or vocational training. Qualified tuition and related expenses do not include room and board, student health fees, or transportation.[71]

Hope Scholarship Credit. To qualify for the Hope Scholarship Credit the student:[72]

- must not have elected the Hope credit in any two earlier years;
- not completed the first two years of postsecondary education before the beginning of the current tax year;
- be enrolled at least half-time in a program that leads to a degree, certificate, or other recognized educational credentials; and
- not been convicted of any Federal or State felony class drug offense for possession or distribution.

For the student who qualifies for the Hope Scholarship Credit (now called the American Opportunity Tax Credit), he may claim a maximum credit of $2,500.[73] (The amounts are indexed for inflation.[74])

Lifetime Learning Credit. To qualify for the Lifetime Learning Credit the student must be enrolled in one or more courses at a qualified educational institution.[75] For the student who qualifies for the Lifetime Learning Credit, he may claim 20 percent of the amount of qualified tuition expenses paid on the first $10,000 of tuition.[76] (The amount is not adjusted for inflation.[77]) The credit is phased out for taxpayers with modified adjusted gross income above certain amounts.[78]

---

65. Section 117(d)(2)(B).
66. Section 117(c).
67. Section 127(c)(1).
68. Section 127(a)(1), (b).
69. Section 127(c)(1).
70. Section 25A(a).
71. Section 25A(f).
72. Section 25A(b)(2).
73. Section 25A(b)(1), (4).
74. Section 25A(h).
75. Section 25A(c), (f).
76. Section 25A(c)(1).
77. Section 25A(c)(1).
78. Section 25A(d).

E. Application of Rules

Example 1. Catherine won a scholarship to attend Academic University, an accredited four-year university. She enrolled as a botany major. The amount of the scholarship is $50,000. Her tuition and fees for the year were $40,000. She used the remainder of the scholarship to pay her rent.

Catherine can exclude the scholarship to the extent it was used for qualified tuition and related expenses. She cannot exclude the amount paid for rent. Accordingly, she can exclude $40,000 and must include the remaining $10,000.

Example 2. Daniel is a graduate student. As part of his course of study he is required to teach Psychology 101. In exchange, the university reduces his tuition for the term.

The amount of tuition reduction represents compensation for services. As such, it is not a qualified scholarship and Daniel cannot exclude the amount from his gross income.

Example 3. Ivan receives a $10,000 scholarship from Invest Co. As a condition to receiving the scholarship, Ivan agrees to work for Invest Co. after he graduates. The scholarship is compensation for future services and cannot be excluded from Ivan's gross income.

Example 4. Charlie receives a fellowship from University to pursue a research project to be determined by University. After conducting the research, Charlie must prepare and submit a paper to University. He will not receive any academic credit for his work and University is entitled to use the results of his research. The fellowship is compensation for service and cannot be exclude from Charlie's gross income.

Example 5. Jennifer is enrolled full time as a freshman at the local university, majoring in political science. For her first term of classes she paid $5,000 in tuition. Jennifer is entitled to a $1,500 Hope Scholarship Credit (100 percent of the first $1,000, plus 50 percent of the second $1,000 of qualified tuition).

F. Problems

1. Tim receives a $50,000 scholarship to attend the local university. The tuition for the year is $45,000. What are the tax consequences to Tim from receiving the scholarship?

2. Caitlyn works for a car manufacturer. Her employer has developed a program through which it will pay the education expenses of some of its employees. Under the program, an employee can submit an application to the program. In the application, the employee must outline the intended course work, the anticipated degree, and the relevance of the degree to the employee's position with the company. If approved, the employer will pay the education expenses of the employee. If the employee terminates his or her employment with the employer within three years of obtaining the degree, the employee agrees to reimburse the employer for the education expenses. What are the tax consequences to Caitlyn if she is accepted into the employer's program?

3. Malcolm has been accepted into the masters program at his local university. He intends to complete a master's degree in economics. As part of the course work he is required to teach microeconomics, an introductory economic course for undergraduate

students. In exchange, he receives a $10,000 credit toward the cost of his master's coursework. What are the tax consequences to Malcolm from this arrangement?

G. Analysis and Application

1. Is the exclusion for qualified tuition justified? Does the exclusion require that similarly situated taxpayers (students who did and those who did not receive a scholarship) be treated differently?

2. Louise and her daughter, Amanda, have been actively involved in exploring various colleges to which Amanda might apply. Amanda will also be applying for a variety of scholarships. Louise wants to better understand when a scholarship will be tax free. What do you tell her?

3. Carolyn is a law student and was selected for law review. All students on law review receive a $10,000 scholarship from the law school. As part of her law review duties, Carolyn must review articles submitted for publication, help select which submitted articles will be published, from those selected for publication review and edit two articles, and assist with the final proofreading.

    What are the tax consequences to Carolyn upon receipt of the scholarship? In formulating your analysis and response, you may want to consider:
    *   Commissioner v. Glenshaw Glass, 348 U.S. 426 (1955)
    *   Bingler v. Johnson, 394 U.S. 741 (1969)

4. Mark has been a stand-out baseball player all through high school and wants to continue playing in college. He was approached by the local university, which offered him a $20,000 scholarship. He has asked your advice as to the tax consequences if he accepts the scholarship.
    a.   Make a list of the additional information you need to be able to give him advice.
    b.   What concerns do you have?

    In formulating your analysis and response, you may want to consider:
    *   Commissioner v. Glenshaw Glass, 348 U.S. 426 (1955)
    *   Bingler v. Johnson, 394 U.S. 741 (1969)
    *   Rev. Rul. 77-263, 1977-2 C.B. 47

5. Jan, a senior in high school, always planned on attending the local university. At the beginning of the year she entered a national beauty contest. The winner of the contest would be awarded a four-year scholarship. In addition, the winner of the contest was required to perform certain services for the pageant sponsors during the year until a beauty pageant winner for the following year was selected. Jan won the competition and received the four-year scholarship.

    What are the tax consequences to Jan of winning the four-year scholarship? In formulating your analysis and response, you may want to consider:
    *   Commissioner v. Glenshaw Glass, 348 U.S. 426 (1955)
    *   Bingler v. Johnson, 394 U.S. 741 (1969)
    *   Rev. Rul. 77-263, 1977-2 C.B. 47

Chapter 12

Damages

Gross Income

Includes all accessions to wealth, such as:	Excludes:
• Compensation for services	• Loans and deposits
• Business profits	• Gifts and inheritances
• Profit from the sale of property	• Life insurance
• Interest	• Certain prizes and awards
• Rents	• Qualified scholarships
• Royalties	• **Personal injury damages**
• Dividends	• Fringe benefits
• Alimony	• Health insurance
• Cancellation of debt	• Workers' compensation

Read

Code Section 104(a)(2)

Treas. Reg. § 1.104-1(c)

A. Background

Gross income includes income (accessions to wealth) derived from any and all sources.[79] It includes every accession to wealth, unless there is an exception. Receiving an award for damages may be an accession to wealth.

B. General Rule for Damages

The tax consequences of damages cannot be determined by simply recognizing the taxpayer has received damages. Rather, the reason why the taxpayer is receiving the damage payment will dictate whether the damages are taxable.

---

79. Section 61(a).

In *Raytheon Production Corp. v. Commissioner*[80] Raytheon had brought suit against RCA for violation of federal anti-trust laws. The parties settled the dispute, with RCA paying damages to Raytheon. The issue before the Tax Court was whether damages from the anti-trust suit had to be included in Raytheon's gross income. The court considered the underlying litigation and concluded the payment was not for lost profits. While the amount of the damage award was measured by the amount of lost profits, what had been destroyed was Raytheon's goodwill. The court concluded that the payment represented a recovery of Raytheon's capital. To the extent of Raytheon's basis in the goodwill, the amount was not taxable. To the extent it exceeded Raytheon's basis, it was a taxable gain. The court provided the following illustration:

> Thus A buys Blackacre for $5,000. It appreciates in value to $50,000. B tortuously destroys it by fire. A sues and recovers $50,000 tort damages from B. Although no gain was derived by A from the suit, his prior gain due to the appreciation in value of Blackacre is realized when it is turned into cash by the money damages.[81]

Based on the *Raytheon Production* opinion, the test is often described as "in lieu of what are the damages being paid?" If the underlying reason represents gross income, the damages are includible in gross income. For example (with some specific and narrow exceptions), if the damages are for lost profits, they are taxable. If the damages are punitive damages, they are taxable. If the damages represent lost wages, they are taxable. To the extent the damages represent a return of capital, they are not taxable; any amount in excess of the capital investment is taxable.

C. Special Rule for Damages on Account of a Personal Physical Injury

When a taxpayer has received damages to compensate him for a personal, physical injury or physical sickness there is a sense that the taxpayer has not received an accession to wealth, but rather is simply being made whole. It is as if the taxpayer were receiving a return of capital that is his body. While Section 104(a)(2) has not always been limited to physical damages, it has always included the idea that the taxpayer is being made whole and, therefore, that the damages payment does not represent an accession to wealth.

Section 104(a)(2) provides that any damages (except punitive damages) received on account of a personal, physical injury or physical sickness are excludable from gross income. (If the taxpayer has deducted an amount paid for medical expenses,[82] he is not entitled to also exclude the recovery of the amount from his income; to claim both an exclusion and a deduction would give the taxpayer a double benefit.)

Tell Me More

Prior to the enactment of Section 104(a)(2) and under an earlier version of Section 61 (and sometimes even after its enactment) the Commissioner and the

---

80. 144 F.2d 110, 113–14 (1st Cir. 1944).
81. Raytheon Production Corp. v. Commissioner, 144 F.2d 110, 114 (1st Cir. 1944).
82. See Section 213 and related discussion in Chapter 16.

courts took the position that no gain was realized from damages received for alienation of affection or defamation of personal character or other similar types of personal injuries. Because the amounts did not constitute gross income, no exclusionary provision was needed.

Prior to 1997, to come with the exclusion of Section 104(a)(2) the taxpayer need only have shown that the damages were paid on account of a personal injury or sickness. There was no requirement that the injury be a physical injury. Accordingly, there are many cases under the prior version of Section 104(a)(2) discussing whether damages (even damages representing lost wages or profits) paid for defamation, age discrimination, or gender discrimination were excludable from income.

Finally, prior to the legislative change in 1996, it was unclear whether punitive damages were excludable under Section 104(a)(2). Congress made the statute clear by prohibiting any exclusion of punitive damages.

Damages on account of emotional distress. If the damages paid are on account of a personal, physical injury and the injury caused emotional distress, the damages related to the emotional distress are excludable. While the statute does not define emotional distress, the legislative history suggests it encompasses insomnia, headaches, and stomach disorders.

If the injury is the emotional distress, even when the emotional distress manifests in physical ailments, the exclusion is more limited. The taxpayer can exclude only the amount paid for medical care attributable to the emotional distress.[83] Accordingly, to determine the extent to which the exclusion is available, the parties must determine the underlying basis for the cause of action.

Summary of Tests — Damages

General rule: In lieu of what were the damages awarded? If the underlying reason for the payment of the amount represents gross income, the damages are gross income.

Special rule for personal physical injury or physical sickness: Any damages (except punitive damages) paid on account of a personal, physical injury or physical sickness are excludable from gross income.

Settlements. Damages can be paid through a court awarded judgment or a settlement reached by the parties.[84] When the parties have settled their dispute, it may not be clear the extent to which the payment is on account of a personal, physical injury or physical sickness or is an award that would not come within the exclusion. An attorney knowledgeable about the tax implications of different types of awards may structure the payment such that in form it qualifies for the exclusion, even if in substance it is not, or at least not entirely, such a payment. In addition, the taxpayer will be against characterizing any portion of the payment as punitive damages as they would be taxable; similarly, the

---

83. Section 104(a), flush language.
84. Section 104(a)(2).

defendant is unlikely to want to characterize any portion of the payment as punitive damages because it might infer acceptance of culpability on its part.

Because the parties will not always be in an adversarial position with respect to characterization of the payments, where the parties have settled their disagreement the Tax Court has resorted to the "in lieu of test" to determine how much of the damages payment is excludable. It asks in lieu of what the settlement payment is being made and the answer to that question depends on the facts and circumstances. Any of the following factors may be relevant:

- The allegations made in the complaint and the strength of each allegation;
- The content of any settlement negotiations;
- Which party drafted the settlement agreement; and
- The tax motivations of each party.

If the settlement agreement was not the result of arm's-length negotiations, the characterization of the payment in the settlement agreement can be disregarded and other factors used to determine the parties' true intent. If the settlement was the result of arm's-length negotiations, it should reflect the intent of both parties and the excludability of the payment will flow from the characterization of the payment given by the parties.

Sample of Cases Addressing the Issue of Allocation of Damages Awarded in a Settlement Agreement[85]

- *Bagley v. Commissioner.*[86] The taxpayer won a jury verdict of $7.2 million, which was followed by appeals and orders for retrials. Eventually, the parties entered into a settlement agreement for $1.5 million, all allocated to personal injuries.

  The issue before the Tax Court was whether the allocation of damages should be respected. The Tax Court considered all the facts and circumstances, including what might have occurred if the case continued on in the judicial system, the payments the defendant might have been required to make, and the positions taken by the parties in settlement negotiations. The court concluded that $1 million was allocated to damages that were (at that time) excludable and $500,000 represented taxable punitive damages.

- *McKay v. Commissioner.*[87] Taxpayer won a jury verdict for $1.6 million in lost compensation, $12.8 million for future damages due to the taxpayer's wrongful discharge, and punitive damages. Because the employer had violated the Racketeer Influenced and Corrupt Organizations Act (RICO), the damages were trebled. After the employer appealed, the parties settled for damages of $16 million, allocated almost entirely to the employee's wrongful discharge tort claim (excludable at that time).

  The issue before the Tax Court was whether the allocation of damages should be respected. Based on the facts and circumstances, the court noted that the parties were in an adversarial relationship and that the employer did not

---

85. Each of these cases was decided before the statute was changed to require a physical, not just personal, injury.

86. 105 T.C. 396 (1995).

87. 102 T.C. 465 (1994), vacated on other grounds, 84 F.3d 433 (5th Cir. 1996).

want an allocation to RICO violations or punitive damages. The Tax Court respected the allocation reached by the parties.

- *Robinson v. Commissioner.*[88] Taxpayer won a jury verdict for, among other things, lost business profits, personal injuries, and $50 million in punitive damages. After the defendant appealed, the parties settled for $10 million. The taxpayer prepared the settlement agreement, allocating 95 percent of the payment to tort-like personal injuries (excludable at that time). The defendant agreed without commenting on or contesting the taxpayer's allocation. Without a review on the merits of the settlement agreement, the state court entered a judgment reflecting the settlement.

The issue before the Tax Court was whether the allocation of the damages should be respected. Based on the facts and circumstances, including the defendant's non-adversarial position regarding the allocation, the relative amounts allocated by the jury, and the likelihood of the jury award being reduced on appeal, the court determined that the taxpayer could exclude 63 percent of the award, but had to include the remainder.

D. Application of Rules

Example 1. Jan owned and operated a small hotel. In a fit of anger, one of her customers started a fire in the lobby. The fire spread and destroyed the entire hotel. At the time of the fire the hotel was worth $100,000 and Jan's adjusted basis in the building was $30,000. Jan filed a civil lawsuit against the tortfeasor. The jury awarded her $100,000 for the loss of her building, $50,000 in lost profits, and $10,000 in punitive damages.

With respect to the building, Jan must include $70,000 in her income. (The $100,000 recovery can be offset by her $30,000 return of capital). In addition, Jan must report the $50,000 of lost profits and $10,000 of punitive damages.

Example 2. Maglio is a professional hockey player. During a game last season, a player from the opposing team hit Maglio with his stick, breaking his leg in two places. Because of the unusually violent nature of the attack and extent of the injury, Maglio brought a lawsuit against the player and won a judgment in the amount of $1 million. The amount of the judgment was based on the physical damage to his leg and his lost wages due to his inability to play hockey for the next two seasons.

The damages were award on account of a personal, physical injury. Accordingly, Maglio may exclude the entire $1 million.

Example 3. The facts are the same as in Example 2, except the award also included $500,000 in punitive damages. Maglio may exclude the $1 million paid on account of a personal, physical injury, but may not exclude the $500,000 of punitive damages.

Example 4. Marcia is employed as a school teacher. She has worked at the same school for over thirty years. When a new principal was hired, he fired all teachers over 50, including Marcia, and hired younger teachers. Marcia brought a claim of wrongful termination and age discrimination. She was successful in her lawsuit, and the court

---

88. 102 T.C. 116 (1994), aff'd in part and remanded, 70 F.3d 34 (5th Cir. 1995).

awarded her $500,000 in damages representing lost wages. Because Marcia did not suffer a personal, physical injury, no portion of the award is excludable from her income.

Example 5. Tracey is a receptionist at the local spa and gym. Her boss, an older gentleman, made continued and frequent sexual advances towards Tracey. When she objected, he noted that she was an employee of a spa and gym and should expect such attention. He continued to make advances and she continued to rebuff them. However, due to the stress caused by her boss's actions, she developed an ulcer and the beginning stages of agoraphobia. In a fit of rage over her continued refusals, her boss fired her.

Tracey hired a law firm to represent her in a wrongful termination claim against her former employer. After a lengthy trial Tracey was successful in her claim and won a $1 million judgment against her former employer for wrongful termination. Because Tracey's boss did not cause a personal, physical injury, she cannot exclude any of the damages award to her. She can exclude the amount paid for medical care attributable to the ulcer and agoraphobia.

Example 6. When walking through his downtown neighborhood Chris was injured when an icicle fell from his neighbor's eave and hit him on the head. He threatened to file a lawsuit against his neighbor for the damage caused to him by the icicle. After several contentious rounds of settlement negotiations, the neighbor agreed to pay Chris $5,000 and Chris agreed to forgo filing a complaint against his neighbor based on the event.

The damages Chris's neighbor paid to him were on account of a personal, physical injury. Accordingly, he may exclude the entire $5,000.

E. Problems

1. Jocelyn brought a cause of action against Miguel for breach of contract. After a lengthy trial, the jury awarded her $40,000 in lost profits and $10,000 of punitive damages. How much of the award must Jocelyn include in her income?

2. Phillip became very angry at Charles and used a sledge hammer to damage Charles's boat, totally destroying it. Charles sued Phillip and obtained a $50,000 judgment. At the time Phillip damaged the boat, Charles's basis in the boat was $40,000. How much of the award must Charles include in his income?

3. Will is a professional baseball umpire. During the last game, he made a controversial call. A fan, enraged by the call, jumped onto the field and assaulted him. He suffered a broken nose and fractured arm. Will sued the fan for damages based on the injuries he suffered and was awarded $50,000 in lost wages, $10,000 in punitive damages, and $15,000 for the anxiety spells Will suffered following the attack. How much of the award must Will include in his income?

4. Jill is a professional singer. At her last concert an attendee seated in the front row called out to her that he believed she had "lost her ability to sing and perform and should just get off the stage." Since that time, Jill has been unable to perform. She rarely goes out into public and when she does she refuses to speak with any fan who approaches her. She lost an unhealthy amount of weight, and the weight loss has led to a heart condition. Jill brought suit against the attendee for intentional infliction of emotional distress and was awarded a $5,000 judgment. How much of the award must Jill include in her income?

F. Analysis and Application

1. Is the exclusion for damages received on account of a personal physical injury or sickness justified? Is it appropriate to tax wages earned by one taxpayer and but not tax wages received by another when paid in the form of damages on account of a physical injury?

2. Gabbie is a college student who struggles to make ends meet. In her search for ways to make a small amount of spending money she discovered she could sell her blood plasma. In exchange for her plasma, the blood bank would pay her $2,000 per "bleed." Every Thursday during the school term she would go to the blood bank and have an intravenous line inserted into her arm. She would wait for close to three hours as her blood circulated into a separation machine, the machine removed her plasma, and the remainder of her blood was returned into her arm. The process caused Gabbie a fair amount of pain and discomfort.

    May Gabbie exclude the amounts the blood bank pays to her as damages on account of a personal physical injury? Are there additional facts you would like to know?

    In formulating your analysis and response, you may want to consider:

    *   Commissioner v. Glenshaw Glass Co., 348 U.S. 426 (1955)
    *   Commissioner v. Schleier, 515 U.S. 323 (1995)
    *   Vincent v. Commissioner, T.C. Memo. 2005-95
    *   Parkinson v. Commissioner, T.C. Memo. 2010-142

3. Julie, who had been diagnosed with multiple sclerosis (MS), was employed as a professional fundraiser. A few years ago her employer hired a new executive director. Julie had a strained relationship with the new director and the tension with the director caused Julie's MS symptoms to flare up. When Julie discovered that the director was embezzling from her employer, she informed the board of directors. The board stated it would address the situation, but failed to take any action. Meanwhile, the tension between Julie and director increased, and Julie's MS symptoms intensified to the point that she could not return to work. After notifying her employer of her inability to work for a length of time her employer terminated her.

    Julie contacted an attorney who represented her in a wrongful termination action. Eventually, she and her former employer entered into a settlement in which her former employer agreed to pay her $33,000.

    a. What language might you expect to be included in the settlement?

    b. To what extent would any part of the payment be excludable from Julie's income?

    c. If contested by the government, how would you support an amount being excludable?

    In formulating your analysis and response, you may want to consider:

    *   Commissioner v. Glenshaw Glass Co., 348 U.S. 426 (1955)
    *   Commissioner v. Schleier, 515 U.S. 323 (1995)
    *   Vincent v. Commissioner, T.C. Memo. 2005-95
    *   Parkinson v. Commissioner, T.C. Memo. 2010-142

Chapter 13

Fringe Benefits

Gross Income

Includes all accessions to wealth, such as:	Excludes:
• Compensation for services	• Loans and deposits
• Business profits	• Gifts and inheritances
• Profit from the sale of property	• Life insurance
• Interest	• Certain prizes and awards
• Rents	• Qualified scholarships
• Royalties	• Personal injury damages
• Dividends	• **Fringe benefits**
• Alimony	• Health insurance
• Cancellation of debt	• Workers' compensation

Read

Code Sections 119; 132

Treas. Reg. §§ 1.61-21; 1.119-1(a), (b), (c)(1); 1.132-2(a)(1), (2), (3), (5)(i); 1.132-3(a)(1), (c)(1)(i), (ii); 1.132-4(a)(1)(i), (iii); 1.132-6(a), (b), (d)(2)(i)

A. Background

Gross income includes income (accessions to wealth) derived from any and all sources.[89] It includes every accession to wealth, unless there is an exception.

Compensation for services is an accession to wealth.[90] The form of the payment—cash, services, property, debt relief—is not relevant. Nor does the type of compensation matter. Whether the payment is characterized as salary, wages, tips, bonus, etc., compensation for services is gross income.[91] Similarly, receiving a fringe benefit from an employer is a form of compensation for services. As such, unless there is an exclusion, a fringe benefit is an accession to wealth.[92]

---

89. Section 61(a).
90. Section 61(a)(1).
91. See discussion in Chapter 3.
92. Section 61(a)(1).

B. Section 119 —
Excludable Meals and Lodging

An employer may provide meals and lodging for the employee. The taxpayer-employee is better off for not having to pay for these items himself. In the past, before there was a relevant Code provision, the taxpayer-employee would argue the benefit was excludable if he could show the meals and lodging were made "for the convenience of the employer." After inconsistencies in tax results between courts and between the courts and the Service, Congress enacted Section 119 to address this issue.

Section 119. Meals or Lodging Furnished for the Convenience of the Employer

(a) Meals or Lodging Furnished to Employee, His Spouse, and His Dependents, Pursuant to Employment. — There shall be excluded from gross income of an employee the value of any meals or lodging furnished to him, his spouse, or any of his dependents by or on behalf of his employer for the convenience of the employer, but only if—

> (1) in the case of meals, the meals are furnished on the business premises of the employer, or
>
> (2) in the case of lodging, the employee is required to accept such lodging on the business premises of his employer as a condition of his employment....

Meals. Based on the statutory provisions and the underlying regulations, the employee can exclude meals provided to him by the employer if the following conditions are met:[93]

- The meals are furnished on the business premises of the employer; and
- The meals are provided for the convenience of the employer.

Meals furnished by the employer will be treated as furnished for the convenience of the employer if they are furnished for a substantial noncompensatory business reason. For example, the meals are furnished for a noncompensatory business reason if they are furnished:[94]

- To have the employee available for emergency calls during the meal period;
- Because the employer's business is such that the employee must be restricted to a short meal period and the employee could not be expected to eat elsewhere in such a short period of time;
- Because there are insufficient eating facilities in the vicinity of the employer's premises; or
- The meals are furnished to a restaurant employee.

---

93. Section 119(a).
94. Treas. Reg. § 1.119-1(a)(2)(ii).

If the employer provides meals that an employee may purchase, the meals are not considered as furnished for the convenience of the employer.[95] If the employee receives a cash reimbursement, the cash is not excludable from gross income.[96]

Lodging. Based on the statutory provisions and the underlying regulations, an employee can exclude lodging provided to him by the employer if the following conditions are met:[97]

- The lodging is on the business premises of the employer;
- The lodging is provided for the convenience of the employer; and
- The employee is required to accept such lodging as a condition of his employment.

It is a condition of his employment if the employee is required to accept the lodging to enable him to perform the duties of employment. For example, this element is met when the lodging is furnished because the employee is required to be available for duty at all times or because the employee could not perform the services required of him unless he is furnished such lodging.[98]

Sample of Cases Addressing the "Business Premises" Requirement of Section 119

- *Commissioner v. Anderson:*[99] The taxpayer was a motel manager and, as part of his responsibilities, he was always "on call" for any issues that might arise at the motel. As a condition of his employment, he was required to reside in a single family residence owned by his employer and located two blocks from the motel.

  The court defined "on the business premises of the employer" to mean the place where the employee performs a significant portion of his duties or conducts a significant portion of his business. Because the employee performed his duties at the motel and not the residence, the court concluded that the residence was not on the business premises of the employer and that the exclusion of Section 119 did not apply.

- *Lindeman v. Commissioner:*[100] Taxpayer was a manager for a hotel and was on-call for any issues that might arise. His employer provided him with a residence adjacent to the motel. The court noted that what constituted the "business premises" required consideration of the employee's duties and the nature of the employer's business. Because the residence was "part and parcel" of the hotel property, it was "on the business premises." He was entitled to the exclude the value of the free housing under Section 119.

---

95. Treas. Reg. § 1.119-1(a)(3)(i).
96. Treas. Reg. § 1.119-1(e).
97. Section 119.
98. Treas. Reg. § 1.119-1(b).
99. 371 F.2d 59 (6th Cir. 1966), cert denied 387 U.S. 906 (1967).
100. 60 T.C. 609 (1973).

Whether a taxpayer meets the above requirements for the exclusion of employer-provided meals or lodging depends in large part on the facts.[101] Because the facts of each case differ so widely, there is little common ground in the opinions that have applied Section 119.

C. Section 132 — Excludable Fringe Benefits

A fringe benefit is a benefit provided by the employer because of the employment relationship. While the benefit represents an accession to wealth in the form of compensation for services, in the past such benefits were traditionally excluded from gross income even though no Code provision allowed for such an exclusion. The exclusion is now codified in Section 132 and includes seven different types of fringe benefits:[102]

- No-additional-cost service
- Qualified employee discount
- Working condition fringe
- De minimis fringe
- Qualified transportation fringe
- Qualified moving expense reimbursement
- Qualified retirement planning services.

If a fringe benefit comes within any of the above types, the value of the benefit is excludable to the extent provided in the Code.

Tell Me More

Other Code provisions, besides Section 132, exclude benefits provided by the employer to the employee. They include:

- Section 79: excluding the value of group term life insurance to the extent the benefit is not more than $50,000.

- Section 105: excluding the insurance benefits received from an employer-provided insurance plan.

- Section 106: excluding the health insurance premiums paid by an employer on behalf of an employee.

- Section 117(d): excluding benefits received under a qualified tuition reduction program.

- Section 129: excluding the value of a dependent care assistance program.

- Section 401, et. seq: excluding contributions an employer makes on behalf of an employee to a qualified retirement plan.

---

101. Treas. Reg. § 1.119-1(a)(1).
102. Section 132(a).

1. No Additional Cost Service

There are some industries where the employer incurs the same cost to provide a service, regardless of how many people participate in the service. For example, the cost of driving a bus from San Francisco to Los Angeles will be the same if the bus is half-empty or completely full. Employers in these industries often make the unused space available to their employees and their families at no charge. It is this type of service that generated the exclusion for no additional cost service fringe benefits.

To qualify, the service must be:[103]

- offered by the employer to the employee;
- offered for sale to customers in the ordinary course of business;
- offered in the line of business of the employer in which the employee is performing services;
- one for which the employer incurs no substantial additional cost (including forgone revenue); and
- one that does not discriminate in favor of highly compensated employees.

2. Qualified Employee Discount

Over the years, as a benefit to their employees, some businesses made their goods and services available to their employees at a price discounted from the price paid by the general public. Such discounts can provide intangible benefits to the employer, ranging from increased sales to increased employee morale to free advertising. Accordingly, when Congress was considering what should be an excludable fringe benefit, retailers presented a strong lobby and were successful in having the benefit excluded. It became the qualified employee discount.

The exclusion applies to property or services offered for sale to customers in the line of business in which the employee is performing services. The amount of the discount is the difference between what the employee pays and what a non-employee customer would pay.[104]

There is a limit on the amount of benefit the taxpayer can exclude. If the employee is purchasing services, the exclusion applies only to the extent of 20 percent of the price at which the service is offered for purchase by non-employee customers. If the employee is purchasing property, the exclusion applies only to the extent of the gross profit percentage of the price at which the property is offered for sale to non-employee customers. The gross profit percentage is:

$$\frac{(\text{aggregate sales price} - \text{cost})}{\text{aggregate sales price}}$$

The percentage is determined by considering all sales of property in the employee's line of business, not just the discounted item.[105]

---

103. Section 132(b), (j)(1).

104. Section 132(c). The benefit cannot discriminate in favor of highly compensated employees. Section 132(j)(1).

105. Section 132(c).

3. Working Condition Fringe Benefit

Employers often provide the items an employee needs to do his job. While this can include items such as office space, access to a computer, and support staff, it can include other job-specific items like trade journals, internet access, and coffee. If the employee had paid for these items directly, because they are costs associated with earning his salary, he would most likely have been entitled to deduct the costs. It seemed to Congress the same result would be reached if the employer provided the items and the employee was not required to include them in income. This correlation provides the basis for the exclusion for working condition fringe benefits.

An employee can exclude the value of property or services provided by the employer to the extent that, if the employee had paid for the item, he would have been allowed a business deduction.[106] Note that the exclusion does not extend to cash payments unless the employee is required to use the cash for an item that would qualify for the exclusion.[107]

4. De Minimis Fringe Benefit

An employee can exclude a fringe benefit that is de minimus. To be de minimis, the value of the property has to be so small that it would be administratively impractical to account for it. The value of the benefit includes consideration of how frequently the benefit is provided by the employer to its employees.[108] The determination is made based on the frequency with which the employer provides the fringe benefit to each individual employee.[109]

If the employer operates an eating facility and the employees can dine there at reduced rates, the benefit of the reduced cost of the meal is treated as a de minimus fringe benefit. To qualify for the exclusion, the facility must be located on or near the employer's business and the revenue from the facility must normally equal or exceed the operating cost.[110]

The regulations identify certain fringe benefits that are excludable from gross income as de minimis fringe benefits:[111]

- Occasional typing of personal letters by a company secretary;
- Occasional personal use of an employer's copying machine;
- Occasional cocktail parties, group meals, or picnics for employees and their guests;
- Traditional birthday or holiday gifts of property (not cash) with a low fair market value;
- Occasional theater or sporting event tickets;
- Coffee, doughnuts, and soft drinks;
- Local telephone calls; and

---

106. Section 132(d).
107. Treas. Reg. § 1.132-5(a)(1)(v).
108. Section 132(e)(1).
109. Treas. Reg. § 1.132-6(b)(1).
110. Section 132(e)(2).
111. Treas. Reg. § 1.132-6(e)(1).

- Flowers, fruit, books or similar property provided to employees under special circumstances.

They also identify certain fringe benefits that are not excludable from gross income as de minimis fringe benefits:[112]

- season tickets to sporting or theatrical events;
- commuting use of an employer-provided car more than one day a month;
- membership in a private country club or athletic facility, regardless of the frequency with which the employee uses the facility; and
- use of employer-owned or leased facilities for a weekend.

D. Application of Rules

Example 1. Holly is a waitress at the local diner, working the 7 am to 4 pm shift. Her employer permits Holly to have two meals at the diner each day she works, without charge. While she may have breakfast on the business premises, she is required to have lunch there. Holly is permitted to exclude the value of the meals provided by her employer.

Example 2. Bernadine is a waitress at a local diner, working the 7 am to 4 pm shift. Her employer permits her to eat two meals at the diner on her days off, without charge. Bernadine may not exclude the value of the meals provided by her employer on her days off.

Example 3. Evan is a bank teller, working from 9 am to 5 pm. His employer provides him a lunch without charge at a cafeteria the bank maintains on the business premises. Because the bank's peak work load is during the lunch period, the tellers are required to eat in the cafeteria so that their lunch periods will not exceed 30 minutes. If Evan had to get lunch other than at the cafeteria, it would take him longer than 30 minutes. Evan may exclude the value of the meals the bank provides him.

Example 4. Charlene is a construction worker and is working on a project located at a remote site. Because there is no lodging around the work site, the employer has provided lodging for the workers at the site. Charlene can exclude the value of the lodging from her gross income.

Example 5. Kenneth is a flight attendant for a commercial airline. The airline permits its employees to fly on the airline at no charge. The employee may reserve seating.

Because the employee is permitted to reserve seating, the employer potentially is forgoing revenue. Accordingly, the fringe benefit does not qualify for the no additional cost service exclusion.

Example 6. The employer offers an employee discount to its sales clerks on its clothing. Clothing sales totaled $800,000. The cost to the employer of the clothing was $600,000. Thus, the gross profit percentage is:

$$\frac{\text{(aggregate sales price} - \text{cost)}}{\text{aggregate sales price}} = \frac{(\$800,000 - \$600,000)}{\$800,000} = 25\%$$

---

112. Treas. Reg. § 1.132-6(e)(2).

The employee's excludable discount is limited to the price at which the property is offered to customers in the ordinary course of business, multiplied by 25%.

Example 7. Grover is an associate at a local law firm. The firm provides him an office and allows him to use the kitchen area and conference room as needed. Use of the office, kitchen area, and conference room are working condition fringe benefits. He can exclude the use value of the rooms from his gross income.

Example 8. Elaine is an associate at a local law firm that specializes in personal injury claims. On occasion, when the trial team is preparing for a trial, the firm will have a meal delivered to the office. That way the team can continue with its preparations. The value of the meal is a de minimis fringe benefit. Elaine can exclude the value of the meals from her gross income.

Example 9. Janette works for an accounting firm. Every day, her employer provides lunch for her, but not for any other employees. The value of the meal is not a de minimis fringe benefit. While the frequency of the meals with respect to the entire workforce is provided "infrequently," it is not de minimis with respect to Janette. She cannot exclude the value of the meals from her gross income.

Example 10. Tony works for a law firm. On occasion, he uses the firm's copy machine to copy his personal documents. The use of his employer's copy machine is a de minimis fringe benefit, and he can exclude the value of making the copies from his gross income.

E. Problems

1. Denny lived in a farm house located on a farm. At the farm he assisted with planting, cultivating, harvesting, drying, storing, and selling corn and soybeans. He assisted with all farm activities. His employment contract required him to live on the farm so he could manage the general operations of the farm, secure the farm equipment, supervise the drying and storing of grain, and perform any necessary duties on a 24-hour-per-day basis. Residences were available for rent in the nearby towns. What are the tax consequences to Denny from use of the farm house?

2. Georgia works for a high end fashion boutique. She is permitted to purchase clothing from the store at a 25 percent discount. May she exclude the value of the fringe benefit from her gross income? Do you need any additional information to make this determination?

3. Sam works at a theme park. He is permitted access to the park (and is able to ride on the rides) without charge on his days off. May he exclude the value of the fringe benefit from his gross income?

4. Ted works for Buses Unlimited, a company that provides interstate bus transportation. He works in the service bay providing mechanical maintenance services. He assures that the oil is changed, the tires rotated, and other miscellaneous upkeep is performed on the buses on a regular basis. Buses Unlimited allows Ted to travel on any of the buses free of charge, as long as there is an empty seat available for him. If Ted travels to El Paso, Texas, can he exclude the value of the trip from his gross income?

5. Monty is an anesthesiologist at the local hospital. On the days he is working, he is required to be on-site the entire time. He is permitted to eat at the hospital cafeteria

free of charge during the times he is working. May he exclude the value of the free meals from his gross income?

6. Randy is an associate at Howard and Stable, LLC. Each Monday at noon all the attorneys meet in the conference room to discuss progress on client files. The firm has lunch delivered. May Randy exclude the value of the free meals from his gross income?

7. Tom works for his father's business. At the end of the year, his father gave all of his employees a box of imported Belgian chocolates. In addition, his father gave Tom three tins of imported Greek coffee beans. Must Tom and the employees include the value of the chocolates in their gross income?

F. Analysis and Application

1. Is the exclusion for meals and lodging provided by the employer justified? Is it appropriate to tax wages earned by one taxpayer and but not wages received by another in the form of benefits?

2. Should it make a difference if a fringe benefit is paid in-kind or with cash?

3. Does the exclusion for meals and lodging provided by the employer extend to meals and lodging provided to the employee's family? Should it?

4. Which fringe benefits excluded from income under Section 132 extend to retired or disabled employees? To spouses of the employee? To dependents of the employee?

5. Under what situations might it be for the convenience of the employer to provide meals to its employees? To provide lodging to its employees?

6. If a fringe benefit were not excluded from the taxpayer's income, how would you determine the value of the benefit?

7. Carter works for a home improvement store. Each year his employer provides all employees a gift during the holiday. Can he exclude the value of the gift if he receives:

   a. A turkey.

   b. A $50 gift card.

8. Max was employed by the Federal Aviation Agency (FAA) and stationed at Wake Island (located in the middle of the Pacific Ocean). He worked on electronic systems located at various places on the island. He was on call 24 hours a day and worked about 54 hours a week. He was required, as a condition of his employment, to live in housing provided by the FAA. He paid his rent through a payroll deduction and purchased supplies at the commissary maintained on the island by the FAA. Without the commissary, there would not have been enough food on the island to accommodate FAA employees.

   a. Can Max exclude from his income the rent that was deducted from his salary?

   b. Can Max exclude from his income the cost of supplies he purchased from the commissary?

   In formulating your analysis and response, you may want to consider:

   • Commissioner v. Glenshaw Glass Co., 348 U.S. 426 (1955)

   • Commissioner v. Kowalski, 434 U.S. 77 (1977)

- Lindeman v. Commissioner, 60 T.C. 609 (1973)
- Commissioner v. Anderson, 371 F.2d 59 (6th Cir. 1966)

9. Sam was employed as a dentist by the state mental hospital. The hospital provided a cottage on the hospital grounds in which he could live. While he was not required to be on duty at all hours, he was expected to be available in case of an emergency. Sam paid the hospital $300 per month for use of the cottage. The fair rental value of the cottage was $500. What are the tax consequences to Sam from use of the cottage?

In formulating your analysis and response, you may want to consider:

- Commissioner v. Glenshaw Glass Co., 348 U.S. 426 (1955)
- Commissioner v. Kowalski, 434 U.S. 77 (1977)
- Lindeman v. Commissioner, 60 T.C. 609 (1973)
- Commissioner v. Anderson, 371 F.2d 59 (6th Cir. 1966)

10. Sarah worked for a casino in Las Vegas. For security reasons (and ability of the employer to maintain control over its workforce and reduce the number of employees succumbing to the temptations of the festive Las Vegas atmosphere), the employer required all casino employees to remain on the business premises throughout the work shift. All employees could receive free meals at the on-site cafeteria. What are the tax consequences to Sarah from the free meals?

In formulating your analysis and response, you may want to consider:

- Commissioner v. Glenshaw Glass Co., 348 U.S. 426 (1955)
- Commissioner v. Kowalski, 434 U.S. 77 (1977)
- Lindeman v. Commissioner, 60 T.C. 609 (1973)
- Commissioner v. Anderson, 371 F.2d 59 (6th Cir. 1966)

Chapter 14

Health Insurance and Workers' Compensation

Gross Income

Includes all accessions to wealth, such as:	Excludes:
• Compensation for services • Business profits • Profit from the sale of property • Interest • Rents • Royalties • Dividends • Alimony • Cancellation of debt	• Loans and deposits • Gifts and inheritances • Life insurance • Certain prizes and awards • Qualified scholarships • Personal injury damages • Fringe benefits • **Health insurance** • **Workers' compensation**

Read

Code Sections 104(a)(1), (a)(3), 105, 106.

Treas. Reg. §§ 1.61-21; 1.119-1(a)(1), (b), (c)

A. Background

Gross income includes income (accessions to wealth) derived from any and all sources. It includes every accession to wealth, unless there is an exception.

B. Health Insurance and Medical Expenses

When considering the payment of medical expenses, it is helpful to recognize that the tax impact may be an exclusion from gross income or a deduction. The taxpayer may be allowed to exclude amounts he has been reimbursed by his insurance company. And, the taxpayer may be allowed to claim a deduction for medical expenses he has paid. It should not be a surprise that Congress did not want taxpayers to be able to claim both an exclusion and a deduction. Congress resolved the tension between the two possibilities by providing that, to the extent the taxpayer has claimed a deduction for medical expenses he paid, he is not entitled to exclude such amount when reimbursed by his insurance company.

Whether the taxpayer is entitled to claim a deduction for medical expenses he has paid is considered in Chapter 16. This chapter considers whether an amount received from an insurance company is excludable from gross income.

Whether an amount received from an insurance company through an insurance policy is excludable from the taxpayer's gross income depends on whether the policy was paid for by the employee or by the employer.

1. Employee-Purchased Insurance

A taxpayer may purchase his own health insurance with after-tax dollars. Based on the terms of the health insurance policy, the taxpayer may file a claim, requesting a payment from the insurance company. If the insurance company agrees to make the payments, to the extent they are for medical care for the taxpayer, the taxpayer's spouse, or dependents, the taxpayer can exclude the entire amount received. The exclusion is permitted even if the amount received from the insurance company exceeds the taxpayer's actual medical costs.

Section 104. Compensation for Injuries or Sickness

(a) In general. — Except in the case of amounts attributable to (and not in excess of) deductions allowed under section 213 (relating to medical, etc., expenses) for any prior taxable year, gross income does not include —

* * *

(3) amounts received through accident or health insurance (or through an arrangement having the effect of an accident or health insurance) for personal injuries or sickness (other than amounts received by an employee, to the extent such amounts (A) are attributable to contributions by the employer which were not includible in the gross income of the employee, or (B) are paid by the employer); ...

---

2. Employer-Purchased Insurance

Employer-sponsored plans have two aspects from a tax perspective. The first aspect is the tax consequences to the employee when the employer pays the employee's insurance premiums. The taxpayer is better off because he receives the benefit of health insurance coverage without having to pay the premiums and has an accession to wealth equal to the value of the premium payments. The Code allows the taxpayer to exclude this accession to wealth.

Section 106. Contributions by Employers to Accident and Health Plans

(a) General Rule.—Except as otherwise provided in this section, gross income of an employee does not include employer-provided coverage under an accident or health plan.

The second aspect is the tax consequence of any amount received from the insurance company as a result of a claim filed by the taxpayer. The general rule is that any recovery is not excludable. However, this general rule is subject to several large exceptions.

105. Amounts Received under Accident and Health Plans

(a) Amounts Attributable to Employer Contributions.—Except as otherwise provided in this section, amounts received by an employee through accident or health insurance for personal injuries or sickness shall be included in gross income to the ext such amounts (1) are attributable to contributions by the employer which were not includible in the gross income of the employee, or (2) are paid by the employer.

(b) Amounts Expended for Medical Care.—Except in the case of amounts attributable to (and not in excess of) deductions allowed under section 213 (relating to medical, etc., expenses) for any prior taxable year, gross income does not include amounts referred to in subjection (a) if such amount are paid, directly or indirectly, to the taxpayer to reimburse the taxpayer for expenses incurred by him for the medical care (as defined in section 213(d)) of the taxpayer, his spouse, his dependents (as defined in section 152, determined without regard to subsections (b)(1), (b)(2), and (d)(1)(B) thereof), and any child (as defined in section 152(f)(1)) of the taxpayer who as of the end of the taxable year has not attained age 27. Any child to whom section 152(e) applies shall be treated as a dependent of both parents for purposes of this subsection.

(c) Payments Unrelated to Absence From Work.—Gross income does not include amounts referred to in subsection (a) to the extent such amounts—

(1) constitute payment for the permanent loss or use of a member or function of the body, or the permanent disfigurement, of the taxpayer, his spouse, or a dependent (as defined in section 152, determined without regard to subsections (b)(1), (b)(2), and (d)(1)(B) thereof), and

(2) are computed with reference to the nature of the injury without regard to the period the employee is absent from work.

First, the taxpayer can exclude reimbursed medical care expenses. The exclusion applies to reimbursed medical expenses incurred for himself, his spouse, and any children under 27. If the amount the insurance company pays the taxpayer exceeds his medical expenses, he cannot exclude that excess amount from his gross income.

Second, the taxpayer can exclude payments made by the insurance company for the loss or use of a member or function of the body or permanent disfigurement as long as the amount of the payment is based on the nature of the injury and not on the period of time the employee is absent from work. The exclusion applies to amounts paid on behalf of the taxpayer, his spouse, or a dependent.

After taking into consideration the two large exceptions, payments that continue to be included in income include sick pay and wage continuation payments.

	Employee-Purchased	Employer-Purchased
Sick pay or wage continuation payments	Excludable	Taxable
Medical care for taxpayer, taxpayer's spouse, and dependents	All excludable (even to the extent it exceeds medical costs incurred)	Excludable up to amount of medical expenses incurred.
Payments to compensate for permanent bodily injury or disfigurement	Excludable if the amount of the payment is based on the nature of the injury	Excludable

3. Allocation between Plans

Allocation between employee-purchased and employer-purchased plans is required in at least two situations. First, an allocation may be required if the taxpayer has two policies, one for which he paid the premiums and one for which his employer paid the premiums. When the taxpayer receives a payment from the insurance companies and the total of the payments exceeds his actual medical expenses, the excess amount must be allocated between the two policies based on the relative payment made by each policy.

Second, an allocation may be required if the taxpayer has one policy and the premiums are paid in part by the employee (with after-tax funds) and in part by the employer. When the taxpayer receives a payment from the insurance company that exceeds his actual medical expenses, the excess amount must be allocated based on the relative amount of the premium paid by the employee and paid by the employer. The payment is bifurcated between the two based on how much of the premiums each party made. In other words, if the taxpayer paid 2/3 of the cost of the premiums, the tax consequences of 2/3 of the payment would be considered under the rules for employee-purchased coverage and 1/3 would be considered under the rules for employer-purchased coverage.

C. Workers' Compensation

If a taxpayer receives a payment through a workers' compensation act and the payment is for personal injuries or sickness, he can exclude the amount from his gross income. To come within the exclusion, the payment must be for an occupational injury or illness. If it is not, even if the payment is labeled workers' compensation, it is not excludable.

The exclusion does not extend to payments that are for retirement if based on age, length or service, or employee contributions, even if the retirement is due to an occupation-related personal injury or sickness.

D. Application of Rules

Example 1. Joan purchased a health insurance policy, agreeing to make monthly premium payments. Later, she incurred $1,000 in medical expenses and submitted a claim to her insurance company. She did not claim a deduction for any of the expenses she incurred.

The insurance company agreed to pay her $1,000. Because the insurance company agreed to make a payment to Joan for her medical care, she may exclude the $1,000 from her gross income.

Example 2. Mark purchased a health insurance policy, agreeing to make monthly premium payments. Later, he incurred $1,000 in medical expenses and submitted a claim to his insurance company. He did not claim a deduction for any of the expenses he incurred.

The insurance company paid him $1,500. Because the insurance company agreed to make a payment to Mark for his medical care, he may exclude the $1,500 from his gross income. The exclusion is permitted even though the amount received from the insurance company exceeds his actual medical costs.

Example 3. Nora's employer provides health insurance coverage for its employees. Nora can exclude the cost of the premiums her employer pays on her behalf from her gross income.

Example 4. Kristy's employer provides health insurance coverage for its employees. Kristy was sick and unable to work for five days. The insurance company paid her $50 for each day she was unable to work. Kristy may not exclude the $250 from her gross income.

Example 5. Ken's employer provides health insurance coverage for its employees. Ken incurred $1,000 in medical expenses and submitted a claim to the insurance company. He did not claim a deduction for any of the expenses he incurred.

The insurance company paid him $1,000. Because the insurance company agreed to make a payment to Ken for his medical care, he may exclude the $1,000 from his gross income.

Example 6. Stanley's employer provides health insurance coverage for its employees. Stanley incurred $1,000 in medical expenses and submitted a claim to the insurance company. He did not claim a deduction for any of the expenses he incurred.

The insurance company paid him $1,500. Stanley may exclude the amount paid to reimburse him for his medical expenses ($1,000). He cannot exclude the remaining $500 payment.

Example 7. Sarah purchased a health insurance policy, agreeing to make monthly premium payments. In addition, her employer provides health insurance coverage for its employees. Later, Sarah incurred $1,000 in medical expenses and submitted a claim to both insurance companies. She did not claim a deduction for any of the expenses she incurred.

Her insurance company paid her $720 and her employer's insurance company paid her $480. The total amount she received, $1,200, exceeds her actual medical expenses by $200. This excess amount is allocated between the two polices based on the relative payment made by each policy. Of the $1,200 she received, 60 percent (720/1200) was from her insurance company and 40 percent (480/1200) was from her employer's insurance company. Accordingly, 60 percent of the $200 can be excluded from gross income ($120) and 40 percent ($80) cannot be excluded. In summary, of the $1,200 payment she can exclude $1,120 ($1000, plus $120) and must include $80.

Example 8. Mike's employer provides health insurance coverage for its employees. However, the employee must make one-fourth of the premium payments. Later, Mike incurred $1,000 in medical expenses and submitted a claim to the insurance company. He did not claim a deduction for any of the expenses he incurred.

The insurance company paid him $1,500. The total amount he received, $1,500, exceeds his actual medical expenses by $500. This excess amount is allocated based on the relative amount of the premium amount paid by the employee and the amount paid by the employer. Because Mike paid one-fourth of the premiums, Mike may exclude $125 (the excess amount attributable to the portion of the policy he purchased) and cannot exclude $375 (the excess amount attributable to the portion of the policy the employer purchased).

Example 9. Stefani was injured at work. She filed a workers' compensation claim. The claim was granted and she received a $2,000 payment. Because the payment was through a workers' compensation act and was for occupational injuries, Stefani can exclude the $2,000 payment from her gross income.

Example 10. Don filed a workers' compensation claim. The claim was granted and he received a $2,000 payment. The amount of the payment was based on the number of years he worked for his employer. While the payment was through a worker's compensation act, because the payment was based on length of service, Don may not exclude the $2,000 payment from his gross income.

Example 11. Phil was injured at work. Because he was of retirement age, he elected to retire. He received workers' compensation benefits computed based on his number of years of service.

Even though Phil's retirement was based on an occupation-related injury, the amount of the payments was based on his length of service. The exclusion for workers' compensation payments does not extend to payments for retirement if they are based on length of service. Phil cannot exclude the payments from his gross income.

E. Problems

Except for problem 5, in each of the following problems, the taxpayer did not claim a deduction for any expenses he or she incurred.

1. Shelby was injured at the annual company softball game. She incurred $5,000 in medical expenses and submitted a claim to her insurance company. Her insurance company paid her $6,000. How much is Shelby required to include in her gross income?

2. Max's employer provides health insurance coverage for all its employees. If Max had made the premium payments for the year, it would have cost him $20,000. Is Max required to include the benefit of the premium payments in his gross income?

3. Otto's wife was injured while playing pick-up basketball at the local gym. He incurred $5,000 in medical expense and submitted a claim to his employer's insurance company. (His employer made all premium payments on the policy.) The insurance company agreed to pay him $6,000. How much is Otto required to include in his gross income?

4. Charlie fell ill after eating at his employer's annual employee-appreciation picnic. He was unable to work for three days. He filed a claim with his employer's insurance company. (His employer made all the premium payments on the policy.) The insurance company agreed to pay him $225 in sick pay. How much is Charlie required to include in his gross income?

5. Chuck was injured while skiing. He incurred $5,000 in medical expense and submitted a claim to his insurance company. He properly claimed a medical expense deduction under Section 213 on his income tax return. Later, the insurance company agreed to pay him $6,000. How much is Chuck required to include in his gross income?

6. Torie purchased a health insurance policy, agreeing to make monthly premium payments. Later, she accepted a job with an employer who provided health insurance coverage to its employees. Torie was in a boating accident and incurred $10,000 in medical expenses. She submitted a claim to both insurance companies. Her insurance company paid her $8,000 and her employer's insurance company paid her $7,000. How much is Torie required to include in her gross income?

7. Lacie's employer provided health insurance coverage. However, each employee was required to pay for one-half of the cost of the premiums. Lacie was injured while learning to in-line skate and incurred $10,000 in medical expenses. She submitted a claim to the insurance company and the company paid her $15,000. How much is Lacie required to include in her gross income?

8. Carolyn works in a sheet metal factory and was injured when carrying a heavy piece of equipment. She filed a workers' compensation claim. The claim was granted and she received a $5,000 payment. The amount of the claim was based on Carolyn's injuries. How much is Carolyn required to include in her gross income?

9. Larry works at a car manufacturing plant. He was injured when one of the power tools malfunctioned. He filed a workers' compensation claim. The claim was granted and he received a $5,000 payment. The amount of the payment was determined based on the number of days Larry was unable to work. How much is Larry required to include in his gross income?

F. Analysis and Application

1. Is the exclusion for recoveries related to the taxpayer's spouse or dependents justified? Why or why not?

2. With respect to employee-sponsored coverage, is the exclusion for all insurance payments, even those that exceed actual medical costs, justified?

3. Why is the amount that exceeds actual medical costs excludable if the plan is paid for by the employee but not excludible if the plan is paid for by the employer? Is there a justification for this difference in treatment?

IV

Personal Deductions

Personal:	Investment:	Business:
• Interest • Taxes • Medical expenses • Education expenses • Moving expenses • Child care expenses • Charitable contributions • Casualty loses • Non-business bad debts • Alimony	• Expenses • Depreciation and amortization • Loss from the disposition of property • Non-business bad debts	• Start up expenses • Expenses • Depreciation and amortization • Losses from the disposition of property • Business bad debts

Chapter 15

Interest

Deductions

Personal:	Investment:	Business:
• Interest • Taxes • Medical expenses • Education expenses • Moving expenses • Child care expenses • Charitable contributions • Casualty loses • Non-business bad debts • Alimony	• Expenses • Depreciation and amortization • Loss from the disposition of property • Non-business bad debts	• Start up expenses • Expenses • Depreciation and amortization • Losses from the disposition of property • Business bad debts

Read

Code Sections 163(a), (h)(1), (2), (3), (4)(A); 221; 262

A. Background

In general, personal expenses are not deductible.[1] Congress does not consider a personal expense an item that should offset the taxpayer's gross income. In other words, it is not considered part of the cost of earning or generating gross income. Any deduction permitted for a personal expense is an exception to this broad-based rule. Accordingly, if the taxpayer wants to claim a deduction on his income tax return for a personal expense, he must establish that Congress specifically provided an exception to the general rule.

B. Exception — Interest

Interest is the amount paid for the use of borrowed money. In general, a taxpayer is not entitled to claim a deduction for personal interest he has paid.[2]

---

1. Section 262.
2. Section 163(a), (h)(1), (2).

Section 163. Interest

(h) Disallowance of Deduction for Personal Interest. —

(1) In General. In the case of a taxpayer other than a corporation, no deduction shall be allowed under this chapter for personal interest paid or accrued during the taxable year.

There are two broad exceptions to this prohibition. The first is for home mortgage interest.[3] The second is for interest on a student loan.[4]

Home mortgage interest. The Code excludes qualified residence interest from the definition (and thus the prohibition on deduction) of personal interest.[5] There are two different types of qualified residence interest: acquisition indebtedness and home equity indebtedness.

Acquisition indebtedness is indebtedness incurred in "acquiring, constructing, or substantially improving any qualified residence of the taxpayer."[6] It does not apply to interest to the extent the loan exceeds $1,000,000.[7]

Home equity indebtedness is indebtedness secured by a qualified residence.[8] It does not apply to indebtedness to the extent it qualifies as acquisition indebtedness. The relevant amount of the loan cannot exceed the excess of the fair market value of the qualified residence over the amount of the acquisition indebtedness.[9] Nor does it apply to interest to the extent the loan exceeds $100,000.[10]

A qualified residence is the taxpayer's principal residence (as defined by Section 121[11]) and one other residence of the taxpayer that is used by the taxpayer as a residence.[12]

Tell Me More

A taxpayer may be required to pay "points" when obtaining a loan. Points are a fee paid to the lender. One point is equal to one percent of the amount of the loan. Points are pre-paid interest but are deductible if incurred in connection

3. Section 163(h)(2)(D), (3).
4. Sections 163(h)(2)(F); 221.
5. Section 163(h)(3)(A).
6. Section 163(h)(3)(B).
7. Section 163(h)(3)(B)(ii). The applicable amount of the loan is $500,000 if the taxpayer is married, filing a separate return. See Bronstein v. Commissioner, 138 T.C. No. 21 (2012).
8. Section 163(h)(3)(C)(i).
9. Id.
10. Section 163(h)(3)(C)(ii). The applicable amount of the loan is $50,000 if the taxpayer is married, filing a separate return.
11. Section 121 is discussed in Chapter 42. If the taxpayer uses more than one home, Section 121 provides guidance, if needed, to determine which home is the principal residence. In general, the residence he uses the majority of the time during the year is his principal residence. Treas. Reg. § 1.121-1(a)(2). The regulations set forth other, non-exclusive, factors to consider, including the taxpayer's place of employment; where the family members live; the address used for the taxpayer's federal income tax return, state tax return, driver's license, automobile registration, voter registration card; mailing address used for bills and correspondence; location of the taxpayer's bank; and location of the taxpayer's religious organizations and recreational clubs. Treas. Reg. § 1.121-1(a)(2).
12. Section 163(h)(4)(A).

with the purchase or improvement of, or secured by, the taxpayer's principal residence.[13]

When property is co-owned by two owners who are not married to each other, the limitations are applied on a per-residence (as opposed to per taxpayer) basis.[14] For example, Charles and Bruce are co-owners of a house and are jointly and severally liable for the mortgage. They qualify for the maximum amount of acquisition and home equity indebtedness. Each may deduct a proportionate share of the interest on $1.1 million.

Interest paid on student loans. The Code excludes interest paid on a "qualified education loan" from the definition (and thus from the prohibition on deduction) of personal interest.[15] Qualified loans include those incurred to pay for higher education expenses of the taxpayer, the taxpayer's spouse, or the taxpayer's dependents. Expenses include tuition, fees, room and board, and other related expenses.[16] Qualified loans do not include loans from a related person (as defined in Section 267(d) or 707(b)(1)).[17]

The maximum amount of interest that can be claimed as a deduction is $2,500.[18] This deduction amount begins to be phased out for a taxpayer with a modified adjusted gross income of $50,000 or more ($100,000 or more for a joint return) and completely phased out for a taxpayer with a modified adjusted gross income over $65,000 ($130,000 for a joint return).[19]

C. Application of Rules

Example 1. During the year Bill paid $3,000 in interest on his credit cards. He had used the credit cards to purchase food, gas, and household items. Because the interest is personal, not subject to any exception, he cannot deduct the interest.

Example 2. Irene purchased a home for $300,000 and used it as her principal residence. She paid $50,000 down and obtained a $250,000 mortgage. The mortgage qualifies as acquisition indebtedness; she is entitled to deduct the interest she pays on the loan.

Example 3. Candace purchased a home for $300,000 and used it as her principal residence. Several years later she obtained a $50,000 loan, secured by the home. She used the proceeds to remodel her home. The debt qualifies as acquisition indebtedness; she is entitled to deduct the interest she pays on the loan.

Example 4. Dirk purchased a home for $300,000 and used it as his principal residence. He paid $50,000 down and obtained a $250,000 mortgage. The mortgage qualifies as acquisition indebtedness; he is entitled to deduct the interest he pays on the $250,000 loan.

This year Dirk borrowed an additional $100,000, secured by the home. He used $25,000 to add a garage and the remaining $75,000 for items not related to the home. The $25,000

---

13. Section 461(g)(2).
14. Sophy v. Commissioner, 138 T.C. No. 8 (2012).
15. Sections 163(h)(2)(F); 221.
16. Section 221(d).
17. Section 221(d)(1).
18. Section 221(b)(1).
19. Section 221(b). These amounts are adjusted for inflation. Section 221(f). For 2011 the phase out amounts are $60,000 to $75,000 ($120,000 to $150,000 for joint returns).

used for the garage is acquisition indebtedness. The remaining $75,000 is home equity indebtedness. He is entitled to deduct the interest he pays on the $100,000 loan.

Example 5. Sebastian owns a home worth $500,000 that he uses as his principal residence. He borrowed $150,000, secured by the house. He used the money to purchase a large boat. The loan qualifies as home equity indebtedness, but he can deduct interest only to the extent of $100,000 of the loan. With respect to the remaining $50,000 of indebtedness the interest is not deductible.

Example 6. Maureen, a single individual, obtained student loans to attend college. In the year after she graduated she obtained a job and earned $45,000 per year. She paid $2,000 in interest on her student loans. Maureen can deduct the interest she paid on her student loans.

D. Problems

1. Bill has a gas card he uses for all the gas purchased for his personal car. During the year he paid $500 in interest for gas charged on the card. Can he deduct this interest?

2. Bobby purchased a home for $500,000 and will use the home as his principal residence. He paid $50,000 down and obtained a $450,000 mortgage. Will Bobby be entitled to a deduction for the interest he pays on the mortgage?

3. Inez obtained a $50,000 line of credit, secured by her home (which is her principal residence). She used the money to spend an entire year traveling. Will Inez be entitled to a deduction for the interest she pays on the line of credit?

4. Alfred obtained a $50,000 loan to add a three-season room to his home (which is his principal residence). He has no other outstanding debt. Is Alfred entitled to a deduction for the interest he pays on the loan?

5. Carl, a single individual, obtained student loans to attend college. After he graduated he obtained a job, earning $30,000 per year. During the year he paid $5,000 in interest on the student loans. Is Carl entitled to a deduction for the interest he pays on the loans?

E. Analysis and Application

1. Is the deduction for acquisition indebtedness interest justified?
    a. Why or why not?
    b. Are there more efficient ways to support home ownership?
    c. Would you consider the deduction a "loophole," allowing a taxpayer with a larger amount of gross income to unfairly reduce his tax liability by obtaining a loan to purchase his residence?

2. Is the deduction for home equity indebtedness interest justified?
    a. Why or why not?
    b. Would you consider the deduction a "loophole," allowing a taxpayer with a larger amount of gross income to unfairly reduce his tax liability by obtaining a loan, secured by his residence?

3. Mary pays $15,000 in qualified residence interest. Her highest marginal tax rate is 35 percent. Considering the tax benefit from the interest deduction, how much did she actually pay?

4. Is the deduction for interest paid on student loans justified?

   a. Why or why not?

   b. Is the deduction "fair" to those for whom the deduction is phased out?

   c. Would you consider the deduction a "loophole," allowing some taxpayers to unfairly reduce their tax liability by financing their college education?

Chapter 16

Taxes and Medical Expenses

Deductions

Personal:	Investment:	Business:
• Interest • **Taxes** • **Medical expenses** • Education expenses • Moving expenses • Child care expenses • Charitable contributions • Casualty loses • Non-business bad debts • Alimony	• Expenses • Depreciation and amortization • Loss from the disposition of property • Non-business bad debts	• Start up expenses • Expenses • Depreciation and amortization • Losses from the disposition of property • Business bad debts

Read

Code Sections 164(a), (b)(1), (b)(2), (b)(5)(A), (B), (c), (d)(1), (f); 213(a), (b), (d)(1), (d)(3), (d)(9); 275

Treas. Reg. §§ 1.164-3(a), (b); 1.164-4(a), (b)(1); 1.164-6(a); 1.213-1(a)(1)(i)-(iii)

A. Background

In general, personal expenses are not deductible.[20] Congress does not consider a personal expense an item that should offset the taxpayer's gross income. In other words, it is not considered part of the cost of earning or generating gross income. Any deduction permitted for a personal expense is an exception to this broad-based rule. Accordingly, if the taxpayer wants to claim a deduction on his income tax return for a personal expense, he must establish that Congress specifically provided an exception to the general rule.

---

20. Section 262

129

B. Exception — Taxes

1. General Rule

In addition to paying federal income taxes, most taxpayers also will have to pay state and local taxes. The Code allows the taxpayer to deduct the following taxes if they have been paid:[21]

- State and local real property taxes;

- State and local personal property taxes;

- State and local income taxes; or, in lieu of state and local income taxes, state and local sales taxes; and

- Foreign income taxes.

To be deductible, the amount must constitute a tax. Local governments may make an assessment for a variety of reasons, not all of which constitute a tax.

- An assessment for water and sewer services is not a tax;[22] and

- An assessment for funds to be used to maintain streets, sidewalks, or other benefits that increase the value of the property assessed and are assessed only on properties that directly benefit is not a tax.[23]

The deduction is allowed only to the person on whom the tax is imposed.[24] If a third party pays the taxpayer's state or local taxes, the third party is not entitled to a deduction.

To be deductible, the tax liability must have been paid.[25]

Summary of Rule — Deduction for Taxes:

To be deductible, the taxes —

- Must have been imposed on the taxpayer; and

- Must have been paid by the taxpayer.

---

21. Section 164(a), (b)(5). Note that if the taxpayer pays taxes related to his investment activity, they could be deducted under Section 212 and if the taxpayer pays taxes related to his business activity, they could be deducted under Section 162(a).

22. Rev. Rul. 79-201, 1979-1 C.B. 97.

23. Section 164(c)(1); Treas. Reg. § 1.164-4(a). Such amounts paid may be considered capital expenditures and added to the basis of the property. If the amount is allocable to maintenance or interest, it can be considered at tax. Section 164(c)(1).

24. Treas. Reg. § 1.164-1(a).

25. Whether the taxes have been paid may depend on whether the taxpayer is a cash or accrual basis taxpayer. These accounting method concepts are discussed in Part VII. In addition, certain timing rules apply regarding the sale of real property. See Section 164(c), (d); Treas. Reg. § 1.164-6(d).

2. Exceptions

Federal taxes. No deduction is allowed for the payment of Social Security taxes[26] or the payment of federal income taxes.[27] Only one-half of employment taxes are deductible.[28]

Sale of real property during the year. The general rule is that taxes are deductible only by the person on whom they are imposed. However, if real property is sold during the year, the state or local tax liability must be apportioned between the buyer and seller irrespective of which party is liable for the taxes under state or local law. The seller is allocated the taxes attributable to the beginning of the real property tax year[29] to the day before the sale. The seller is allocated the taxes attributable to the day of sale to the end of the real property tax year.[30] Each party is entitled to deduct their allocable share, irrespective of how the taxes are allocated for state or local purposes and irrespective who actually effectively pays them. An agreement between the seller and buyer to allocate the taxes between them in a different manner does not change the allocation for tax purposes.[31]

Co-ownership of property. If the property is co-owned, each co-owner is entitled to deduct the amount of taxes paid, even if the portion paid is greater than that owner's respective ownership interest in the property. In *Powell v. Commissioner*[32] the taxpayer was a co-owner of property and paid more than her allocable share of state property taxes. In deciding whether she could deduct the entire amount of taxes paid, the court noted that, by paying the taxes, the taxpayer was protecting her interest in the property.[33]

C. Exception — Medical Expenses

Section 213 provides an exception to the general rule that no deduction is permitted for personal expenses. To be deductible, the amount must have been paid for medical care, not have been reimbursed, and be a qualifying expense. In addition, the deduction is limited to the amount that exceeds a percentage of adjusted gross income.[34]

Qualifying medical care expenses. To be deductible, the expense must be a qualifying medical care expense. The Code provides a broad definition of medical care, including:

- Amounts paid for "diagnosis, cure, mitigation, treatment, or prevention of disease, or for the purpose of affecting any structure or function of the body."[35]

---

26. Section 275(a)(1)(A); Treas. Reg. § 1.164-2(a).
27. Section 275(a)(1)(C); Treas. Reg. § 1.164-2(a).
28. Section 164(f)(1).
29. The real property tax year is determined under local law and is the period to which the tax imposed relates. Treas. Reg. § 1.164-6(c).
30. Section 164(d),
31. Section 164(c)(2).
32. T.C. Memo. 1867-32.
33. Powell v. Commissioner, T.C. Memo. 1967-32.
34. Section 213(a).
35. Section 213(d)(1)(A).

- Amounts paid for medically-related transportation costs and qualified long-term care services;[36]

- Medical insurance;[37] and

- Lodging costs while away from home for medical care.[38]

Amounts paid for qualified long-term care services include amounts paid for diagnostic, preventive, therapeutic, curing, treating, mitigating, and rehabilitative services that are required by a chronically ill individual and provided pursuant to a plan of care prescribed by a licensed health care practitioner.[39] It includes a portion of the premiums paid for long-term care insurance.[40]

The deduction does not extend to amounts paid to promote general health (such as for a vacation).[41] A vast amount of expenses may fall between specifically-identified deductible expenses and those for general health care. To determine if an expense is deductible the Tax Court uses the following test: can the taxpayer establish that the expenditures were an essential element of the treatment and that they would not otherwise have been incurred for non-medical reasons.[42]

With respect to drugs, only the amount paid for prescription drugs (i.e., those requiring a prescription) and insulin is a qualified expense.[43]

The Code also includes in the definition of medical expenses amounts paid for the purpose of affecting any structure or function of the body.[44] This provision has been the source of disagreements regarding deductibility. Amounts paid for breast reconstruction surgery following a mastectomy for cancer, vision correction surgery to correct myopia,[45] and the costs of hormone therapy and sex reassignment surgery incurred by a taxpayer with gender identity disorder[46] have been held to come within this provision and be deductible. In contrast, amounts paid to whiten teeth[47] or for breast augmentation surgery did not.[48]

Amounts that otherwise would constitute capital expenditures may come within the definition of a deductible medical expenses.[49] A capital expenditure made by the taxpayer with the primary purpose of medical care may be currently deductible. For example, if the cost otherwise qualifies, the taxpayer may deduct the cost of wheelchairs, eye glasses, artificial teeth and limbs, and crutches. If the capital expenditure relates to a permanent improvement or betterment of property and would not otherwise be for

---

36. Section 213(d)(1)(B), (C).
37. Section 213(d)(1)(D)
38. Section 213(d)(2).
39. Sections 213(d)(1)(C); 7702B(c). If the provider is a relative, the payment may not qualify. Section 213(d)(1)(D), (d)(11).
40. Section 213(d)(1)D), (d)(10).
41. Treas. Reg. § 1.213-1(e)(1)(ii).
42. Magdalin v. Commissioner, T.C. Memo. 2008-293.
43. Section 213(b), (d)(3).
44. Section 213(d)(1)(A).
45. Rev. Rul. 2003-57, 2003-1 C.B. 959.
46. O'Donnabhain v. Commissioner, 134 T.C. 34 (2010).
47. Rev. Rul. 2003-57, 2003-1 C.B. 959.
48. O'Donnabhain v. Commissioner, 134 T.C. 34 (2010).
49. Treas. Reg. § 1.213-1(e)(1)(iii).

medical care, a deduction is still allowed, but the amount of the deduction is limited. It cannot exceed the extent to which the cost of the item does not increase the value of the property.[50]

Unreimbursed expenses. To be deductible, the expenses must be unreimbursed. To the extent a taxpayer recovers the cost of medical expenses through insurance, he is not entitled to a deduction. The deduction is not permitted regardless of whether the taxpayer's employer provided the insurance coverage or the taxpayer paid for the coverage himself.[51]

Floor on deduction. The deduction is allowed only to the extent the expenses exceed 10 percent of adjusted gross income. (For taxpayers who are 65 or whose spouses are 65 or older, the percentage is 7.5 percent.[52]) By making a portion of medical expenses non-deductible, Congress retains the personal, nondeductible nature of a certain portion of the expenses. Only to the extent the medical expenses go beyond what might be considered normal or expected is the deduction permitted.

D. Application of Rules

Taxes

Example 1. For the year Lillie paid $5,000 in state incomes taxes. She may deduct the amount paid.

Example 2. Josh sold his personal residence to Karlene on July 1. Under state law, the real property tax year was the calendar year and taxes due for the year were $5,000. Josh is entitled to deduct the real property taxes from January 1 through June 30, or $2,500. Karlene is entitled to deduct the real property taxes due from July 1 through December 31, or $2,500.

Example 3. Kaylie, Lennie, and Martha were co-owners of a cabin. Kaylie paid the entire amount of state property taxes. Even though Kaylie owns only one-third of the cabin, she may deduct the entire amount of taxes she paid.

Medical Expenses

Example 4. Nan paid $100 for prescription drugs. She may claim the cost as a medical expense.

Example 5. Samantha and Ted attending marriage counseling sessions each month for the entire year, paying $3,000. Because the counseling was not related to a medical condition, the cost does not qualify as a medical expense.

Example 6. Jane has heart disease and cannot climb stairs. Her doctor recommended she install an elevator in her home so she would not have to climb the stairs. The cost of

---

50. Treas. Reg. § 1.213-1(e)(1)(iii).
51. Section 213(a).
52. Section 213(f).

installing the elevator is $5,000. Having an elevator in the home will increase its value by only $3,000. Jane may claim as a deductible medical expense the excess, the difference between the cost and the increase in value, or $2,000 ($5,000 cost, less $3,000 increase in value).

Example 7. Coral incurred $3,000 in qualified medical expenses. Her adjusted gross income for the year was $20,000. She can claim a deduction for the medical expenses only to the extent they exceed 10 percent of her adjusted gross income (10 percent of her adjusted gross income is $2,000). She may claim a $1,000 medical expense deduction.

E. Problems

Taxes

1. Nan worked in Charlotte, North Carolina. In addition to paying federal income tax, Nan also paid state and city income taxes. Can Nan deduct the federal, state, and city income taxes she paid?

2. Drew sold his house to Efrin on March 1. Under state law, the real property tax year is the calendar year and the taxes due for the year of sale were $5,000.

   a. How much of the taxes are allocable to Drew?

   b. How much of the taxes are allocable to Efrin?

3. Fred sold his house to Gregg on March 1. Under state law, the real property tax year is the calendar year and the taxes due for the year of sale were $5,000. As part of the sales agreement, Gregg agreed to pay the taxes due for the entire year (and he did so).

   c. How much of the taxes are allocable to and deductible by Fred?

   d. How much of the taxes are allocable to and deductible by Gregg?

Medical Expenses

For each expense, the taxpayer did not receive any reimbursement.

4. Ossie injured her foot and was required to use crutches for one week. May she deduct the cost of the crutches as a medical expense?

5. During the year Maley paid $200 for vitamins and protein powder. May she deduct the costs as medical expenses?

6. Sue paid $500 for a year-long membership to the health club. May she deduct the cost as a medical expense?

7. Tom paid $300 for cosmetic surgery to reduce the lines on his forehead. May he deduct the cost as a medical expense?

8. Jeff, determined to get healthy, attended a clinic to stop smoking and joined a weight loss program. May he deduct the cost of the clinic and the program?

9. Karl has a degenerative spinal disorder. His doctor recommended he install a swimming pool so that he could swim every day. The cost of installing the swimming pool is $15,000. The pool will increase the value of his home by $10,000. What is the amount of deductible medical expense Karl may claim?

F. Analysis and Application

Taxes

1. Ted sold his house to Jane on March 1. Under state law, the real property tax year is the calendar year and taxes due for the year of sale were $10,000. Ted had failed to pay the taxes in the prior year. As part of the sales agreement, Jane agreed to pay the $10,000 due for the previous year.

    a. How much of the taxes in the prior year are allocable to Ted? To Jane? If she pays the tax due for the previous year how much is Jane entitled to deduct?

    b. How much of the taxes due in the year of sale are allocable to Ted? To Jane? If Jane pays the entire amount, how much is she entitled to deduct?

2. Look through Form 1040 and Schedule A. Where on the forms do you find the amount paid for real property taxes taken into consideration?

3. Janice sold her home to Vince on a land sale contract. As part of their agreement, Vince was to pay the real property taxes. When Vince failed to pay the real property taxes, Janice paid them. Eventually, Vince defaulted on the contract; Janice instituted foreclosure proceedings and recovered possession of the house.

    Is Janice entitled to claim a deduction for the amount of real property taxes she paid? In formulating your analysis and response, you may want to consider:

    • Powell v. Commissioner, T.C. Memo. 1967-32

    • Peters v. Commissioner, T.C. Memo. 1970-314

Medical Expenses

4. Look through From 1040 and Schedule A. Where on the forms do you find the amount of medical expenses paid taken into consideration?

5. Jonathan suffered from chronic fatigue syndrome. When traditional medicine did not relieve his symptoms, he researched non-traditional remedies. He learned of healing sessions provided through Navajo healing ceremonies. He spent $5,000 traveling to and attending a ceremony. May he deduct the $5,000 as a medical expense?

6. Drew was an attorney practicing in Minnesota. By the age of 43 he had suffered four heart attacks. A heart specialist advised him to spend the winter season in a warm climate. Accordingly, he spent December, January, and February in Orlando, Florida. For each month he paid $2,000 in rent. May Drew deduct the $6,000 of rent payments ($2,000 in the first year, $4,000 in the following year) as a medical expense?

Chapter 17

Education Expenses, Moving Expenses, Child Care Expenses

Deductions

Personal:	Investment:	Business:
• Interest • Taxes • Medical expenses • **Education expenses** • **Moving expenses** • **Child care expenses** • Charitable contributions • Casualty loses • Non-business bad debts • Alimony	• Expenses • Depreciation and amortization • Loss from the disposition of property • Non-business bad debts	• Start up expenses • Expenses • Depreciation and amortization • Losses from the disposition of property • Business bad debts

Read

Code Sections (a), (b), (c), 217(a)-(d)

Treas. Reg. §§ 1.162-5(a)-(c) ; 1.217-2(a)(1), (b)(3), (c)(3), (c)(4)

A. Background

In general, personal expenses are not deductible.[53] Congress does not consider a personal expense an item that should offset the taxpayer's gross income. In other words, it is not considered part of the cost of earning or generating gross income. Any deduction permitted for a personal expense is an exception to this broad-based rule. Accordingly, if the taxpayer wants to claim a deduction on his income tax return for a personal expense, he must establish that Congress specifically provided an exception to the general rule.

---

53. Section 262

B. Exception — Education Expenses

Expenses for education often have both personal elements and business elements. It is when the business element plays a large enough role that these expenses are deductible. Accordingly, it should not be surprising that the primary provision dealing with these expenses is found in the regulations under Section 162, the provision allowing a deduction for business expenses. It sets forth a two part test.

A taxpayer may claim a deduction for educational expenses that either:[54]

- Maintain or improve skills required in his employment or business; or
- Meet the express requirements of his employer (or applicable law) necessary to retain his established employment relationship, status, or rate of compensation.

At the same time, the expenses are not deductible if the education either:[55]

- Meets the minimum educational requirements for qualification in the taxpayer's employment or business; or
- Qualifies the taxpayer for a new business.

1. Skills Required for Employment

Under the first part of the test, the taxpayer must establish that the education either maintained or improved skills required in his employment or business or met the express requirements of his employer (or applicable law) necessary to retain his established employment relationship, status, or rate of compensation.[56]

Maintaining or improving skills. A taxpayer is considered as maintaining business skills when he takes a course dealing with current developments or he takes an academic or vocation course.[57] The courses must be related to his business, which requires that he be engaged in a business.

Examples

- Expense of a practicing tax attorney to attend the annual New York University Institute on Taxation: deductible.[58]
- Expense of courses toward a major in philosophy taken by a police detective: not deductible (no connection between course work and job).[59]
- Expense of seminar in Hawaii on "Hawaiian Cultural Transition in a Diverse Society" taken by science teachers: not deductible (no connection between seminar and job; seminar not sufficiently germane to teaching science).[60]

---

54. Treas. Reg. § 1.162-5(a).
55. Treas. Reg. § 1.162-5(b)(2), (3).
56. Treas. Reg. § 1.162-5(a), (c)(1).
57. Treas. Reg. § 1.162-5(c)(1).
58. Coughlin v. Commissioner, 203 F.2d 307 (2d Cir. 1953).
59. Carroll v. Commissioner, 418 F.2d 91 (7th Cir. 1969).
60. Takahashi v. Commissioner, 87 T.C. 126 (1986) (participation in the seminar did not maintain or improve the skills required to perform their jobs).

- Expense of obtaining an LL.M. by a taxpayer who had not begun the practice of law: not deductible (not engaged in a business at time expense was incurred).[61]

- Expense of obtaining an MBA by a taxpayer who had worked only 3 months in the field: not deductible (taxpayer not established in the business).[62]

- Expense of obtaining a masters degree by a taxpayer who had been employed as a teacher, but resigned to attend school full-time: deductible (taxpayer did not have to be on leave to still be in the business; she expected to return to teaching after study and graduate study was a normal incident of carrying on the business of teaching).[63]

Required to retain employment. The education must have been undertaken to meet the express requirements of his employer (or applicable law) necessary to retain his established employment relationship, status, or rate of compensation.[64] The requirements must be express and imposed for bona fide business purposes. It includes only the minimum education necessary to retain the job, status, or pay.[65] This requirement applies to a taxpayer who has continuing education requirements or education requirements as a condition of renewing a license or certificate.[66]

2. Minimum Education or Qualifies for a New Business

Under the second part of the test, the expense is not deductible if the education either meets the minimum educational requirements for qualification in the taxpayer's employment or business or qualifies the taxpayer for a new business.[67]

Minimum educational requirements. The taxpayer cannot deduct the cost of the minimum education needed for employment.[68] If the individual has met the minimum educational requirements to qualify for his job, he will be treated as continuing to meet the requirements, even if they are changed.[69] For teachers, the minimum educational requirements are the minimum required to initially be employed.[70]

Qualifies for a new business. The taxpayer cannot deduct the cost of education that qualifies him for a new business.[71] It is not relevant whether the taxpayer intends to pursue the new business. Accordingly, the courts have noted that obtaining a bachelor's degree almost always qualifies the taxpayer for a new line of business.[72] A mere change in duties is not a new business if the new duties are in the same general type of work as the original

61. Wassenaar v. Commissioner, 72 T.C. 1195 (1979).
62. Link v. Commissioner, 90 T.C. 460 (1988).
63. Furner v. Commissioner, 393 F.2d 292 (7th Cir. 1968).
64. Treas. Reg. § 1.162-5(a), (c)(2).
65. Treas. Reg. § 1.162-5(c)(2).
66. See, e.g., Hill v. Commissioner, 181 F.2d 906 (4th Cir. 1950).
67. Treas. Reg. § 1.162-5(b).
68. Treas. Reg. § 1.162-5(b)(2).
69. Treas. Reg. § 1.162-5(b)(2)(i).
70. Treas. Reg. § 1.162-5(b)(2)(ii). The regulations provide several examples. Treas. Reg. § 1.162-5(b)(2)(iii).
71. Treas. Reg. § 1.162-5(b)(3)(i).
72. Warren v. Commissioner, T.C. Memo. 2003-175.

employment.[73] All teaching is considered to involve the same general type of work. The regulations give the following examples as changes in duties that are not new businesses:[74]

- Elementary to secondary school classroom teacher
- Classroom teacher of one subject to a classroom teacher of a different subject
- Classroom teacher to guidance counselor
- Classroom teacher to principal.

Examples

- Cost of bachelor's degree earned by a Methodist minister: not deductible (even though courses related to his current employment, they qualified him for a new business).[75]
- Cost of law school incurred by a law librarian: not deductible (even though the degree would be helpful to her in her work, degree would allow her to enter the practice of law if she chose to do so).[76]
- Cost of obtaining a law license in a different state: not deductible (the license qualified the taxpayer for a new business).[77]

Summary — Test for Deduction of Education Expenses

A taxpayer may claim a deduction for educational expenses that either:

- Maintain or improve skills required in his employment or business; or
- Meet the express requirements of his employer (or applicable law) necessary to retain his established employment relationship, status, or rate of compensation.

At the same time, the expenses are not deductible if the education either:

- Meets the minimum educational requirements for qualification in the taxpayer's employment or business; or
- Qualifies the taxpayer for a new business.

C. Moving Expenses

A taxpayer can claim a deduction for moving expenses incurred "in connection with the commencement of work" at a new principal place of work.[78] While the move must have a reasonable proximity in time and place to the new principal place of work, the

---

73. Treas. Reg. § 1.162-5(b)(3)(i).
74. Treas. Reg. § 1.162-5(b)(3)(i).
75. Warren v. Commissioner, T.C. Memo. 2003-175.
76. Galligan v. Commissioner, T.C. Memo. 2002-150, aff'd, 2003-1 U.S.T.C. 50,381 (8th Cir. 2003).
77. Sharon v. Commissioner, 66 T.C. 515 (1976), aff'd, 591 F.2d 1273 (9th Cir. 1978).
78. Section 217(a). The deduction is an "above-the-line" deduction.

taxpayer can be self-employed or an employee, changing jobs with the same employer, entering the workforce for the first time, beginning work for a new employer, or self-employed taxpayers entering a new business or moving to a new location.[79]

To qualify, the taxpayer's new principal place of work must be at least 50 miles farther from his former residence than was his former principal place of work.[80] In addition, the employment cannot be temporary; the taxpayer must be a full-time employee in the general location of the new principal place of work for at least 39 weeks during the 12-month period immediately following the move.[81]

If the taxpayer meets the criteria of Section 217(c), he can deduct the reasonable cost of:[82]

- Transporting the taxpayer, other household members, and household belongings from the old residence to the new residence; and

- Reasonable cost of lodging en route.

Note

When an employer pays or reimburses an employee's moving expenses, it might qualify as a "qualified moving expense reimbursement" excludable fringe benefit. See Section 132(a)(6), (g).

If the taxpayer's employer pays the moving expenses or reimburses the taxpayer, the taxpayer may not claim a deduction for the moving expenses.[83]

Timing of deduction. The cost is deductible in the year in which it is paid or incurred, based on the taxpayer's method of accounting. He does not have to wait until he has satisfied the minimum period of employment.[84] However, if he claimed the deduction and subsequently cannot satisfy the minimum period of employment, he must include the amount previously deducted in income in the first year the requirement cannot be met.[85] If his employer paid his moving expenses or reimbursed the taxpayer (making it an excludable fringe benefit), the taxpayer must include the amount excluded in income if the minimum period of employment criteria cannot be met.[86]

The taxpayer is permitted to delay claiming the deduction on the original return. When the minimum period of employment is met, the taxpayer can file either an amended return or a claim for refund.[87]

---

79. Treas. Reg. § 1.217-2(a)(3)(i).
80. Section 217(c)(1). If the taxpayer had no former principal place of work, the new principal place of work must be at least 50 miles from his former residence. Section 217(c)(2).
81. Section 217(c)(2)(A). Alternatively, a self-employed individual must perform services on a full-time basis in the general location during at least 78 weeks during the 24-month period following his arrival in the new location. Not less than 39 of those weeks must be during the 12-month period following his arrival. Section 217(c)(2)(B).
82. Section 217(b); Treas. Reg. § 1.217-2(b)(3). The cost of meals is not deductible.
83. See Section 132(a)(6).
84. Section 217(d)(2).
85. Section 217(d)(3).
86. See Section 82.
87. Treas. Reg. § 1.217-2(d)(2)(ii).

D. Child Care Expenses

While child care may be necessary to enable parents to work, the cost of child care is considered personal in nature and not deductible unless specifically authorized. Currently, while no deduction is permitted, a taxpayer is entitled to a credit if he meets the criteria of Section 21. In addition, a taxpayer can exclude from income the value of services provided under a dependent care assistant program.

1. Child Care Credit

Section 21 provides a credit for some child care expenses. To come within Section 21, the taxpayer must have "employment-related expenses" and there must be one or more "qualifying individuals."[88] An expense is employment-related if paid for household services or for the care of a qualifying individual paid to enable the taxpayer to be employed.[89] A qualifying individual is:[90]

- A dependent of the taxpayer under 13 for whom the taxpayer is eligible to claim a dependency exemption;
- A dependent of the taxpayer who is physically or mentally incapable of caring for himself and who has the same home as the taxpayer; or
- The spouse of the taxpayer if the spouse is physically or mentally incapable of caring for himself and who has the same home as the taxpayer.

Computation of amount of credit. The credit amount is 35 percent of the employment-related expenses.[91] If there is one qualifying individual, the amount of employment-related expenses taken into account cannot exceed $3,000. If there are two or more qualifying individuals, the amount of employment-related expenses cannot exceed $6,000.[92] In either event, employment-related expenses cannot exceed the individual's earned income for the year.[93] The amount of the credit is phased out based on the taxpayer's adjusted gross income. The percentage is reduced (but not below 20 percent) by one percentage point for each $2,000 by which the taxpayer's adjusted gross income exceeds $15,000.[94]

2. Dependent Care Assistant Program

The taxpayer can exclude from income amounts incurred or paid by the employer pursuant to a dependent care assistant program.[95] The excluded amount cannot exceed $5,000.[96]

---

88. Section 21(a)(1).
89. Section 21(b)(2)(A).
90. Section 21(b)(1).
91. Section 21(a).
92. Section 21(c).
93. Section 21(d)(1). For married couples, the amount of the earned income is the lesser of the two incomes.
94. Section 21(a)(2).
95. Section 129(a)(1). What qualifies as a dependent care assistant program is set forth in Section 129(d).
96. Section 129(a)(2)(A). If the taxpayer is married and files a separate return, the maximum amount he can exclude is $2,500.

If the amount is excluded under this provision, it cannot be deducted or be the basis for a credit under any other provision. If the taxpayer also qualifies for the credit under Section 21, the dollar limit of Section 21 is reduced by the total amount excluded through the dependent care assistant program.[97]

E. Application of Rules

Education Expenses

Example 1. Carrie was employed by a law firm to conduct legal research. She had completed 2 years of law school. To continue working for the law firm, Carrie was required to complete her law degree and pass the bar examination. Carrie finished her final year of law school and took a bar review course.

The law degree and bar review course are education required to meet the minimum educational requirements for qualification in Carrie's business. The cost is personal and not deductible.

Example 2. Derrick was an accountant. He attended night school and completed his law degree. Because the law degree qualified him for a new trade or business the cost of law school is personal and not deductible.

Example 3. Evan was a medical doctor specializing in internal medicine. He attended a three day seminar covering the latest techniques in enteric medicine. Because the seminar maintains or improves the skills required in his business and does not qualify him for a new business, the cost of the seminar is deductible.

Moving Expenses

Example 4. Angie's employer transferred her from the Seattle office to the San Francisco office. Angie can deduct the cost of moving from Seattle to San Francisco.

Example 5. Xena's employer transferred her from the Orlando office to the Dallas office. Her employer paid her moving expenses. Xena is not entitled to claim a deduction for her moving expenses.

Child Care Expenses

Example 6. Bonnie paid $5,000 in child care expenses for her daughter. Her earned income for the year was $15,000. She may claim a $1,050 credit (the lesser of $3,000 and $15,000, × 35 percent).

Example 7. Kellie paid $6,000 in child care expenses for her two children. Her earned income for the year was $15,000. She may claim a $2,100 credit (the lesser of $6,000 and $15,000, × 35 percent).

---

97. Section 21(c).

Example 8. Mary Anne paid $6,000 in child care expenses for her son. Her earned income for the year was $31,000. Because her income exceeds $15,000, the credit is reduced by one percentage point for each $2,000 of adjusted gross income above $15,000. The amount of adjusted gross income above $15,000 is $16,000, and the reduction is 8 percent. She is entitled to a credit of 27 percent (35 percent, less 8 percent). She may claim a $810 credit (the lesser of $3,000 or $31,000, x 27 percent).

F. Problems

Educational Expenses

1. Robert was an attorney. In order to maintain his law license, he was required to earn 10 CLE credits each year. This past year the cost of the CLE courses he took was $3,000. May Robert deduct the cost of the CLE courses?

2. Nancy was an ordained minister. During the year, she took two philosophy courses at the local university. May Nancy deduct the cost of the courses?

3. Lori had been employed for 15 years as a director of nursing at a long-term care facility. She decided that obtaining a MBA degree would give her greater credibility when dealing with the highly-educated doctors. She also believed the courses would allow her to be more effective in her job. She purposefully selected courses that focused on health care infrastructure and management. Can Lori deduct the cost of obtaining the MBA degree?

Moving Expenses

4. Jerrod's employer transferred him from the Seattle office to the Portland office. He sold his house in Seattle and purchased one in Portland. He worked in the Portland office for 8 months, then left to take a different job. Can Jerrod claim a deduction for the cost of moving from Portland to Seattle?

5. Courtney's employer transferred her from the Miami office to the Washington, D.C. office. Her employer reimbursed her for the cost of the move. What are the tax consequences to Courtney?

6. Molly was a self-employed computer consultant. She moved from San Diego to Denver and pursued her consulting business in the Denver area. May Molly deduct the cost of moving from San Diego to Denver?

Child Care Expenses

7. Lexi spent $7,000 in child care expenses for her 3-year old daughter. Her earned income for the year was $15,000. May she claim the child care credit? If so, what is the amount of the credit?

8. Taylor's employer provides a dependent care assistant program which she can utilize free of charge. Each work day she drops off her 2-year old son at the day care. The value of the day care services for the year was $4,000. Must Taylor include the value of the services in her gross income?

Chapter 18

Charitable Contributions

Deductions

Personal:	Investment:	Business:
• Interest • Taxes • Medical expenses • Education expenses • Moving expenses • Child care expenses • **Charitable contributions** • Casualty loses • Non-business bad debts • Alimony	• Expenses • Depreciation and amortization • Loss from the disposition of property • Non-business bad debts	• Start up expenses • Expenses • Depreciation and amortization • Losses from the disposition of property • Business bad debts

Read

Code Sections 262; 170(a)(1), (c), (f)(1), (3), (8), (16), (17), (l)

Treas. Reg. §§ 1.170A-1(a), (b), (g); 1.170A-13(f)(1)-(3); Prop. Reg. § 1.170A-15(a); Prop. Reg. § 1.170A-16(a), (b), (c)(1)

A. Background

In general, personal expenses are not deductible.[98] Congress does not consider a personal expense an item that should offset the taxpayer's gross income. In other words, it is not considered part of the cost of earning or generating gross income. Any deduction permitted for a personal expense is an exception to this broad-based rule. Accordingly, if the taxpayer wants to claim a deduction on his income tax return for a personal expense, he must establish that Congress specifically provided an exception to the general rule.

---

98. Section 262.

B. Background — Charitable Contribution Deduction

Charitable organizations provide services and support to a wide variety of worthwhile causes. Congress recognized that several policy objectives could be achieved if a deduction were provided for contributions made to such charities. First, to the extent the public provided financial support for these causes the public would not look to the government for support. Second, given that contributions are voluntarily made, each person could select those charitable organizations he believed were most deserving of his financial support. Accordingly, the Code provides a deduction for contributions made to a charity, to the extent it is a qualifying charitable contribution.

Contribution of appreciated property. When a taxpayer contributes property to a charitable organization, he has disposed of property. When a taxpayer disposes of appreciated property, he usually must realize and recognize any gain. When a taxpayer transfers appreciated property to a charitable organization he is not required to recognize any gain realized.[99]

C. Criteria for a Charitable Contribution Deduction

Section 170 is a very complex Code section. It contains several criteria the taxpayer must meet to be entitled to a charitable contribution deduction. It then sets forth many limitations on the amount that can be deducted.

To qualify for a charitable contribution deduction, the following criteria must be met. The contribution must be:[100]

- To or for the use of a qualified recipient;
- Made with no expectation of a return benefit;
- Actually paid during the taxable year; and
- Sufficiently substantiated.

1. To or for the Use of a Qualified Recipient

A contribution is for the use of a qualified organization if it is held in a legally enforceable trust (or similar arrangement) for the organization. The Code defines several "qualified

---

99. Note that this is the same result as when a taxpayer makes a gift. Because the taxpayer does not receive any cash, property, or services in the exchange, he does not realize any gain. In addition, any loss realized could not be recognized as it would be a personal, nondeductible loss.

100. Section 170(a), (c).

recipients," including the United States, a state, or a political subdivision if the contribution is made exclusively for public purposes.[101]

A qualified organization also includes a United States corporation, trust, or foundation. The organization must be organized and operated exclusively for religious, charitable, scientific, literary, or educational purposes; to foster national or international amateur sports competition; or for the prevention of cruelty to children or animals. The earnings of the organizations cannot inure to the benefit of a private shareholder or an individual. Finally, it cannot be engaged in lobbying or political activities to an extent that would disqualify it for tax exemption purposes.[102]

Note that an individual will never constitute a qualified recipient.[103]

2. No Expectation of a Return Benefit

Just as with a gift, a charitable contribution must be given with "detached and disinterested generosity."[104] There can be no expectation of a return benefit. "A contribution for purposes of section 170 of the Code is a voluntary transfer of money or property that is made with no expectation of procuring a financial benefit commensurate with the amount of the transfer."[105] In this area, as with gifts, the intent of the donor will be of paramount importance and that intent will be determined based on the facts and circumstances surrounding the transfer.

Examples — Taxpayer Had Expectation of Return Benefit

Hernandez v. Commissioner:[106] The taxpayer paid fees to the Church of Scientology for special auditing and training sessions. The amount of the fee was dependent on the length and sophistication of the session. A refund was given if the session was not provided, and no sessions where provided for free. The taxpayer was not entitled to a charitable contribution deduction because the fee was paid in exchange for the auditing and training sessions.

Rev. Rul. 67-246:[107] A charity sponsored a symphony concert to raise funds for its charitable programs. The charity sold tickets to the charity performance for $5. The ticket cost was approximately equal to regular, established admission prices. Even though the concert was promoted as a charity event, a taxpayer who purchased a ticket was not entitled to a charitable contribution deduction because the value of the benefit (the concert) was equal to what the taxpayer paid.

---

101. Section 170(c)(1).
102. Section 170(c)(2).
103. See, e.g., Davis v. United States, 495 U.S. 472 (1990).
104. See Commissioner v. Duberstein, 363 U.S. 278, 285 (1960).
105. Rev. Rul. 83-104, 1983-2 C.B. 46.
106. 490 U.S. 680 (1989).
107. 1976-2 C.B. 104.

If the taxpayer does receive a return benefit but the benefit is less than the contribution, the taxpayer may claim a charitable contribution deduction for the difference, to the extent he intended to make a charitable contribution.[108] In such situations where the contribution exceeds $75, the organization is required to inform the taxpayer that the amount of the deduction cannot exceed the excess of the contribution over the value of the benefit received.[109]

3. Actually Paid

To meet this portion of the requirements, the taxpayer must have actually paid the amounts in issue.[110] It is not sufficient to have promised to pay. The timing rules, providing when amounts are included in income and deducted, may allow a deduction before any payment is actually made. The rules of Section 170 take precedence over the timing rules; irrespective of the accounting method used by the taxpayer, no deduction is allowed until the amount is actually paid.[111]

If the taxpayer is paying in cash, the amount is paid when the cash is unconditionally delivered or mailed. If the taxpayer is paying by check, the amount is paid when the check is unconditionally delivered or mailed (as long as the check subsequently clears).[112] If the taxpayer pays by credit card, the amount is paid in the year the charge is made. (It does not matter when the taxpayer makes payment on the credit card debt.[113])

4. Adequate Substantiation

A theme running through the allowance by the Code of any deduction is that the taxpayer must be able to substantiate the amount of the deduction. With respect to charitable contributions, this requirements means the taxpayer must be able to substantiate the amount paid or the property donated, with the rules varying depending on the amount of the contribution and whether the contribution was of cash or property.[114]

If the taxpayer is donating property with a value of less than $250 and it is impractical to obtain a receipt, for example if the contribution is made at a charity's unattended drop site, no receipt is required.[115] If the taxpayer is donating clothing or household items (furniture, furnishings, electronic, appliances, linens, and other similar items), the items must be in a good used condition or better. If they are not, the taxpayer is not entitled to a charitable contribution deduction.[116]

---

108. Treas. Reg. § 1.170A-1(h)(1), (2); Rev. Rul. 67-246, 1967-2 C.B. 104.
109. Section 6115.
110. Section 170(a)(1).
111. Treas. Reg. § 1.170A-1(a).
112. Treas. Reg. § 1.170A-1(b).
113. Rev. Rul. 78-38, 1978-1 C.B. 67.
114. Section 170(f)(1), (8), (11), (17); Treas. Reg. § 1.170A-13; Prop. Reg. § 1.170A-15 (addressing cash contributions); Prop. Reg. § 1.171A-16 (addressing non-cash contributions).
115. Prop. Reg. § 1.170A-16(a)(2).
116. Section 170(f)(16).

Contribution	Cash, Check, Credit Card	Property
Less than $250	• Bank record showing name of the qualified organization, date of contribution, and amount; or • Receipt (or other written communication) from qualified organization with name of organization, date of contribution, and amount	• Receipt (or other communication) from organization showing name of the charitable organization, date and location of contribution, and description of the property; or • Written records for each item donated that include name of the organization; date and location of contribution; description, value, and basis of property; year deduction claimed
At least $250, but not more than $500	• Written acknowledgment from the qualified organization of amount, whether the organization provided goods or services in return, description and estimate of value of such goods or services, or alternatively a statement that the only benefit received was an intangible religious benefit • Bank record or other communication showing the date of contribution	• Receipt (or other communication) as described above for property contributions of less than $250, but also including whether the organization provided goods or services in return, description and estimate of value of such goods or services, or alternatively a statement that the only benefit received was an intangible religious benefit; and • Written records for each item donated as described above
At least $500, but not more than $5,000	Same requirements as for cash contributions of less than $500	• Receipt (or letter or other communication) as described above for property contributions of less than $500; and • Written records for each item donated as described above, also including how property had been obtained, date obtained, and information related to its basis
$5,000 or more	Same requirements as for cash contributions of less than $500	Acknowledgement and written records as described for contributions of less than $5,000, plus a qualified written appraisal (Form 8283)

Checklist for Qualifying Charitable Contributions

❏   Was the client's contribution to a qualified recipient?

❏   Did the client receive services or property in return for the benefit? To the extent he did, the amount of the contribution must be reduced.

❏   Did the client actually pay in cash, deliver a check, or place a charge on his credit card?

❏   Does the client have the necessary documentation to substantiate the contribution?

D. Limitations on the Amount of the Deduction

The general rule is that the amount of the charitable contribution deduction is the amount of cash contributed or the fair market value of the property contributed.[117]

Limitations Based on the Type of Property Contributed. In some situations Congress has limited the amount a taxpayer may claim as a charitable contribution deduction for appreciated property to the basis in the property. Whether the limitation applies depends on the type of property contributed (ordinary or capital[118]) and the use the charitable organization makes of the property.[119]

If a taxpayer makes a contribute to an institution of higher education and, in return, receives the right to purchase tickets for seating at an athletic event in an athletic stadium of the institution, only 80 percent of the amount contributed can be deducted as a charitable contribution.[120] (Of course, the amount given in exchange for the purchase of tickets would not be deductible.)

Percentage Limitations on Amount of Deduction. In general, the total amount of charitable contributions cannot exceed 50 percent of the taxpayer's contribution base (the contribution basis is usually equal to the taxpayer's adjusted gross income). For contributions to most organizations, this will be the only percentage limitation that will apply. However, in some situations, depending on the type of property contributed and the organization the contribution is made to, the percentage limitation may be reduced to 30 percent or 20 percent of the contribution base.[121] (Note that, if the total amount of charitable contributions is 20 percent or less of the taxpayer's contribution base, no percentage limitation will apply.) A deduction that is not allowed due to a limitation may be carried forward for five years.[122]

E. Special Rules

Contribution of services. The deduction allowed for charitable contributions does not extend to a contribution of services. However, if the taxpayer incurs certain expenses in providing the services and the expenses are not reimbursed, he may claim a charitable deduction for those amounts.[123]

Contributions of partial interests. The general rule is that a taxpayer is not entitled to claim a charitable contribution deduction if he contributes less than his entire interest in the property.[124] However, if all the taxpayer owns is a partial interest and he contributes

---

117. Treas. Reg. § 1.170A-1(c)(1).
118. Capital assets are discussed in Chapter 37.
119. Section 170(e)(1). There are numerous, complex limitations and exceptions. They are beyond the scope of this text.
120. Section 170(l).
121. Section 170(b)(1)(A), (B). As with limitations based on the type of property, percentage limitations are also complex and the Code should be consulted for specific limitations.
122. Section 170(d)(1)(A).
123. Treas. Reg. § 1.170A-1(g).
124. Section 170(f)(3)(A).

all of his partial interest, he is entitled to a charitable contribution deduction. A taxpayer may not transfer an interest in property to create such a partial interest.[125]

The general rule is subject to several exceptions. A taxpayer is entitled to a charitable contribution deduction if he contributes a partial interest if it is:[126]

- a remainder interest in a personal residence or farm;
- undivided portions of the entire interest in property; or
- a qualified conservation easement.

Bargain sales. A taxpayer may sell property to a qualifying charitable organization at a selling price that is less than fair market value. To determine if the taxpayer is entitled to a charitable contribution deduction, rules similar to the part gift/part sale rules apply. The taxpayer's basis in the property is allocated between the sale and the contribution, based on the relative value of the sale and the contribution.[127] Then two separate transactions are considered.

Example. A taxpayer sold property worth $100,000 to a charity for $20,000. The property had a basis of $10,000. The proportion of the basis allocated to the sale is $20,000/$100,000 (20 percent) of $10,000, or $2,000. The proportion of the basis allocated to the contribution is $80,000/$100,000 (80 percent) of $10,000, or $8,000. The taxpayer is treated as disposing of property with a basis of $2,000 for $20,000, realizing a $18,000 gain and contributing property with a basis of $8,000 and fair market value of $80,000.

F. Application of Rules

Example 1. Patsy made a charitable contribution to her local animal shelter (a qualified organization) by mailing a check on December 31. She made a charitable contribution in the year she mailed the payment.

Example 2. Charla contributed appreciated stock to a qualified charitable organization. Her basis in the stock was $2,000 and at the time of contribution the stock was worth $10,000. Charla had $8,000 gain realized but she is not required to recognize the gain.

Example 3. A charity sponsored a symphony concert to raise funds for its charitable programs. The charity sold tickets to the charity performance for $15, including in their advertising the fact that it was soliciting gifts to support the organization. The materials also noted the usual cost of a ticket was $5.

Agnes wanted to support the symphony so purchased two tickets, paying $30. Because the amount she paid exceeded the usual cost of the tickets by $20 and she intended to make a gift to the symphony, Agnes made a $20 charitable contribution.

Example 4. Jim is a huge football fan and supports the college and its football team. Each year Jim contributed $15,000 to the college. As a "premium contributor," Jim was entitled to receive, without charge, two season tickets. The two tickets were worth $1,000.

Because the amount Jim paid exceeded the cost of the tickets and he intended to make a gift to the college, Jim made a $14,000 charitable contribution. However, the amount

---

125. Treas. Reg. § 1.170A-7(a)(2)(i).
126. Section 170(f)(3)(B).
127. Section 1011(b).

of his charitable contribution deduction is subject to the limitation on contributions to institutes of higher learning. Jim can deduct 80 percent of the amount of the charitable contribution, or $11,200.

Example 5. Jill frequently listens to a public radio station. During the last week of December the radio station held its annual fund drive. Jill called into the station and pledged a contribution of $100. On January 5th she mailed her check to the station.

Jill is not entitled to claim a charitable contribution deduction in the year she made the pledge. Rather, she can claim the deduction in the year she made payment by mailing her check to the station.

Example 6. Mike agreed to provide free legal services to the local YMCA (a qualified organization). If he had charged for his services, he would have received $1,000.

Because Mike was not compensated for his services, he does not have to include $1,000 in his income. Because he contributed services, he is not entitled to a charitable contribution deduction for the amount of his services.

Example 7. Adam owned Blackacre. His basis in the property was $15,000 and its fair market value was $150,000. He agreed to sell it to a qualified charitable organization for $50,000.

The proportion of the basis allocated to the sale is $50,000/$150,000 (1/3) of $15,000, or $5,000. The proportion of the basis allocated to the contribution is $100,000/$150,000 (2/3) of $15,000, or $10,000.

Adam is treated as disposing of property with a basis of $5,000 for $50,000, realizing a $45,000 gain and contributing property with a basis of $10,000 and fair market value of $100,000.

G. Problems

1. Quinn agreed to make a charitable contribution by using his credit card. The charge was placed last year; Quinn paid the credit card bill this year. Assuming the contribution was to a qualified organization, in which year can Quinn claim a charitable contribution deduction?

2. Charlie supports the art center, a qualified organization. At their annual auction Charlie was the highest bidder on a three-day cruise for two to the Bahamas. His bid was $3,000. What additional information do you need to determine whether Charlie is entitled to a charitable contribution deduction?

3. When called during the annual pledge drive Maxine pledged $1,000 to the March of Dimes. She mailed a $700 check to the organization (a qualifying organization), but was unable to pay the remainder. Is Maxine entitled to a charitable contribution deduction? If so, in what amount?

4. The Boy Scouts (a qualified organization) held the annual Soap Box Derby on the last Saturday in March. Kent volunteered at the event, giving over eight hours of his time. If he had instead worked that day he would have earned $2,000. Is Kent entitled to a charitable contribution deduction?

5. Scott's niece is a member of the Girl Scouts. Each year the local Girl Scouts have a week-long camp at Kamp Tawageneo. Because his niece's parents cannot afford to

have their daughter attend, Scott makes a donation to the Girl Scouts in his niece's name in an amount that covers the cost of the camp; his niece is able to attend. Is Scott entitled to a charitable contribution deduction?

6. Willie owns and operates a small diner in town. Once a month he allows a local organization dedicated to the welfare of animals to use the banquet room located in the back of the diner, free of charge, for its meeting. The organization is a qualified organization. Is Willie entitled to a charitable contribution deduction?

7. Every year Rustine purchases ten boxes of Girl Scout cookies. Is she entitled to a charitable contribution deduction?

8. President Obama was awarded the Nobel Peace Prize in 2009. The award included a medal, a diploma, and $1.4 million. He donated the cash award to a qualified charity. What were the tax consequences from the donation?

H. Analysis and Application

1. Is the deduction for charitable contributions justified?

   a. Why or why not?

   b. Are there more efficient ways for the public to support charitable organizations?

   c. Would you consider the deduction a "loophole," allowing those with a larger amount of gross income to unfairly reduce their tax liability by making charitable contributions?

2. Mary makes a $5,000 qualifying contribution to a charitable organization. Her marginal tax rate is 35 percent. Considering the tax benefit from the charitable contribution deduction, how much did the contribution actually cost her?

3. Ann explains to you that she would like to make a large contribution to an animal rescue charity. However, before she does so she would like to know for certain that the entity is a qualified organization. Locate the Internal Revenue Service's "Cumulative List of Organizations Described in § 170(c)" so you can determine if the organization is included in the list.

4. This year Maureen contributed $10,000 worth of stock to a qualified organization. In order to claim a charitable contribution deduction on her income tax return she must complete and attach a Form 8283, Noncash Charitable Contributions. She would like for you to provide her a copy of this form. Can you locate the form for her?

5. Jasmine enjoys supporting the arts. She often is willing to purchase tickets to the local symphony, but with her busy schedule she rarely is able to attend a performance. She pays $500 for a season ticket (five performances), even though the actual charge for the tickets is only $400.

   a. Is Jasmine entitled to a charitable contribution deduction? If so, in what amount?

   b. With respect to the performances Jasmine is unable to attend, can she claim a charitable contribution deduction for the cost of the unused ticket?

   c. If Jasmine believes her schedule is such that she will not be able to attend any performances, and she wants to maximize her charitable contribution deductions, what advice might you give her?

d.   Jasmine is particularly fond of the flute and would like to make a contribution to assist the symphony's principal flautist (even though she is not aware who holds that position with the symphony). If she makes such a contribution, will she be entitled to a charitable contribution deduction?

In formulating your analysis and response, you may want to consider:

- Davis v. United States, 495 U.S. 472 (1990)
- Tripp v. Commissioner, 337 F.2d 432 (7th Cir. 1964)
- Rev. Rul. 67-246, 1976-2 C.B. 104

6.   Members of the local Boy Scout Troup came to Deanne's door. They asked her to support the organization (a qualified organization) by purchasing a raffle ticket. Each ticket cost $5 and the items being raffled off included a large tent, a high-altitude winter coat, and a set of camping chairs. Deanne bought three tickets. If she does not win any items from the raffle may she claim a $15 charitable contribution deduction?

In formulating your analysis and response, you may want to consider:

- Davis v. United States, 495 U.S. 472 (1990)
- Tripp v. Commissioner, 337 F.2d 432 (7th Cir. 1964)
- Rev. Rul. 67-246, 1976-2 C.B. 104

Chapter 19

Casualty Losses

Deductions

Personal:	Investment:	Business:
• Interest	• Expenses	• Start up expenses
• Taxes	• Depreciation and	• Expenses
• Medical expenses	amortization	• Depreciation and
• Education expenses	• Loss from the	amortization
• Moving expenses	disposition of property	• Losses from the
• Child care expenses	• Non-business bad debts	disposition of property
• Charitable contributions		• Business bad debts
• **Casualty loses**		
• Non-business bad debts		
• Alimony		

Read

Code Sections 165(c)(3), (h)(1), (2)

A. Background

Basis. The basis of property is the amount the taxpayer originally paid for the property.[128] In general, a taxpayer will purchase an item for its fair market value. The adjusted basis reflects an increase for any subsequent capital expenditures.[129]

Amount realized. The amount realized is the amount the taxpayer sold the property for.[130] In general, a taxpayer will sell an item for its fair market value. What types of assets the taxpayer receives as payment for the item he is selling is irrelevant; the focus is on the value of the payment. Most often the taxpayer will be paid in cash, property, services, debt relief, or a combination of those items.

---

128. Section 1012(a).
129. Section 1016(a).
130. Section 1001(b).

Loss realized and recognized. When the property has decreased in value the difference between the amount realized and the adjusted basis of the property sold or otherwise disposed of by the taxpayer is the loss realized.[131]

> Amount realized
> − <u>Adjusted basis</u>
> Loss realized

To recognize a loss, the taxpayer must provide authority. In general, the taxpayer may not recognize any loss from the disposition of property used for personal purposes.[132]

B. Exception — Casualty Loss

Once a taxpayer acquires property, the property may decrease in value. The Code does not permit the taxpayer to report that decrease in wealth until he has disposed of the property. In general, the decrease in wealth is the amount of loss the taxpayer has in the property, or the difference between the amount the taxpayer sold the property for and the amount he paid for it, as adjusted.[133]

> Amount realized
> − <u>Adjusted basis</u>
> Loss realized

Section 1001. Determination of Amount of and Recognition of Gain or Loss

(a) Computation of Gain or Loss. — ... the loss shall be the excess of the adjusted basis provided in such section [Section 1011] for determining loss over the amount realized....

Unless the Code provides authority, no loss realized may be recognized, or reported, on the taxpayer's income tax return. Section 165(c)(3) allows a taxpayer to recognize a casualty loss or theft of personal property. The taxpayer is not allowed to claim a loss in excess of his basis in the property.[134]

Section 165. Losses

(a) General Rule. — There shall be allowed as a deduction any loss sustained during the taxable year and not compensated for by insurance or otherwise.

(b) Amount of Deduction. — For purposes of subsection (a), the basis for determining the amount of the deduction for any loss shall be the adjusted basis

---

131. Section 1001(a).
132. Section 165(c)(3).
133. Sections 1001(a); 1016(a).
134. Section 165(b).

provided in section 1011 for determining the loss from the sale or other disposition of property.

(c) Limitation on Losses of Individuals. — In the case of an individual, the deduction under subsection (a) shall be limited to —

> (3) except as provided in subsection (h), losses of property not connected with a trade or business or a transaction entered into for profit, if such losses arise from fire, storm, shipwreck, or other casualty, or from theft.

Loss Realized and Loss Recognized

Loss realized is the difference between the amount realized and the adjusted basis of the property.

Loss recognized is the amount of loss realized the taxpayer can report on his income tax return.

Tell Me More

The Code provides that, in specific situations, the taxpayer must defer the recognition of loss until a later time. These provisions are addressed in Chapters 43 and 47.

Casualty or theft loss. The taxpayer's property may be destroyed through a casualty, such as a fire, storm, tornado, or hurricane. Or it may be stolen.

While there is rarely little doubt about whether a loss from fire, storm, tornado, or hurricane comes within the statutory provision, disagreement may arise as to what falls within "other casualty." The Service has interpreted "other casualty" as an "identifiable event of a sudden, unexpected, and unusual nature."[135] The Service has consistently taken the position that an event that is sudden cannot be gradual or progressive.

Examples of Revenue Rulings Addressing "Sudden"

- Rev. Rul. 70-91:[136] water heater burst from rust and corrosion over a period of time: damage to the water heater was not sudden, therefore not a casualty; damage to rugs, carpet, and drapes was a casualty.

- Rev. Rul. 63-232:[137] damage caused by termites to property was not sudden, therefore not a casualty.

- Rev. Rul. 79-174:[138] damage caused to ornamental pine trees by mass attack of southern pine beetles over a 5–10 day period was sudden and unexpected and, therefore, a casualty loss.

---

135. Rev. Rul. 72-592, 1972-2 C.B. 101.
136. 1970-1 C.B. 37.
137. 1963-2 C.B. 97.
138. 1979-1 C.B. 99.

Generally, the taxpayer must establish that the property has suffered physical damage. In *Chamales v. Commissioner*[139] the taxpayers lived adjacent to O.J. Simpson. When Simpson was arrested for the murder of Nicole Brown Simpson and Ronald Goldman, the media and general public blocked streets and trespassed on their land. The taxpayers argued that, as a result of all the media attention in the area, the value of their property had decreased in value. The court disagreed, finding that there was no physical damage to the property (i.e., no permanent decrease in value).

Sometimes the problem the taxpayer encounters is being able to show what happened to the property, to establish that he suffered a theft or casualty loss. In *Popa v. Commissioner*[140] the taxpayer lived in Saigon, Vietnam. He was away from his home on a business trip when Saigon fell to the North Vietnamese. He never was able to return to Saigon to reclaim his possessions. The Service argued that the taxpayer could not know what had happened to his possessions. The Tax Court agreed with the taxpayer that, most likely, his property was either destroyed or pilfered. It allowed him to claim the casualty loss.

The dissent took the majority to task for not requiring the taxpayer to meet his burden of proof as to what had happened to his possessions. It reviewed prior casualty loss cases. In *Powers v. Commissioner*,[141] the taxpayer's car was seized by the East German police. Because what occurred did not happen by chance, accident, or contingency, the court held it was not a casualty. The dissent noted that, similarly, if the taxpayer's possessions had been confiscated by the government, the taxpayer would not have been entitled to a casualty loss deduction. Because the taxpayer could not establish if his possessions had been destroyed or pilfered, he could not satisfy his burden regarding what happened to his property. The dissent would not have permitted the casualty loss deduction.

An issue similar to *Popa* previously had been before the court. In *Allen v. Commissioner*[142] the taxpayer went to the Metropolitan Museum of Art in New York. She arrived with a brooch on her dress. When she left, the brooch was no longer there. In order to claim a casualty loss, the brooch had to have been stolen. Merely having lost the brooch was not sufficient. Because she did not know what happened to the brooch (theft or loss), she was not entitled to claim a theft loss deduction.

Computation of amount of loss. The general rule is that the amount of the loss is the lesser of the basis or the decrease in value caused by the casualty or theft. Note that, if the value of the property exceeds the property's basis, there is no loss attributed to this excess (i.e. lost profit). Because the increase in value (the appreciation) had never been reported, no offsetting loss is permitted.

Once the amount of loss has been determined, it is reduced by any insurance proceeds received.[143] It is further reduced based on two statutory limitations. First, the loss is allowed only to the extent it exceeds $100. This computation is made for each casualty or theft.[144] The taxpayer totals all remaining casualty loss amounts. If there is a net loss, the taxpayer may recognize the loss only to the extent it exceeds 10 percent of his adjusted gross income.[145]

---

139. T.C. Memo. 2000-33.

140. 73 T.C. 130 (1979).

141. 36 T.C. 1191 (1961).

142. 16 T.C. 163 (1951).

143. See Section 165(h)(5)(E). Note that, upon receiving insurance proceeds, the taxpayer may have a gain on the disposition.

144. Section 165(h)(1).

145. Section 165(h)(2)(A). If the taxpayer also has casualty gains, these gains are taken into consideration in computing the amount of allowable casualty loss. Section 165(h)(2)(A). There is also a rule that applies if the taxpayer has a net casualty gain. Section 165(h)(2)(B).

Timing. When the taxpayer has submitted an insurance claim and there is a reasonable prospect of recovery, the taxpayer may not claim the loss until the amount of insurance recovery is determined with reasonable certainty.[146] If the property has been stolen, the loss is allowed in the year the taxpayer discovers the theft.[147]

C. Application of Rules

Example 1. Dennis owned a boat he used for personal purposes. This year a large storm struck the area, causing the boat to sink. He did not have the boat insured. Dennis was not able to salvage any part of the boat. He had purchased the boat for $5,000 and at the time of the storm its fair market was $4,000. For the year, Dennis's adjusted gross income was $30,000.

Dennis suffered a casualty loss. The amount of the loss is the lesser of the basis or the decrease in value. The lesser amount is the decrease in value, $4,000. The loss is allowed only to the extent it exceeds $100, or $3,900. Next, the loss is allowed only to the extent it exceeds $3,000 (10 percent of adjusted gross income), or $900. Dennis can claim a $900 casualty loss.

Example 2. Rich owned a boat he used for personal purposes. This year a large storm struck the area, causing the boat to sink. He did not have the boat insured. Rich was not able to salvage any part of the boat. He had purchased the boat for $5,000 and at the time of the storm its fair market value was $7,000. For the year, Rich's adjusted gross income was $30,000.

Rich suffered a casualty loss. The amount of the loss is the lesser of the basis or the decrease in value. The lesser amount is the basis, or $5,000. The difference between the fair market value ($7,000) and adjusted basis ($5,000) represents appreciation Rich did not have to recognize. Accordingly, he is not entitled to an offsetting loss for the unrecognized appreciation when the boat was destroyed.

The $5,000 loss is allowed only to the extent it exceeds $100, or $4,900. Next, the loss is allowed only to the extent it exceeds $3,000 (10 percent of adjusted gross income), or $1,900. Rich can claim a $1,900 casualty loss.

Example 3. Cassandra owned a boat she used for personal purposes. This year a large storm struck the area, causing the boat to sink. She did not have the boat insured. Cassandra was not able to salvage any part of the boat. She had purchased the boat for $5,000 and at the time of the storm its fair market value was $4,000. For the year, Cassandra's adjusted gross income was $60,000.

Cassandra suffered a casualty loss. The amount of the loss is the lesser of the basis or the decrease in value. The lesser amount is the decrease in value, or $4,000. The $4,000 loss is allowed only to the extent it exceeds $100, or $3,900. Next, the loss is allowed only to the extent it exceeds $6,000 (10 percent of adjusted gross income). Because the loss ($3,900) does not exceed $6,000, Cassandra is not entitled to claim a casualty loss.

---

146. Treas. Reg. § 1.165-1(d)(2).
147. Treas. Reg. § 1.165-8(a)(2).

Example 4. Heidi owned a boat she used for personal purposes. This year a large storm struck the area, causing the boat to sink. Heidi was not able to salvage any part of the boat. Heidi purchased the boat for $5,000 and at the time of the storm its fair market value was $5,000. Heidi had the boat insured and was able to recover $5,000 from the insurance company.

Heidi suffered a casualty loss. Because the boat was completely destroyed, the amount of the loss is $5,000. However, the loss is completely offset by the insurance proceeds and Heidi is not able to claim any loss ($5,000 loss, less $5,000 insurance recovery).

Example 5. Metta owned a boat she used for personal purposes. This year a large storm struck the area, causing damage to the boat. Metta purchased the boat for $10,000. Before the storm, its value was $8,000 and after the storm its value was $5,000. Metta did not have the boat insured and her adjusted gross income was $40,000.

Metta suffered a casualty loss. The amount of the loss is the lesser of the basis or the decrease in value. The lesser amount is the decrease in value, or $3,000 ($8,000 reduced to $5,000). The $3,000 loss is allowed only to the extent it exceeds $100, or $2,900. Next, the loss is allowed only to the extent it exceeds $4,000. Because the loss ($2,900) does not exceed $4,000, Metta is not allowed to claim a casualty loss.

Example 6. Misty owned a valuable pendant with a basis and fair market value of $10,000. Unfortunately this year a robber broke into her house. Among the items he took was the pendant, which she did not have insured. Misty's adjusted gross income was $50,000.

Misty suffered a theft loss. The amount of the theft loss is the basis in the pendant, or $10,000. The $10,000 loss is allowed only to the extent it exceeds $100, or $9,900. Next, the loss is allowed only to the extent it exceeds $5,000 (10 percent of adjusted gross income), or $4,900. Cassandra can claim a $4,900 theft loss.

D. Problems

1. Evan owns a boat. This year there was a large storm that caused the boat to sink. He paid $8,000 for the boat and before the storm it had a fair market value of $8,000. He did not have the boat insured, and his adjusted gross income was $40,000. What are the tax consequences to Evan?

2. Caroline owns a tractor. This year it suffered damage from a large hail storm. She paid $15,000 for the tractor. Before the storm the fair market value was $10,000 and after the storm its value was $7,000. Caroline did not have the tractor insured and her adjusted gross income was $40,000. What are the tax consequences to Caroline?

3. Emma owns a cabin. This year it suffered damage from a large wind storm. She paid $80,000 for the cabin. Before the storm the fair market value was $100,000 and after the storm its value was $90,000. Emma received $3,000 from her insurance company and her adjusted gross income was $40,000. What are the tax consequences to Emma?

4. Gigi owns a van. This year it was stolen. At the time of the theft her basis in the van was $8,000 and the fair market value was $7,000. Gigi received $6,000 from her insurance company and her adjusted gross income was $40,000. What are the tax consequences to Gigi?

Chapter 20

Non-Business Bad Debts

Deductions

Personal:	Investment:	Business:
• Interest • Taxes • Medical expenses • Education expenses • Moving expenses • Child care expenses • Charitable contributions • Casualty loses • **Non-business bad debts** • Alimony	• Expenses • Depreciation and amortization • Loss from the disposition of property • Non-business bad debts	• Start up expenses • Expenses • Depreciation and amortization • Losses from the disposition of property • Business bad debts

Read

Code Section 166

Treas. Reg. §§ 1.166-1(a), (c), (d)(1); 1.166-2(a), (b), (c)(1); 1.166-5(a), (b)

A. Background

Personal expenditures. In general, personal expenses are not deductible.[148] Congress does not consider a personal expense an item that should offset the taxpayer's gross income. In other words, it is not considered part of the cost of earning or generating gross income. Any deduction permitted for a personal expense is an exception to this broad-based rule. Accordingly, if the taxpayer wants to claim a deduction on his income tax return for a personal expense, he must establish that Congress specifically provided an exception to the general rule.

Forgiveness of debt. If a taxpayer has borrowed money that he has an obligation to repay and part of the obligation to repay is later forgiven, the taxpayer has gross income to the extent he no longer is required to repay the borrowed amount.[149]

---

148. Section 262.
149. Section 61(a)(12); United States v. Kirby Lumber Co., 284 U.S. 1 (1931).

B. Non-Business Bad Debts

If the borrower cannot repay a debt, the lender has experienced a decrease in wealth. The Code provides a bad debt deduction in such situations.[150] To be entitled to claim a bad debt deduction, there must be a debt and the borrower must be unable to repay the borrowed amount. The amount of the deduction cannot exceed the lender's basis in the debt.[151] In order for a non-business bad debt to be deductible, the entire amount of the debt must become worthless.[152]

Note

If the debt is represented by a "security" (i.e., stock), any deduction is permitted by the loss provisions of Section 165 and not the bad debt provisions of Section 166.[153]

Debt. A bad debt deduction can arise only in those situations where a valid debt exists.[154] It does not extend to other situations, such as where money has been transferred as a gift. Accordingly, when money has been transferred between family members, the Service will closely scrutinize the transaction to verify it is a valid, enforceable obligation to pay a fixed sum of money.

Worthless debt. The debtor must be unable to repay the debt. The creditor is not entitled to a bad debt deduction if he forgives the debt or otherwise cancels the debt. To determine if the debt has become worthless, the creditor must consider "all pertinent evidence," but is not required to seek a court judgment.[155]

Tell Me More

It may be difficult to ascertain when a debt has become worthless. Accordingly, the Code provides some flexibility in making this determination. The taxpayer has seven years from the time the debt becomes worthless to file a claim for refund.[156]

Amount of deduction. The amount of the non-business bad debt deduction cannot exceed the taxpayer's basis in the debt.[157] When the transaction is an unpaid loan, the taxpayer's basis in the debt will be the unpaid portion of the loan.

Character of a non-business bad debt. If the debt is a non-business bad debt, it is characterized as a short-term capital loss.[158] Capital gains and losses are addressed in Chapter

---

150. Section 166. The Code also provides a deduction for business bad debts. Business bad debts are discussed in Chapter 27.
151. Section 166(b).
152. Section 166(a), (d).
153. Section 166(e).
154. Treas. Reg. § 1.166-1(c).
155. Treas. Reg. § 1.166-2.
156. Section 6511(d)(1).
157. Section 166(b).
158. Section 166(d)(1).

37. It is sufficient here if you understand that the maximum net capital loss a taxpayer may claim each year is $3,000.[159] Any remaining loss must be carried forward.[160] (Business bad debts are characterized as ordinary losses. There is no limit on the amount of ordinary loss that can be claimed. See discussion in Chapter 27.)

Characterization Summary

Type of Debt	Character
Business bad debt	Ordinary loss
Non-business bad debt	Short-term capital loss

A business bad debt is a debt acquired in connection with the taxpayer's business. All other debts will be characterized as non-business bad debts. These debts include personal loans (i.e., a loan to a family member or friend) or debts incurred in connection with a taxpayer's investment.

Section 166. Bad Debts

(d)(2) Nonbusiness debt defined.— For purposes of paragraph (1), the term "nonbusiness bad debt" means a debt other than—

(A) a debt created or acquired (as the case may be) in connection with a trade or business of the taxpayer; or

(B) a debt the loss from the worthlessness of which is incurred in the taxpayer's trade or business.

Business	Non-Business
– employee (a taxpayer can be in the business of being an employee)	– personal loans
	– shareholder (investor)
– in the business of buying and selling corporations	– other type of investor

---

Tell Me More

If the taxpayer has a business bad debt, he is allowed to claim a deduction for any portion of the debt that has become worthless; deductions for partially worthless business bad debts are allowed.[161]

---

159. Section 1211(b).
160. Section 1212(b).
161. Business bad debts are discussed in Chapter 27.

C. Application of Rules

Example 1. Theodore loaned $10,000 to his brother, saying "pay me back when you can." His brother was not able to repay Theodore. Because the transaction more closely resembles a gift, Theodore is not entitled to a non-business bad debt deduction.

Example 2. William loaned his friend $10,000. His friend signed a promissory note containing a stated rate of interest, repayment schedule, and penalties for late payment. Unfortunately, his friend had financial difficulties and was unable to pay the remaining outstanding $9,000 debt. The debt is a non-business bad debt, and William may claim a $9,000 short-term capital loss.

Example 3. William loaned his friend $10,000. His friend signed a promissory note containing a stated rate of interest, repayment schedule, and penalties for late payment. Unfortunately, after making payments for a year, his friend had financial difficulties and was unable to repay the debt. William told his friend, "don't worry about paying me back!" Because William forgave the debt, he is not entitled to a bad debt deduction.

Example 4. William loaned his friend $10,000. His friend signed a promissory note containing a stated rate of interest, repayment schedule, and penalties for late payment. Unfortunately, after making payments for a year, his friend had financial difficulties and stated he was uncertain if he would be able to repay the remainder of the outstanding debt.

The debt is a non-business bad debt. To be deductible, the entire debt must be worthless. Until it is determined whether his friend is able to repay any portion of the debt, William may not claim a non-business bad debt deduction.

D. Problems

1. Alex owns and operates a small kiosk that sells watches. Each Friday Kevin works for him at the kiosk. In January Alex loaned Kevin $5,000. In June Kevin told Alex that he was unable to repay the loan. Alex and Kevin agreed that Kevin would work at the kiosk each weekend (Saturday and Sunday) for the remainder of the year and Alex would "forgive" the debt.

   a. What are the tax consequences to Alex?

   b. What are the tax consequences to Kevin?

2. Susan loaned her good friend Mary $10,000. Mary fell on hard times and was unable to repay Susan. Susan told Mary, "Don't worry about it. Pay me back if you ever have the money."

   a. What are the tax consequences to Susan?

   b. What are the tax consequences to Mary?

3. Joshua loaned his brother, Jonathan, $10,000. Jonathan signed a promissory note containing a stated rate of interest, repayment schedule, and penalties for late payment. Unfortunately, after Jonathan had repaid only $2,000 of the amount, he encountered financial difficulties and was unable to repay the remainder.

   a. What are the tax consequences to Joshua?

   b. What are the tax consequences to Jonathan?

E. Analysis and Application

1. Cherie has come to you wanting to know if she can claim a non-business bad debt deduction. Last year she loaned $10,000 to her niece and her niece has failed to repay the debt. In order to make a decision, what questions should you ask Cherie?

2. Can you explain to your client the difference between a business and a non-business bad debt?

3. Prepare a check list of those items that should exist when creating a loan so that it will be deductible as a nonbusiness bad debt if the borrower is unable to repay the loan.

V

Businesses

Personal:	Investment:	Business:
• Interest • Taxes • Medical expenses • Education expenses • Moving expenses • Child care expenses • Charitable contributions • Casualty loses • Non-business bad debts • Alimony	• Expenses • Depreciation and amortization • Loss from the disposition of property • Non-business bad debts	• **Start up expenses** • **Expenses** • **Depreciation and amortization** • **Losses from the disposition of property** • **Business bad debts**

Chapter 21

Overview: Business Expenditures

Deductions

Personal:	Investment:	Business:
• Interest	• Expenses	• Start up expenses
• Taxes	• Depreciation and	• Expenses
• Medical expenses	amortization	• Depreciation and
• Education expenses	• Loss from the	amortization
• Moving expenses	disposition of property	• Losses from the
• Child care expenses	• Non-business bad debts	disposition of property
• Charitable contributions		• Business bad debts
• Casualty loses		
• Non-business bad debts		
• Alimony		

One of the overarching objectives of the Code is to impose tax on a taxpayer's accession to wealth. When the taxpayer operates his own business, his taxable increase in wealth is not his gross income. Rather, it is his gross income less the costs he incurred to generate the income.

> Business gross income
> − <u>Costs of operating business for the year</u>
> Taxable income

The Code provides several business-related deductions. For an individual income tax class, the reference to business generally is to a taxpayer's sole proprietorship. All tax items from a sole proprietorship are reported by the taxpayer on his individual income tax return.[1]

Expenditures. By way of example we consider a taxpayer with a legal practice. The amount his clients pay him for his legal services is his gross income. However, it would be unfair to impose tax based on this amount as he had to spend money to operate his practice. Specifically, if we took a simplified look at the costs he incurred in operating his practice, it might include amounts he paid for the following:

---

1. If the business were operated through a partnership or corporation, the entity itself also would be filing a return. The tax treatment of an ownership interest in a partnership or corporation is beyond the scope of this text.

- Computer
- Desk
- Copy machine
- Pens
- Paper
- Salary paid to paralegal
- Salary paid to receptionist
- Building
- Land

If we look closer at these costs, we see that some of them impact only one taxable year. Others impact more than one taxable year. Still others may impact one or more taxable years—we may not know for sure. If we organized the costs into categories based on whether they impact one or more taxable years, we might arrange them as follows:

One Taxable Year	More Than One Taxable Year
Pens	Computer
Paper	Desk
Salaries	Copy machine
	Building
	Land

The Code deals with the two categories differently. The first category, expenditures that impact only one taxable year, is discussed in Chapter 23. The second category, expenditures that impact more than one taxable year, is discussed in Chapter 25. For some assets, it might be unclear into which category it should be placed. This issue is discussed in Chapter 22.

Losses. Chapter 4 addressed appreciation in property and the requirement that the profit be recognized when the property is disposed of. As a corollary, if the property has decreased in value from the date of purchase to the time of sale, there is a loss in the property. In that instance, a loss is allowed if a Code section permits the taxpayer to claim the loss. Losses from the sale of property used in a business are discussed in Chapter 26.

Bad debts. When a taxpayer loans money or extends credit to a business customer and is not repaid, the taxpayer has a decrease in his wealth. In some situations, the taxpayer can deduct the amount of the bad debt on his income tax return. Business bad debts are discussed in Chapter 27.

Many sole proprietorships are reported on Schedule C. Take a moment and review Schedule C. Consider the following:

- Where is the income reported?
- What expense deductions are allowed?
- Where is depreciation or amortization taken into account?
- How does the total income or loss from the business relate to the Form 1040?

Exhibit: First Page of Schedule C

SCHEDULE C (Form 1040) Department of the Treasury Internal Revenue Service (99)	**Profit or Loss From Business** (Sole Proprietorship) ⊠ For information on Schedule C and its instructions, go to www.irs.gov/schedulec. ⊠ Attach to Form 1040, 1040NR, or 1041; partnerships generally must file Form 1065.	OMB No. 1545-0074 **20 12** Attachment Sequence No. 09

Name of proprietor		Social security number (SSN)
A	Principal business or profession, including product or service (see instructions)	B Enter code from instructions ⊠
C	Business name. If no separate business name, leave blank.	D Employer ID number (EIN), (see instr.)

E   Business address (including suite or room no.   ) ⊠ --

      City, town or post office, state, and ZIP code

F   Accounting method: (1) ☐ Cash   (2) ☐ Accrual   (3) ☐ Other (specify) ⊠ ---

G   Did you "materially participate" in the operation of this business during 2012? If "No," see instructions for limit on losses   . ☐ Yes ☐ No

H   If you started or acquired this business during 2012, check here . . . . ⊠ ☐

I   Did you make any payments in 2012 that would require you to file Form(s) 1099? (see instructions)   . . . . . ☐ Yes ☐ No

J   If "Yes," did you or will you file required Forms 1099? . . . . ☐ Yes ☐ No

Part I   Income

1	Gross receipts or sales. See instructions for line 1 and check the box if this income was reported to you on Form W-2 and the "Statutory employee" box on that form was checked . . . . ⊠ ☐	1
2	Returns and allowances (see instructions)	2
3	Subtract line 2 from line 1	3
4	Cost of goods sold (from line 42)	4
5	Gross profit. Subtract line 4 from line 3	5
6	Other income, including federal and state gasoline or fuel tax credit or refund (see instructions)	6
7	Gross income. Add lines 5 and 6 . . . . ⊠	7

Part II   Expenses   Enter expenses for business use of your home only on line 30.

8	Advertising	8	18	Office expense (see instructions)	18
9	Car and truck expenses (see instructions)	9	19	Pension and profit-sharing plans .	19
10	Commissions and fees .	10	20	Rent or lease (see instructions):	
11	Contract labor (see instructions)	11	a	Vehicles, machinery, and equipment	20a
12	Depletion	12	b	Other business property . . .	20b
13	Depreciation and section 179 expense deduction (not included in Part III) (see instructions)	13	21	Repairs and maintenance . . .	21
			22	Supplies (not included in Part III)	22
			23	Taxes and licenses	23
			24	Travel, meals, and entertainment:	
14	Employee benefit programs (other than on line 19) . .	14	a	Travel	24a
			b	Deductible meals and entertainment (see instructions) .	24b
15	Insurance (other than health)	15			
16	Interest:		25	Utilities	25
a	Mortgage (paid to banks, etc.)	16a	26	Wages (less employment credits) .	26
b	Other	16b	27a	Other expenses (from line 48) . .	27a
17	Legal and professional services	17	b	Reserved for future use . . .	27b

28	Total expenses before expenses for business use of home. Add lines 8 through 27a . . . . . ⊠	28	
29	Tentative profit or (loss). Subtract line 28 from line 7	29	
30	Expenses for business use of your home. Attach Form 8829. Do not report such expenses elsewhere . .	30	

31	Net profit or (loss). Subtract line 30 from line 29.
	   • If a profit, enter on both Form 1040, line 12 (or Form 1040NR, line 13) and on Schedule SE, line 2.
	   (If you checked the box on line 1, see instructions). Estates and trusts, enter on Form 1041, line 3.
	   • If a loss, you must go to line 32.
		31	

32	If you have a loss, check the box that describes your investment in this activity (see instructions).
	   • If you checked 32a, enter the loss on both Form 1040, line 12, (or Form 1040NR, line 13) and on Schedule SE, line 2. (If you checked the box on line 1, see the line 31 instructions). Estates and trusts, enter on Form 1041, line 3.
	   • If you checked 32b, you must attach Form 6198. Your loss may be limited.
		32a ☐ All investment is at risk.
		32b ☐ Some investment is not at risk.	

For Paperwork Reduction Act Notice, see your tax return instructions.   Cat. No. 11334P   Schedule C (Form 1040) 2012

Chapter 22

Capital Expenditures

Deductions

Personal:	Investment:	Business:
• Interest • Taxes • Medical expenses • Education expenses • Moving expenses • Child care expenses • Charitable contributions • Casualty loses • Non-business bad debts • Alimony	• Expenses • Depreciation and amortization • Loss from the disposition of property • Non-business bad debts	• Start up expenses • Expenses • Depreciation and amortization • Losses from the disposition of property • Business bad debts

Read

Code Section 263(a)

Treas. Reg. §§ 1.162-4; 1.263(a)-1(a), (b); 1.263(a)-2(a), (c), (h); 1.263(a)-4(f)(1)

A. Background

Gross income. Gross income includes income (accessions to wealth) derived from any and all sources.[2] It includes every accession to wealth, unless there is an exception.

Basis. The basis of property is the amount the taxpayer originally paid for the property.[3] In general, a taxpayer will purchase an item for its fair market value. Thus, a taxpayer's basis in property is the fair market value of the property at the time of purchase.

---

2. Section 61(a).
3. Section 1012(a).

Taxable income. In general, taxable income is the taxpayer's gross income, less all allowable deductions.[4] The taxpayer's liability is based on the amount of the taxpayer's taxable income.[5]

B. Capital Expenditures

The Code aims to tax an accession to wealth, or a taxpayer's net business income. To determine the accession to wealth, the taxpayer is allowed to deduct the cost of earning the business income. If the expenditure impacts only one year and is an ordinary and necessary expense, the taxpayer may currently deduct the cost.[6] If the expenditure impacts more than year and the asset wears out over time, the taxpayer recovers the cost over a number of years through depreciation or amortization.[7] If the asset doesn't wear out, the taxpayer will recognize any decrease in value when he sells the asset.

While the rules for how to treat an item that impacts one year or more than one year are fairly straight forward, a lot of difficulty remains in determining into which category an item falls. This chapter explores some of the tests available to help the taxpayer and the Commissioner make that determination.

1. The Supreme Court

On several occasions the Supreme Court has had the opportunity to provide guidance on the distinction between an expense (an asset that has a life less than one year) and a capital expenditure (an asset that has a life more than one year).

In *Lincoln Savings and Loan Ass'n,*[8] a state savings and loan was required to pay an "additional premium" to the Federal Savings and Loan Insurance Corporation when insuring its deposits. The issue before the court was whether the additional premium payments were an expense or a capital expenditure. The Supreme Court set forth a specific test: if the expenditure created a "separate and distinct asset," then the expenditure was a capital expenditure. Because the payment created a specific type of asset protection, the Supreme Court found it created a separate and distinct asset and, accordingly, was a capital expenditure.

Over twenty years later the issue of whether an item was an expense or a capital expenditure was again before the Supreme Court. In *INDOPCO, Inc. v. Commissioner*[9] the corporate taxpayer was approached by a third party that wanted to carry out a friendly take-over. The corporate taxpayer incurred consulting and legal fees in investigating whether the take-over would be in its best interests. It ultimately agreed to the takeover.

The issue before the court was whether the consulting and legal fees were currently deductible or were capital expenditures. The corporate-taxpayer applied the test set forth in *Lincoln Savings & Loan* and argued that the fees did not create a separate and distinct

---

4. Section 63(a).
5. Section 1.
6. Section 162(a). Business expenses are discussed in Chapter 23.
7. Sections 167; 168. Depreciation is discussed in Chapter 25.
8. 403 U.S. 345 (1971).
9. 503 U.S. 79 (1992).

asset and, therefore, that the fees were currently deductible expenses. In deciding against the corporate-taxpayer, the Supreme Court recognized the limitations of the definition set forth in *Lincoln Savings & Loan* and provided further guidance regarding the distinction between expenses and capital expenditures.

> *Lincoln Savings* stands for the simple proposition that a taxpayer's expenditure that "serves to create or enhance ... a separate and distinct" asset should be capitalized under § 263. It by no means follows, however, that *only* expenditures that create or enhance separate and distinct assets are to be capitalized under § 263.... In short, *Lincoln Savings* holds that the creation of a separate and distinct asset well may be a sufficient, but not a necessary, condition to classification as a capital expenditure....

> Nor does our statement in Lincoln Savings.... that "the presence of an ensuing benefit that may have some future aspect is not controlling" prohibit reliance on future benefit as a means of distinguishing an ordinary business expense from a capital expenditure. Although the mere presence of an incidental future benefit ... may not warrant capitalization, a taxpayer's realization of benefits beyond the year in which the expenditure is incurred is undeniably important in determining whether the appropriate tax treatment is immediate deduction or capitalization ... Indeed, the text of the Code's capitalization provision, § 263(a)(1), which refers to "permanent improvements or betterments," itself envisions an inquiry into the duration and extent of the benefits realized by the taxpayer.[10]

The Supreme Court held that the costs generated substantial future benefits and, accordingly, were capital expenditures.[11]

2. Regulations

The Service has made a concerted effort to assist the taxpayer by placing certain costs into either the expense or the capital expenditure category. Over the last five years there has been a history of proposed regulations, public hearings, and regulations being withdrawn. It is a difficult area of the law and one significantly lacking in bright lines or bright line tests. The following chart summarizes a few of the more common costs a business might incur and its characterization based on the regulations or other Service guidance.

---

10. INDOPCO, Inc., 503 U.S. 86, at 87.
11. INDOPCO, Inc., 503 U.S. 86, at 86–87.

Expense	Capital Expenditure
• rent for business property • supplies (used and consumed in business operation) • advertising and selling costs • training costs • incidental repairs or maintenance • severance payments made to downsize a company • defending right to income from property • expanding an existing business	• improvements made that increase the value of property, substantially prolong the useful of the property, or adapt it to a new or different use • billboard or business sign • acquisition costs • restoration of property or expenditure that is part of a general plan of rehabilitation, modernization, and improvement of property • construction of a building, machinery, equipment, furniture, etc. • defending or perfecting title to property • cost of disposing of an asset • goodwill, when the assets of a going concern are acquired • expanding into a new line of business

Acquisition costs. Costs associated with the acquisition of an asset must be added to the adjusted basis of the asset.[12]

Example. The taxpayer purchased a building for $100,000. As part of the transaction the taxpayer purchased title insurance for $10,000. The title insurance is an acquisition costs, a capital expenditure. The cost of the insurance is added to the basis of the property, resulting in an adjusted basis in the building of $110,000.

In some situations, it may be unclear whether costs were incurred in the acquisition of an asset or for another purpose. The Supreme Court has held that the issue is resolved by considering the "origin of the claim." In *United States v. Hilton Hotels Corp.*[13] the taxpayer was required to repurchase stock from certain shareholders. The corporation argued that it incurred litigation costs to determine the fair market value of the stock, thereby determining the amount the shareholders would receive for their stock; the litigation did not involve determining who owned the stock. Considering the "origin of the claim," the Supreme Court stated that the claim being litigated was the acquisition of the stock. Accordingly, it held the litigation costs were capital expenditures.

Defending and perfecting title. Costs associated with defending or perfecting title of an asset must be added to the adjusted basis of the asset.[14]

Example. The taxpayer and his neighbor disputed the location of the property line between their two properties. At a cost of $10,000 the taxpayer is able to resolve the dispute

---

12. Temp. Reg. § 1.263(a)-2T(a).
13. 397 U.S. 580 (1970). A companion case, Woodward v. Commissioner, 397 U.S. 572 (1970), addressing the same issue was issued at the same time.
14. Treas. Reg. § 1.212-1(k); Temp. Reg. § 1.263(a)-2T(e).

in his favor. The cost of defending and perfecting title to his land, $10,000, is a capital expenditure and must be added to his basis in the land.

Additions and improvement. If the taxpayer makes an addition to the property or improves the property, the cost of the addition or improvement must be added to the adjusted basis of the property.[15] Temporary regulations provide a taxpayer must capitalize amounts paid to improve the property. Property is improved if the amounts paid[16] —

- result in a betterment of the property;
- restore the property; or
- adapt the unit to a new or different use.

Example. The taxpayer owns a building with an adjusted basis of $100,000. At a cost of $10,000, the taxpayer adds an atrium to the east side of the building. The cost of the atrium is a capital expenditure. The cost is added to the basis of the building, resulting in an adjusted basis for the building (including the atrium) of $110,000.

Disposing of or retiring an asset. The Supreme Court has held that the cost of disposing of an asset is a capital expenditure. But, because the asset will not have a continuing useful life to the taxpayer (because he is disposing of it), the practical impact of the court's holding is either to reduce the taxpayer's gain or increase the loss by the amount of the disposal cost.[17]

Example. The taxpayer removed and discarded old telephone poles, replacing them with new telephone poles. The taxpayer could increase the amount of the loss from the disposition of the old telephone poles by the cost of removing them.[18]

Cost of constructing an asset. When a taxpayer constructs an asset, each individual cost he incurs may be either an expense (i.e., rent, salary) or a capital expenditure (i.e., steel beams, concrete, boards).[19] However, rather than consider the nature of the individual costs, the relevant inquiry is whether the end product is an expense or capital expenditure. In *Commissioner v. Idaho Power Co.*[20] the taxpayer had to consider all the costs that went into constructing a building. These costs were represented by the building, a capital asset. All costs associated with the construction of the asset were capital expenditures.

Improvements. If the taxpayer replaces or improves an asset, the cost of the addition or improvement must be added to the adjusted basis of the property.[21] The temporary regulations have a safe harbor, allowing routine maintenance on property other than a building to be considered not an improvement. Routine maintenance is the recurring activities a taxpayer expects to perform as a result of use of the property to keep the unit in its ordinary efficient operating condition. It includes cleaning and replacement of parts. The activity is routine only if the taxpayer reasonably expects to perform the activities more than once during the class life of the property.[22]

Example. The taxpayer owns a building with an adjusted basis of $100,000. At a cost of $50,000 the taxpayer rehabilitates the property by replacing the wiring and upgrading

---

15. Temp. Reg. § 1.263(a)-3T(a), (d).
16. Temp. Reg. § 1.263(a)-3T(d).
17. Woodward v. Commissioner, 397 U.S. 572 (1970).
18. See Rev. Rul. 2000-7, 2000-1 C.B. 712.
19. Temp. Reg. § 1.263(a)-2T(d)(1), (d)(2), Ex. 8.
20. 418 U.S.1 (1974).
21. Treas. Reg. § 1.263(a)-3T(a).
22. Temp. Reg. § 1.263(a)-3T(g).

the pipes. The cost of the improvements is added to the basis of the building, resulting in an adjusted basis for the building of $150,000.

Case Law Sample: Repair or Improvement

Test: Under prior regulations, to repair is to restore to a sound state or to mend, while a replacement connotes a substitution. A repair is an expenditure for the purpose of keeping the property in an ordinarily efficient operating condition. It does not add to the value of the property, nor does it appreciably prolong its life. It merely keeps the property in an operating condition over its probably useful life for the uses for which it was acquired. Expenditures for that purpose are distinguishable from those for replacements, alterations, improvements, or additions which prolong the life of the property, increase its value, or make it adaptable to a different use. The one is a maintenance charge, while the other are additions to capital investment which should not be applied against current earnings.[23]

Repair: The taxpayer was in the business of curing ham. After oil from a nearby factory began leaking into the taxpayer's basement, the taxpayer installed a liner. The liner was a repair and, therefore, currently deductible.[24]

Capital Improvement: The taxpayer owned and operated an outdoor movie theatre. After water began draining from the grounds onto a neighboring farmer's field, the taxpayer installed a drainage pipe. The pipe was an improvement and, therefore, was a capital expenditure.[25]

Signs and billboards. While advertising can provide a benefit that extends beyond the current year, the government has agreed to treat advertising expenses as currently deductible expenses. The only exceptions are the costs for signs and billboards. The costs of these items are capital expenditures.[26]

Expansion in to a new area of business. If the taxpayer incurs costs associated with expanding into a new area of business, the costs must be capitalized. This treatment is contrasted with expanding a current line of business, which costs, if otherwise qualified, continue to be currently deductible.

Case Law: Expanding a Business or Expanding into a New Area of Business

Currently deductible:

Briarcliff Candy Corp v. Commissioner:[27] the taxpayer incurred costs for establishing a division to promote sales in new retail outlets. The costs were currently deductible.

---

23. Treas. Reg. § 1.263(a)-1(b) (prior regulation); Midland Empire Packing Company v. Commissioner, 14 T.C. 635 (1950).
24. Midland Empire Packing Co. v. Commissioner 14 T.C. 635 (1950).
25. Mt. Morris Drive-In Theatre v. Commissioner, 25 T.C. 272 (1955).
26. Rev. Rul. 92-80, 1992-2 C.B. 57.
27. 475 F.2d 775 (2d Cir. 1973).

Colorado Springs National Bank v. United States:[28] taxpayer incurred costs in creating credit card services for customers. The court held the credit card services were merely new ways of offering letters of credit. The costs were currently deductible.

Revenue Ruling 2000-4:[29] the taxpayer incurred costs in obtaining, maintaining, and renewing certifications of compliance with international quality standards. The costs were currently deductible.

One-year rule. For those costs that are close to one year, the regulations provide a test to help the taxpayer determine if the costs should be capitalized. If the taxpayer makes a prepayment and the right or benefit paid for does not extend beyond the earlier of 12 months after the first date on which the taxpayer realizes the benefit or the end of the taxable year following the taxable year in which the payment is made, the taxpayer is not required to capitalize the amount of the payment.[30]

C. Application of Rules

Example 1. Jeb repainted the outside of the building where his business is located. The cost of repainting is an expense.

Example 2. Marcus replaced a few broken tiles on the floor of his business show room. The cost of replacing the tiles is an expense.

Example 3. Terrance replaced the entire roof of the building where his business is located. The cost of the roof replacement is a capital expenditure

Example 4. Sandy spent $6,000 to train all of her employees on use of new computer software that would automatically track the store's inventory. The cost of the training is an expense.

Example 5. Clyde had the plumbing and wiring in the building where his business is located completely replaced. The cost of the replacements is a capital expenditure.

Example 6. Kelley purchased a building for her business. As part of the transaction, she obtained an inspection. The cost of the inspection is an acquisition cost and, therefore, a capital expenditure. The cost of the inspection is added to the basis of the property.

Example 7. Karlene had a dispute with Linda about the ownership of the building used for Karlene's business. Karlene paid $15,000 in attorney fees. The dispute was eventually settled in Karlene's favor. The cost of defending and perfecting title to the building is a capital expenditure and must be added to her basis in the building.

Example 8. Cindy's business was doing well and she needed more room to store her inventory. She added a large storeroom to the back of the building. The cost of the storeroom is a capital expenditure and the cost must be added to her basis in the building.

---

28. 505 F.2d 1185 (10th Cir. 1974).
29. 2000-1 C.B. 331.
30. Treas. Reg. § 1.263(a)-4(f)(1).

Example 9. Dennis needed a storage unit to store rakes, lawn mowers, gas cans, and other items used to maintain the lawn at his business. He paid $500 for a permit, $5,000 in construction wages, and $7,000 for supplies. Because Dennis constructed an asset, all costs associated with the storage unit must be considered together. The cost of the storage unit, $12,500, is a capital expenditure.

Example 10. Francine paid $20,000 for an advertising company to prepare new promotional pieces to be run as advertisements on local television channels. She plans to use the ads for the next two years. Because it is for advertising, the $20,000 paid to the advertising company is an expense.

Example 11. Beth paid $10,000 for a new sign to be installed in front of her business. The cost of the sign is a capital expenditure.

Example 12. Darren owns and operates a consulting service. In November he purchased 12 months worth of fire insurance. The insurance creates a benefit lasting beyond the year of purchase. However, because the benefit does not extend beyond 12 months or the following year, the cost is an expense.

Example 13. Albert owns and operates a small business. In November he purchased 24 months worth of flood insurance. The insurance creates a benefit lasting beyond the year of purchase. In addition, the benefit extends beyond 12 months and extends beyond the following year. The cost is a capital expenditure.

D. Problems

With respect to the following costs, discuss whether each is an expense or a capital expenditure.

1. Janice owns and operates a small diner. This year she changed the decorating motif from southern-country to French antique. As part of the redesign she painted the walls and purchased new window treatments, artwork, centerpieces, lamps, tablecloths, placemats, plates, silverware, and glasses. She spent $10,000 on the new items.

2. Arlene owns and operates a car repair shop. This year she paid $15,000 to have the parking lot re-sealed.

3. Holly owns a paint shop. This year the heating and cooling system broke and she paid $20,000 to have it replaced.

4. Reba owns a recording studio. This year she updated the studio's recording equipment, paying $50,000 for the equipment.

5. Sarah owns a small used book store. This year she paid $2,000 for software she could use to track the store's inventory.

6. Mike owns an ice cream shoppe. This year he paid a contractor $10,000 to build a storage unit attached to the back of the building. He also paid $40,000 for building supplies.

7. Kieran paid $5,000 to purchase three year's worth of casualty insurance for his business.

8. On April 1 Norbert entered into an agreement with Snow-Removal Express for snow removal services for his business. He paid them $5,000 and the contract extended through March 31 of the following year.

9. Janson entered into a lease agreement with Furniture Direct. He agreed to pay Furniture Direct $100 each month for two years for the use of office furniture. At the end of the two years, Janson has the option to purchase the leased furniture for $50. What are the tax consequences to Janson?

E. Analysis and Application

Science Books, Inc. hired another publishing company to research, prepare, edit, and arrange a book on physics. It paid the publishing company a lump sum for the completed manuscript. Is the amount paid to the publishing company an expense or a capital expenditure?

In formulating your analysis and response, you may want to consider:

- INDOPCO, Inc. v. Commissioner, 503 U.S. 79 (1992)
- Commissioner v. Idaho Power Co 418 U.S. 1 (1974)
- Midland Empire Packing Co. v. Commissioner, 14 T.C. 635 (1950)
- Mt. Morris Drive-In Theatre Co. v. Commissioner, 25 T.C. 272 (1955)

Chapter 23

Business Expenses

Deductions

Personal:	Investment:	Business:
• Interest	• Expenses	• **Start up expenses**
• Taxes	• Depreciation and	• **Expenses**
• Medical expenses	amortization	• Depreciation and
• Education expenses	• Loss from the	amortization
• Moving expenses	disposition of property	• Losses from the
• Child care expenses	• Non-business bad debts	disposition of property
• Charitable contributions		• Business bad debts
• Casualty loses		
• Non-business bad debts		
• Alimony		

Read

Code Sections 161; 162(a); 195

Treas. Reg. §§ 1.162-1(a); 1.162-3; 1.162-6; 1.162-7; 1.162-8; 1.162-9

A. Background

Gross income. Gross income includes income (accessions to wealth) derived from any and all sources.[31] It includes every accession to wealth, unless there is an exception.

Basis. The basis of property is the amount the taxpayer originally paid for the property.[32] In general, a taxpayer will purchase an item for its fair market value. Thus, a taxpayer's basis in property is the fair market value of the property at the time of purchase.

Taxable income. In general, taxable income is the taxpayer's gross income, less all allowable deductions.[33] The taxpayer's liability is based on the amount of the taxpayer's taxable income.[34]

---

31. Section 61(a).
32. Section 1012(a).
33. Section 63(a).
34. Section 1.

B. Expense Deduction

One of the overarching objectives of the Code is to impose tax on a taxpayer's accession to wealth. When the taxpayer operates his own business, his taxable increase in wealth is not his gross income. Rather, it is his gross income less the expenses he incurred to generate the income.[35]

Consistent with the concept of taxing net income, the Code provides several business-related deductions.[36] One provision allows a deduction for expenditures that impact only one taxable year. Specifically, the expenditure must be:

- Ordinary

- Necessary

- Expense

- Paid or incurred during the taxable year

- In carrying on any business

Section 162. Trade or Business Expenses

(a) In general. There shall be allowed as a deduction all the ordinary and necessary expenses paid or incurred during the taxable year in carrying on any trade or business....

If the payment comes within Section 162, the taxpayer can deduct the amount of the expense (the basis of the asset).

Ordinary. While the Code does not provide a definition of "ordinary" the Supreme Court has. In *Welch v. Helvering*,[37] Mr. Welch had been the secretary of the E.L. Welch Company, which was in the grain business. The Company went bankrupt and was unable to pay many of its creditors.

Mr. Welch then obtained a job with the Kellogg Company purchasing grain on behalf of the Company. To reestablish his relations with customers of the Welch Company and solidify his credit and standing, over several years he paid some of the debts of the Welch Company (his previous employer). Mr. Welch wanted to deduct the payments as expenses under Section 162.

The Supreme Court considered whether the debt payments were deductible expenditures under Section 162(a). In considering the requirement that the expenditure be ordinary, the Court noted that the payment does not have to be "habitual or normal in the sense that the same taxpayer will have to make them often."[38] Rather, the expense has to be common and accepted in the group or community of which the taxpayer is part. The court held that "life in all its fullness must supply the answer to the riddle."[39] In other words, determination of whether the payment is ordinary is based on the facts and circumstances.

---

35. As discussed later in this chapter, a taxpayer may also be in the business of being an employee.
36. Section 212 provides a similar deduction for expenses incurred in an investment activity. Section 212 deductions are discussed in Chapter 29.
37. 290 U.S. 111 (1933).
38. Welch v. Helvering, 290 U.S. 111, 115 (1933).
39. Id.

Looking at the facts and circumstances before it, the court considered that people do not ordinarily pay the debts of others. Accordingly, the expenditure was not an ordinary expense and could not be deducted under Section 162.

Necessary. In the same case, the Supreme Court considered what constituted a necessary expenditure. The Court defined "necessary" as an expenditure that is appropriate or helpful.[40] The court agreed that the payments were necessary in that they were helpful to Mr. Welch's business.

Expense. Expenditures that impact the taxpayer's business in only one taxable year or have a life less than one year (and otherwise qualify) are currently deductible. Expenses can be contrasted with capital expenditures. Because a capital expenditure impacts more than one taxable year, it affects profits in more than one year and the cost should be recovered by the taxpayer over time.[41]

Paid or incurred in the taxable year. The issue of whether an expense is paid or incurred during the taxable year depends on the taxpayer's method of accounting.[42]

Business. The taxpayer must be engaged in a business. Neither the Code nor the regulations provides a definition of business. In *Commissioner v. Groetzinger*[43] the taxpayer was a full-time gambler. In determining whether his gambling activities constituted a business, the court noted that to be engaged in a business the taxpayer had to be "involved in the activity with continuity and regularity and that the taxpayer's primary purpose for engaging in the activity must be for income or profit. A sporadic activity, a hobby, or an amusement diversion does not qualify."[44] The determination is based on an examination of the facts. The court went on to find that the taxpayer was engaged in gambling full time, in good faith, and with regularity. Accordingly, he was engaged in a business.[45]

Requirements for an Expense to Be Deductible under Section 162

The expense must be:

- **Ordinary:** common and accepted in the industry (based on the facts and circumstances).

- **Necessary:** appropriate and helpful.

- **Expense:** have a life of less than one year, or otherwise impact only one taxable year.

- **Paid or incurred during the taxable year.**

- **In carrying on a business:** involved in the activity with continuity and regularity; the taxpayer's primary purpose must be for income or profit. A sporadic activity or hobby does not qualify.

The amount that can be deducted is the amount the taxpayer paid for the item — its basis.

---

40. Welch, 290 U.S. at 113.
41. See Sections 167; 168. See discussion in Chapter 25.
42. Methods of accounting are discussed in Chapters 32 and 33.
43. 480 U.S. 23 (1987).
44. Commissioner v. Groetzinger, 480 U.S. 23, 35 (1987).
45. Groetzinger, 480 U.S. at 35–36.

Salaries. One of the most common expense deductions a business may have is for salaries. To be deductible, a salary must satisfy the requirements of Section 162(a). The Code provides additional guidance with respect to salaries by requiring they must be reasonable.[46] Of course, since an unreasonably large salary would not meet the "ordinary" requirement, it is doubtful that the provision adds any additional requirement for salaries to be deductible. However, it does serve to focus attention on the reasonableness of salaries paid.

Tell Me More

What incentive does a business have to pay unreasonably large salaries?

The incentive usually arises when related taxpayers want to shift income between themselves.

Example: A corporation is treated as a separate taxpayer, meaning that it pays tax on the net income it generates. As with sole proprietorships, a corporation is entitled to claim a deduction for salaries.

Beauty Shop Corporation operates a beauty salon. It is owned equally by two shareholders who also are employed by the corporation as stylists. The corporation pays each shareholder a reasonable salary of $50,000. Its abbreviated tax return might appear as follows:

Income:	$300,000
Salary deduction:	<u>100,000</u>
Taxable income:	$200,000

Beauty Shop Corporation pays out the amount of its net income in dividends, or $100,000 to each of its two shareholders. Thus, each shareholder receives $150,000 from the corporation ($50,000 in salary and $100,000 in dividends).

In sum, the parties report and pay tax on the following net income:

Taxpayer	Net Income
Beauty Shop Corporation	$200,000
Shareholder/Stylist 1	150,000
Shareholder/Stylist 2	<u>150,000</u>
Total taxable income:	$500,000

Because the two shareholders are also the employees of the corporation, they have an incentive to pay themselves an excessive salary. If they paid themselves $150,000 each in salary, the corporation's abbreviated tax return would appear as follows:

---

46. Section 162(a)(1).

Income:	$300,000
Salary deduction:	300,000
Taxable income:	$-0-

Because there is no net income, the corporation does not pay any dividends. Thus, each shareholder receives $150,000 from the corporation in salary (and no dividends).

In sum, the parties report and pay tax on the following net income:

Taxpayer	Net Income
Beauty Shop Corp	$0
Shareholder/Stylist 1	150,000
Shareholder/Stylist 2	150,000
Total taxable income:	$300,000

By paying themselves an excessive salary, the shareholders have reduced taxable income of the combined group of Beauty Shop Corporation and its shareholders by $200,000 (from $500,000 down to $300,000).

Historically, the Tax Court analyzed whether a salary was reasonable based on a list of factors. The factors are not weighted, nor does the presence or absence of any one factor determine the outcome. No factor is determinative.[47]

Factors the Tax Court Has Considered in Determining If Salary Is Reasonable

The following factors have been considered. The factors are not weighted.

- Position held by the employee
- Hours worked by employee.
- Employee duties and responsibilities.
- Contribution of employee to success of company.
- Comparison of past duties and salary with current responsibilities and compensation.
- Amount paid to employees employed by other companies who have similar duties and responsibilities.
- The size of the company, complexities of the company's business, and general economic conditions.

outline

47. See, e.g., Eberl's Claim Service, Inc. v. Commissioner, 249 F.3d 994 (10th Cir. 2001), aff'g, T.C. Memo. 1977-2336; Haffner's Service Stations, Inc. v. Commissioner, 326 F.3d 1 (1st Cir. 2003).

- Whether the employee and employer are "related."
- Computation of salaries in such a way that results in the company not having any taxable income.

Some courts have shifted to using an "independent investor test."[48] Rather than the court looking at a variety of non-directive or determinative factors, the court suggested the focus should be on the economic benefit the employee brings to the business. Whether the salary is reasonable should be evaluated from the perspective of a hypothetical independent investor:

> A relevant inquiry is whether an inactive, independent investor would be willing to compensate the employee as he was compensated. The nature and quality of the services should be considered, as well as the effect of those services on the return the investor is seeing on his investment. The corporation's rate of return on equity would be relevant to the independent investor in assessing the reasonableness of compensation in a small corporation where excessive compensation would noticeably decrease the rate of return.[49]

Clothing. A taxpayer may be in the business of being an employee.[50] As an employee, the taxpayer may be required to wear certain clothing to work. Recall that as a general rule no deduction is allowed for personal expenses. Thus, even though expenditures for clothing are helpful or even essential to the taxpayer's business, they are personal expenditures and are not deductible.

There are, however, situations when a taxpayer is required to wear clothing to work that he would not wear when not working. For example, the work uniform worn by policemen, nurses, and postal carriers would not be suitable wear during non-work hours. The cost of these types of uniforms can qualify as a deductible business expense.[51]

What about the situation where the clothing the taxpayer is required to wear while working is not clothing the taxpayer would chose to wear while not working? In *Pevsner v. Commissioner*[52] the taxpayer worked at an upscale clothing boutique. She was required to wear designer clothing while working. While she could have worn the clothing when not working, she chose not to because they did not fit with her lifestyle and she wanted the clothes to last as long as possible.

The Fifth Circuit considered the test for deductibility of clothing expense and found that the clothing must be of a type specifically required as a condition of employment, not adaptable to general usage as ordinary clothing, and not so worn. To determine whether or not the cost of the clothing at issue met the test, the court had to decide if the test was an objective or a subjective test. In reversing the Tax Court and holding that the test is an objective test, the Fifth Circuit stated:

---

48. See, e.g., Metro Leasing & Dev. Corp. v. Commissioner, 376 F.3d 1015 (9th Cir. 2004); Exacto Spring Corp. v. Commissioner, 196 F.3d 833 (7th Cir. 1999); Dexsil Corp. v. Commissioner, 147 F.3d 96 (2d Cir. 1998); Owensby & Kritikos, Inc., 819 F.2d 1315 (5th Cir. 1987); Elliotts, Inc. v. Commissioner, 716 F.2d 1241, 1245 (9th Cir. 1983).

49. Elliotts, Inc. v. Commissioner, 716 F.2d 1241, 1245 (9th Cir. 1983).

50. See generally United States v. Generes, 405 U.S. 93 (1971); Pevsner v. Commissioner, 628 F.2d 467 (5h Cir. 1980).

51. Rev. Rul. 70-474, 1970-2 C.B. 34. Such employee business expense deductions are "below the line" deductions, subject to the 2 percent floor. Sections 62(a)(1); 67(a), (b).

52. 628 F.2d 467 (5th Cir. 1980).

Under an objective test, no reference is made to the individual taxpayer's lifestyle or personal taste. Instead, adaptability for personal or general use depends upon what is generally accepted for ordinary street wear.

The principal argument in support of an objective test is, of course, administrative necessity. The Commissioner argues that, as a practical matter, it is virtually impossible to determine at what point either price or style makes clothing inconsistent with or inappropriate to a taxpayer's lifestyle. Moreover, the Commissioner argues that the price one pays for the styles one selects are inherently personal choices governed by taste, fashion, and other unmeasurable values. Indeed, the tax court has rejected the argument that a taxpayer's personal taste can dictate whether clothing is appropriate for general use. An objective test, although not perfect, provides a practical administrative approach that allows a taxpayer or revenue agent to look only to objective facts in determining whether clothing required as a condition of employment is adaptable to general use as ordinary streetwear. Conversely, the tax court's reliance on subjective factors provides no concrete guidelines in determining the deductibility of clothing purchased as a condition of employment.

In addition to achieving a practical administrative result, an objective test also tends to promote substantial fairness among the greatest number of taxpayers. As the Commissioner suggests, it apparently would be the tax court's position that two similarly situated YSL boutique managers with identical wardrobes would be subject to disparate tax consequences depending upon the particular manager's lifestyle and "socio-economic level."[53]

Clothing Expenditures That Qualify as a Business Expense

Test: The cost of clothing is deductible if the clothing is:

1. Of a type specifically required as a condition of employment;

2. Not adaptable to general usage as ordinary clothing; and

3. Not so worn.

Application: The cost of the following uniforms qualifies as a deductible expense:

- Uniforms worn by police officers, firemen, letter carriers, nurses, bus drivers.[54]

- Uniforms worn by those in the armed services and reservists.[55]

- Military fatigue uniforms.[56]

Expenses for seeking employment. A taxpayer who is seeking new employment may be in the business of performing services as an employee. If the taxpayer is seeking new employment in the same business, the expenses are currently deductible if directly connected with his business, based on the facts and circumstances. If the taxpayer is seeking

---

53. Pevsner v. Commissioner, 628 F.2d 467, 470–71 (5th Cir. 1980), citations omitted.
54. Rev. Rul. 70-474, 1970-2 C.B. 34.
55. Treas. Reg. § 1.262-1(b)(8).
56. Rev. Rul. 67-115, 1967-1 C.B. 30.

employment in a new business, the expenses are not deductible. If the taxpayer is not employed, his business would consist of the services performed for his past employer if no substantial lack of continuity occurred between the past employment and the seeking of new employment. If there is a substantial lack of continuity or if the taxpayer is seeking employment for the first time, the expenses are not deductible.[57]

Taxpayer's Taxable Income

> Gross income
> – <u>Business expenses</u>
> Taxable income

C. Start Up Costs

To qualify as a currently deductible expense under Section 162, the taxpayer must be carrying on a business. If the taxpayer is only investigating or otherwise preparing to begin a business, the costs do not qualify. To assist taxpayers who have generated such start up costs, Congress enacted Section 195.

Start up costs include expenses for:[58]

- investigating the creation or acquisition of an active business;

- creating an active business; or

- for any activity engaged in for profit and for the production of income before the day on which the active business begins in anticipation of such activity becoming an active business.

To claim a deduction for start up costs, the taxpayer must enter into the business after the costs were incurred and elect to amortize the costs.[59]

If he makes the election, the taxpayer can claim a deduction for start up costs in the year he begins his business. The amount he can deduct is determined by a two-step process. First, he can take an amount in the year he begins his business. The amount is the lesser of two amounts: the total amount of start up costs or $5,000 reduced by the amount by which the start up costs exceed $50,000 (but not below zero).[60] Thus, if he incurs more than $55,000 in start up costs, he is not entitled to any deduction under the first step and the costs must be recovered entirely through the second step. Conversely, if the total amount of start up costs can be claimed under the first step no calculation need be done under the second step.

---

57. Rev. Rul. 75-120, 1970-1 C.B. 55.
58. Section 195(c)(1).
59. Section 195(b).
60. Section 195(b)(1)(A).

Under the second step, any remaining start up costs are amortized ratably over 180 months beginning in the month the taxpayer begins his business.[61]

If a taxpayer goes out of business and the business is liquidated prior to the end of the amortization period, any remaining unamortized start up costs can be deducted as provided under Section 165 in the business's final taxable year.[62]

Steps for Determining Amount of Deductible Start Up Costs

Step One: Identify all start up costs.

Step Two: Determine the amount by which the start up costs exceed $50,000. Subtract that number from $5,000 (but do not go below zero).

Step Three: Determine which is the lesser amount, the amount determined in Step Two or $5,000.

Step Four: Subtract the amount determined in Step Three from the total amount of start up costs.

Step Five: Divide the amount determined in Step Four by 180.

Step Six: Multiply the amount determined in Step Five by the number of months the taxpayer was in business during the year.

Step Seven: In the first year the taxpayer can deduct the total of the amount determined in Step Three plus the amount determined in Step Six. For each subsequent year the taxpayer can deduct the amount determined in Step Six until the total amount of start up costs has been deducted.

Example: Cindy paid $53,000 in start up costs when investigating the creation or acquisition of a bakery. She began her business in March and properly elected to amortize the costs.

Step One: Cindy has $53,000 in start up costs.

Step Two: The start up costs exceed $50,000 by $3,000 ($53,000, less $50,000). Thus, the amount for Step Two is $5,000 − $3,000 = $2,000

Step Three: The lesser amount of the amount determined in Step Two, $2,000, or $5,000 is $2,000.

Step Four: The total amount of start up costs, $53,000, less the amount determined in Step Three, $2,000, is $51,000.

Step Five: The amount determined in Step Four, $51,000, divided by 180 is $283.

Step Six: In the first year, Cindy was in business ten months (March through December). The amount determined in Step Five, $283, multiplied by 10 is $2,830.

Step Seven: In the first year Cindy can deduction the total of the amount determined in Step Three, $2,000, plus the amount determined in Step Six, $2,830, or $4,830. In each subsequent years Cindy can

---

61. Section 195(b)(1)(B).
62. Section 195(b)(2).

deduction $3,396 ($283 × 12 months) until she has recovered the
$53,000 of start up costs.

D. Application of Rules

Example 1. Mariah operates a party supply business out of a small store located in the local mall. As part of her operating expenses, every month she pays the rent, electric bill, and water bill.

To be deductible, the cost of the rent, electricity, and water must be ordinary and necessary expenses paid or incurred in carrying on her business. Because they each satisfy the criteria, she may deduct the payments as business expenses.

Example 2. Noreen operates a print shop. This year she purchased a new copy machine for $20,000.

To be deductible, the cost of the copy machine must be an ordinary and necessary expense paid or incurred in carrying on her business. Because the machine has a life of more than one year, it is not an expense and Noreen may not currently deduct the cost of the machine.

Example 3. Olivia works at a pottery shop. Because the clay she works with is very messy, she wears jeans to work every day.

To be deductible, the jeans must be required as a condition of her employment, they must not be adaptable to general usage as ordinary clothing, and must not be so worn. Because jeans are adaptable to general wear, Olivia may not deduct the cost of her jeans.

Example 4. Paul operates a pizza parlor. His son works for him as a waiter. While Paul pays the other employees $10 per hour (the going rate in the area), he pays his son $15 per hour.

To be deductible, a salary must be an ordinary and necessary expense paid or incurred in carrying on a business. The salaries paid to the other employees meet the criteria and may be deducted. To the extent the amount Paul pays his son exceeds reasonable compensation, it does not meet the criteria and Paul would not be entitled to a deduction.

Example 5. Quimby would like to operate a yoga center. She conducts a feasibility study to help her decide if she should open such a center. Based on the study, she decides to open a yoga center in the southern part of town.

To be deductible, the cost of the feasibility study must be an ordinary and necessary expense paid or incurred in carrying on a business. Because she is not yet engaged in a business, she may not deduct the cost of the feasibility study under Section 162. (If she does begin the business, the costs may be addressed as start up costs under Section 195).

Example 6. Danielle paid $4,000 when investigating the creation or acquisition of a gas station. She properly elected to amortize the start up costs. She can deduct the entire $4,000 in the year she begins the business.

Example 7. Dirk paid $60,000 when investigating the creation or acquisition of a dude ranch. He properly elected to amortize the start up costs. Under the first step, he can deduct the lesser of two amounts: the total amount of start up costs or $5,000 reduced by the amount by which the start up costs exceed $50,000 (but not below zero). Because the start up costs exceed $50,000 by $10,000, the $5,000 is reduced to zero and Dirk is not entitled to any deduction under the first step. Under the second step, Dirk may amortize the entire $60,000 of start up costs ratably over 180 months beginning in the month he begins business.

Example 8. Drew paid $52,000 in start up costs when investigating the creation or acquisition of a fashion boutique. He properly elected to amortize the costs. Under the first step, he can deduct the lesser of two amounts: the total amount of start up costs or $5,000 reduced by the amount by which the start up costs exceed $50,000 (but not below zero). Because the start up costs exceed $50,000 by $2,000, Drew may deduct $3,000 under the first step in the year he begins business. Under the second step, Drew may amortize the remaining $49,000 ($52,000 less $3,000) of start up costs ratably over 180 months beginning in the month he begins business.

E. Problems

1. Able owns and operates a novelty store. Which of the following expenditures would be deductible as a business expense under Section 162?

   a. Lease payment.

   b. Employee salaries.

   c. Amount paid for a new cash register.

   d. Amount paid for a new computer.

   e. Paper for the copy machine.

   f. Cleaning supplies.

2. Beth operates a small cattle farm. Her daughter owns land adjacent to her farm and Beth leases that land and uses it for grazing the cattle. Each year she pays her daughter $50,000 for use of the land. Beth could have leased land, equally good for grazing, located about one mile away for $40,000 per year. May Beth claim as a business expense the $50,000 lease payment made to her daughter?

3. Carrie operates a bookkeeping service. To reduce the tedium of the work, every week she has fresh cut flowers delivered to the office. May Carrie deduct the cost of the flowers?

4. Carl works as a mechanic for a car repair shop. All the mechanics are required to wear a standard uniform that contains the shop's logo and the mechanic's name. May Carl deduct the cost of the uniforms?

5. Caroline owns and operates a yoga center. When she is teaching a yoga class she wears yoga pants. May Caroline deduct the cost of the yoga pants?

6. Randy incurred start up costs when investigating the creation or acquisition of a racing track. He properly elected to amortize the costs. How much of the costs can he claim as an amortization expense on his return in the year he begins his business:

   a. If the start up costs are $3,000?

   b. If the start up costs are $5,000?

   c. If the start up costs are $56,000?

F. Analysis and Application

1. Consider a business you might be interested in operating. Identify at least ten expenses you would expect to incur in running the business.

2. Can you explain to your client the test for determining what expenditures are currently deductible?

3. Your client is considering entering into the car repair business. What start-up expenses might you expect your client to incur?

4. Bejeir was a certified public accountant and member of the Florida bar. His law practice was primarily tax, but he did practice in other areas such as admiralty and probate. Bejeir purchased a sailboat hoping that, through the sailboat, he would make connections among yacht owners. He also created a flag with the numbers "1040" that he flew on the boat. He made some contacts both through the use of the boat and from conversations that arose from flag. He did not use the boat for entertaining or meeting with clients. He did make some use of the boat for personal purposes. For the year he incurred $8,000 in maintenance expenses for the sailboat. May Bejeir deduct the expenses?

    In formulating your analysis and response, you may want to consider:

    *   Welch v. Helvering, 290 U.S. 111 (1933)
    *   Jenkins v. Commissioner, T.C. Memo. 1983-667
    *   Palo Alto Town & Country Village, Inc. v. Commissioner, 565 F.2d 1388 (9th Cir. 1977)

5. Tiffany was well-known in the equestrian world but, due to a divorce, had to restructure her life. To support herself, she decided to begin a business designing horse barns and homes. She discussed her plan with her accountant and a longtime friend who had successfully started her own business. She did not prepare a formal business plan or any cash flow projections.

    Tiffany used her contacts in the industry to obtain clients. She also continued her presence in the equestrian world by competing in and attending horse shows. Through her equestrian-related activities she was able to interact with a large concentration of extraordinarily wealthy people. Moreover, she believed that, to maintain the trust of potential clients, she needed to continue her ownership of horses and active competition. During the year she spent a substantial sum on horse-related care, competition fees, and club memberships. Can Tiffany deduct the cost of her horse-related activities?

    In formulating your analysis and response, you may want to consider:

    *   Welch v. Helvering, 290 U.S. 111 (1933)
    *   Jenkins v. Commissioner, T.C. Memo. 1983-667
    *   Palo Alto Town & Country Village, Inc. v. Commissioner, 565 F.2d 1388 (9th Cir. 1977)

6. Research project: Research Tax Court opinions addressing expenses that do not qualify as "necessary." Prepare a presentation.

7. Research project: Research opinions addressing whether a salary is "reasonable." Prepare a presentation.

Chapter 24

Travel, Entertainment, and Business Meals

Deductions

Personal:	Investment:	**Business:**
• Interest	• Expenses	• Start up expenses
• Taxes	• Depreciation and	• **Expenses**
• Medical expenses	amortization	• Depreciation and
• Education expenses	• Loss from the	amortization
• Moving expenses	disposition of property	• Losses from the
• Child care expenses	• Non-business bad debts	disposition of property
• Charitable contributions		• Business bad debts
• Casualty loses		
• Non-business bad debts		
• Alimony		

Read

Code Sections 161; 162(a); 195

Treas. Reg. §§ 1.162-1(a); 1.162-3; 1.162-6; 1.162-7; 1.162-8; 1.162-9

A. Background

Gross income. Gross income includes income (accessions to wealth) derived from any and all sources.[63] It includes every accession to wealth, unless there is an exception.

Basis. The basis of property is the amount the taxpayer originally paid for the property.[64] In general, a taxpayer will purchase an item for its fair market value. Thus, a taxpayer's basis in property is the fair market value of the property at the time of purchase.

Taxable income. In general, taxable income is the taxpayer's gross income, less all allowable deductions.[65] The taxpayer's liability is based on the amount of the taxpayer's taxable income.[66]

---

63. Section 61(a).
64. Section 1012(a).
65. Section 63(a).
66. Section 1.

The cost of travel, meals, and lodging is inherently personal. However, when associated with a business there is some justification for allowing a deduction as a business expense. Over the years Congress and the courts have struggled to find the right balance between non-deductible personal expenses and deductible business expenses associated with the cost of generating business income.

B. Travel Expenses

Travel costs related to carrying out the taxpayer's business are deductible.[67] For example, the cost of a taxi to visit a client, the cost of flying to take a deposition, and the cost of driving to the courthouse to try a case would all be deductible business expenses. If the taxpayer travels for both personal and business reasons, whether the travel costs are deductible depends on the primary purpose of the travel. If the primary purpose is business, the cost of the travel is deductible. If the primary purpose is personal, the cost of the travel is not deductible, but any expenses incurred at the destination related to the business would be deductible.

Limitations. Because of the overwhelming personal taint, Congress imposed rules that limit the amount that may be deducted when the travel is via a cruise ship or other form of luxury water transportation.[68] It also prohibited any deduction for the amount of travel expenses for travel as a form of education.[69] For example, a Spanish teacher who spends time in Mexico may not deduct the travel expenses as ordinary and necessary business expenses.

If a spouse or dependent travels with the taxpayer, no deduction for expenses related to the travel of the spouse or dependent is allowed unless the spouse or dependent:[70]

- Is a bona fide employee of the taxpayer;
- Is traveling for a bona fide business purpose; and
- The spouse or dependent could otherwise deduct the expense.

1. Commuting Expenses

The cost of commuting to work is a personal expense.[71] Even when the commute to work is substantial, the Supreme Court has found the cost is not deductible as a business expense. In *Commissioner v. Flowers*[72] the taxpayer lived in Jackson, Mississippi, and worked in Mobile, Alabama. While he often used an office in Jackson, on occasion he was required to drive to Mobile to work. The taxpayer claimed a deduction for the cost of the trips, meals, and lodging when he had to travel to Mobile.

The Supreme Court held that, to be deductible, travel expenses had to be reasonable and necessary, incurred away from home, and be incurred in pursuit of business. The

---

67. Section 162.
68. Section 274(m)(1).
69. Section 274(m)(2).
70. Section 274(m)(3).
71. Section 262; Treas. Reg. § 1.262-1(b)(5).
72. 326 U.S. 465 (1946).

court noted that the taxpayer's decision to live so far from his work was not related to the business; the business received no benefit. Accordingly, the court found the travel expenses were personal, non-deductible expenses.[73]

If the taxpayer is required to perform work duties while traveling to work, the courts have allowed the taxpayer to deduct the travel cost. In *Pollei v. Commissioner*[74] the taxpayers were police captains who were considered to be on duty from the time they left their house until the time they returned home. The court allowed them to deduct the travel and maintenance costs of driving their personal cars to work and from work home. The court noted that the deduction would be allowed only in similar situations.

A taxpayer, once at work, may be required to travel for work-related reasons. If the taxpayer has to work in two different locations on the same day for the same employer, he may deduct the cost of travel between the work locations.[75] If the taxpayer works in two different locations on the same day for two different employers, he may deduct the cost of travel between the first work location and the second. The Service considered the taxpayer as being in a business and the travel between the two locations necessary to carry out his business.[76]

Temporary jobs. If the taxpayer has a temporary job, the taxpayer is considered to be traveling. Travel expenses paid or incurred in connection with the temporary assignment away from home are deductible. If the taxpayer is away from home for more than one year, the position is not treated as indefinite and the expenses are not subject to the same rules as temporary jobs.[77] The Service has applied this rule to various fact patterns.[78]

2. Away from Home Expenses

If a taxpayer is away from home on business-related travel he is incurring duplicate costs. Thus, if the taxpayer is away from home, the taxpayer can deduct the cost of meals and lodging.[79] The Code does not define when a taxpayer is away from home. The Service has provided a definition that focuses not on the traditional meaning of home, but rather on the location of the taxpayer's principal place of business. If the taxpayer has more than one employer or works in more than one location, which location is his "home" is determined based on the facts and circumstances.[80] Some appellate courts have followed the Service's definition,[81] others have rejected it in favor of a more traditional definition of "home."[82]

---

73. Id.
74. 877 F.2d 838 (10th Cir. 1989).
75. Rev. Rul. 55-109, 1955-1 C.B. 261.
76. Rev. Rul. 55-109, 1955-1 C.B. 261.
77. Section 162(a).
78. Rev. Rul. 93-86, 1993-2 C.B. 71.
79. Section 162(a)(2).
80. Rev. Rul. 75-432, 1975-2 C.B. 60.
81. See, e.g., Robertson v. Commissioner, 190 F.3d 392, 395–96 (5th Cir. 1999) (noting that "home" was not used in its usual meaning, but rather to refers to the place where the taxpayer performs his most important duties or spends the most time).
82. See, e.g., Rosenspan v. United States, 438 F.2d 905 (2d Cir. 1971) ("home" should be defined as ordinary people would define it).

Meals. In order for the cost of meals to be deductible, the taxpayer has to satisfy the "overnight rule" or "sleep and rest rule." To meet this test, the taxpayer must be released from his employment responsibilities to obtain substantial sleep or rest prior to returning to work. While the release from work need not be a full day, it must be sufficient time to obtain substantial sleep or rest.[83]

Lodging. If the taxpayer is required to pay for a hotel room while on a business trip, the cost is deductible. The basis for the deduction is that the cost of the hotel room is duplicating the taxpayer's cost of maintaining a personal residence.[84]

C. Entertainment Expenses

The cost of entertainment is a personal expense. When the entertainment is undertaken as part of a business activity, it takes on a business aspect. While the Code does provide a business deduction, because entertainment has an inherently personal aspect, it limits the amount the taxpayer can deduct.

First, the cost of the entertainment needs to be established as a business expense. The taxpayer must be able to satisfy Section 162 by establishing the expense was ordinary, necessary, and paid or incurred while engaged in a business. Next, the taxpayer must meet one of two tests.[85]

"Directly related to" test. Under the first test, the expenditure must be "directly related to" the active conduct of the taxpayer's business.[86] In general, to meet this test, the taxpayer must:[87]

- Have more than a general expectation of deriving income or other business benefit at some indefinite future time from the making of the expenditure;

- During the entertainment actively engage in a business meeting, negotiation, discussion, or other bona fide business transaction for the purpose of obtaining income or business benefit;

- Have as the principal aspect of the combined business and entertainment the active conduct of the taxpayer's business; and

- Establish the expenditure is allocable to the taxpayer and persons with whom the taxpayer is engaged in the active conduct of business.

If the taxpayers are not present or there are substantial distractions, the expenditure is generally considered not to directly relate to the taxpayer's business. For example, it is

---

83. Rev. Rul. 75-170, 1975-1 C.B. 60.

84. Section 162(a)(2); Glazer v. Commissioner, T.C. Memo. 1990-645. In those situations were the taxpayer did not duplicate his costs (i.e., would change his residence for longer-term employments), the taxpayer is not permitted to deduct lodging expenses as he is not away from home when he moves to a different job.

85. Section 274(n).

86. Section 274(a)(1)(A).

87. Treas. Reg. § 1.274-2(c)(3).

likely the distractions will be substantial when a meeting is held at a night club, sporting event, or cocktail party.[88]

"Associated with" test. Under the second test, the expenditure must be "associated with" the active conduct of the business.[89] The expenditure will be considered not directly related to the active conduct of the taxpayer's business unless:[90]

- It was associated with the active conduct of a business; and
- The entertainment directly preceded or followed a substantial and bona fide business discussion.

The taxpayer's purpose for making the expenditure must be a "clear business purpose." An intent to maintain business goodwill or obtain new business will meet this test.[91] Whether there is a substantial and bona fide business discussion depends on the facts and circumstances. To meet this requirement, the taxpayer does not need to spend more time on business than on entertainment.[92]

If the taxpayer can meet one of these tests he can deduct one-half of the amount otherwise allowable.[93]

D. Business Meals

The cost of meals is a personal expense. When the meal is part of business entertainment, it takes on a business aspect. While the Code does provide a business deduction, because meals have an inherently personal aspect, it limits the amount the taxpayer can deduct.

First, the expense of the meal needs to be established as a business expense. The taxpayer must be able to satisfy Section 162 by establishing the expense was ordinary, necessary, and paid or incurred while engaged in a business. Next, the taxpayer must establish:[94]

- The meal is not lavish or extravagant; and
- The taxpayer (or an employee of the taxpayer) is present at the meal.

If the taxpayer can meet these requirements he can deduct one-half of the amount otherwise allowable.[95]

Meals for the taxpayer. Section 274 does not directly address whether a taxpayer can deduct the cost of his own meals. The general rule is that the cost of meals (while not away from home) are personal, nondeductible expenses.[96] If the taxpayer can establish that the cost is different from or in excess of what the taxpayer would usually spend, the excess cost might be deductible.

---

88. Treas. Reg. § 1.274-2(c)(7).
89. Section 274(a)(1)(A).
90. Treas. Reg. § 1.274-2(d)(1).
91. Treas. Reg. § 1.274-2(d)(2).
92. Treas. Reg. § 1.274-2(d)(3)(i)(a).
93. Section 274(n)(1).
94. Section 274(k).
95. Section 274(n)(1).
96. Section 262: Sutter v. Commissioner, 21 T.C. 170 (1953).

E. Substantiation

Section 274 sets forth specific substantiation requirements for expenses that constitute entertainment. The taxpayer must have either adequate records or have sufficient evidence to corroborate his statement of the following:[97]

- Amount of the expense;
- Time and place of the travel, entertainment, or amusement;
- Business purpose for the expense; and
- The business relationship to the taxpayer of the persons entertained.

To constitute adequate records, generally the taxpayer must maintain an account book, diary, or similar record with entries made at or near the time of the expense with documents that support the entries.[98] No substantiation is needed for per diem and mileage allowances.[99]

If the taxpayer cannot provide the substantiation, no deduction is allowed.[100]

F. Application of Rules

Example 1. Joan lives in Fairfax, Virginia, and works in Washington, D.C. Every day she takes the metro to work. Joan is not entitled to deduct the cost of taking the metro from home to work or from work to home.

Example 2. Louise is a large animal veterinarian. Every day she travels from farm to farm to meet with clients. Louise is entitled to deduct the travel cost of driving between farms.

Example 3. Margaret was an estate planning attorney. When she completed a complex estate plan, she would take the client to lunch and explain the documents and review the plan. She would make reservations at a nice, but not extravagant, restaurant. Margaret maintained adequate records regarding the amount of the expense, the date and location of the restaurant, and the name of the client. Margaret can deduct one-half of the cost of the lunch.

G. Problems

1. Gidget lived in an apartment that was three blocks from her work. She decided to purchase a house. When she bought a small bungalow in the suburbs, her commute to work increased to a 20 minutes drive each way. After she moved to the suburbs, may Gidget deduct the cost of commuting to work?

2. Stuart is a real estate appraiser with a business office in town.

    a. May Stuart deduct the cost of travel from home to work or from work to home?

---

97. Section 274(d).
98. Treas. Reg. § 1.274-5T(c)(2).
99. Treas. Reg. § 1.274-5(g).
100. Section 274(d).

b. When Stuart travels from real estate location to real estate location during the day, may he deduct the travel cost?

c. If Stuart travels from home directly to a real estate location, may he deduct the travel cost?

3. Theresa is a financial consultant. Once a month she would invite a client to a five-star restaurant. During the dinner she would discuss a variety of general financial investment possibilities and the client's specific investment strategies. Sometimes, but not at every dinner, the client would chose to make some additional investments. May Theresa deduct the cost of her meal and her client's meal?

H. Analysis and Application

1. Ethel is an actor who lived in Hollywood. She obtained a job acting in a Broadway play. Because the play was expected to run for some time, she rented an apartment in New York. Is Ethel's home for tax purposes in Hollywood or New York?

2. Richard played the tuba for the San Francisco orchestra. It was not possible for him to commute to work with the tuba on public transportation. Accordingly, he would travel by cab. May Richard deduct the cost of the cab?

Chapter 25

Depreciation and Amortization

Deductions

Personal:	Investment:	Business:
• Interest • Taxes • Medical expenses • Education expenses • Moving expenses • Child care expenses • Charitable contributions • Casualty loses • Non-business bad debts • Alimony	• Expenses • Depreciation and amortization • Loss from the disposition of property • Non-business bad debts	• Start up expenses • Expenses • **Depreciation and amortization** • Losses from the disposition of property • Business bad debts

Read

Code Sections 167(a); 168(a), (c), (d)(1), (d)(2), (d)(4)(A), (d)(4)(B)

Treas. Reg. §§ 1.167(a)-1(a); 1.167(a)-10(a); 1.167(g)-1

A. Background

Gross income. Gross income includes income (accessions to wealth) derived from any and all sources.[101] It includes every accession to wealth, unless there is an exception.

Basis. The basis of property is the amount the taxpayer originally paid for the property.[102] In general, a taxpayer will purchase an item for its fair market value. Thus, a taxpayer's basis in property is the fair market value of the property at the time of purchase.

Taxable income. In general, taxable income is the taxpayer's gross income, less all allowable deductions.[103] The taxpayer's liability is based on the amount of the taxpayer's taxable income.[104]

---

101. Section 61(a).
102. Section 1012(a).
103. Section 63(a).
104. Section 1.

B. Depreciation

One of the overarching objectives of the Code is to impose tax on a taxpayer's accession to wealth. When the taxpayer operates his own business, his taxable increase in wealth is not his gross income. Rather, it is his gross income less the costs he incurred to generate the income.

The previous chapter discussed the allowance of a deduction for the expenses a taxpayer incurs in his business.[105] A taxpayer's accession to wealth would be skewed if he were similarly allowed to deduct expenditures that had an impact on his business spanning more than one year. For example, if a taxpayer was allowed to deduct the entire cost of a computer, desk, copy machine, building, and land in the year of purchase, his income would be artificially low in that year. In subsequent years, while he was still using those items in his business (but not getting a deduction for the cost of those items), his income would be artificially high.

The more economically correct solution is to recover a portion of the cost over the length of time the asset is used in the business. In essence, the decrease in value of the asset is the cost associated with using the asset in the business. This method of recovering the cost of the property is called "depreciation" when associated with tangible property and "amortization" when associated with intangible property.

For an asset to qualify for depreciation or amortization, the asset must:[106]

- Be purchased and used in the taxpayer's business,[107]
- Have a life extending more than one year, and
- Wear out over time.

Section 167. Depreciation.

(a) General Rule. — There shall be allowed as a depreciation deduction a reasonable allowance for the exhaustion, wear and tear (including a reasonable allowance for obsolescence) —

(1) of property used in the trade or business....

Consider

- Depreciation is the cost of the property broken down into the equivalent of expense deductions allowed each year, continuing for the tax life of the property (i.e., until the cost of the property is fully recovered).

---

105. See Section 162.
106. Section 167(a)(1).
107. Depreciation also is allowed for assets purchased and used in a taxpayer's investment activities that have a life extending more than one year and wear out over time. See the discussion in Chapter 29.

- Even though the taxpayer may have recovered the entire cost of the property through depreciation, the property may still be of use in his business. The actual life and the "tax life" may not coincide.

While the Code provides that a taxpayer is entitled to claim depreciation based on the cost of the property and the life of the property, the taxpayer and the Commissioner often disagreed on the useful life of an asset. To eliminate this controversy Congress provided for standardized useful lives for some assets. It also provided for alternative methods of recovering the cost of the asset.[108]

1. Tangible Personal Property

Tangible person property is placed into class lives based generally on the length of time over which Congress expects the taxpayer to recover the cost of the property.[109]

Examples

- Tangible personal property includes items such as computers, stoves, copy machines, cars, trees, equipment, desks, sidewalks, and furniture.
- Class lives and an example of a few of the assets included in that class life are as follows.

    3-year property: tractor unit for over-the-road use, race horse.

    5-year property: automobile, taxi, truck, computer, office machinery.

    7-year property: desk, files, agricultural machinery and equipment.

    10-year property: barge, tug, tree, vine bearing fruits or nuts.

With the class life dictating how long it will take the taxpayer to recover the cost of the property for tax purposes, a percentage of the cost is recovered each year.[110]

Because Congress wanted the taxpayer to be able to claim more depreciation in the early years (which leaves less to be claimed in later year), the amount of depreciation the taxpayer is entitled to claim changes from year to year. The amount is determined by multiplying the cost of the property by the applicable percentage from the depreciation chart.[111] When the depreciation allowed during each of the years is totaled it equals the original cost of the property. This recovery methodology is the modified accelerated cost recovery system (MACRS).

The depreciation charts are as follows:[112]

---

108. Section 168 carries out Section 167 by providing for the depreciation of property based on specific rules.
109. Section 168(c), (e); Rev. Proc. 87-56, 1987-2 C.B. 674.
110. Section 168(b)(1).
111. Rev. Proc. 87-57, 1987-2 C.B. 687.
112. Id. Property also can be classified as fifteen- or twenty-year property.
The taxpayer may elect out of using the method represented in the chart (the double-declining

Recovery Period	3-Year	5-Year	7-Year	10-Year
Year 1	33.33%	20.00%	14.28%	10.00%
Year 2	44.45%	32.00%	24.49%	18.00%
Year 3	14.81%	19.20%	17.49%	14.40%
Year 4	7.41%	11.52%	12.49%	11.52%
Year 5		11.52%	8.93%	9.22%
Year 6		5.76%	8.93%	7.37%
Year 7			8.93%	6.55%
Year 8			4.46%	6.55%
Year 9				6.56%
Year 10				6.55%
Year 11				3.28%

Example. Mary purchased a piece of equipment for $100,000 and used the equipment in her business. The equipment is classified as 5-year property. Mary is entitled to recover the cost of the equipment over time, as follows:

Year	Calculation	Yearly Depreciation
1	$100,000 × 20%	$20,000
2	$100,000 × 32%	$32,000
3	$100,000 × 19.2%	$19,200
4	$100,000 × 11.52%	$11,520
5	$100,000 × 11.52%	$11,520
6	$100,000 × 5.76%	$5,760
Total Depreciation:		$100,000

Convention. To be entitled to claim depreciation the taxpayer must place the property in service in his business. For the year the taxpayer places the property in service he will not have used it in his business for the entire taxable year. While the taxpayer could compute exactly how many days the asset was used in his business during the initial year

method) and recover the cost of the property using the straight-line method, or in equal amounts over the life of the property. See the "Tell Me More" discussion box for more information on the straight-line method of depreciation.

and prorate the first-year's depreciation, Congress elected a much simpler method. For the first year, the taxpayer is entitled to claim one-half of the year's depreciation.[113] Note that the chart already takes this into consideration and provides a percentage for one-half of the first year's depreciation.

If the taxpayer sells the property prior to claiming all available depreciation, the same issue arises. During the year of sale, the taxpayer does not use the property in his business the entire taxable year. As with the first year, for the year of sale the taxpayer is entitled to claim one-half of the year's depreciation.[114] The taxpayer must make this calculation.

This method of computing a partial year's worth of depreciation is referred to as the convention. Tangible personal property uses a one-half year convention.

Example. Mary purchased a piece of equipment in June for $100,000 and used the equipment in her business. The equipment is classified as 5-year property. In the first year, Mary is entitled to a $20,000 depreciation deduction ($100,000 × 20%). Note that the percentage from the chart has already been adjusted to calculate one-half year's worth of depreciation (1/2 × 40% = 20%).

In Year 4 Mary sells the property. During the year of sale Mary does not use the property in her business for the entire taxable year. Applying the one-half year convention, Mary is entitled to one-half of the depreciation allowed in Year 4, or $100,000 × 11.52% × ½ = $5,760.

Because of the half-year convention and only a portion of the first year's depreciation being recovered in the first year, depreciation continues into the year following the asset's actual class life. For example, for property with a three-year class life, it will take the taxpayer at total of four years to recover the cost. For property with a five-year class life, it will take the taxpayer six years to recover the cost. For property with a fifteen-year class life, it will take the taxpayer sixteen years to recover the cost of the property.

Tell Me More

To prevent taxpayers from abusing the one-half year convention by placing all or a majority of assets into service in the later part of the year (and receiving one-half year's worth of depreciation), the Code may provide that the taxpayer use the mid-quarter convention.[115]

If the amount of tangible personal property placed in service during the last three months of the year has an aggregate basis greater than 40 percent of the aggregate basis of all properties placed in service that year, the mid-quarter convention applies in place of the half year convention. Tables that can be used to compute the amount of allowable depreciation using the one-quarter convention can be found in Revenue Procedure 87-57.

---

113. Section 168(d)(1).
114. Id.
115. Section 168(d)(3).

Relationship with Adjusted Basis. The basis of property is the cost of the property at the time it was purchased. As the cost is "recovered" by the taxpayer through depreciation, the basis is reduced (adjusted).[116] Depreciation must be taken based on the depreciation method. In other words, it cannot be saved for a later date. This result is accomplished by the basis always being reduced by the allowable amount of depreciation for that year. Similarly, if the taxpayer miscalculates the amount of allowable depreciation and claims too much, the basis is reduced by the amount claimed. In sum, the basis is reduced by the greater of the amount the taxpayer claimed or should have claimed.[117]

Once the basis in the property is reduced to zero, the taxpayer has completely recovered the cost of the property and the depreciation deductions have been used to reduce the taxpayer's income over time. Once fully depreciated, no further deductions with respect to that property are allowed.

Formula — Adjusted Basis

Adjusted basis = original cost + capital expenditures − depreciation

Adjusted basis cannot be less than zero.

Example. Mary purchased a piece of equipment for $100,000 and used the equipment in her business. The equipment is classified as 5-year property. Mary is entitled to recover the cost of the equipment over time and must reduce her basis as follows:

Year	Calculation	Depreciation	Adjusted Basis
1	$100,000 × 20%	$20,000	$80,000
2	$100,000 × 32%	32,000	48,000
3	$100,000 × 19.2%	19,200	28,800
4	$100,000 × 11.52%	11,520	17,280
5	$100,000 × 11.52%	11,520	5,760
6	$100,000 × 5.76%	<u>5,760</u>	-0-
		$100,000	

Tell Me More

The depreciation methodology that applies to tangible personal property is the modified accelerated cost recovery system (MACRS) and is set forth in Section

---

116. Section 1016(a)(1).
117. Treas. Reg. § 1.1016-3(a).

168. It incorporates a "double declining" method. Under this method, using the adjusted basis of the property, the taxpayer is permitted to claim twice what he could be entitled to under straight-line. In the year straight-line depreciation would result in a larger depreciation deduction, the taxpayer must switch to the straight-line method. Rather than use the charts provided by the Service, the taxpayer could compute the allowable amount of depreciation.

Example. Mary purchased a piece of equipment for $100,000 and used the equipment in her business. The equipment is classified as 5-year property. Under the straight-line method Mary would be able to recover the cost of the property ratably over 5 years, or 20% each year (20,000 each year). Under the double-declining method, Mary is entitled to recover double that amount, or 40% each year. In the first year, the half-year convention applies. Mary is entitled to recover the cost of the equipment over time as follows:

Year	Calculation	Depreciation	Adjusted Basis
1	$100,000 × 40% × ½	$20,000	$80,000
2	$80,000 × 40%	32,000	48,000
3	$48,000 × 40%	19,200	28,800
4	$28,800 × 40%	11,520	17,280
	- switch to straight-line -		
5	$17,280 × 2/3	11,520	5,760
6	$5,760	5,760	-0-
Totals:		$100,000	

Note the allowable amount of depreciation is the same as that determined using the depreciation chart.

2. Real Property

Section 168 provides that a taxpayer depreciates real property using the straightline method.[118] Real property is divided into residential and non-residential property based on the use of the property.[119] For example, apartment buildings would be classified as residential property and shopping malls would be characterized as nonresidential property. For residential property, it will take the taxpayer 27.5 years to recover the cost. For non-

118. Section 168(b)(3).
119. Section 168(b)(3), (c).

residential property, it will take the taxpayer 39 years to recover the cost.[120] The amount of allowable depreciation is determined by multiplying the cost of the property by the applicable percentage, determined by the month the taxpayer placed the building in service, from the depreciation chart.

The depreciation charts are as follows:

Residential Rental Property (%)

Year	Jan	Feb	Mar	Apr	May	June	July	Aug	Sep	Oct	Nov	Dec
1	3.485	3.182	2.879	2.576	2.273	1.97	1.667	1.364	1.061	.758	.455	.152
2–27	3.636	3.636	3.636	3.636	3.636	3.636	3.636	3.636	3.636	3.636	3.636	3.636
28	1.87	2.273	2.576	2.879	3.182	3.485	3.636	3.636	3.636	3.636	3.636	3.636
29	0	0	0	0	0	0	.152	.455	.758	1.061	1.364	1.667

Non-Residential Rental Property (%)

Year	Jan	Feb	Mar	Apr	May	June	July	Aug	Sep	Oct	Nov	Dec
1	2.461	2.247	2.033	1.819	1.605	1.391	1.177	.963	.749	.535	.321	.107
2–39	2.564	2.564	2.564	2.564	2.564	2.564	2.564	2.564	2.564	2.564	2.564	2.564
40	.107	.321	.535	.749	.963	1.177	1.391	1.605	1.819	2.033	2.247	2.461

120. Section 168(c).

Example. Nancy purchased a shopping mall in April for $1,000,000. The real property is non-residential real property, and Nancy is entitled to recover the cost of the shopping mall over time as follows:

Year	Calculation	Yearly Depreciation
1	$1,000,000 × 1.819%	$18,190
2	$1,000,000 × 2.564%	$25,640
3	$1,000,000 × 2.564%	$25,640
	. . .	
38	$1,000,000 × 2.564%	$25,640
39	$1,000,000 × 2.564%	$25,640
40	$1,000,000 × .749%	$7,490
Total Depreciation:		$1,000,000

Convention. To be entitled to claim depreciation, the taxpayer must place the property in service in his business. For the year the taxpayer places the property in service, he will not have used it in his business for the entire taxable year. While the taxpayer could compute exactly how many days the asset was used in his business during the initial year and prorate the first-year's depreciation, Congress elected a simpler route. For the first year, the taxpayer is entitled to claim one-half of the depreciation for the month the building was placed in service and the depreciation for the remaining months.[121] Note that the chart already takes this into consideration and calculates one-half of the month the asset was placed in service and the remaining month's depreciation for the first year.

If the taxpayer sells the property prior to claiming all available depreciation, the same issue arises. During the year of sale, the taxpayer does not use the property in his business the entire taxable year. As with the first year, for the year of sale the taxpayer is entitled to claim depreciation for one-half of the month the asset was sold and all prior months. The taxpayer must make this calculation. This convention for real property is called the one-half month convention.

Example. Nancy purchased a shopping mall in April for $1,000,000. The real property is non-residential real property. In the first year Nancy is entitled to a $18,190 depreciation deduction. Note that the percentage from the chart has already been adjusted to calculate the depreciation allocable to half of April and all of May through December.

In June of Year 5 Nancy sells the property. During the year of sale Nancy does not use the property in her business for the entire taxable year. Applying the one-half month convention Nancy is entitled to one-half of June and all of January through May, or 5.5/12 × 2.564% × $1,000,000 = $11,772.

---

121. Section 168(d)(2).

Tell Me More

The depreciation methodology that applies to real property is the straight-line method. It allows the cost to be recovered ratably (evenly) over the life of the asset. Rather than use the charts provided by the Service, the taxpayer could compute the allowable amount of depreciation.

Example. Nancy purchased a shopping mall in April for $1,000,000. The building is non-residential real property, and Nancy is entitled to recover the cost of the shopping mall over 39 years, applying the one-half month convention, as follows:

Year	Calculation	Yearly Depreciation*
1	$1,000,000 \times 8.5/12 \times 1/39$	$18,162
2	$1,000,000 \times 1/39$	$25,641
3	$1,000,000 \times 1/39$	$25,641
	. . .	
38	$1,000,000 \times 1/39$	$25,641
39	$1,000,000 \times 1/39$	$25,641
40	$1,000,000 \times 3.5/12 \times 1/39$	$7,478
Total Depreciation:		$1,000,000

Note that the first year of depreciation is split between year 1 and year 40. The depreciation allocable to January through March and one-half of April are claimed in year one. The remainder of the year, one-half of April and May through December, are claimed in year 40.

* The numbers are slightly different due to rounding.

Relationship with Adjusted Basis. The basis of property is the cost of the property at the time it was purchased. As the cost is "recovered" by the taxpayer through depreciation, the basis is reduced (adjusted).[122] Once the basis in the property is reduced to zero, the taxpayer has completely recovered the cost of the property and the depreciation deductions have been used to reduce the taxpayer's income over time. Once fully depreciated, no further deductions with respect to that property are allowed.

Example. Nancy purchased a shopping mall in April for $1,000,000. The building is non-residential real property, and Nancy is entitled to recover the cost of the shopping mall over time, reducing her basis, as follows:

---

122. Section 1016(a).

Year	Calculation	Yearly Depreciation	Adjusted Basis
1	$1,000,000 × 1.819%	$18,190	$981,810
2	$1,000,000 × 2.564%	$25,640	956,170
3	$1,000,000 × 2.564%	$25,640	930,530
	. . .		
38	$1,000,000 × 2.564%	$25,640	33,130
39	$1,000,000 × 2.564%	$25,640	7,490
40	$1,000,000 × .749%	$7,490	-0-
Total:		$1,000,000	

3. Intangible Property

Section 168 does not address intangible property. Congress eventually filled this gap by enacting Section 197. Section 197 provides that the cost of certain intangible assets is recovered ratably over 15 years (180 months) beginning in the month the intangible asset is placed in service. Because the property is an intangible asset, the deduction is referred to as amortization.

Definition — Intangible Property

Intangible property that is depreciated over 15 years includes:[123]

- Goodwill
- Going-concern value
- Workforce in place
- Customer lists
- Patent
- Copyright
- License
- Covenant not to compete
- Franchise
- Trademark

Example. Ollie purchased a business, including goodwill, in March. He paid $36,000 for the goodwill. Goodwill is intangible property, and Ollie is entitled to recover the cost over 180 months as follows:

---

123. Section 197(d).

Year	Calculation	Yearly Amortization
1	$36,000 × 10 × 1/180	$2,000
2	$36,000 × 12/180	$2,400
3	$36,000 × 12/180	$2,400
	. . .	
15	$36,000 × 12/180	$2,400
16	$36,000 × 2/180	$400
Total Amortization:	$36,000	

Relationship with Adjusted Basis. The basis of the intangible asset is the cost of the asset at the time it was purchased. As the cost is "recovered" by the taxpayer through amortization, the basis is reduced (adjusted).[124] Once the basis in the intangible asset is reduced to zero, the taxpayer has been able to completely recover the cost of the asset and the amortization deductions have been used to reduce the taxpayer's income over time. Once fully amortized, no further deductions with respect to that asset are allowed.

Example. Using the same example as from above, Ollie purchased a business, including goodwill, in March. He paid $36,000 for the goodwill. Goodwill is intangible property, and Ollie entitled to recover the cost over 180 months, as follows:

Year	Calculation	Amortization	Adjusted Basis
1	$36,000 × 10 × 1/180	$2,000	$34,000
2	$36,000 × 12/180	2,400	31,600
3	$36,000 × 12/180	2,400	29,200
	. . .		
14	$36,000 × 12/180	2,400	2,800
15	$36,000 × 12/180	2,400	400
16	$36,000 × 2/180	400	-0-
Total Amortization		$36,000	

4. Other Property

If the property is not tangible person property (Section 168), real property (Section 168), or intangible property (Section 197), the cost can be recovered ratably under the straight-line method (Section 167) if the taxpayer can establish:

- That the taxpayer purchased the asset and placed it in service;
- The cost of the property

---

124. Section 1016(a).

- That the property wears out over time; and
- The length of time it will take the asset to wear out.

Tell Me More

Under the straight-line method, the taxpayer recovers the cost of the property ratably over its useful life.

Example. On July 1 the taxpayer paid $3,000 for fire insurance for his business. The insurance extends for three years. Because the useful life of the insurance is three years, the taxpayer recovers the cost ratably over that time.

Year	Calculation	Yearly Amortization
1	$3,000/3 × ½	$500
2	$3,000/3	1,000
3	$3,000/3	1,000
4	$3,000/3 × ½	500
Total Amortization:		$3,000

Summary — Depreciation

To qualify for depreciation or amortization, the asset must:
- Be purchased by the taxpayer
- Be used in the taxpayer's business;
- Have a life or benefit of more than one year; and
- Wear out over time.

The determination of how much depreciation is allowed each year depends on whether the asset is:
- Tangible personal property
- Real property
- Intangible property
- Another type of property

---

5. Bonus Depreciation

In certain situations a taxpayer may elect to claim bonus depreciation.[125] Bonus depreciation does not mean the taxpayer is entitled to depreciation totaling an amount

---

125. Section 179(a). Note that bonus depreciation is not available for property purchased for an investment activity. Depreciation of investment property is discussed in Chapter 29.

greater than what he paid for the property. Rather, it means that the taxpayer may claim more depreciation in the year he places the asset in service (and, therefore, less in later years).

Bonus depreciation is one area of the Code that has seen many changes over the years. Thus, it is important to make sure you have read the most recent version of Section 179 before giving advice to a client.

Tell Me More

On many occasions Congress has implemented additional bonus-type depreciation provisions, allowing the taxpayer to claim additional amounts of depreciation in the first year the property is placed in service (with corresponding less depreciation in the following years). These provisions often are available only for a limited amount of time, operating as an incentive for the taxpayers to utilize them before they expire. See for example Section 168(k). If the taxpayer is interested in maximizing depreciation deductions in the year the property is placed in service, it is worth reviewing Section 168 for additional, temporary provisions allowing such additional depreciation.

Applicable property. If the taxpayer has placed tangible personal property depreciated using MACRS or qualifying real property into service during the taxable year, he may elect to claim bonus depreciation.[126]

Impact of making election. If the taxpayer elects to claim bonus depreciation, he may claim up to $500,000 of depreciation in the year he places the asset in service.[127] The remainder of the cost of the property is recovered under the usual depreciation method. Note this means that in the first year the taxpayer can claim both bonus depreciation and regular (MACRS) depreciation.

Limitations on amount of bonus depreciation. There are three applicable limitations on the amount of bonus depreciation that can be claimed. The first limitation is that the amount of bonus depreciation claimed cannot exceed the cost of the property.[128]

Example. The taxpayer purchased an oven for $5,000 and elected to claim bonus depreciation. The most bonus depreciation he can claim is $5,000. Note that, after claiming the bonus depreciation, he has recovered all of his basis in the oven (his adjusted basis is zero) and he is not entitled to any additional depreciation.

The second limitation is that the amount of bonus depreciation claimed cannot exceed the taxable income derived from the business (before considering any bonus depreciation).[129]

Example. Taxpayer purchased a piece of equipment for $600,000 and elected to claim bonus depreciation. The taxable income from his business is $20,000. The most bonus depreciation he can claim is $20,000. After claiming $20,000 of bonus depreciation, the

---

126. Section 179(d)(1).
127. Section 179(b)(1)(D).
128. Section 179.
129. Section 179(b)(3).

remaining $580,000 ($600,000 less $20,000 of bonus depreciation) can be recovered using his regular depreciation method.

The third limitation is that, for every dollar over $2,000,000 that the taxpayer spends on tangible personal property, he must reduce the amount of bonus depreciation he can claim.[130]

Example. Taxpayer purchased a total of $2,100,000 of tangible personal property. Because the cost of the purchased tangible personal property exceeds $2,000,000 by $100,000, he must reduce the amount of bonus depreciation by that amount. Thus, the taxpayer can claim $400,000 ($500,000 - $100,000) of bonus depreciation.

Examples

Amount Spent on Tangible Personal Property	Amount Spent over $200,000	Amount of Allowable Bonus Depreciation
$2,200,000	$200,000	$300,000
$2,300,000	300,000	200,000
$2,400,000	400,000	100,000
$2,600,000	600,000	-0-

Example. Bob purchased a piece of equipment for $800,000. He will use the equipment in his business and the equipment has a five year class life. It is the only tangible personal property he purchased that year and his business had taxable income of $900,000. He elected bonus depreciation.

None of the three limitations apply and Bob can claim $500,000 of bonus depreciation. Bob recovers the remaining $300,000 cost of his property ($800,000 cost, less $500,000 bonus depreciation) using his regular depreciation method.

Year	Calculation	Depreciation	Adjusted Basis
1	Bonus	$500,000	300,000
1	$300,000 × 20%	60,000	240,000
2	300,000 × 32%	96,000	144,000
3	300,000 × 19.2%	57,600	86,400
4	300,000 × 11.52%	34,560	51,840
5	300,000 × 11.52%	34,560	17,280
6	300,000 × 5.76%	17,280	-0-
Total Depreciation:		$800,000	

---

130. Section 179(b)(2)(D).

Note that in the first year Bob's total amount of depreciation was equal to the bonus depreciation plus the regular depreciation. Thus, Bob claimed $560,000 of depreciation in that year.

Summary — A Difference in Timing

A business expenditure is recovered using one of the following methods:
- If the expenditure has a benefit that impacts only one year, the entire cost is recovered during that year.
- If the expenditure has a benefit that impacts more than one year and the asset wears out over time, the cost is recovered over time.
- If the expenditure has a benefit that impacts more than one year and the asset does not wear out over time, the taxpayer's capital investment (i.e., basis) is recovered only upon sale of the property.

Taxpayer's Taxable Income

   Gross income
 − Business expenses
 − <u>Depreciation and/or amortization</u>
   Taxable income

C. Application of Rules

Example 1. Tangible personal property. Flo owns and operates a small business. She purchased for use in her business a new desk for $20,000. The desk is classified as 7-year property. She made no elections. Flo is entitled to recover the cost of the desk over time as follows:

Year	Calculation	Yearly Depreciation
1	$20,000 × 14.28%	$2,856
2	$20,000 × 24.49%	4,898
3	$20,000 × 17.49%	3,498
4	$20,000 × 12.49%	2,498
5	$20,000 × 8.93%	1,786
6	$20,000 × 8.93%	1,786
7	$20,000 × 8.93%	1,786
8	$20,000 × 4.46%	<u>892</u>
Total Depreciation:		$20,000

Example 2. Real property. Gregg purchased an apartment building in June, paying $500,000. He made no elections. The real property is residential real property, and Gregg is entitled to recover the cost of the apartment building over time as follows:

Year	Calculation	Yearly Depreciation
1	$500,000 × 1.97%	$9,850
2	$500,000 × 3.636%	18,180
3	$500,000 × 3.636%	18,180
	. . .	
26	$500,000 × 3.636%	18,180
27	$500,000 × 3.636%	18,180
28	$500,000 × 3.485%	17,425
Total Depreciation:		$500,000

Example 3. Intangible property. Harry purchased a business in November. As part of the purchase price he paid the seller $25,000 for the going-concerning value of the business.

The going-concern value is an intangible asset, and Harry is entitled to recover the cost over 15 years, or 180 months, as follows:

Year	Calculation	Amortization
1	$25,000 × 2 × 1/180	$277
2	$25,000 × 12/180	1,666
3	$25,000 × 12/180	1,666
	. . .	
15	$25,000 × 12/180	1,666
16	$25,000 × 10/180	1,388
Total Amortization:		$25,000

Example 4. Tangible personal property and bonus depreciation. Arlie owns and operates a soda shop. She purchased for use in her business a new piece of equipment (5-year property) for $900,000 and elected bonus depreciation. It was the only tangible personal property she purchased that year, and her business had taxable income of $600,000.

None of the three limitations apply, and Arlie can claim $500,000 of bonus depreciation in the first year. Arlie recovers the remaining $400,000 cost of her property ($900,000 cost, less $500,000 of bonus depreciation) using her regular depreciation method.

Year	Calculation	Depreciation
1	Bonus	$500,000
1	$400,000 × 20%	80,000
2	400,000 × 32%	128,000
3	400,000 × 19.2%	76,800
4	400,000 × 11.52%	46,080
5	400,000 × 11.52%	46,080
6	400,000 × 5.76%	23,040
		$900,000

Note that Arlie will claim a total of $580,000 of depreciation in the first year.

Example 5. Tangible personal property and bonus depreciation. Betsy owns and operates a bakery. She purchased for use in her business a new piece of equipment (5-year property) for $300,000 and elected bonus depreciation. It was the only tangible personal property she purchased that year, and her business had taxable income of $600,000.

Because the cost of the property is less than $500,000, the most bonus depreciation she can claim is the cost of the property, or $300,000. After claiming bonus depreciation in the first year, Betsy has completely recovered the cost of the equipment.

Example 6. Tangible personal property and bonus depreciation. Chris owns and operates a candy store. He purchased for use in his business a new piece of equipment (5-year property) for $600,000 and elected bonus depreciation. It was the only tangible personal property he purchased that year, and his business had taxable income of $200,000.

Because the taxable income from his business is less than $500,000, the most bonus depreciation he can claim is the amount of taxable income, or $200,000. Chris recovers the remaining $400,000 cost of his property ($600,000 cost, less $200,000 of bonus deprecation) using his regular depreciation method.

Year	Calculation	Depreciation
1	Bonus	$200,000
1	$400,000 × 20%	80,000
2	400,000 × 32%	128,000
3	400,000 × 19.2%	76,800
4	400,000 × 11.52%	46,080
5	400,000 × 11.52%	46,080
6	400,000 × 5.76%	23,040
		$600,000

Note that Chris will claim a total of $280,000 of depreciation in the first year.

Example 7. Tangible personal property and bonus depreciation. Danny owns and operates a department store. He purchased for use in his business a new piece of equipment (5-year property) for $2,200,000 and elected bonus depreciation. It was the only tangible personal property he purchased that year, and his business had taxable income of $500,000.

Because he spent more than $2,000,000 on tangible personal property, the amount of bonus depreciation he can claim is reduced for every dollar he spent on tangible personal property over $2,000,000, or reduced by $200,000. Thus, he can claim $300,000 of bonus depreciation ($500,000 less $200,000) in the first year. Danny recovers the remaining $1,900,000 cost of his property ($2,200,000 cost, less $300,000 of bonus depreciation) using his regular depreciation method.

Year	Calculation	Depreciation
1	Bonus	$300,000
1	$1,900,000 × 20%	380,000
2	1,900,000 × 32%	608,000
3	1,900,000 × 19.2%	364,800
4	1,900,000 × 11.52%	218,880
5	1,900,000 × 11.52%	218,880
6	1,900,000 × 5.76%	109,440
		$2,200,000

Note that Danny will claim a total of $680,000 of depreciation in the first year.

D. Problems

1. Charlie purchased a hydraulic lift for use at his car repair shop (which he operates as a sole proprietorship). He paid $30,000 and, for tax purposes, the lift has a life of seven years. He makes no elections. How much deprecation is Charlie entitled to claim during each of the next eight years?

2. Dennis purchased an x-ray machine for use in his business. He paid $300,000 and, for tax purposes, the x-ray machine has a life of five years. He elected to claim bonus depreciation and his business had taxable income (before taking into consideration the depreciation) of $600,000 for the year. How much depreciation is he entitled to claim during each of the next six years?

3. Evan purchased a piece of equipment for use in his business. He paid $700,000 and, for tax purposes, the equipment has a life of five years. His business had taxable income (before taking into consideration the depreciation) of $600,000 for the year. How much depreciation is he entitled to claim during each of the next six years under the following alternative situations:

    a. He makes no elections.

b.   He elects to claim bonus depreciation.

c.   He makes no elections and sells the equipment in year three.

d.   He elects bonus depreciation and sells the equipment in year three.

4.   Frank purchased a piece of equipment for use in his business. The equipment has a life of five years. He elected to claim bonus depreciation. For the year his business had taxable income (before taking into consideration the depreciation) of $700,000. How much depreciation is he entitled to claim during in the first year if the cost of the equipment is:

a. $900,000

b. $1,300,000

c. $2,600,000

5.   Jack purchased a piece of equipment for use in his business. He paid $600,000 and, for tax purposes, the equipment has a life of five years. He elected to claim bonus depreciation. For the year his business had taxable income (before taking into consideration the depreciation) of $300,000. How much depreciation is he entitled to claim during in the first year?

6.   George purchased a shopping center in June. He paid $1,000,000 for the building and $500,000 for the land. He made no elections.

a.   How much depreciation is he entitled to claim in the first year?

b.   How much depreciation is he entitled to claim in the second year?

c.   How much depreciation is he entitled to claim in the third year?

7.   Hal purchased an apartment building November. He paid $1,000,000 for the building and $500,000 for the land. He made no elections.

a.   How much depreciation is he entitled to claim in the first year?

b.   How much depreciation is he entitled to claim in the second year?

c.   How much depreciation is he entitled to claim in the third year?

8.   Inez purchased a coffee shop. One of the assets she purchased was the customer list. It cost her $20,000. How will she recover the cost of the list?

E. Analysis and Application

1.   Consider a business you might be interested in operating. Identify at least ten expenditures (life of more than one year) you would expect to incur in running the business.

a.   How many of the items wear out over time?

b.   If the asset does not wear out over time, how do you recover the cost of the asset?

2.   Under what circumstances would you advise your client to elect bonus depreciation? When would you advise your client to not elect bonus depreciation?

3.   Javier owns and operates a high-end hotel in Colorado. Throughout the common areas Javier has displayed a variety of antiques unique to Colorado and its gold mining era. While the majority is maintained in glass display cases, a few are incorporated as functional pieces through out the lobby.

   a.   Can Javier claim depreciation deductions on the antiques kept in the glass display cases?

   b.   Can Javier claim depreciation deductions on the antiques used as functional pieces? In formulating your analysis and response, you may want to consider:

- Simon v. Commissioner, 103 T.C. 247 (1994), aff'd, 68 F.3d 41 (2d Cir. 1995)
- Liddle v. Commissioner, 103 T.C. 285 (1994), aff'd, 65 F.3d 329 (3d Cir. 1995)
- Rev. Rul. 68-232, 1968-1 C.B. 79

4.   Create a chart showing the application of depreciation of tangible personal property, real property, and intangible property. Incorporate the application of bonus depreciation where relevant.

5.   Create a flow chart explaining the deductibility of expenses and depreciation related to a business.

6.   Concept Map: Prepare a concept map covering deductions (including expenses and capital expenditures) that might be encountered by a taxpayer who operates a bakery as a sole proprietorship.

A concept map is a visual diagram showing links between and among important related concepts. The process of creating a concept map requires the integration of new information with prior knowledge. A concept map can be used to clarify what has been read and heard by creating a visual representation of key terms around a central idea or concept. It is not intended to establish a hierarchy between concepts (as an outline would), only the existence of a relationship between concepts.

Chapter 26

Loss From Disposition of Business Property

Deductions

Personal:	Investment:	Business:
• Interest • Taxes • Medical expenses • Education expenses • Moving expenses • Child care expenses • Charitable contributions • Casualty loses • Non-business bad debts • Alimony	• Expenses • Depreciation and amortization • Loss from the disposition of property • Non-business bad debts	• Start up expenses • Expenses • Depreciation and amortization • **Losses from the disposition of property** • Business bad debts

Read

Code Sections 165(a), (b), (c)(1); 267(a)(1), (b)(1), (c)(4), (d)

Treas. Reg. §§ 1.165-1(a), (b), (d)(2),(3); 1.165-7(b)(1); 1.165-9(a)(2)

A. Background

In Chapter 4 we considered the tax consequences of the disposition of property. Recall that gross income includes income (accessions to wealth) derived from any and all sources.[131] Once a taxpayer acquires property, the property can increase in value. However, the Code does not require the taxpayer to report that increase in wealth until he has disposed of the property.[132] In general, the accession to wealth is the amount of profit the taxpayer has in the property, or the difference between the amount the taxpayer sold the property

---

131. Section 61(a).
132. Sections 1001; 61(a)(3).

for and the amount he paid for it.[133] To measure this profit, the Code provides specific terminology.

Adjusted basis. The basis of property is the amount the taxpayer originally paid for the property.[134] In general, a taxpayer will purchase an item for its fair market value. The adjusted basis reflects an increase for any subsequent capital expenditures and a decrease for depreciation.[135]

Amount realized. The amount realized is the amount the taxpayer sold the property for.[136] In general, a taxpayer will sell an item for its fair market value. What types of assets the taxpayer receives as payment for the item he is selling is irrelevant; the focus is on the value of the payment. Most often the taxpayer will be paid in cash, property, services, debt relief, or a combination of those items.

Gain realized and recognized. The difference between the amount realized and the adjusted basis of the property sold or otherwise disposed of by the taxpayer is the gain realized.[137] This formula permits the taxpayer to recover the amount he paid for the property tax free. This recovery sometimes is called a return of capital.

> Amount realized
> − Adjusted basis
> Gain realized

Unless the Code provides otherwise, any gain realized must be recognized.[138] To recognize gain means to report it on the taxpayer's income tax return.

Business. Neither the Code nor the regulations provides a definition of business. The Supreme Court held that, to be engaged in a business, the taxpayer had to be involved in the activity with continuity and regularity; the taxpayer's primary purpose for engaging in the activity must be for income or profit. A sporadic activity, a hobby, or an amusement diversion does not qualify. The determination is based on an examination of the facts.[139]

Personal losses. In general, the taxpayer may not recognize any loss from the disposition of property used for personal purposes.[140]

B. General Rule — Loss from Disposition of Business Property

Once a taxpayer acquires property, the property may decrease in value. The Code does not permit the taxpayer to report that decrease in wealth until he has disposed of the

---

133. Section 1001(a).
134. Section 1012(a).
135. Section 1016(a).
136. Section 1001(b).
137. Section 1001(a).
138. Section 1001(c).
139. Commissioner v. Groetzinger, 480 U.S. 23 (1987).
140. Section 165(c)(3).

property. In general, the decrease in wealth is the amount of loss the taxpayer has in the property, or the difference between the amount the taxpayer sold the property for and the amount he paid for it, as adjusted.[141]

> Amount realized
> – <u>Adjusted basis</u>
> Loss realized

Section 1001. Determination of Amount of and Recognition of Gain or Loss

(a) Computation of Gain or Loss. — ... the loss shall be the excess of the adjusted basis provided in such section [Section 1011] for determining loss over the amount realized....

Unless the Code provides authority, no loss realized may be recognized, or reported, on the taxpayer's income tax return. Section 165(c)(1) allows a taxpayer to recognize a loss from the sale of business property. The taxpayer is not allowed to claim a loss in excess of his basis in the property.[142]

Section 165. Losses

(a) General Rule. — There shall be allowed as a deduction any loss sustained during the taxable year and not compensated for by insurance or otherwise.

(b) Amount of Deduction. — For purposes of subsection (a), the basis for determining the amount of the deduction for any loss shall be the adjusted basis provided in section 1011 for determining the loss from the sale or other disposition of property.

(c) Limitation on Losses of Individuals. — In the case of an individual, the deduction under subsection (a) shall be limited to —

> (1) losses incurred in a trade or business....

Loss Realized and Loss Recognized

Loss realized is the difference between the amount realized and the adjusted basis of the property.

Loss recognized is the amount of loss realized the taxpayer can report on his income tax return.

---

141. Sections 1001(a); 1016(a).
142. Section 165(b).

Note

Losses related to the disposition of investment property are discussed in Chapter 30.

Tell Me More

The Code provides that, in specific situations, the taxpayer must defer the recognition of loss until a later time. These provisions are addressed in Chapters 43 and 47.

C. Special Rules

1. Property Converted from Personal Use

If the taxpayer disposes of property and the property had been used for personal purposes, the loss during the time the property was held for personal purposes may not be recognized. The recognized loss is limited to the loss that occurred while the property was used for business purposes. The regulations achieve this result through the "lesser-of" rule. The taxpayer may not claim a loss in excess of his basis in the property. His basis in the property is the lesser of the value of the property or the basis at the time of conversion, as adjusted.[143]

Note that the "lesser-of rule" only applies to basis for purposes of computing depreciation and calculating the amount of loss realized. To calculate the amount of gain on disposition of the property, the basis in the property is the usual adjusted basis — cost, plus any capital expenditures, less depreciation.[144]

2. Business Property Casualty Losses

One way a taxpayer may suffer a loss related to business property is through a casualty loss.[145] The taxpayer's property may be destroyed or harmed by a casualty, such as a fire, storm, tornado, or hurricane. Or it may be stolen. The general rule is that the amount of the loss is the lesser of the adjusted basis or the decrease in value caused by the casualty or theft. However, if the property has been completely destroyed, the amount of the loss is the

---

143. See Treas. Reg. § 1.165-9(b)(2); Rev. Rul. 72-111, 1972-1 C.B. 56.

144. Id.

145. Section 165(c)(1). Casualty losses also are allowed for personal property. Section 165(c)(3). See the discussion in Chapter 19.

adjusted basis of the property.[146] Note that, if the value of the property exceeds the property's adjusted basis, there is no loss attributed to this excess (i.e. lost profit). Because the increase in value (the appreciation) had never been reported, no offsetting loss is permitted.

Once the amount of loss has been determined, it is reduced by any insurance proceeds received.[147] The taxpayer may recognize any remaining loss.[148]

Timing. When the taxpayer has submitted an insurance claim and there is a reasonable prospect of recovery, the taxpayer may not claim the loss until the amount of insurance recovery is determined with reasonable certainty.[149] If the property has been stolen, the loss is allowed in the year the taxpayer discovers the theft.[150]

D. Sales to Related Parties

When the taxpayer recognizes a loss, he may use the loss to offset his gross income, resulting in less taxable income and a lower tax liability. Given this tax benefit, some taxpayer would "sell" property that had decreased in value to a related party. By selling to a related party, the taxpayer would recognize a loss and, perhaps, still maintain control over the property.

Example. Through his sole proprietorship Mitch owns land with a basis of $5,000 and fair market value of $2,000. If he sold the land to his teenage daughter for $2,000, he would have a $3,000 loss realized (amount realized of $2,000, less basis of $5,000); he could use the loss to offset his income. As his daughter is a minor, arguable he still has control over the land.

Congress responded to these types of potentially abusive transactions by enacting Section 267, which prohibits the taxpayer from recognizing a loss when the sale is to a related party.[151] In the previous example, because the sale was to Mitch's daughter, under Section 267 he would not be able to recognize the $3,000 loss realized.

Parties are related if they are members of the same family.[152] Family members include brothers and sisters, spouse, ancestors, and lineal descendants.[153]

Section 267 has an additional provision that applies on a subsequent sale by the related party. It allows the buyer-turned-seller to offset any gain by the loss previously disallowed. While it allows the related party to offset the gain realized, it cannot be used to create a loss.[154]

Example. Through his sole proprietorship Mitch owned land with a basis of $5,000 and fair market value of $2,000. He sold the land to his daughter for $2,000. He had a $3,000 loss realized but could not recognize the loss because it was a sale to a related party.

---

146. Treas. Reg. § 1.165-7(b)(1).
147. See Section 165(h)(5)(E).
148. Section 16(c)(1).
149. Treas. Reg. § 1.165-1(d)(2).
150. Treas. Reg. § 1.165-8(a)(2).
151. Section 267(a)(1).
152. Section 267(b)(1). A person can also be related to an entity, such as a trust, corporation, or partnership. Those rules are beyond the scope of this text.
153. Section 267(c)(4).
154. Section 267(d).

Five years later Mitch's daughter sold the land for $10,000. She had a $8,000 gain realized (amount realized of $10,000, less $2,000 basis). She can offset this gain by the $3,000 loss Mitch was not able to recognize, reporting only $5,000 of gain (gain of $8,000, less the $3,000 loss previously disallowed).

Summary of Rules — Sale of Business Property at a Loss

General rule: A taxpayer may recognize a loss from the disposition of property used in his business. However, if the sale is to a related party, the taxpayer may not recognize the loss.

Property converted from personal use: The amount of recognized loss cannot exceed the loss while the property was used for business purposes. For determining loss, the adjusted basis is the lesser of the fair market value or the basis at the time of conversion to business use, as adjusted.

Casualty or theft losses: The amount of loss is the lesser of the adjusted basis in the property or the decrease in value caused by the casualty. However, if the property was completely destroyed or stolen, the loss is equal to the property's adjusted basis. The recognized loss is the loss reduced by any insurance proceeds received.

E. Application of Rules

Example 1. Otto owns and operates a small business. This year he sold a piece of equipment used in his business for $10,000. At the time of the sale his adjusted basis in the equipment was $12,000. Otto may recognize the $2,000 loss ($10,000 amount realized, less $12,000 adjusted basis).

Example 2. Larry owns a van he uses for personal purposes. He had purchased the van several years earlier for $20,000. He also owns and operates a bakery. This year he began offering a delivery service. To make the deliveries, Larry converted the van to business use. At the time of the conversion the value of the van was $6,000. After claiming $2,000 of depreciation, Larry sold the van for $1,000.

Larry's adjusted basis in the van is the lesser of the value of the property ($6,000) or the basis at the time of conversion ($20,000), as adjusted for depreciation. Accordingly, Larry's adjusted basis is $4,000 ($6,000 basis, less $2,000 of depreciation) and he may recognize a $3,000 loss ($1,000 amount realized, less $4,000 basis).

Example 3. Mabel owns a van she uses for personal purposes. She had purchased the van several years earlier for $20,000. She also owns and operates a printing company. This year she began offering a delivery service. To make the deliveries, Mabel converted the van to business use. At the time of the conversion the value of the van was $6,000. After claiming $2,000 of depreciation, Mabel sold the van for $21,000.

For purposes of measuring gain, Mabel's adjusted basis in the van is the cost, less depreciation or $18,000 ($20,000 cost, less $2,000 depreciation). Mabel must recognize a $3,000 gain ($21,000 amount realized, less $18,000 adjusted basis).

Example 4. Mike owns a van he uses for personal purposes. He had purchased the van several years earlier for $20,000. He also owns and operates a repair business. This year, because he needed a van to use in his business, he converted the van to business use. At the time of the conversion the value of the van was $6,000. After claiming $2,000 of depreciation, Mike sold the van for $7,000.

For purposes of measuring loss, Mike's adjusted basis in the van is the lesser of the value of the property ($6,000) or the basis at the time of conversion ($20,000), less depreciation. His adjusted basis is $4,000 ($6,000 basis, less $2,000 of depreciation). There is no loss realized ($7,000 amount realized, less $4,000 basis).

For purposes of measuring gain, his adjusted basis in the van is the cost less depreciation. His adjusted basis is $18,000 ($20,000 cost, less $2,000 depreciation). There is no gain realized ($7,000 amount realized, less $18,000 adjusted basis). Mike reports neither a gain nor a loss.

Example 5. Dennis owned a boat he used in his sight-seeing business. This year a large storm struck the area, causing the boat to sink. He did not have the boat insured. Dennis was not able to salvage any part of the boat. At the time of the storm Dennis' adjusted basis in the boat was $5,000 and its fair market value was $4,000.

Dennis suffered a casualty loss. Because the boat was completely destroyed, the amount of the loss is the adjusted basis in the boat, or $5,000.

Example 6. Rich owned a boat he used in his sight-seeing business. This year a large storm struck the area, causing the boat to sink. He did not have the boat insured. Rich was not able to salvage any part of the boat. At the time of the storm Rich's adjusted basis in the boat was $5,000 and its fair market value was $7,000.

Rich suffered a casualty loss. Because the boat was completely destroyed, the amount of the loss is the adjusted basis in the boat, or $5,000. The difference between the fair market value ($7,000) and adjusted basis ($5,000) represents appreciation Rich did not have to recognize. Accordingly, he is not entitled to an offsetting loss for the unrecognized appreciation when the boat was destroyed.

Example 7. Keith owned a boat he used in his sight-seeing business. This year a large storm struck the area causing $2,000 damage to the boat. He did not have the boat insured. Just before the storm, Keith's adjusted basis in the boat was $5,000 and its fair market value was $6,000.

Keith suffered a casualty loss. The amount of the loss is the lesser of his adjusted basis ($5,000) or decrease in value caused by the casualty ($2,000). Thus, the amount of the loss is $2,000.

Example 8. Heidi owned a boat she used in her sight-seeing business. This year a large storm struck the area, causing the boat to sink. Heidi was not able to salvage any part of the boat. At the time of the storm Heidi's adjusted basis in the boat was $5,000 and its fair market value was $4,000. Heidi had the boat insured and was able to recover $5,000 from the insurance company.

Heidi suffered a casualty loss. Because the boat was completely destroyed, the amount of the loss is the adjusted basis in the boat, or $5,000. However, the loss is completely offset by the insurance proceeds and Heidi is not able to claim any loss ($5,000 loss, less $5,000 insurance recovery).

Example 9. James owns and operates a small business. This year he sold a piece of equipment used in his business to his brother, Gregg, for $10,000. At the time of the sale his adjusted basis in the equipment was 12,000. James realized a $2,000 loss ($10,000 amount realized, less $12,000 adjusted basis). However, he cannot recognize the loss because he sold the equipment to a related party.

Subsequently, Gregg sold the equipment for $15,000. At the time of the sale, Gregg's adjusted basis in the equipment was $9,000. Gregg has a gain realized of $6,000. However, he can offset this gain by the loss James was not allowed to claim, or by $2,000. Gregg recognizes a $4,000 gain ($6,000 gain, less the $2,000 disallowed loss).

Example 10. Charlie owns and operates a small business. This year he sold a piece of equipment used in his business to his brother, Dan, for $10,000. At the time of the sale his adjusted basis in the equipment was 15,000. Charlie realized a $5,000 loss ($10,000 amount realized, less $15,000 adjusted basis). However, he cannot recognize the loss because he sold the equipment to a related party.

Subsequently, Dan sold the equipment for $11,000. At the time of the sale, Dan's adjusted basis in the equipment was $10,000. Dan has a gain realized of $1,000. However, he can offset this gain by the loss Charlie was not allowed to claim, or by $5,000. He cannot use the loss to create a loss for himself; Dan does not recognize a gain or a loss ($1,000 gain, less the $1,000 of disallowed loss).

F. Problems

1.   Amy owns and operates a small business. This year she sold a piece of equipment used in her business for $10,000. Her adjusted basis in the equipment was $15,000. What are the tax consequences to Amy?

2.   Beth owns and operates a small business. This year she sold a piece of equipment used in her business to her sister, Cathy, for $10,000. Her adjusted basis in the equipment was $15,000. The following year, Cathy sells the equipment for $16,000.

   a.   What are the tax consequences to Beth?

   b.   What are the tax consequences to Cathy?

3.   Arnold owned a freezer he used for personal purposes. He paid $8,000 for the freezer. When he began operating a cake baking business as a sole proprietorship, he transferred the freezer to the business. At the time of the conversion, the value of the freezer was $5,000.

   The following year, after claiming $1,000 of depreciation, Arnold sold the freezer for $3,000. What are the tax consequences to Arnold?

4.   Evan owned a computer he used for personal purposes. He paid $3,000 for the computer. When he began operating an investment consulting business as a sole proprietorship, he transferred the computer to the business. At the time of the conversion, the value of the computer was $2,500.

   The following year, after claiming $500 of depreciation, Evan sold the computer for $2,800. What are the tax consequences to Evan?

5.   Fred operates a taxi-cab business. This year while driving his taxi-cab, he was in an accident. At the time of the accident, his adjusted basis in the taxi-cab was $5,000. Its value before the accident was $4,000 and its value after was $2,000. He filed a claim with his insurance company and recovered $1,000. What are the tax consequences to Fred?

6. Gigi operates a package delivery service. This year one of the vans used in her business was stolen. At the time of the theft her adjusted basis in the van was $8,000 and the fair market value was $10,000. Gigi did not receive any recovery from her insurance company. What are the tax consequences to Gigi?

G. Analysis and Application

Mike and Ted have been best friends since grade school. They are not related.

In January, Mike purchased a freezer for use in his business for $10,000; Ted purchased a diamond-bladed cutting saw for use in his business for $20,000. In December of the same year, the freezer had decreased in value to $8,000 and the value of the saw had decreased to $16,000. After talking over their options, Mike agreed to buy Ted's saw for $16,000 and Ted agreed to buy Mike's freezer for $8,000. Mike reported a $2,000 loss, and Ted reported a $4,000 loss. In January of the following year Mike repurchased the freezer from Ted for $8,000; Ted repurchased the saw from Mike for $16,000.

What are the tax consequences to Mike and Ted from the above transactions? In formulating your analysis and response, you may want to consider:

- Wolder v. Commissioner, 493 F.2d 608 (1974)
- Salvatore v. Commissioner, T.C. Memo. 1970-30

Chapter 27

Business Bad Debts

Deductions

Personal:	Investment:	**Business:**

• Interest
• Taxes
• Medical expenses
• Education expenses
• Moving expenses
• Child care expenses
• Charitable contributions
• Casualty loses
• Non-business bad debts
• Alimony
	• Expenses
	• Depreciation and
	  amortization
	• Loss from the
	  disposition of property
	• Non-business bad debts
		• Start up expenses
		• Expenses
		• Depreciation and
		  amortization
		• Losses from the
		  disposition of property
		• **Business bad debts**

Read

Code Section 166

Treas. Reg. §§ 1.166-1(a), (c), (d)(1), (e); 1.166-2(a), (b), (c)(1)

A. Background

Forgiveness of debt. If a taxpayer has borrowed money that he has an obligation to repay and part of the obligation to repay is later forgiven, the taxpayer has gross income to the extent he no longer is required to repay the borrowed amount.[155]

Deductions. Deductions are a matter of legislative grace. To be entitled to claim a deduction, the taxpayer must provide authority for allowance of the deduction.[156]

---

155. Section 61(a)(12); United States v. Kirby Lumber Co., 284 U.S. 1 (1931).
156. Welch v. Helvering, 290 U.S. 111 (1933).

B. Business Bad Debts

If the borrower cannot repay a debt, the lender has experienced a decrease in wealth. The Code provides a bad deduction in such situations.[157] To be entitled to claim a bad debt deduction, there must be a debt and the borrower must be unable to repay the borrowed amount. The amount of the deduction cannot exceed the lender's basis in the debt.[158] For business bad debts, a deduction is permitted for any portion of the debt that has become worthless.[159]

Note

If the debt is represented by a "security" (i.e., stock), any deduction is permitted by the loss provisions of Section 165 and not the bad debt provisions of Section 166.[160]

Debt. A bad debt deduction can arise only in those situations where a valid debt exists.[161] It does not extend to other situations, such as where money has been transferred as a gift. Accordingly, when money has been transferred between related parties, the Service will closely scrutinize the transaction to verify it is a valid, enforceable obligation to pay a fixed sum of money.

Worthless debt. The debtor must be unable to repay the debt. The creditor is not entitled to a bad debt deduction if he forgives the debt or otherwise cancels the debt. To determine if the debt has become worthless, the creditor must consider "all pertinent evidence," but is not required to seek a court judgment.[162]

Tell Me More

It may be difficult to ascertain when a debt has become worthless. Accordingly, the Code provides some flexibility in making this determination. The taxpayer has seven years from the time the debt becomes worthless to file a claim for refund.[163]

Amount of deduction. The amount of the business bad debt deduction cannot exceed the taxpayer's basis in the debt.[164] When the transaction is an unpaid loan, the taxpayer's basis in the debt will be the unpaid portion of the loan. If the transaction is a payment owed for services rendered and the taxpayer is a cash basis taxpayer, the taxpayer's basis in the account receivable (i.e., debt) will be zero and no deduction permitted.[165]

---

157. Section 166.
158. Section 166(b).
159. Section 166(a).
160. Section 166(e).
161. Treas. Reg. 1.166-1(c).
162. Treas. Reg. § 1.166-2.
163. Section 6511(d)(1).
164. Section 166(b).
165. Cash basis accounting is discussed in Chapter 32.

Character of a business bad debt. If the debt is a business bad debt, it is characterized as an ordinary loss. There are no limits on the amount of ordinary loss a taxpayer can claim. (Non-business bad debts are characterized as short-term capital losses. See discussion in Chapters 20 and 29.)

Characterization Summary

Type of Debt	Character
Business bad debt	Ordinary loss
Non-business bad debt	Short-term capital loss

A business bad debt is a debt acquired in connection with the taxpayer's business. Note that the taxpayer can be in the business of being an employee. All other debts will be characterized as non-business bad debts. These debts include personal loans (i.e., a loan to a family member or friend) or debts incurred in connection with a taxpayer's investment.

Business	Non-Business
– employee (a taxpayer can be in the business of being an employee) – in the business of buying and selling corporations	– personal loans – shareholder (investor) – other type of investor

In those situations where the taxpayer has a dual relationship with a corporation (employee and shareholder) and loans money to the corporation, the characterization of the debt will depend on the dominate reason the taxpayer made the loan to the corporation.

In *United States v. Generes*,[166] Mr. Generes owned about 44 percent of a construction corporation, originally investing $38,900. He also was the president of the corporation. As president, he worked six to eight hours a week and earned $12,000 per year.[167]

Over the years, Mr. Generes loaned money to the corporation. He also guaranteed loans made by banks to the corporation and agreed to indemnify bid and performance bonds issued to the corporation from an underwriter. After many years of success, the corporation significantly underbid two projects and defaulted on the contracts. The underwriter completed the work and Mr. Generes was called upon to indemnify the underwriter in the amount of $162,104. Mr. Generes also loaned the corporation $158,814. The corporation went into receivership and Mr. Generes was unable to obtain reimbursement for either amount.

The issue before the court was whether the unreimbursed debt (composed of the direct loan to the corporation and the payments to indemnify the underwriter) was a business or a non-business bad debt. To resolve this issue, the regulations considered whether the debt had a "proximate relationship" to the taxpayer's business. If so, it was a business bad debt. If the debt had a "proximate relationship" to his stock ownership,

---

166. 405 U.S. 93 (1972).
167. The court noted that, after considering the taxes due on this salary, the taxpayer would net approximately $7,000.

it was a non-business bad debt. With the debt able to have a proximate relationship to both the business and the stock ownership, the regulation failed to resolve the issue. The Supreme Court interpreted the term "proximate relationship" as meaning dominant motivation. "By making the dominant motivation the measure, the logical tax consequence ensues and prevents the mere presence of a business motive, however small and however insignificant, from controlling the tax result at the taxpayer's convenience."[168] Because Mr. Generes' dominant motivation for loaning the funds was to protect his investment in the corporation (and not to protect his salary), the bad debt was a non-business bad debt.[169]

Note

A deduction is permitted for personal and investment non-business bad debts, but the amount of deduction allowed may be limited. Non-business bad debts are discussed in Chapters 20 and 29.

Tell Me More

A taxpayer who is a shareholder in a closely-held corporation may make advances to the corporation. If the corporation is unable to repay these advances, the bad debt must be characterized as a business or a non-business bad debt. Based on the court's holding in *Generes*, this determination depends on the shareholder's dominate motivation in advancing funds to the corporation; given the factual nature of the inquiry, the determination has been the subject of much litigation.

In *Whipple v. Commissioner*[170] the Supreme Court noted that a taxpayer's investment in a closely-held corporation is not a business. Rather, the taxpayer is investing in the business of the corporation. "Even if the taxpayer demonstrates an independent trade or business of his own, care must be taken to distinguish bad debt losses arising from his own business and those actually arising from activities peculiar to an investor concerned with, and participating in, the conduct of the corporate business.... furnishing management and other services to corporations for a reward not different from that flowing to an investor in those corporations is not a trade or business."[171]

Guaranty. A taxpayer may guaranty the debt of a third party. In the event the third party cannot pay the debt, the guarantor must make the payment. When that occurs, the third party is obligated to reimburse the guarantor. To the extent the third party cannot, the grantor is entitled to a bad debt deduction. If the guaranty is connected with the taxpayer's business, the bad debt deduction is a business bad debt, characterized as an ordinary loss.[172]

---

168. United States v. Generes, 405 U.S. 93, 105 (1972).
169. United States v. Generes, 405 U.S. 93, 106, 107 (1972).
170. 373 U.S. 193 (1963).
171. Whipple v. Commissioner, 373 U.S. 193, 202, 203 (1963).
172. Treas. Reg. 1.166-9.

C. Application of Rules

Example 1. Theodore operates a car wash as a sole proprietorship. Last year, when his soap supplier was having financial difficulties, Theodore loaned the supplier $10,000. Even though the supplier signed a promissory note, he was unable to repay the debt. The debt is a business bad debt, and Theodore is entitled to claim a $10,000 ordinary loss.

Example 2. William operates a feed supply store and is a cash basis taxpayer. Jed, who is one of his best customers, owed William $5,000 for feed he had purchased. Unfortunately, Jed fell on hard times, declared bankruptcy, and the debt to William was discharged.

The debt (an account receivable) is a business bad debt, and William can deduct his basis in the debt. As a cash basis taxpayer, William's basis in the account receivable is zero; he is not entitled to a bad debt deduction.

Example 3. Kinsley operates a small convenience store and is an accrual basis taxpayer. Hudson, who is one of her best customers, owed Kinsley $6,000 for supplies he had purchased. Unfortunately, Hudson fell on hard times and was unable to pay his debt to Kinsley.

The debt (an account receivable) is a business bad debt, and Kinsley can deduct her basis in the debt. As an accrual basis taxpayer, Kinsley's basis in the account receivable is $6,000. The debt is a business bad debt, and Kinsley is entitled to claim a $6,000 ordinary loss.

D. Problems

1. Paul operates a dog wash as a sole proprietorship. Last year he paid $10,000 for stock in Soapy Dog Inc., a corporation that made organic dog shampoo. Unfortunately, the corporation had difficulty finding distributors for the shampoo and went out of business. Is Paul entitled to a business bad debt deduction for the amount he paid for the Soapy Dog stock?

2. Joy loaned $10,000 to her sister so her sister could start a consulting business. When the business failed, Joy's sister was unable to repay her. Is Joy entitled to a business bad debt deduction for the loan to her sister?

3. Angelo owns and operates an ice cream shop as a sole proprietorship. Last year, when his ice cream supplier was having financial difficulties, Angelo loaned the supplier $50,000. Even though the supplier signed a promissory note, he was unable to repay the debt. Is Angelo entitled to a business bad debt deduction for the loan to the supplier?

E. Analysis and Application

1. Can you explain to your client the difference between a business and a non-business bad debt?

2. Your client, Jerome, operates a financial consulting firm. He is a cash basis taxpayer. Every month, several of Jerome's clients are unable to pay all or part of their bill. Can you explain to Jerome why he is not entitled to a business bad debt deduction for the amounts he is unable to collect?

3. Make a checklist of the facts you might ask your client about to determine the client's dominant motive behind making a loan to a corporation.

VI

Investment Activities

Personal:	Investment:	Business:
• Interest • Taxes • Medical expenses • Education expenses • Moving expenses • Child care expenses • Charitable contributions • Casualty loses • Non-business bad debts • Alimony	• **Expenses** • **Depreciation and amortization** • **Loss from the disposition of property** • **Non-business bad debts**	• Start up expenses • Expenses • Depreciation and amortization • Losses from the disposition of property • Business bad debts

Chapter 28

Overview:
Investment Expenditures

Deductions

Personal:	Investment:	Business:
• Interest • Taxes • Medical expenses • Education expenses • Moving expenses • Child care expenses • Charitable contributions • Casualty loses • Non-business bad debts • Alimony	• **Expenses** • **Depreciation and amortization** • **Loss from the disposition of property** • **Non-business bad debts**	• Start up expenses • Expenses • Depreciation and amortization • Losses from the disposition of property • Business bad debts

One of the overarching objectives of the Code is to impose tax on a taxpayer's accession to wealth. When the taxpayer has investment activities, his taxable increase in wealth is not his gross investment income. Rather, it is his gross income less the costs he incurred to generate the investment income.

Investment income
– <u>Costs of generating investment income for the year</u>
Taxable investment income

The Code provides several deductions related to investment activities. The treatment of costs incurred in an investment activity is substantially the same as the treatment of business deductions, with the two major types of deductions being expenses and depreciation related to capital expenditures.

Reminder — Business Expenditures

Expense: Deduction for an item that impacts one year or is consumed within one year. The expense must be ordinary, necessary, and paid or incurred while engaged in a business.[1]

---

1. Section 162(a).

Capital expenditure: Expenditure that impacts more than one year or has a benefit that extends beyond one year.

Depreciation: Deduction methodology for recovering the cost of a capital expenditure where the asset wears out over time.[2]

The deductibility of expenses and depreciation are discussed in Chapter 29.[3]

Losses. Chapter 4 addressed profit in property and the requirement that that profit be recognized when the property is disposed of. As a corollary, if the property has decreased in value from the date of purchase to the time of sale, there would be a loss in the property. In that instance, a loss is allowed if a Code section permits the taxpayer to claim the loss. Losses from the disposition of assets acquired for an investment activity are discussed in Chapter 30.

Bad debts. When a taxpayer loans money as part of his investment activity and is not repaid, the taxpayer has a decrease in his wealth. In some situations, the taxpayer can deduct the amount of the bad debt on his income tax return. Non-business bad debts are discussed in Chapter 29.

Many investments item are reported on Schedule E, Supplemental Income and Loss. Take a moment and review Schedule E. Consider the following:

- Where is the investment income reported?

- What expense deductions are allowed?

- Where is depreciation or amortization taken into account?

- Where are losses taken into account?

- How does the total income or loss from the investment activity relate to the Form 1040?

---

2. Sections 167; 168.

3. Whether a cost is an expense or capital expenditure is discussed in Chapter 22 in conjunction with business costs.

Exhibit: First Page of Schedule E

SCHEDULE E (Form 1040)	Supplemental Income and Loss	OMB No. 1545-0074
	(From rental real estate, royalties, partnerships, S corporations, estates, trusts, REMICs, etc.)	**20 12**
Department of the Treasury Internal Revenue Service (99)	⊠ Attach to Form 1040, 1040NR, or Form 1041. ⊠ Information about Schedule E and its separate instructions is at www.irs.gov/form1040.	Attachment Sequence No. 13

Name(s) shown on return	Your social security number

Part I Income or Loss From Rental Real Estate and Royalties   Note. If you are in the business of renting personal property, use Schedule C or C-EZ (see instructions). If you are an individual, report farm rental income or loss from   Form 4835 on page 2, line 40.

A Did you make any payments in 2012 that would require you to file Form(s) 1099? (see instructions)   ☐ Yes ☐ No
B If "Yes," did you or will you file required Forms 1099?   ☐ Yes ☐ No

1a	Physical address of each property (street, city, state, ZIP code)
A	
B	
C	

1b	Type of Property (from list below)	2 For each rental real estate property listed above, report the number of fair rental and personal use days. Check the QJV box only if you meet the requirements to file as a qualified joint venture. See instructions.		Fair Rental Days	Personal Use Days	QJV
A			A			
B			B			
C			C			

Type of Property:
1 Single Family Residence   3 Vacation/Short-Term Rental   5 Land   7 Self-Rental
2 Multi-Family Residence   4 Commercial   6 Royalties   8 Other (describe)

Income:	Properties:		A	B	C
3 Rents received	3				
4 Royalties received	4				
Expenses:					
5 Advertising	5				
6 Auto and travel (see instructions)	6				
7 Cleaning and maintenance	7				
8 Commissions	8				
9 Insurance	9				
10 Legal and other professional fees	10				
11 Management fees	11				
12 Mortgage interest paid to banks, etc. (see instructions)	12				
13 Other interest	13				
14 Repairs	14				
15 Supplies	15				
16 Taxes	16				
17 Utilities	17				
18 Depreciation expense or depletion	18				
19 Other (list) ⊠ _____	19				
20 Total expenses. Add lines 5 through 19	20				
21 Subtract line 20 from line 3 (rents) and/or 4 (royalties). If result is a (loss), see instructions to find out if you must file Form 6198	21				
22 Deductible rental real estate loss after limitation, if any, on Form 8582 (see instructions)	22	( )	( )	( )	( )

23a	Total of all amounts reported on line 3 for all rental properties	23a	
b	Total of all amounts reported on line 4 for all royalty properties	23b	
c	Total of all amounts reported on line 12 for all properties	23c	
d	Total of all amounts reported on line 18 for all properties	23d	
e	Total of all amounts reported on line 20 for all properties	23e	
24	Income. Add positive amounts shown on line 21. Do not include any losses	24	
25	Losses. Add royalty losses from line 21 and rental real estate losses from line 22. Enter total losses here	25	( )
26	Total rental real estate and royalty income or (loss). Combine lines 24 and 25. Enter the result here. If Parts II, III, IV, and line 40 on page 2 do not apply to you, also enter this amount on Form 1040, line 17, or Form 1040NR, line 18. Otherwise, include this amount in the total on line 41 on page 2	26	

For Paperwork Reduction Act Notice, see your tax return instructions.   Cat. No. 11344L   Schedule E (Form 1040) 2012

Chapter 29

Expenses, Depreciation, and Non-Business Bad Debts

Deductions

Personal:	Investment:	Business:
• Interest • Taxes • Medical expenses • Education expenses • Moving expenses • Child care expenses • Charitable contributions • Casualty loses • Non-business bad debts • Alimony	• **Expenses** • **Depreciation and amortization** • **Loss from the disposition of property** • **Non-business bad debts**	• Start up expenses • Expenses • Depreciation and amortization • Losses from the disposition of property • Business bad debts

Read

Code Sections 166; 168(a)(2); 212

Treas. Reg. §§ 1.166-1(c), (d)(1); 1.166-2(a), (b), 1.166-5(a), (b); 1.212-1(a), (d), (e), (g), (h), (k), (l)

A. Background

Business expenses. Expenses (items that have a life or benefit of less than one year) paid or incurred while engaged in a business are currently deductible if they are ordinary and necessary expenses.[4]

Capital expenditures and depreciation. A taxpayer's basis in property is the amount the taxpayer paid for the property.[5] In general, when a taxpayer purchases property, he pays fair market value for the property. Thus, a taxpayer's basis in property is the fair market value of the property at the time of purchase. If the taxpayer uses the asset in his business

---

4. Section 162(a).
5. Section 1012(a).

and the asset wears out over time, the taxpayer can recover the cost of the property through depreciation.[6]

Forgiveness of debt. If a taxpayer has borrowed money that he has an obligation to repay and part of the obligation to repay is later forgiven, the taxpayer has gross income to the extent he no longer is required to repay the borrowed amount.[7]

Business bad debts. For business bad debts, the lender is allowed to claim a deduction for any portion of the debt that has become worthless. Bad debt deductions for partially worthless debts are allowed. A business bad debt is characterized as an ordinary loss.[8]

B. Investors

One of the overarching objectives of the Code is to impose tax on a taxpayer's accession to wealth. When the taxpayer purchases investment property (e.g., rental property or stock) his taxable increase in wealth is not his gross income. Rather, it is his gross income less the costs he incurred to generate the income.

1. Expenses

Consistent with the concept of taxing net income, the Code provides several investment-related deductions. One provision allows a deduction for expenditures that impact only one taxable year. Specifically, the expenditure must be:

- Ordinary
- Necessary
- Expense
- Paid or incurred during the taxable year
- For the production of income

Section 212. Expenses for Production of Income

In the case of an individual, there shall be allowed as a deduction all the ordinary and necessary expenses paid or incurred during the taxable year—

(1) for the production or collection of income;

(2) for the management, conservation, or maintenance of property held for the production of income; or

(3) in connection with the determination, collection, or refund of any tax.

The Code originally did not have a provision that addressed deductions related to investments. The absence of such a provision was the subject of the Supreme Court opinion

---

6. Sections 167; 168; 1016(a).

7. Section 61(a)(12); United States v. Kirby Lumber Co., 284 U.S. 1 (1931).

8. Section 166.

Higgins v. Commissioner.[9] Mr. Higgins lived in Paris and had employees who worked for him in the United States. The employees managed his stock portfolio and rental properties. Mr. Higgins paid the employees' salaries and the rent for the employees' office space. He claimed a deduction for the salaries and rent. At that time, the only Code section available to him to claim these deductions was Section 162. The government argued that Mr. Higgins was not engaged in a business. The Supreme Court agreed, holding that Mr. Higgins "merely kept records and collected interest and dividends from his securities, through managerial attention to his investments."[10] Because he was not engaged in a business, he was not entitled to a deduction for the salaries and rent. To resolve this problem, and provide taxpayers like Mr. Higgins a deduction for the cost of making money from investment property, Congress enacted Section 212.

Note that the first four elements are the same as those under Section 162, dealing with business expenses. Conveniently, the courts have interpreted these elements the same, regardless of whether they are considering the element in connection with Section 162 or Section 212.[11] If the payment comes within Section 212, the taxpayer can deduct the amount of the expense (i.e., the basis of the asset).

Requirements for an Expense to Be Deductible under Section 212

The expense must be:

- **Ordinary:** common and accepted in the industry (based on the facts and circumstances).
- **Necessary:** appropriate and helpful.
- **Expense:** have a life of less than one year, or impact only one taxable year.
- **Paid or incurred during the taxable year.**
- **Production of income:** related to the production of income.

The amount that can be deducted is the amount the taxpayer paid for the item, its basis.

Tell Me More

Higgins v. Commissioner was decided before day-traders were commonplace. Currently, the tax consequences of a taxpayer who buys and sells stock will vary, depending on whether the taxpayer is a dealer, investor, or day-trader.

A dealer regularly purchases securities from and sells to customers in the ordinary course of business. (Gains and losses are ordinary.)

An investor trades only occasionally for his own account. (Gains and losses are subject to the capital gains and losses rules.[12])

A day-trader buys and sells for his own account and seeks to profit from short-term changes in value. The trading activity is substantial, frequent, regular, and

---

9. 312 U.S. 212 (1941).
10. Higgins v. Commissioner, 312 U.S. 212, 218 (1941).
11. See further discussion of the elements in Chapter 23.
12. See discussion of capital gains and losses in Chapter 38.

> continuous. Day-traders are treated as being in the business of trading. (Generally, the gains and losses are subject to the capital gains and losses rules.)
>
> Mr. Higgins was an investor.

Tax-free income. Some expenses are associated with income that is not required to be included in income, such as income from tax-exempt bonds. Because the tax-exempt income is not included in the taxpayer's accession to wealth, it would be a double benefit for the taxpayer to both be able to exclude the income and claim a deduction for expenses related to that income. Accordingly, no deduction is allowed for expenses associated with tax-exempt income.[13]

Section 212(2). An individual is permitted to deduct the ordinary and necessary expenses paid or incurred during the taxable year for the management, conservation, or maintenance of property held for the production of income. While this Section appears to be broad, after those items that are capital expenditures are taken into consideration, the provision applies to few expenditures. Recall that acquisition costs and costs associated with defending or perfecting title of an asset are capital expenditures.

> Expenses paid or incurred in defending or perfecting title to property ... or in developing or improving property, constitute a part of the cost of the property and are not deductible expenses. Attorneys' fees paid in a suit to quiet title to lands are not deductible; but if the suit is also to collect accrued rents thereon, that portion of such fees is deductible which is properly allocable to the services rendered in collecting such rents.[14]

Section 212(3). Section 212 allows a deduction for expenses incurred in connection with the determination, collection, or refund of tax.[15]

2. Depreciation

As was discussed in connection with a taxpayer's business,[16] a taxpayer is permitted to recover the cost of capital expenditures through depreciation. Specifically, for an asset to qualify for depreciation or amortization, the asset must:[17]

- Be purchased and used in the taxpayer's investment activity,
- Have a life extending more than one year, and
- Wear out over time.

---

13. Treas. Reg. § 1.212-1(e).
14. Treas. Reg. § 1.212-1(k).
15. See also Treas. Reg. § 1.212-1(l).
16. See discussion in Chapter 25.
17. Section 167(a)(2).

Section 167. Depreciation

(a) General Rule. — There shall be allowed as a depreciation deduction a reasonable allowance for the exhaustion, wear and tear (including a reasonable allowance for obsolescence) — ...

(2) of property held for the production of income.…

The categories for investment property are the same as those for business property: tangible personal property, real property, intangible property, and all other property. The method of recovering the cost is the same as with business property.[18] The only difference is that investment property is not eligible for bonus depreciation.

Bonus Depreciation

Capital expenditures used for investment purposes are not eligible for the bonus depreciation provided for in Section 179.[19]

The adjusted basis for investment property is calculated the same as it is for business property.

Formula — Adjusted Basis

Adjusted basis = original cost + capital expenditures – depreciation
Adjusted basis cannot be less than zero.

Summary — Depreciation

To qualify for depreciation or amortization, the asset must:
- Be purchased by the taxpayer
- Be used in the taxpayer's investment activity;
- Have a life or benefit of more than one year; and
- Wear out over time.

The determination of how much depreciation is allowed each year depends on whether the asset is:
- Tangible personal property
- Real property
- Another type of property

---

18. If necessary, please review Chapter 25.
19. For more information on bonus depreciation, see Chapter 25.

Taxpayer's Taxable Income

Gross investment income
– Investment expenses
– <u>Depreciation from investment property</u>
Taxable investment income

3. Non-Business Bad Debts

If a borrower cannot repay a debt, the lender has experienced a decrease in wealth. The Code provides a bad debt deduction in such situations.[20] To be entitled to claim a bad debt deduction, there must be a debt and the borrower must be unable to repay the borrowed amount. The amount of the deduction cannot exceed the lender's basis in the debt.[21] In order for a non-business bad debt to be deductible, the entire amount of the debt must become worthless.[22] These requirements were discussed in Chapter 27 in conjunction with business bad debts.

Note

If the debt is represented by a "security" (i.e., stock), any deduction is permitted by the loss provisions of Section 165 and not the bad debt provisions of Section 166.[23]

Character of a non-business bad debt. If the debt is a non-business bad debt, it is characterized as a short-term capital loss.[24] Capital gains and losses are addressed in Chapter 37. It is sufficient here if you understand that the maximum net capital loss a taxpayer may claim each year is $3,000.[25] Any remaining loss must be carried forward.[26] (Business bad debts are characterized as ordinary losses. There is no limit on the amount of ordinary loss that can be claimed. See discussion in Chapter 27.)

Characterization Summary

Type of Debt	Character
Business bad debt	Ordinary loss
Non-business bad debt	Short-term capital loss

---

20. Section 166.
21. Section 166(b).
22. Section 166(a), (d).
23. Section 166(e).
24. Section 166(d)(1).
25. Section 1211(b).
26. Section 1212(b).

A business bad debt is a debt acquired in connection with the taxpayer's business. Note that the taxpayer can be in the business of being an employee. All other debts will be characterized as non-business bad debts. These debts include personal loans (i.e., a loan to a family member or friend) or debts incurred in connection with a taxpayer's investment.

Section 166

(d)(2) Nonbusiness debt defined. — For purposes of paragraph (1), the term "nonbusiness bad debt" means a debt other than —

(A) a debt created or acquired (as the case may be) in connection with a trade or business of the taxpayer; or

(B) a debt the loss from the worthlessness of which is incurred in the taxpayer's trade or business.

Business	Non-Business
– employee (a taxpayer can be in the business of being an employee) – in the business of buying and selling corporations	– personal loans – shareholder (investor) – other type of investor

In those situations where the taxpayer has a dual relationship with a corporation (employee and shareholder) and loans money to the corporation, the characterization of the debt will depend on the dominate reason the taxpayer made the loan to the corporation. (See *United States v. Generes*,[27] discussed in Chapter 27.) Thus, when the taxpayer is a shareholder and employee of the corporation, to determine the tax consequences of a bad debt, the dominate reason for making the loan must be determined. Factors that may be relevant include his percentage ownership in the corporation (including whether he is a controlling or minority shareholder), the amount of salary he is paid, the value of his stock, and the loan amount.

Note

A deduction is permitted for personal non-business bad debts, but the amount of deduction allowed may be limited. Personal non-business bad debts are discussed in Chapter 20.

Tell Me More

A taxpayer who is a shareholder in a closely-held corporation may make advances to the corporation. If the corporation is unable to repay these advances, the bad

---

27. 405 U.S. 93 (1972).

debt must be characterized as a business or a non-business bad debt. Based on the court's holding in *Generes*, this determination depends on the shareholder's dominate motivation in advancing funds to the corporation; given the factual nature of the inquiry, the determination has been the subject of much litigation.

In *Whipple v. Commissioner*[28] the Supreme Court noted that a taxpayer's investment in a closely-held corporation is not a business. Rather, the taxpayer is investing in the business of the corporation. "Even if the taxpayer demonstrates an independent trade or business of his own, care must be taken to distinguish bad debt losses arising from his own business and those actually arising from activities peculiar to an investor concerned with, and participating in, the conduct of the corporate business.... furnishing management and other services to corporations for a reward not different from that flowing to an investor in those corporations is not a trade or business."[29]

Guaranty. A taxpayer may guaranty the debt of a third party. In the event the third party cannot pay the debt, the guarantor must make the payment. When that occurs, the third party is obligated to reimburse the guarantor. To the extent the third party cannot, the grantor is entitled to a bad debt deduction. If the guaranty is connected with a taxpayer's investment, the bad debt deduction is a non-business bad debt, characterized as a short-term capital loss.[30]

C. Application of Rules

Example 1. Derris owns a substantial amount of stock. To help him monitor and manage his investments he hired an assistant. Because the salary paid to the assistant is an ordinary and necessary expense incurred in the production of income, Derris is entitled to a deduction for the amount of the salary.

Example 2. Jack invests in only tax-exempt bonds. To better understand tax-exempt bonds, Jack enrolled in a class on managing tax-free investments. Because the income from the tax-exempt bonds is not included in income, any expense he incurs related to that income is not deductible. He may not deduct the cost of the class.

Example 3. Windsor owns a substantial amount of investments, including stock and investment properties. Windsor paid $5,000 to an attorney to help him determine the tax liability associated with the investments. Section 212(3) allows a deduction for tax advice. Thus, Windsor can claim a deduction for the $5,000 he paid his attorney.

Example 4. Gregg purchased an apartment building in June, paying $500,000. The real property is residential real property and Gregg uses it in his investment activity. Gregg is entitled to recover the cost of apartment building over time, as follows:

---

28. 373 U.S. 193 (1963).
29. Whipple v. Commissioner, 373 U.S. 193, 202, 203 (1963).
30. Treas. Reg. § 1.166-9.

Year	Calculation	Yearly Depreciation
1	$500,000 × 1.97%	$9,850
2	$500,000 × 3.636%	18,180
3	$500,000 × 3.636%	18,180
	. . .	
26	$500,000 × 3.636%	18,180
27	$500,000 × 3.636%	18,180
28	$500,000 × 3.485%	<u>17,425</u>
Total Depreciation:		$500,000

Example 5. Jean-Claude invested $10,000 in Corporation, receiving in exchange 20 percent of the stock. This year Corporation filed bankruptcy and was liquidated. Jean-Claude received nothing for his shares.

Jean-Claude has invested in Corporation; the transaction is not a loan. Thus he is not permitted to claim a bad debt deduction under Section 166. (Because the stock is a "security", he may claim a loss under Section 165.)

Example 6. Marco owned 30 percent of Production Corp. Several years ago he loaned Production Corp. $10,000. This year Production Corp. filed bankruptcy and was unable to repay the loan. The debt is a non-business bad debt, and Marco may claim a $10,000 short-term capital loss.

Example 7. On occasion Jon-Luc was willing to make loans to his friends. However, before making each loan, Jon-Luc insisted that the borrower have a plan for use of the money and a plan for repayment. Each borrower was required to sign a promissory note which contained a stated rate of interest, a repayment schedule, and remedies in the event of default.

This past year Jon-Luc was less careful than he should have been when making a loan to his friend Todd. When Todd still owed Jon-Luc $10,000, he filed bankruptcy and the debt was discharged. The debt is a non-business bad debt, and Jon-Luc may claim a $10,000 short-term capital loss.

Example 8. Nadine owned 30 percent of Square Corp. Several years ago she loaned Square Corp. $10,000. This year Square Corp. fell on hard times. Natalie, wanting Square Corp. to succeed, informed the board of directors that Square Corp. need not repay the debt. Because Nadine forgave the debt, she is not entitled to claim a bad debt deduction.

D. Problems

1. Renee purchased a computer for use in her investment activities. She paid $3,000 and, for tax purposes, the computer has a life of five years. How much deprecation is Renee entitled to claim during each of the next six years?

2. Jason spent $1,000 on advertising in a newspaper for vacancies in an apartment building he owned. May he deduct the cost of the advertising?

3.   Wesley purchased an apartment building in November. He paid $1,000,000 for the building and $500,000 for the land.

    a.   How much depreciation is he entitled to claim in the first year?

    b.   How much depreciation is he entitled to claim in the second year?

    c.   How much depreciation is he entitled to claim in the third year?

4.   Jonathan owns an apartment building. He paid his attorney $2,000 to prepare a lease agreement he could use with new tenants. May Jonathan deduct the amount he paid his attorney?

5.   Prada owns and manages a small apartment building. A dispute arose as to whether she had clear title to the building. While the dispute continued, the tenants refused to pay rent, not knowing for sure to whom the amount should be paid. Prada hired an attorney who filed suit to quiet title and collect accrued rents. Can Prada deduct the amount she paid the attorney?

6.   Percy owned 60 percent of Food Corp. and was employed by the corporation. Several years ago she guaranteed a $10,000 loan from the bank to Food Corp. This year Food Corp. suffered large losses due to food it sold tainted with salmonella; it was unable to pay its debts. Percy was called upon to pay the $10,000 debt Food Corp. owed to the bank. What are the tax consequences to Percy?

E. Analysis and Application

1.   Name seven expenditures you may have related to an investment activity.

    a.   How many of those costs would qualify as an expense?

    b.   How many of those costs would qualify as a capital expenditure?

    c.   How many of the capital expenditures would be depreciable?

2.   Create a chart showing the application of depreciation of tangible personal property and real property.

3.   Create a flow chart explaining the deductibility of expenses and depreciation related to an investment activity.

4.   Can you explain to your client the difference between a business and a non-business bad debt?

5.   Prepare a check list of those items that should exist when creating a loan so that it will be deductible as a non-business bad debt if the borrower is unable to repay the loan.

6.   Don owns all the stock of Business Enterprises, Inc. This past year he contributed $40,000 to the corporation.

    a.   In what ways might you characterize the transaction?

    b.   What additional information do you need to decide which characterization is correct?

7.   Marjorie has come to you, wanting to know if she can claim a non-business bad debt deduction. Last year, she loaned $10,000 to a corporation and the corporation has failed to repay the debt.

In order to make a decision, what questions should you ask Marjorie?

8. In *United States v. Generes* the Supreme Court compared the taxpayer's salary of $12,000 to his investment in the corporation of at least $38,900. The court noted that the salary was "pre-tax" income and the investment was "taxpaid" income. Can you explain the distinction and why it is important?

Chapter 30

Losses From Disposition of Investment Property

Deductions

Personal:	Investment:	Business:
• Interest • Taxes • Medical expenses • Education expenses • Moving expenses • Child care expenses • Charitable contributions • Casualty loses • Non-business bad debts • Alimony	• Expenses • Depreciation and amortization • **Loss from the disposition of property** • Non-business bad debts	• Start up expenses • Expenses • Depreciation and amortization • Losses from the disposition of property • Business bad debts

Read

Code Sections 165(a), (b), (c)(1); 267(a)(1), (b)(1), (c)(4), (d)

Treas. Reg. §§ 1.165-1(a), (b), (d)(2), (3); 1.165-7(b)(1); 1.165-9(a)(2)

A. Background

In Chapter 4 we considered the tax consequences of the disposition of property. Recall that gross income includes income (accessions to wealth) derived from any and all sources.[31] Once a taxpayer acquires property, the property can increase in value. However, the Code does not require the taxpayer to report that increase in wealth until he has disposed of the property.[32] In general, the accession to wealth is the amount of profit the taxpayer has in the property, or the difference between the amount the taxpayer sold the property

---

31. Section 61(a).
32. Sections 1001; 61(a)(3).

for and the amount he paid for it.[33] To measure this profit, the Code provides specific terminology.

Adjusted basis. The basis of property is the amount the taxpayer originally paid for the property.[34] In general, a taxpayer will purchase an item for its fair market value. The adjusted basis reflects an increase for any subsequent capital expenditures and a decrease for depreciation.[35]

Amount realized. The amount realized is the amount the taxpayer sold the property for.[36] In general, a taxpayer will sell an item for its fair market value. What types of assets the taxpayer receives as payment for the item he is selling is irrelevant; the focus is on the value of the payment. Most often the taxpayer will be paid in cash, property, services, debt relief, or a combination of those items.

Gain realized and recognized. The difference between the amount realized and the adjusted basis of the property sold or otherwise disposed of by the taxpayer is the gain realized.[37] This formula permits the taxpayer to recover the amount he paid for the property tax free. This recovery is sometimes called a return of capital.

> Amount realized
> − <u>Adjusted basis</u>
> Gain realized

Unless the Code provides otherwise, any gain realized must be recognized.[38] To recognize gain means to report it on the taxpayer's income tax return.

Personal losses. In general, the taxpayer may not recognize any loss from the disposition of property used for personal purposes.[39]

B. Loss from Disposition of Investment Property

Once a taxpayer acquires property, the property may decrease in value. The Code does not permit the taxpayer to report that decrease in wealth until he has disposed of the property. In general, the decrease in wealth is the amount of loss the taxpayer has in the property, or the difference between the amount the taxpayer sold the property for and the amount he paid for it, as adjusted.[40]

> Amount realized
> − <u>Adjusted basis</u>
> Loss realized

---

33. Section 1001(a).
34. Section 1012(a).
35. Section 1016(a).
36. Section 1001(b).
37. Section 1001(a).
38. Section 1001(c).
39. Section 165(c)(3).
40. Sections 1001(a); 1016(a).

Section 1001. Determination of Amount of and Recognition of Gain or Loss

(a) Computation of Gain or Loss. — … the loss shall be the excess of the adjusted basis provided in such section [Section 1011] for determining loss over the amount realized....

Unless the Code provides authority, no loss realized may be recognized, or reported, on the taxpayer's income tax return. Section 165(c)(2) allows a taxpayer to recognize a loss from a transaction entered into for profit. Accordingly, this provision allows a taxpayer to recognize losses from the sale of investment property. The taxpayer is not allowed to claim a loss in excess of his basis in the property.[41]

Section 165. Losses

(a) General Rule. — There shall be allowed as a deduction any loss sustained during the taxable year and not compensated for by insurance or otherwise.

(b) Amount of Deduction. — For purposes of subsection (a), the basis for determining the amount of the deduction for any loss shall be the adjusted basis provided in section 1011 for determining the loss from the sale or other disposition of property.

(c) Limitation on Losses of Individuals. — In the case of an individual, the deduction under subsection (a) shall be limited to — …

> (2) losses incurred in any transaction entered into for profit, though not connected with a trade or business....

Loss Realized and Loss Recognized

Loss realized is the difference between the amount realized and the adjusted basis of the property.

Loss recognized is the amount of loss realized the taxpayer can report on his income tax return.

Tell Me More

The Code provides that, in specific situations, the taxpayer must defer the recognition of loss until a later time. These provisions are addressed in Chapters 43 and 47.

---

41. Section 165(b).

Note

Losses related to the disposition of property used in a business are discussed in Chapter 26.

1. Transaction Entered into for Profit

Property that is traditionally purchased for investment purposes, such as stock and rental properties, easily comes within the requirement that the transaction was entered into for profit. The more complex situations are those where the taxpayer purchased the asset for personal purposes and wants to convert the use from personal to investment.

Personal residence. While there may be investment benefits in purchasing a personal residence, the primary or dominant motivation behind purchasing a home is to use it as a residence. As such, the taxpayer's residence is a personal asset (one not used for investment purposes or in a business).

When a taxpayer moves out of a residence, there are at least two different objectives he can have with respect to the property. First, he can try and sell the home. Sometimes, it will take time to sell and the taxpayer may incur expenses related to the home between moving out and the sale. Second, he can convert the property into rental property. Each scenario has a different tax result.

If the taxpayer sells the residence, any loss realized from the sale cannot be recognized because the loss is personal.[42]

If the taxpayer converts the property to rental property, then eventually sells the rental property, he can recognize the loss attributable to the time the property was rental property.[43] In order for the property to be considered rental property, the taxpayer must adequately convert the property from personal use (residence) to rental property. The courts have stated that this is accomplished by renting out the property. The requirement that the property be rented out applies only with respect to the loss from the sale of the property.[44] It does not apply to operating expenses[45] or depreciation. The result is that, if the property is offered for rent but never rented out, a taxpayer is allowed operating expense deductions and depreciation, but not a loss on disposition.

In *Cowles v. Commissioner*[46] the taxpayers were unable to sell their residence in a timely manner. The taxpayers then listed the property for sale and for rent. The taxpayers received two offers to rent the property. Neither was accepted. The first offer was not for a sufficient amount of rent. The second offer was withdrawn as the potential renters decided to buy their own residence. The taxpayers eventually sold the house without ever having rented it and realized a loss on disposition.

There was no dispute over whether the taxpayers were entitled to claim operating expenses or depreciation during the time the home was offered for rent. The government

---

42. See Sections 165(c)(3); 262.
43. Section 165(c)(2).
44. Id.
45. Such as those allowed under Section 212.
46. T.C. Memo. 1970-198.

conceded that offering the property for rent was sufficient to bring the property within Section 212 and Section 168. The issue was whether the taxpayers were entitled to recognize the loss realized on disposition. More specifically, the taxpayers had to establish that the purchase of the residence was a "transaction entered into for profit." The court held it was not.

> Concededly this case reflects some conceptual difficulties. It is not readily apparent how a mere offer to rent property is sufficient to justify a holding that it is "held for the production of income" within the meaning of sections 212 and 167 but not sufficient to permit a holding that it is "otherwise appropriated to income-producing purposes" within the meaning of section 1.165-9, Income Tax Regs. But such a distinction has long been established in the decided cases.... Perhaps if we were writing on a clean slate, we would be inclined to re-examine this distinction. But, in light of the foregoing decisions, as well as those hereinafter cited, we are unwilling to chart a new course.... Nor does the fact that the sale of the property was incident to Theodore's transfer of employment support a conclusion in petitioners' favor....
>
> We hold that mere offers to sell or rent are insufficient to provide the necessary foundation for the deduction of a loss incurred in a "transaction entered into for profit," as required by section 165(c)(2).[47]

Conversion of Personal Residence to Investment Property	Section 212(1) Management expenses ("production or collection of income")	Section 165(c)(2) Loss on sale ("transaction entered into for profit")
Offered for rent, but never rented out	Allowed	Not allowed
Actually rented	Allowed	Allowed (to extent of loss after conversion)

2. Basis Rules for Property Converted from Personal Use

If the taxpayer disposes of property and the property had been used for personal purposes, the loss during the time the property was held for personal purposes may not be recognized. The recognized loss is limited to the loss that occurred while the property was used for investment purposes. The regulations achieve this result through the "lesser-of" rule. The taxpayer may not claim a loss in excess of his basis in the property. His basis in the property is the lesser basis or value of the property at the time of conversion, as adjusted.[48]

Note that the "lesser-of rule" only applies to basis for purposes of computing depreciation and calculating the amount of loss realized. To calculate the amount of gain on disposition

---

47. Cowles v. Commissioner, T.C. Memo. 1970-198.
48. See Treas. Reg. § 1.165-9(b); Rev. Rul. 72-111, 1972-1 C.B. 56.

of the property, the basis in the property is the usual adjusted basis—cost, plus any capital expenditures, less depreciation.[49]

These rules apply to the above-discussed situations where the taxpayer has successfully converted the personal residence into investment property and sold the property at a loss. The maximum loss he is entitled to claim is the loss that occurred while the property was held for investment purposes. Any loss that occurred while the taxpayer used the property as his personal residence is not permitted because it is a personal loss. Thus, for purposes of determining the amount of loss that can be recognized, the taxpayer's basis is the fair market value of the property at the time of conversion, adjusted for depreciation.[50]

Pictorial Example of Basis Rules for Personal Property Converted to Investment Property

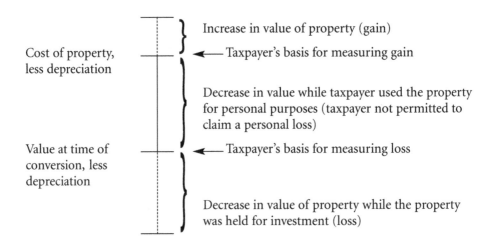

Rules — Taxpayer's Basis in Property Converted from Personal to Investment Property

- **Appreciated property:** If the value of the property at the time of the conversion from personal to investment is greater than what the taxpayer paid for the property, the taxpayer takes a cost basis in the property, less any depreciation claimed.

- **Depreciated property:** If the value of the property at the time of the conversion from personal to investment is less than what the taxpayer paid for the property, the taxpayer's basis depends on what happens to the value of the property after the conversion.

49. Id.
50. See Treas. Reg. § 1.165-9(b), (c); Rev. Rul. 72-111, 1972-1 C.B. 56.

- ○ *Decreases below the fair market value of the property at the time of the conversion.* The taxpayer takes the fair market value of the property as of the time of the conversion as the basis in the property, less depreciation. The taxpayer will have a loss equal to the decrease in value that occurred after the conversion of the property.

- ○ *Increases in excess of the taxpayer's purchase price.* The taxpayer takes a cost basis in the property, less depreciation. The taxpayer will have a gain on disposition of the property.

- ○ *Increases in value, but not in excess of the taxpayer's purchase price.* The decrease in value of the property represents the loss in the property while the taxpayer used it for personal purposes. The taxpayer reports nothing.

3. Special Rule — Investment Property Casualty Losses

One way a taxpayer may suffer a loss related to investment property is through a casualty loss.[51] The taxpayer's property may be destroyed or harmed by a casualty, such as a fire, storm, tornado, or hurricane. Or it may be stolen. The general rule is that the amount of the loss is the lesser of the adjusted basis or the decrease in value caused by the casualty or theft. However, if the property has been completely destroyed, the amount of the loss is the adjusted basis of the property.[52] Note that, if the value of the property exceeds the property's adjusted basis, there is no loss attributed to this excess (i.e. lost profit). Because the increase in value (the appreciation) had never been reported, no offsetting loss is permitted.

Once the amount of loss has been determined, it is reduced by any insurance proceeds received.[53] The taxpayer may recognize any remaining loss.[54]

Timing. When the taxpayer has submitted an insurance claim and there is a reasonable prospect of recovery, the taxpayer may not claim the loss until the amount of insurance recovery is determined with reasonable certainty.[55] If the property has been stolen, the loss is allowed in the year the taxpayer discovers the theft.[56]

C. Sales to Related Parties

When the taxpayer recognizes a loss, he may use the loss to offset his gross income, resulting in less taxable income and a lower tax liability. Given this tax benefit, some

---

51. Section 165(c)(2). Casualty losses also are allowed for personal property. Section 165(c)(3). See the discussion in Chapter 19.
52. Treas. Reg. § 1.165-7(b)(1).
53. See Section 165(h)(5)(E).
54. Section 165(c)(2).
55. Treas. Reg. § 1.165-1(d)(2).
56. Treas. Reg. § 1.165-8(a)(2).

taxpayers would "sell" property that had decreased in value to a related party. By selling to a related party, the taxpayer would recognize a loss and, perhaps, still maintain control over the property.

Example. Mitch owns stock with a basis of $5,000 and fair market value of $2,000. If he sold the stock to his teenage daughter for $2,000, he would have a $3,000 loss realized (amount realized of $2,000, less basis of $5,000); he could use the loss to offset his income. As his daughter is a minor, arguable he still has control over the stock.

Congress responded to these types of potentially abusive transactions by enacting Section 267, which prohibits the taxpayer from recognizing a loss when the sale is to a related party.[57] In the previous example, because the sale was to Mitch's daughter, under Section 267 he would not be able to recognize the $3,000 loss realized.

Parties are related if they are members of the same family.[58] Family members include brothers and sisters, spouse, ancestors, and lineal descendants.[59]

Section 267 has an additional provision that applies on a subsequent sale by the related party. It allows the buyer-turned-seller to offset any gain by the loss previously disallowed. While it allows the related party to offset the gain realized, it cannot be used to create a loss.[60]

Example. Mitch owned stock with a basis of $5,000 and fair market value of $2,000. He sold the stock to his daughter for $2,000. He had a $3,000 loss realized but could not recognize the loss because it was a sale to a related party.

Five years later Mitch's daughter sold the stock for $10,000. She had an $8,000 gain realized (amount realized of $10,000, less $2,000 basis). She can offset this gain by the $3,000 loss Mitch was not able to recognize, reporting only $5,000 of gain (gain of $8,000, less the $3,000 loss previously disallowed).

Summary of Rules — Sale of Investment Property at a Loss

General rule: A taxpayer may recognize a loss from the disposition of investment property. However, if the sale is to a related party, the taxpayer may not recognize the loss.

Property converted from personal use: The amount of recognized loss cannot exceed the loss while the property was used for investment purposes. For determining loss, the adjusted basis is the lesser of the fair market value of the property or the basis at the time of conversion to investment use, as adjusted.

Casualty or theft losses: The amount of loss is the lesser of the adjusted basis in the property or the decrease in value caused by the casualty. However, if the property was completely destroyed or stolen, the loss is equal to the property's adjusted basis. The recognized loss is the loss reduced by any insurance proceeds received.

---

57. Section 267(a)(1).
58. Section 267(b)(1). A person can also be related to an entity, such as a trust, corporation, or partnership. Those rules are beyond the scope of this text.
59. Section 267(c)(4).
60. Section 267(d).

D. Application of Rules

Example 1. Otto owned stock in InvestCo. This year he sold the stock for $100. At the time of the sale his basis was $120. Otto may recognize the $20 loss ($100 amount realized, less $120 basis).

Example 2. Larry converted his personal residence into rental property by renting it out. At the time of the conversion, the fair market value of the building was $100,000 and his adjusted basis was $120,000. For purposes of computing depreciation on the rental property Larry's basis is $100,000.

Example 3. Maynard converted his personal residence into rental property by renting it out. At the time of the conversion the fair market value of the building was $100,000 and his adjusted basis was $120,000. Five years later, when his adjusted basis was $80,000 (basis of $100,000, reduced by allowable depreciation), Maynard sold the property for $60,000. Maynard may recognize a $20,000 loss ($60,000 amount realized, less $80,000 adjusted basis).

Example 4. Nellie converted her personal residence into rental property by renting it out. At the time of the conversion, the fair market value of the building was $100,000 and her adjusted basis was $120,000. Five years later, she sold the property for $150,000. As of the time of the sale, the total amount of depreciation she had claimed (based on the $100,000 value) was $50,000. For purposes of the sale, her adjusted basis is $70,000 ($120,000, less $50,000) and her gain is $80,000 ($150,000 amount realized, less $70,000 adjusted basis).

Example 5. Mabel moved out of her personal residence and put it up for sale. One year later she sold the residence. Mabel is not entitled to claim any maintenance expenses (under Section 212) or depreciation.

Example 6. Mike moved out of his personal residence and put it up for sale or rent. He was unable to find a renter for the building, but did sell the property a year later, realizing a loss. During the time the property was offered for rent, Mike is entitled to claim maintenance expenses (under Section 212) and depreciation. He is not entitled to claim the loss on sale.

Example 7. Dennis owned a computer he used to manage his investment activities. This year a large storm struck the area, and lightening struck his house. Because his computer was plugged in to an outlet, it was completely destroyed. Dennis did not have the computer insured. At the time of the storm, Dennis's adjusted basis in the computer was $1,000 and its fair market value was $500.

Dennis suffered a casualty loss. Because the computer was completely destroyed and it was used in his investment activities, the amount of the loss is the adjusted basis in the computer, or $1,000.

Example 8. Rich owned a computer he used to manage his investment activities. This year a large storm struck the area and his home was flooded. His computer sustained some damage. Just before the storm, Rich's adjusted basis in the computer was $1,000 and its fair market value was $500. After the storm, the fair market value of the computer was $200.

Rich suffered a casualty loss. The amount of the loss is the lesser of his adjusted basis ($1,000) or decrease in value caused by the casualty ($300). Thus, the amount of the loss is $300.

Example 9. Heidi owned a computer she used to manage her investment activities. This year a large storm struck the area, and lightening struck her house. Because her computer was plugged in to an outlet, it was completely destroyed. Heidi had insurance on the computer and recovered $300 from her insurance company. At the time of the storm, Heidi's adjusted basis in the computer was $1,000 and its fair market value was $500.

Heidi suffered a casualty loss. Because the computer was completely destroyed, the amount of the loss is the adjusted basis in the computer, or $1,000. However, the loss is reduced by the insurance proceeds and Heidi is able to recognize a $700 loss ($1,000 loss, less $300 insurance recovery).

Example 10. James owned stock in RelatedCo. This year he sold the stock to his brother, Gregg, for $10,000. At the time of the sale his basis in the stock was 12,000. James realized a $2,000 loss ($10,000 amount realized, less $12,000 basis). However, he cannot recognize the loss because he sold the stock to a related party.

Subsequently, Gregg sold the stock for $15,000. At the time of the sale, Gregg's basis in the stock was $10,000. Gregg had a gain realized of $5,000. However, he can reduce this gain by the loss James was not allowed to claim, or by $2,000. Gregg recognizes a $3,000 gain ($5,000 gain, less the $2,000 previously disallowed loss).

E. Problems

1. Amy collects antiques. This year she sold a piece for $10,000. Her basis in the piece was $15,000. What are the tax consequences to Amy?

2. Beth collects watercolor paintings. This year she sold a painting to her sister, Cathy, for $10,000. Her basis in the painting was $15,000. The following year Cathy sold the painting for $16,000.

   a. What are the tax consequences to Beth?

   b. What are the tax consequences to Cathy?

3. Drew owned a computer he used for personal purposes. He paid $3,000 for the computer. When he began actively managing his investments, he transferred the use of the computer to his investment activities. At the time of the conversion, the value of the computer was $2,000. What are the tax consequences to Drew in the following alternative scenarios:

   a. The following year, after claiming $1,000 of depreciation, Drew sold the computer for $4,000.

   b. The following year, after claiming $1,000 of depreciation, Drew sold the computer for $500.

   c. The following year, after claiming $1,000 of depreciation, Dan sold the computer for $1,500.

4. Fred collects oil paintings. This year a flood in his house damaged one of the paintings. His basis in the painting was $10,000. Its value before the flood was $8,000 and its

value after was $2,000. He filed a claim with his insurance company and recovered $1,000. What are the tax consequences to Fred?

5. Gigi collects antique watches. This year one of her watches was stolen. At the time of the theft, her basis in the watch was $8,000 and the fair market value was $10,000. Gigi did not receive any recovery from her insurance company. What are the tax consequences to Gigi?

6. Each year Whitney holds a garage sale. This year she sold her used microwave oven for $50. She had purchased the microwave three years earlier for $140. What are the tax consequences to Whitney?

7. Last year Claire purchased Circle Co stock for $40,000. This year the stock has decreased in value to $30,000. What are the tax consequences to Claire?

8. Mary purchased her residence for $200,000. When it had decreased in value to $150,000 she converted the property to rental property and successfully rented it. During the time it was rented, she claimed $10,000 of depreciation. What are the tax consequences if she subsequently sells the property for the following alternative amounts:

   a. $250,000

   b. $100,000

   c. $175,000

F. Analysis and Application

1. Tom lives in Michigan and works for an automotive company. With the downturn in the economy he was laid off from work. He moved out of his house and back into his parent's home. He placed his house on the market, offering it for rent and for sale. He received no offers to rent and eventually sold the house at a substantial loss.

   a. What expenses might Tom have incurred in attempting to rent his house? Of those expenses, which would be deductible under Section 212?

   b. During the time Tom offers his house for rent is he entitled to claim depreciation?

   c. May Tom claim the loss realized on the sale of his home?

   d. Do these answers make sense?

2. Besides a personal residence, what other property might a taxpayer own for personal purposes that he might later want to convert to investment use? How would he establish that the property had been so converted?

3. Frank owns and operates a large residential building as a bed and breakfast. Due to a decline in the economy, resulting in fewer guests, he converted the bed and breakfast into his personal residence. At the time of the conversion the fair market value of the property was $5,000 less that its adjusted basis. Three years later Frank sold the home and moved into a small condominium. He realized a $7,000 loss on the sale. Can Frank claim any of the loss?

4. When the fair market value of the property is less than the adjusted basis at the time of conversion, why is depreciation calculated using fair market value? Why isn't is calculated using the adjusted basis?

5. Keith's aunt devised to him her home. The value of the house at the time of his aunt's death was $250,000. Keith did not move into the property. Rather, a year later he sold the home for $200,000. What are the tax consequences to Keith from the sale?

6. Mike and Ted have been best friends since grade school. They are not related.

    In January, Mike purchased Invest Co. for $100 per share; Ted purchased Microchip Co. for $200 per share. In December of the same year Invest Co. stock decreased in value to $80 per share and Microchip Co. decreased to $160 per share. After talking over their options, Mike agreed to buy Ted's stock for $160 per share and Ted agreed to buy Mike's stock for $80 per share. Mike reported a $20 loss per share; Ted reported a $40 loss per share. In January of the following year Mike repurchased Invest Co. stock from Ted for $80 per share; Ted repurchased Microchip Co. stock from Mike for $160 per share.

    What are the tax consequences to Mike and Ted from the above transactions? In formulating your analysis and response, you may want to consider:

    - Wolder v. Commissioner, 493 F.2d 608 (1974)
    - Salvatore v. Commissioner, T.C. Memo. 1970-30

VII

Timing Methodologies

Cash Basis:	Accrual Basis:	Special Rules:
Income: earlier of— • Actual receipt • Receipt of cash equivalent • Constructive receipt • Economic benefit Payment: considered paid when actual payment made	Income: earlier of— • Actual receipt • All events test Payment: considered accrued when meet the all events test	• Installment method • Restoration of amounts received under a claim of right • Tax benefit rule • Net operating loss

Chapter 31

Overview:
Methods of Accounting

Methods of Accounting

Cash Basis:	Accrual Basis:	Special Rules:
Income: earlier of— • Actual receipt • Receipt of cash equivalent • Constructive receipt • Economic benefit Payment: considered paid when actual payment made	Income: earlier of— • Actual receipt • All events test Payment: considered accrued when meet the all events test	• Installment method • Restoration of amounts received under a claim of right • Tax benefit rule • Net operating loss

A taxpayer reports his taxable income and pays the applicable tax on an annual basis. Most often, the taxpayer's taxable year is the calendar year — the 12-month period from January 1 through December 31 — with the return being filed on the following April 15. Some taxpayers may have a fiscal year. A fiscal year covers a 12-month time frame, but does not end on December 31.[1]

Section 441. Period for Computation of Taxable Income

(a) Computation of Taxable Income. — Taxable income shall be computed on the basis of the taxpayer's taxable year.

(b) Taxable Year. — For purposes of this subtitle, the term "taxable year" means —

> (1) the taxpayer's annual accounting period, if it is a calendar year or a fiscal year ...

---

1. Section 441(a).

While the yearly reporting requirement provides a convenient rule, it is not problem-free. First, it is often not clear in which year an item should be reported. For example, if a sole proprietor performs services but is not paid until the following year, in which year is the income reported—the year the services are performed or the year of payment? The same issue can arise with respect to a deduction. For example, if a sole proprietor receives a shipment of supplies but does not pay for them until the following year, in which year can he claim the deduction—the year the supplies were delivered or the year he paid for them?

These issues are resolved based on the taxpayer's accounting method. Cash basis accounting is considered in Chapter 32 and accrual basis accounting is considered in Chapter 33.[2] In general, the taxpayer can select his method of accounting.[3] If the taxpayer has an inventory and the sale of those goods is a material income-producing factor, the taxpayer is required to use the accrual method.[4] If the method of accounting selected by the taxpayer does not clearly reflect his income, the Commissioner can require the taxpayer to change to a method that does.[5]

Section 446. General Rule for Methods of Accounting

(a) General Rule.—Taxable income shall be computed under the method of accounting on the basis of which the taxpayer regularly computes his income in keeping his books.

(b) Exceptions.—If no method of accounting has been regularly used by the taxpayer, or if the method used does not clearly reflect income, the computation of taxable income shall be made under such method as, in the opinion of the Secretary, does clearly reflect income.

(c) Permissible Methods.—Subject to the provisions of subsection (a) and (b), a taxpayer may compute taxable income under any of the following methods of accounting—

(1) the cash receipts and disbursements method;

(2) the accrual method

* * *

Second, some issues take more than one year to be resolved or fully understood. It is possible that what appeared to be income in one year is determined to not be income several years later. Or, it is possible that a deduction claimed in one year is determined to be not a proper deduction several years later. Restoring amounts received under a claim of right, addressing the income issue, is discussed in Chapter 34. The tax benefit rule, addressing the deduction issue, is discussed in Chapter 35.

---

2. There are other methods of accounting, generally designed to address special issues that arise in different industries, but they will not be covered in this textbook.
3. Section 446(a)-(c).
4. Section 461(a); Treas. Reg. § 1.461-1(c)(2).
5. Section 446(b).

Chapter 32

Cash Basis Accounting

Methods of Accounting

Cash Basis:	Accrual Basis:	Special Rules:
Income: earlier of— • **Actual receipt** • **Receipt of cash equivalent** • **Constructive receipt** • **Economic benefit** **Payment: considered paid when actual payment made**	Income: earlier of— • Actual receipt • All events test Payment: considered accrued when meet the all events test	• Installment method • Restoration of amounts received under a claim of right • Tax benefit rule • Net operating loss

Read

Code Sections 441(a)-(e); 446(a)-(c); 451(a), (h); 461(a), (g)

Treas. Reg. §§ 1.446-1(a), (b), (c)(1)(i); 1.451-2; 1.461-1(a)(1)

A. Background

Gross income. Gross income includes income (accessions to wealth) derived from any and all sources.[6] It includes every accession to wealth, unless there is an exception.

Because a loan does not represent an accession to wealth, it is not included in income when the funds are received. Similarly, because a security deposit does not represent an accession to wealth, it is not included in income when received.

Deductions. Deductions are a matter of legislative grace. To be entitled to claim a deduction, the taxpayer must provide authority for allowance of the deduction.[7]

An expense has a life or benefit that last less than one year. If an expense meets the criteria of Section 162, it is currently deductible. The expense must be:

---

6. Section 61(a).
7. Welch v. Helvering, 290 U.S. 111 (1933).

- Ordinary: common and accepted in the industry (based on the facts and circumstances).

- Necessary: appropriate and helpful.

- Expense: have a life of less than one year, or otherwise impact only one taxable year.

- **Paid or incurred during the taxable year.** If a cash basis taxpayer, the amount must have been paid.

- In carrying on a trade or business: involved in the activity with continuity and regularity; the taxpayer's primary purpose must be for income or profit. A sporadic activity or hobby does not qualify.

In contrast, a capital expenditure has a life or benefit that extends beyond one year. It is not currently deductible, even if the amount is paid in full. Rather, if the asset wears out over time, the cost must be capitalized and can be recovered through depreciation or amortization deductions.

Taxable income. In general, taxable income is the taxpayer's gross income, less all allowable deductions.[8] The taxpayer's liability is based on the amount of the taxpayer's taxable income.[9]

B. Cash Basis Accounting

The theory behind cash basis accounting is very simple—the taxpayer reports the income when he receives the payment. It does not matter if the payment is in cash or in property.[10] And, he can claim a deduction that is otherwise allowed by the Code when he has made the payment.[11]

Section 451. General Rule for Taxable Year of Inclusion

(a) General Rule.—The amount of any item of gross income shall be included in the gross income for the taxable year in which received by the taxpayer, unless, under the method of accounting used in computing taxable income, such amount is to be properly accounted for as of a different period.

Section 461. General Rule for Taxable Year of Deduction

(a) General Rule.—The amount of any deduction or credit allowed by this subtitle shall be taken for the taxable year which is the proper taxable year under the method of accounting used in computing taxable income.

---

8. Section 63(a).
9. Section 1.
10. Section 451(a).
11. Section 461(a).

1. Reporting Income

When a taxpayer receives gross income, he must report it.

Cash: When the taxpayer receives gross income in the form of cash, he must report the cash in the year of receipt.

Property: When the taxpayer receives gross income in the form of property, he must report the value of the property in the year of receipt.

Check: When the taxpayer receives gross income in the form of a check, it is treated the same as cash. The taxpayer must include the amount of the check in income, even if received on December 31st after the banks have closed. If the check is post-dated or is subsequently dishonored upon presentation or was delivered subject to a condition that arose after delivery but before the check was presented for payment, the taxpayer does not have to include the check in his income when the check is received.[12]

Sample of Some Cases Involving Checks

Baxter v. Commissioner:[13] the taxpayer earned money in 1978 and the check was dated December 30, 1978 (which was a Saturday). However, to receive the check on that date, he would have had to drive 40 miles. Finally, the bank would not credit the funds to his account until 1979. The taxpayer was required to include the check in income in 1979.

Bright v. United States:[14] the taxpayer deposited a check in 1985. The bank did not allow him access to the funds until 1986, when it could collect the funds from the drawee bank. The taxpayer was required to include the check in income in 1985.

Kahler v. Commissioner:[15] the taxpayer received a check on December 31 and deposited it the following year. The taxpayer was required to include the check in income in the year he received the check.

---

a. Cash Equivalent

An issue may arise when the taxpayer receives something other than cash or property. Whether the taxpayer must include an amount in gross income depends on whether what he received can function the same as cash or easily be converted into cash, i.e., a cash equivalent. The most common example of a cash equivalent is a promissory note. The note is neither cash nor property. Whether receipt of the note must be included in income depends on whether the note can be used the same as cash or readily be converted into cash (without a large discount).

---

12. Some court opinions address checks as cash equivalents. See discussion about cash equivalents below.

13. 816 F.2d 493 (9th Cir. 1987).

14. 926 F.2d 383 (5th Cir. 1991). The taxpayer could have deposited the check at the payor bank and received access to the funds immediately.

15. 18 T.C. 31 (1952).

In *Williams v. Commissioner*[16] the taxpayer received a promissory note in exchange for services he had rendered. The note was payable in eight months, was not secured, and bore no interest. The taxpayer, concerned the obligor would not be able to pay the note, attempted to sell the note to several banks. No banks were willing to purchase the note from him.

The Service argued the taxpayer should include the note in income upon receipt of the note. The taxpayer argued he was not required to report anything until the note was paid. The Tax Court agreed with the taxpayer. The note "was not received in payment of the outstanding debt due him for the performance of his services. A note received only as security, or as an evidence of indebtedness, and not as payment, may not be regarded as income at the time of receipt."[17]

At the other end of the spectrum is *Cowden v. Commissioner.*[18] The taxpayers received two promissory notes in 1951 in exchange for an oil, gas, and mineral lease. The first promissory note was due in 1952. The second promissory note was due in 1953. The obligor on both notes was Stanolind Oil and Gas Company. Later in 1951, the taxpayer assigned the first promissory note to a bank (of which the taxpayer-husband was a director). The face value of the note was $250,192.50. The bank discounted the note by $257.43. In 1952, the taxpayer assigned the second promissory note to the bank. The face value of the note was $250,484.34. The bank discounted the note by $313.14.

The Service argued the notes should have been included in income at the time they were created, 1951, with the amount appropriately discounted from the date of maturity to the date of creation. The Fifth Circuit held—

> If a promise to pay of a solvent obligor is unconditional and assignable, not subject to set-offs, and is of a kind that is frequently transferred to lenders or investors at a discount not substantially greater than the generally prevailing premium for the use of money, such promise is the equivalent of cash and taxable in like manner as cash would have been taxable had it been received by the taxpayer rather than the obligation.[19]

It remanded the case to the Tax Court for a determination of whether the promissory notes met the definition of a cash equivalent. On remand, the Tax Court found that the taxpayers had received a cash equivalent.

The cash equivalency doctrine has been applied narrowly and primarily to promissory notes.

Sample of Cases Involving Cash Equivalents

Kuehner v. Commissioner:[20] amounts were contributed to an escrow account the taxpayer controlled. Because the taxpayer's property interest in the account was the equivalent of cash, he was required to include in his income the value of the amounts contributed to the escrow account during the year.

Revenue Ruling 73-173:[21] the taxpayer received breeding rights in thoroughbred stallions. To the extent the rights were freely transferable, readily marketable, and

---

16. 28 T.C. 1000 (1957).
17. Williams v. Commissioner, 28 T.C. 1000, 1002 (1957).
18. 289 F.2d 20 (5th Cir. 1961).
19. Cowden v. Commissioner, 289 F.2d 20, 24 (5th Cir. 1961).
20. 214 F.2d 437 (1st Cir. 1954).
21. 73-173, 1973-1 C.B. 40.

immediately convertible to cash, the taxpayer was required to include the value of the rights in his income upon receipt because they were a cash equivalent.

b. Constructive Receipt

Because a cash basis taxpayer is required to include in income only amounts received, some taxpayers may try to avoid receipt. To prohibit such inappropriate deferrals of income, the regulations require cash basis taxpayers to include in income any amounts that are constructively received. Income is constructively received if the amount is made available to the taxpayer and there are no limitations or restrictions on the taxpayer's control.[22]

Treas. Reg. § 1.451-2(a)

(a) General rule. — Income although not actually reduced to a taxpayer's possession is constructively received by him in the taxable year during which it is credited to his account, set apart for him, or otherwise made available so that he may draw upon it at any time, or so that he could have drawn upon it during the taxable year if notice of intention to withdraw had been given. However, income is not constructively received if the taxpayer's control of its receipt is subject to substantial limitations or restrictions.

While the constructive receipt doctrine does not allow a taxpayer to defer reporting income, it does not require a taxpayer to accelerate reporting income. If the amount is not yet due and owing, the taxpayer can decline to accept payment.[23]

Example. Baxter owns a duplex. Rent is due on the first day of the month. On December 31, tenant offered him a check for January's rent. Because the rent was not yet due, Baxter was free to decline payment, requesting that the tenant return the following day when the rent was actually due. (Of course, if he does accept the prepayment, he must include the payment in his income in the year of receipt.)

Note that, at the time parties are negotiating a contract, no amounts are due and owing. Accordingly, they are free to structure the transaction (and payment schedule) as they wish without running afoul of the constructive receipt doctrine.[24]

Lottery prize winners. States may allow a lottery winner to elect either a lump sum payout or receive payments over time. If the lottery winner elects to receive payments over time, under the constructive receipt doctrine the total amount of winnings was available to the taxpayer without limitation. Section 451(h) overrides the constructive receipt doctrine and allows the taxpayer to include the payments as they are received. To come within Section 451(h) the lottery winner must be required to exercise the option within sixty days of the date he is entitled to receive payment.

---

22. Treas. Reg. § 1.451-2(a).
23. Cowden v. Commissioner, 289 F.2d 20 (1961); Rev. Rul. 60-31, 1960-1 C.B. 174.
24. Id.

Checklist for Constructive Receipt

❏   The amount is made available to the taxpayer;

❏   There are no limitations or restrictions on the taxpayer's control; and

❏   The amount is due and owing.

Quote

The doctrine of constructive receipt was, no doubt, conceived by the Treasury in order to prevent a taxpayer from choosing the year in which to return income merely by choosing the year in which to reduce it to possession. Thereby the Treasury may subject income to taxation when the only thing preventing its reduction to possession is the volition of the taxpayer.

Ross v. Commissioner, 169 F.2d 483, 491 (1st Cir. 1948)

Tell Me More

A taxpayer may own a controlling interest in a corporation. He may also be employed by the corporation. Courts have recognized the existence of the corporation separate from the shareholder. Thus, even though the shareholder, through his controlling interest, can cause the corporation to pay him, the courts have held that the taxpayer is not required to include compensation in income until it is actually paid by the corporation to the employee. For the taxpayer-shareholder to be treated as having constructively received a salary payment, some facts, in addition to ownership, generally are required.[25]

c. Economic Benefit Doctrine

A taxpayer may have a right to receive income in the future and the right may represent a current benefit. When the taxpayer does not have actual receipt, what is received is not a cash equivalent, and the taxpayer is not in constructive receipt of any amount but there is an economic benefit, courts may turn to the economic benefit doctrine and require the taxpayer to currently report the value of the benefit in income. Thus, gross income includes an economic benefit conferred on the taxpayer to the extent the benefit has an ascertainable fair market value.

The focus generally is on whether a fixed amount has been set aside, secured against the payer's creditors, to be irrevocably paid out to the taxpayer in the future. The economic benefit doctrine is likely to apply when an amount is placed in escrow, to be paid out in the future. Courts have applied this doctrine most often when considering deferred compensation or the deferred payment of a prize or award. For example, in *Sproull v. Commissioner*,[26] as part of a football player's contract, a bonus was placed in escrow, to be

---

25. Hyland v. Commissioner, 175 F.2d 422 (2d Cir. 1979); Rev. Rul. 72-317, 1972-1 C.B. 128.
26. 16 T.C. 244 (1951), *aff'd*, 194 F.2d 541 (6th Cir. 1952).

paid out to the player over a two-year period. The football player received an economic benefit when the amount was placed in escrow.

Example. The taxpayers won the Irish Hospital Sweepstakes. Because they were minor children, the funds were deposited into a bank account until the children turned 21 or their legal representative applied for release of the funds. The taxpayers were required to include the funds in the year deposited to their account. In that year they received the economic benefit from the funds because they had irrevocably been set aside.[27]

d. Claim of Right

A taxpayer may have possession of money, but not be certain he is entitled to keep it. In *North American Oil Consolidated v. Burnet*[28] there was a dispute between North American Oil and the government about beneficial ownership of land with oil. In 1915 the government filed a lawsuit to oust North American Oil from possession of the land. In 1916 the court appointed a receiver to operate the property and hold the income from the property. In 1917 the district court issued a final decree dismissing the bill, and the receiver paid the income to North American Oil. The government appealed. In 1920, the appellate court affirmed the trial court and in 1922 an appeal to the Supreme Court was dismissed.

The issue before the court was the proper year for North American Oil to report the income. The possibilities included:

1915: the year the government filed the lawsuit

1916: the year the funds at issue were earned

1917: the year the funds were paid to North American Oil

1922: the year the case became final and it was certain North American Oil could keep the funds.

The Supreme Court held the funds were included in the taxpayer's income when it had control over them. Inclusion was required even though there was the possibility North American Oil would have to return the funds if it lost the case on appeal. The court stated —

> If a taxpayer receives earnings under a claim or right and without restriction as to its disposition, he has received income which he is required to return [author's note: return means report], even though it may still be claimed that he is not entitled to retain the money, and even though he may still be adjudged liable to restore its equivalent.[29]

The requirement that a taxpayer include in income funds within his control, even if he might have to return the funds in the future, is known as the claim of right doctrine.

Tell Me More

If North American Oil had lost the case on appeal years after having included the amount in income, it would have been entitled to address the reduction in income at the time the funds were repaid.[30]

---

27. Pulsifer v. Commissioner, 64 T.C. 245 (1975).
28. 286 U.S. 417 (1932).
29. North American Oil Consolidated v. Burnett, 286 U.S. 417, 424 (1932).
30. This issue is discussed in Chapter 35.

The Supreme Court expanded the reach of the claim of right doctrine to include illegally obtained funds. In *James v. United States*[31] the taxpayer embezzled funds and one of the issues before the court was the proper year to include the funds. In reaching its decision that the funds should be included in income in the year of embezzlement, the court relied on its holding in *North American Oil*.

> When a taxpayer acquires earnings, lawfully or unlawfully, without the consensual recognition, express or implied, of an obligation to repay and without restriction as to their disposition, "he has received income which he is required to return, even though it may still be claimed that he is not entitled to retain the money, and even though he may still be adjudged liable to restore its equivalent."[32]

Tell Me More

There is a policy issue involved in taxing illegally obtained funds. For example, assume the taxpayer embezzled funds. He must report the funds on his income tax return and pay the applicable tax. Assume he spends none of the embezzled funds, except to the extent necessary to pay the taxes.

When the taxpayer is caught, he is required to make restitution. Unfortunately, the taxpayer only has the amount of embezzled funds less the tax paid. If he returns what he has to the victim, the victim will not be made whole. Instead, a portion of the victim's funds were previously transferred to the government.

Summary of Rule — Claim of Right Doctrine

A taxpayer must include in income funds (whether legally or illegally obtained) received under a claim of right, without an obligation to repay, and without restriction as to their disposition, even though he may have to repay the funds in the future.

2. Claiming a Deduction

Under cash basis accounting, an amount is considered paid when the taxpayer actually makes the payment.[33] The cash or property must leave the control of the taxpayer or any agent of the taxpayer. If the taxpayer pays with a check, the amount is considered paid when the check is delivered or mailed, as long as the check is unconditional and clears in due course. Under cash basis accounting an amount cannot be "constructively paid." Accordingly, a taxpayer who issues his own note as payment has not made a payment for cash basis accounting purposes.

---

31. 366 U.S. 213 (1961).
32. James v. United States, 366 U.S. 213, 219 (1961).
33. Treas. Reg. §§ 1.446-1(c)(1)(i); 1.461-1(a)(1).

The taxpayer can make payment with borrowed funds.[34] For example, when the taxpayer uses a credit card to make a payment, the amount is considered paid even though the taxpayer still owes the third party.

Prepayments. With deductions tied so closely to payments, a taxpayer may chose to pay an amount early to be able to claim the deduction. However, a prepayment may provide the taxpayer with a right or benefit that extends beyond one year. If the taxpayer pays for an asset that has a life of more than one year, the payment must be capitalized and the cost recovered through depreciation, if applicable.[35] For example, if the taxpayer prepaid five years' worth of rent, the benefit extends more than one year. Accordingly, the taxpayer is required to capitalize the expenditure and recover the cost through amortization.

For those costs that are close to one year, the regulations provide a test to help the taxpayer determine if the costs should be capitalized. If the taxpayer makes a prepayment and the right or benefit paid for does not extend beyond the earlier of 12 months after the first date on which the taxpayer realizes the benefit or the end of the taxable year following the taxable year in which the payment is made, the taxpayer is not required to capitalize the amount of the payment.[36]

Prepayments of interest are subject to their own rule. Even if the taxpayer prepays interest, the interest is treated as having been paid in the period to which it is allocable.[37] In effect, the taxpayer is placed on the accrual method of accounting.[38]

Tell Me More

A taxpayer may be required to pay "points" when obtaining a loan. Points are a fee paid to the lender. One point is equal to one percent of the amount of the loan. Points are pre-paid interest but are deductible if incurred in connection with the purchase or improvement of, or secured, by the taxpayer's principal residence.[39]

Summary of Rules — Cash Basis Taxpayer

The taxpayer must include in income all amounts:

- Actually received
- That are a cash equivalent
- Constructively received
- For which he has received an economic benefit

He can claim a deduction, if otherwise allowed, for all amounts actually paid during the year.

---

34. Rev. Rul. 78-39, 1978-1 C.B. 73.
35. Sections 263; 167; 168. See discussion in Chapters 23 and 29.
36. Treas. Reg. § 1.263(a)-4(f)(1).
37. Section 461(g)(1).
38. The accrual method of accounting is discussed in Chapter 34.
39. Section 461(g)(2).

C. Application of Rules

Each taxpayer is a cash basis taxpayer.

Example 1. Alexis provided $1,000 of legal services to her client. After receiving the bill the client called Alexis and said that he was unable to pay the bill until the following year. While he paid her nothing during the current year, he did pay her $800 in the following year. Alexis reports no income during the current year and $800 in the following year.

Example 2. Charlene operates a hair salon as a sole proprietorship. On December 30 of this year she colored, cut, and styled her client's hair. The client gave her a $90 check. Charlene was unable to deposit the check until January 3 of the following year.

If the taxpayer receives a check, the check generally is treated the same as cash. Unless the check is dishonored upon presentation, Charlene must include the check in her income for the first year.

Example 3. Frieda provided $1,000 of legal services to her client. The client paid Frieda by giving her a watch worth $1,000. Frieda must report the value of the watch in her gross income in the year she received the watch.

Example 4. Jennifer provided consulting services to her client. After receiving the bill the client called Jennifer and said he was unable to pay the bill until the following year. He signed a promissory note reflecting the amount he owed Jennifer.

Generally, a promissory note is not treated the same as cash or as a cash equivalent. When Jennifer received the promissory note she was not required to include any amount in her gross income.

Example 5. Francine, a cash basis taxpayer, provided legal services to her client in December. After receiving the bill the client called Francine to tell her he would come to her office that day to pay the bill. Francine asked the client to wait until January to pay the bill, and he did so.

Because the client had made the amount available to Francine in December without limitations or restrictions, and the amount was due and owing, Francine has constructive receipt. She must include the amount the client was willing to pay her in December in her income for that year.

Example 6. Dinah owns and operates a photography studio. This July she met with her client and agreed to provide photography services at the client's November wedding. As part of the negotiations for the services, even though the client was willing and able to pay earlier, the parties agreed Dinah would not bill the client for the services until January of the following year.

At the time of the meeting with the client, no amount was due and owing to Dinah. Accordingly, she was free to negotiate for a payment structure that included a payment in the future. She is not in constructive receipt of any amount.

Example 7. Gladys works for a consulting business. As part of her compensation package her employer agreed to transfer $100,000 to an annuity company. The company will begin paying Gladys a yearly annuity payment when she turns 65, continuing until her death.

While Gladys has received no cash currently, she does currently benefit from the annuity funded by her employer. She must include the present value of the annuity in her gross income in the year the employer creates the account.

Example 8. Henrietta owns and operates a computer software business. This year she paid $100 cash for supplies. For purposes of Section 162 Henrietta has paid for these items.

Example 9. Holly owns and operates a computer software business. This year she paid $100 for supplies by using her business Visa card. For purposes of Section 162 Holly has paid for these items.

Example 10. Heidi has a legal practice. In December she prepared the check for the utility company, entered the check into the business's ledger, but, rather than mailing the payment, kept the envelope in her purse. She dropped the envelope in the first mailbox she came across in January.

For a deduction to be permissible the taxpayer must actually make the payment. There is no constructive payment doctrine. Until Heidi mails the bill, she has not made the payment. If the deduction is otherwise permissible, she may claim it in the year the bill was mailed.

Example 11. Eileen has a legal practice. In December she purchased a copy machine. Even though Eileen paid for the equipment, it was a capital expenditure and the cost must be recovered over time through depreciation.

Example 12. Darren owns and operates a consulting service. In November he purchased 12 months worth of fire insurance. The insurance created a benefit lasting beyond the taxable year of purchase. However, because the benefit does not extend beyond 12 months or the following year, he can deduct the cost of the insurance.

Example 13. Albert owns and operates a small business. In November he purchased 24 months worth of flood insurance. The insurance created a benefit lasting beyond the year of purchase. In addition, the benefit extends beyond 12 months and extends beyond the following year. Accordingly, he cannot currently deduct the cost of the insurance. Rather, it is a capital expenditure and the cost must be recovered over time through amortization.

D. Problems

Each taxpayer is a cash basis taxpayer.

1. Hillary owns a fashion boutique. On Friday, December 29th she had a large sale. At the close of business she added up her receipts, summarized below. From her Friday receipts how much must she include in her income for the year?

   Cash $5,000
   Checks $15,000
   Credit card charges* $45,000

* Note that there is often a two-day delay between when Hillary runs the credit card through her machine and when the company credits her account.

2. Marcus is a successful painter. A local art gallery contacted him about staging an art show. As part of the offer, the gallery would also purchase five of his oil paintings for a total payment of $100,000 and keep them permanently on display. Because he has already earned a substantial amount from sales during the year, Marcus suggests

that the gallery display the paintings during the current year, and then purchase the five paintings next year. The gallery agrees. What are the tax consequences to Marcus this year and next year?

3. Carrie is a medical consultant. In November of this year Carrie performed $50,000 worth of services for Dr. Jones. Based on her practice of billing the client the following month, Carrie did not send a bill to Dr. Jones until late December. Dr. Jones paid the bill in early January of the following year. In which year must Carrie report the $50,000?

4. Darius is a computer consultant. In November of this year Darius performed $50,000 worth of services for Mark. Darius sent Mark the bill at the end of November and Mark mailed a check. While Darius received the check on December 27, he did not deposit it until the following year. In which year must Darius report the $50,000?

5. Ester is a wedding planner. In December of this year Ester planned Florence's wedding at a cost of $10,000. Florence offered to pay Ester as soon as the wedding was over, but Ester insisted that Florence not pay her until January when Florence had returned from her honeymoon. When Florence returned in January, she paid Ester. In which year must Ester report the $10,000?

6. Georgia provided $10,000 of legal services to her client. Upon receiving the bill the client called Georgia and told her that she would not be able to pay the bill until the following year. To provide the most secure position for Georgia as possible, the client offered to sign a promissory note. Georgia agreed and the client signed the note. The following year the client paid the bill in full. In which year must Georgia report the $10,000?

7. Hans is a sales representative for a large shoe company. In addition to a fixed salary Hans receives a commission based on the number of shoes he sells each month. In December he received payment for his November commissions. Although the check seemed larger than he expected it to be, Hans did not question the amount. He deposited the check. In January of the following year, the company notified Hans, telling him that there was a computational error in computing the amount of his check. Hans must return the overpayment to the company. What are the tax consequences to Hans from receiving the commission check?

8. Iris has known Ted for many years. In fact, she has some information about Ted that he does not want revealed. For Iris to not reveal what she knows about Ted, Ted pays her $5,000 each year. What are the tax consequences to Iris each year when she receives the payment from Ted?

9. Anthony makes a $10,000 charitable contribution to his favorite charity by placing a charge on his credit card. For purposes of determining whether Anthony is entitled to a charitable contribution deduction, when is the payment considered as having been made?

10. Franz purchased a computer for use in his business by placing a charge on his credit card. What are the tax consequences to Franz?

11. Kieran paid $5,000 to purchase casualty insurance for his business. To determine the tax consequences of the purchase, what additional information do you need from Kieran?

12. Ernie provided $10,000 of legal services to Brian related to Brian's business. Brian paid Ernie with a negotiable note. In December Ernie was able to sell the note to his bank for $9,900. In January of the following year, Brian paid the $10,000 note.

    a. What are the tax consequences to Ernie?

   b. What are the tax consequences to Brian?

13. Gabby provided $10,000 of legal services to Jordan. Jordan has not yet paid. What is Gabby's basis in the account receivable?

E. Analysis and Application

Each taxpayer is a cash basis taxpayer.

1. How many items can you identify that might be a cash equivalent?

2. If a check is post-dated for the following year, when does the taxpayer have to include the amount in income?

3. Can you think of a situation when the taxpayer would be arguing that constructive receipt applied and the Commissioner would be arguing that it did not apply?

4. Ian owns and operates a small business. In December he prepared the monthly checks for the utility, water, and phone company, entering each check into the business's ledger.

   a. He drops the checks in the mail on December 31. What are the tax consequences to Ian?

   b. Alternatively, he drops the checks into the mail on January 1. What are the tax consequences to Ian?

   c. Given that the above two alternatives involve a difference in time of just one day, is the difference in tax result justified?

5. Jennie, a cash basis taxpayer, lived in a small town in Wisconsin. She entered the Boating Digest's Sweepstakes and, to her surprise, won a new 20-foot boat. The Award Crew knocked on her door at noon on December 31 and gave her the good news. They also told her that the boat was waiting for her in Madison, Wisconsin, whenever she wanted to sign the paper work acknowledging receipt of the prize. Jennie lived fifteen miles away from Madison. In which year must Jennie include the value of the boat?

In formulating your analysis and response, you may want to consider:

- Hornung v. Commissioner, 47 T.C. 428 (1967)
- Ames v. Commissioner, 112 T.C. 304 (1999)
- Schneirs v. Commissioner, 69 T.C. 511 (1977)

6. Cole, a cash basis taxpayer, was a well-known author. In 2010, $50,000 in royalties were paid by the publisher to his agent. His agent embezzled $40,000 of the royalties and paid Cole the remaining $10,000. In 2011 Cole discovered the embezzlement, fired his agent, and sued for recovery of the embezzled amounts. In 2012 Cole recovered $30,000 of the embezzled funds. How much must Cole include in his income in 2010, 2011, and 2012?

In formulating your analysis and response, you may want to consider:

- Kuehner v. Commissioner, 214 F.2d 437 (1st Cir. 1954)
- Busby v. United States, 679 F.2d 48 (5th Cir. 1982)
- Johnston v. Commissioner, 14 T.C. 560 (1950)

7. Zina, a cash basis taxpayer, loves to gamble and lives 100 miles from Atlantic City. Last night she traveled to Atlantic City and spent several hours playing blackjack in

the Sands Casino. Because she was winning most of the hands, she had twice as many chips as when she arrived. When the dealer's shift was over, she was afraid her luck would end and decided to stop gambling while she was ahead. Zina knows that the chips can be used in any of the casinos in Atlantic City (and almost all of the restaurants and stores). She wasn't sure if she was going to gamble at a different casino, so she placed the chips she had won into her backpack and left the casino. What are the tax consequences to Zina?

In formulating your analyses and response, you may want to consider:

- Cowden v. Commissioner, 289 F.2d 20 (5th Cir. 1961)
- Williams v. Commissioner, 28 T.C. 1000 (1957)
- Rev. Rul. 80-52, 1980-1 C.B. 100.

8. Research project: With respect to the constructive receipt doctrine, research the impact of the taxpayer's geographic proximity to the location where the income is being made available. Prepare a presentation.

Chapter 33

Accrual Basis Accounting

Methods of Accounting

Cash Basis:	Accrual Basis:	Special Rules:
Income: earlier of— • Actual receipt • Receipt of cash equivalent • Constructive receipt • Economic benefit Payment: considered paid when actual payment made	Income: earlier of— • Actual receipt • All events test Payment: considered accrued when meet the all events test	• Installment method • Restoration of amounts received under a claim of right • Tax benefit rule • Net operating loss

Read

Code Sections 446(a)-(c); 451(a); 461(a), (f), (g), (h)

Treas. Reg. §§ 1.446-1(a)(2), -1(c)(1)(ii)(A); 1.451-1(a); 1.461-1(a)(2)(i), (ii); 1.461-2(a)(1)

A. Background

Gross income. Gross income includes income (accessions to wealth) derived from any and all sources.[40] It includes every accession to wealth, unless there is an exception.

Because a loan does not represent an accession to wealth, it is not included in income when the funds are received. Similarly, because a security deposit does not represent an accession to wealth, it is not included in income when received.

Deductions. Deductions are a matter of legislative grace. To be entitled to claim a deduction, the taxpayer must provide authority for allowance of the deduction.[41]

An expense has a life or benefit that last less than one year. If an expense meets the criteria of Section 162, it is currently deductible. The expense must be:

---

40. Section 61(a).
41. Welch v. Helvering, 290 U.S. 111 (1933).

- Ordinary: common and accepted in the industry (based on the facts and circumstances).

- Necessary: appropriate and helpful.

- Expense: have a life of less than one year, or otherwise impact only one taxable year.

- **Paid or incurred during the taxable year.** If an accrual basis taxpayer, the amount must have been accrued.

- In carrying on a trade or business: involved in the activity with continuity and regularity; the taxpayer's primary purpose must be for income or profit. A sporadic activity or hobby does not qualify.

In contrast, a capital expenditure has a life or benefit that extends beyond one year. It is not currently deductible, even if the amount is paid in full. Rather, if the asset wears out over time, the cost must be capitalized and can be recovered through depreciation or amortization deductions.

Taxable income. In general, taxable income is the taxpayer's gross income, less all allowable deductions.[42] The taxpayer's liability is based on the amount of the taxpayer's taxable income.[43]

B. Accrual Basis Accounting

Accrual basis accounting is based on the rights and obligations of the taxpayer. These rights and obligations are considered as part of the all-events test. Actual receipt is irrelevant for purposes of the all-events test. However, the taxpayer must report income at the earlier of when the taxpayer receives payment or meets the all-events test for income. With respect to deductions, a taxpayer is entitled to a deduction, if otherwise allowed, when he meets the all-events test for deductions.

1. Reporting Income

The taxpayer must report income at the earlier of when the taxpayer receives payment or meets the all-events test for income.

a. Actual Receipt

The rules for receipt of a payment are the same as those for cash basis taxpayers. When a taxpayer receives gross income, he must report it.

Cash: When the taxpayer receives gross income in the form of cash, he must report the cash in the year of receipt.

Property: When the taxpayer receives gross income in the form of property, he must report the value of the property in the year of receipt.

---

42. Section 63(a).
43. Section 1.

Check: When the taxpayer receives gross income in the form of a check, it is treated the same as cash. The taxpayer must include the amount of the check in income, even if received on December 31st after the banks have closed. If the check is post-dated or is subsequently dishonored upon presentation or was delivered subject to a condition that arose after delivery but before the check was presented for payment, the taxpayer does not have to include the check in his income when the check is received.

Claim of right: A taxpayer must include in income funds (whether legally or illegally obtained) received under a claim of right, without an obligation to repay, and without restriction as to their disposition, even though he may have to repay the funds in the future.[44]

Prepayment for services. If the taxpayer receives an advance payment for services, there may be an issue as to when the taxpayer has to include the amount in income. The general rule applied by the Supreme Court is that the taxpayer must include all advance payments in gross income (even though the services have not yet been rendered).[45]

Nevertheless, some taxpayers have argued that the income is accrued only when the goods have been delivered or the services have been provided. In *Schlude v. Commissioner*[46] the taxpayer provided dance lessons. Some clients signed contracts, agreeing to pay a fixed amount over time. Other clients paid cash in advance for lessons. In both cases, not all of the lessons paid for had been provided by year's end. The taxpayer argued the amounts should be reported not when the cash was received but as the lessons were provided and the money was earned. The Supreme Court noted that it could not be determined at the time the contract was entered into when the clients would request a lesson, allowing the taxpayer to earn the income. Accordingly, it held the taxpayer had to include all prepayments in its gross income at the time of receipt.

The Seventh Circuit created a small exception to the rule the Supreme Court set forth in *Schlude v. Commissioner*. In *Artnell Co. v. Commissioner*[47] the issue before the court was very similar to the issue in *Schulde*. The taxpayer purchased the White Sox baseball team. Due to the change in ownership, the White Sox' season spanned two taxable years. The taxpayer disagreed with the Commissioner about when revenue received from the sale of season tickets, parking, broadcast rights, etc. should be reported. The Commissioner argued that the prepayments had to be reported in the year of receipt- the first year. The taxpayer argued that the prepayments should be reported as the games were played and the money was earned, or spread between the two taxable years.

The Seventh Circuit noted that, factually, *Artnell* could be distinguished from *Schlude*. In *Schlude*, it was not possible to forecast when a lesson would be requested by the client. In contrast, in *Artnell* when the income would be earned could be determined because the baseball games were played on a predetermined schedule. By reporting the income as it was earned, the taxpayer in *Artnell* could more clearly reflect income. The Seventh Circuit allowed the policy behind the reporting methods (clearly reflect income) to take precedence over the specific reporting rules.

The government also has provided for a limited deferral when the taxpayer has received a prepayment for services.[48] The deferral can be used by a taxpayer who was paid in the

---

44. See complete discussion about the claim of right doctrine in Chapter 33.
45. Schlude v. Commissioner, 372 U.S. 128 (1963); American Automobile Ass'n v. United States, 367 U.S. 687 (1961).
46. 372 U.S. 128 (1963).
47. 400 F.2d 981 (7th Cir. 1968).
48. Rev. Proc. 2004-34, 2004-1 C.B. 991.

first year for services to be provided in the year of payment and the subsequent year. The taxpayer must include in income amounts as they are earned over the two-year time frame. This ruling permits the taxpayer to report a portion of the income that otherwise would have been reported in the first year in the second year. However, amounts cannot be deferred beyond the second year.

Example. Cindy, an accrual basis taxpayer, agreed to perform $5,000 worth of consulting services for Dennis during the next two years. In the first year Dennis paid Cindy $5,000 and Cindy provided $4,000 worth of consulting services. Cindy provided the remaining $1,000 worth of consulting services in the following year. Under Rev. Proc. 2004-34 Cindy reports $4,000 of income in the first year and $1,000 in the second year.

The revenue procedure does not apply to prepayments of rent or interest. Nor can the taxpayer take advantage of the deferral if he included the entire advance payment in the first year for financial accounting purposes.

Prepayment for goods. If the taxpayer receives an advance payment for goods, there may be an issue as to when the taxpayer has to include the amount in income. The general rule is that the taxpayer must include all advance payments in gross income (even though the goods have not yet been provided).

Nevertheless, Treas. Reg. § 1.451-5 allows the taxpayer to defer reporting advance payments for goods sold in the ordinary course of business until the goods are shipped. However, the deferral cannot extend farther than the year following the year of payment.

Example. Paul, an accrual basis taxpayer, agreed to provide $5,000 of supplies to his customer. The customer paid for the items in the first year. One-fifth of the supplies were shipped in the first year (the year of payment). Three-fifths of the supplies were shipped in the second year, with the remaining one-fifth shipped in the third year. Under Treas. Reg. § 1.451-5 Paul must include $1,000 in the year the customer pays for the supplies and $4,000 in the second year.

Tell Me More

Congress has provided some statutory relief to businesses who receive payments for goods or services that span more than one year, such as magazine subscriptions[49] and prepaid dues paid to nonprofit membership organizations.[50]

---

b. Accrual of Income — All Events Test

Under the all events test, income accrues when the right to the income is fixed and the amount can be determined with reasonable accuracy. The all events test can be met even though actual payment has not been made.[51]

The fixing of the right to the payment is a facts and circumstances test. It may be tied to when the item is shipped, delivered, accepted, or when title passes. As long as the method is consistent with generally accepted accounting principles, is consistently used,

---

49. Section 455.
50. Section 456.
51. Treas. Reg. §§ 1.446-1(c)(1)(ii); 1.451-1(a)(1).

and consistent with the regulations, the time selected by the taxpayer for fixing the right to payment will be respected.[52]

Treas. Reg. § 1.451-1(a)

(a) General rule—Gains, profits, and income are to be included in gross income for the taxable year.... Under an accrual method of accounting, income is includible in gross income when all the events have occurred which fix the right to receive such income and the amount thereof can be determined with reasonable accuracy....

In *Spring City Foundry Co. v. Commissioner*[53] the taxpayer shipped goods to a buyer but did not receive payment. A bankruptcy petition eventually was filed against the buyer. After several years had passed, the taxpayer received partial payment from the trustee as part of the bankruptcy proceedings. Because the taxpayer had the right to the income in the year the goods were shipped, that was the year it was required to include the amount in income. In other words, doubt as to collectibility did not alter the fact that the all events test had been met.

Thus, a taxpayer must accrue all amounts that satisfy the all events test unless at the time of accrual there is a reasonable expectancy he will not be paid (such as when the payor is insolvent at the time of accrual).

Example. The taxpayer was to receive a commission paid from a trust fund funded with state tax revenue from the sale of beer. Even though it had not been paid the entire amount of commission because there were not enough funds in the trust fund, it could not wait until it was paid to report the commissions. Rather, it was required to accrue the amount of commissions when it had a right to receive them.[54]

Connection to Bad Debt Deduction

If the taxpayer reports income under the all events test, but is never paid, he may be able to claim a bad debt deduction.[55]

Exceptions for amounts received for services. If the taxpayer is to receive amounts for the performance of services and, based on the taxpayer's experience, the amount will not be received, he is not required to accrue it. To come within this special exception, the taxpayer's services must be in a specific service area such as health, law, engineering, architecture, accounting, actuarial science, performing arts, or consulting. Or, the taxpayer does not have more than $5,000,000 in gross receipts for any prior taxable year. In addition, the income cannot be subject to a late fee or bear interest.[56]

---

52. Treas. Reg. § 1.446-1(c)(1)(ii)(C).
53. 292 U.S. 182 (1934).
54. Georgia School-Book Depository, Inc. v. Commissioner, 1 T.C. 463 (1943).
55. Section 166. Business bad debt deductions are discussed in Chapter 27.
56. Section 448(d)(5).

Special rule for interest. Interest accrues as it is earned over the life of the loan. Accrual is not required if the interest cannot be collected at the time of performance.[57]

2. Accrual of Payment

To be considered accrued for purposes of determining when payment has been made, the taxpayer must meet the all events test. The first two prongs of the all events test for deductions mirror those from the all events test for income: there is a fixed liability and the amount of the liability can be determined with reasonable accuracy. Under the third prong, economic performance must have occurred with respect to the liability.[58]

Fixed liability. Whether or not the taxpayer has the ability to actually make the payment is not relevant.[59] To be a fixed liability, the liability cannot be contingent.[60] Similarly, if the liability is contested, it is considered a contingent liability and the amount is not accrued. However, to the extent a taxpayer pays a contested liability, it is considered as meeting the all events test (i.e., it has accrued).[61] To the extent it is not paid, no accrual occurs.

Economic performance. Under the all events test for accrual, the third prong is that economic performance must have occurred. If the payment is for services, the services must have been performed. If the payment is for the use of property, economic performance occurs over the time the taxpayer is entitled to use the property. If the payment is for goods, the goods must have been delivered.[62]

If economic performance has occurred, but the first two prongs of the all events test have not been met, accrual does not occur until all prongs of the all events test have been met. In *United States v. General Dynamics*[63] the taxpayer self-insured its employees, obligating itself to pay certain medical expenses incurred by its employees. For the final quarter of its fiscal year, it estimated the claims incurred by the employees that had not yet been reported. While economic performance had occurred, to the extent it could only estimate the amount of the liability, it failed to meet the all events test. It was not entitled to accrue the fourth quarter estimated costs.

Note that the requirement of economic performance having occurred is necessary even if the taxpayer can establish the asset has a life of less than one year. For example, the taxpayer was a long-haul trucker. He purchased a warranty for his semi-trailer that covered November 1 of the current year through October 31 of next year. Even though the warranty is an asset with a life of one year or less, economic performance occurs only as the warranty coverage is provided during the term of the policy.

Prepayments. With deductions tied so closely to payments, a taxpayer may chose to have an amount accrued as early as possible to be able to claim the deduction at the time

---

57. Clifton Manufacturing Co. v. Commissioner, 137 F.2d 290 (4th Cir. 1943); Rev. Rul. 80-361, 1980-2 C.B. 164; Rev. Rul. 74-607, 1974-2 C.B. 149.
58. Treas. Reg. § 1.461-1(a)(2)(i).
59. Cohen v. Commissioner, 21 T.C. 855 (1954); Rev. Rul. 70-367, 1970-2 C.B. 37.
60. Dixie Pine Products Co. v. Commissioner, 320 U.S. 516 (1944).
61. Section 461(f).
62. Section 461(h).
63. 481 U.S. 239 (1987).

of accrual. However, a prepayment may provide the taxpayer with a right or benefit that extends beyond one year. If the taxpayer pays for an asset that has a life of more than one year, the payment must be capitalized and the cost recovered through depreciation, if applicable. For example, if the taxpayer prepaid five years' worth of rent, the benefit extends more than one year. Accordingly, the taxpayer is required to capitalize the expenditure and recover the cost through amortization.

For those costs that provide a right or benefit close to one year, the regulations provide a test to help the taxpayer determine if the costs should be capitalized. If the taxpayer makes a prepayment and the right or benefit paid for does not extend beyond the earlier of 12 months after the first date on which the taxpayer realizes the benefit or the end of the taxable year following the taxable year in which the payment is made, the taxpayer is not required to capitalize the amount of the payment.[64]

Summary of Rules — Accrual Basis Taxpayer

The taxpayer must include an amount in income at the earlier of when:

- Actually received
- The all events test is met:
  - The right to the income is fixed; and
  - The amount can be determined with reasonable accuracy.

The taxpayer can claim a deduction, if otherwise allowed, for all amounts that meet the all events test:

  - The right to the income is fixed;
  - The amount can be determined with reasonable accuracy; and
  - Economic performance has occurred.

C. Application of Rules

Each taxpayer is an accrual basis taxpayer.

Example 1. Caesar provided $1,000 of legal services to his client. After receiving the bill the client called Caesar and said she was unable to pay the bill until the following year. While she paid him nothing in the current year, she did pay $800 in the following year.

The all events test has been met in the current year—the client owes Caesar $1,000. Caesar must report $1,000 in the current year. The fact the client has not paid him anything in the current year is not relevant.

Example 2. Gregg provided $1,000 of legal services to his client. The client paid Gregg by giving him a watch worth $1,000. Gregg must report the value of the watch in his gross income in the year he received the watch.

---

64. Treas. Reg. § 1.263(a)-4(f)(1).

Example 3. Jennifer provided $5,000 worth of consulting services to her client. After receiving the bill, the client called Jennifer and said he was unable to pay the bill until later the following year. He signed a promissory note reflecting the amount he owned Jennifer.

The all events test has been met in the current year—the client owes Jennifer $5,000. Jennifer must report $5,000 in the first year. The fact that the client believes he will not be able to pay the bill until the following year is not relevant.

Example 4. Dinah owns and operates a photography studio. In November she met with her client and agreed to photograph ski events that were to take place at the client's ski resort. She would take pictures from December through March. The client paid her when they entered into the agreement in November.

Dinah received a pre-payment. Under Rev. Proc. 2004-34, Dinah can report the income from the services provided in December and defer reporting the income from the services provided in January through March until the following year.

Example 5. Nancy is a consultant. Her client hired her to provide consulting services for the next two years. The client paid her when they entered into the contract. She completed one-third of the work in the first year. Unfortunately, she was able to complete only another one-third of the work in the second year and had to work in the third year, providing the final one-third of the work.

Nancy received a pre-payment. Under Rev. Proc. 2004-34, Nancy can report one-third of the income from the services provided in the first year. She can defer reporting the income from the services provided after the first year. Because the deferral cannot go beyond the second year, the fact that she continued to provide services in the third year is not relevant. She must report the remaining two-thirds of the income in the second year.

Example 6. Harry owns and operates a computer software business. This year he paid $100 for supplies. For purposes of Section 162 Harry has accrued these items.

Example 7. Nemo owns and operates a computer software business. This year he purchased a new computer for use in his business. While the amount paid for the computer has been accrued, because the cost is a capital expenditure Nemo must recover the cost over time through depreciation.

Example 8. Henry has a legal practice. In December he prepared the check for the utility company, entered the check into the business's ledger, but, rather than mailing the payment, kept the envelope in his wallet. He dropped the envelope in the first mailbox he came across in January.

For a deduction to be permissible, the all events test must be met. Because the amount of the liability is fixed, can be determined with reasonable accuracy, and the electricity has been provided, the all events test has been met in the first year. The fact that Henry did not actually make the payment until the following year is not relevant.

Example 9. Evan has a consulting business. During the year he hired Maxine to provide legal services. When he received Maxine's bill for $5,000 he was certain there had been a mistake. He immediately called her to disagree with the charges.

For a deduction to be permissible, the all events test must be met. Because the amount of the liability is not fixed, but rather is contested, Evan cannot claim a deduction with respect to the legal services.

Example 10. Jason has a consulting business. In December he ordered six new widgets to be delivered the following January. The widgets cost $5,000 each.

For a deduction to be permissible, the all events test must be met. The amount of the liability is fixed and the amount can be determined with reasonable accuracy. However, in the first year, the goods have not been delivered. Jason is not entitled to a deduction until the second year, when there has been economic performance.

Example 11. Eileen has a legal practice. In December she purchased a copy machine. Even though Eileen paid for the equipment, it is a capital expenditure and the cost must be recovered over time through depreciation.

Example 12. Darren owns and operates a consulting service. In November he purchased 12 months worth of fire insurance. The insurance created a benefit lasting beyond the year of purchase. However, because the benefit did not extend beyond 12 months or the following year, he can deduct the cost of the insurance.

Example 13. Albert owns and operates a small business. In November he purchased 24 months worth of flood insurance. The insurance created a benefit lasting beyond the year of purchase. In addition, the benefit extended beyond 12 months and extended beyond the following year. Accordingly, he cannot currently deduct the cost of the insurance. Rather, it is a capital expenditure and the cost must be recovered over time through amortization.

D. Problems

Each taxpayer is an accrual basis taxpayer.

1. Hillary owns a fashion boutique. On Friday, December 29th she had a large sale. At the close of business she added up her receipts, summarized below. From her Friday receipts, how much must she include in her income for the year?

Cash	$5,000
Checks	$15,000
Credit card charges	$45,000

2. Carrie is a medical consultant. In November of this year Carrie performed $50,000 worth of services for Dr. Jones. Carrie waited until late December to send Dr. Jones a bill. Dr. Jones paid the bill in early January of the following year. In which year must Carrie report the $50,000?

3. Darius is a computer consultant. In November of this year Darius performed $50,000 worth of services for Mark. Darius sent Mark the bill at the end of November and Mark mailed a check. While Darius received the check on December 27, he did not deposit it until the following year. In which year must Darius report the $50,000?

4. Ester is a wedding planner. In December of this year Ester planned Florence's wedding at a cost of $10,000. Florence offered to pay Ester as soon as the wedding was over, but Ester insisted that Florence not pay her until January when Florence had returned from her honeymoon. When Florence returned in January, she paid Ester. In which year must Ester report the $10,000?

5. Hans is a sales representative for a large shoe company. In addition to a fixed salary, Hans receives a commission based on the number of shoes he sells each month. In December he received payment for his November commissions. Although the check seemed larger than he expected it to be, Hans did not question the amount. He deposited the check. In January of the following year, the company notified Hans, telling him that there was a computational error in computing the amount of his

check. Hans must return the overpayment to the company. What are the tax consequences to Hans from receiving the commission check?

6. Gloria owns and operates a wholesale equipment supply store. When a customer purchased an item, a bill was sent to the client. Once she received shipping instructions from the client, she would have the equipment shipped from the general warehouse. Title passed to the client once the item was shipped. When must Gloria report the income from the sale?

7. Anthony makes a $10,000 charitable contribution to his favorite charity by placing a charge on his credit card. For purposes of determining whether Anthony is entitled to a charitable contribution deduction, when is the payment considered as having been made?

8. Franz purchased a computer for use in his business by placing a charge on his credit card. What are the tax consequences to Franz?

9. Kieran paid $5,000 to purchase casualty insurance for his business. To determine the tax consequences of the purchase, what additional information do you need from Kieran?

10. Gabby provided $10,000 of legal services to Jordan. Jordan has not yet paid. What is Gabby's basis in the account receivable?

E. Analysis and Application

Each taxpayer is an accrual basis taxpayer.

1. Liz, an accrual basis, calendar year taxpayer, owned and operated a large farm for more than 20 years. This year she wanted to increase the amount of winter wheat she planted. Accordingly, she leased 100 acres of land from Albert. She agreed to pay Albert $150 an acre (total payment of $15,000). The lease was for one year, running from September 1, 2012, to August 21, 2013.

   Liz made the $15,000 lease payment on September 1, 2012. Can she deduct the lease payment on her 2012 return?

2. Patsy owned and operated a mobile home dealership. Often, as part of the purchase of a mobile home, the customer would sign a mortgage. Patsy would sell the mortgages to a finance company. From the amount the finance company owed Patsy, it would withhold 5 percent, placing that amount in a reserve account. The withheld amount would be paid to Patsy when the purchaser completed all payments on the mortgage.

   Considering the sale of the mortgages to the finance company, must Patsy include the amount held in the reserve account in her income in the year of sale?

3. Casino loaned a customer $3 million dollars for the purchase of casino chips. While the customer signed a promissory note, the debt was not enforceable under state law. When the customer lost all the chips, even though he was solvent, he claimed he was unable to repay the debt. Eventually Casino and customer settled the debt for $1 million.

   a. What are the tax consequences to Casino when the customer signs the promissory note?

b. What are the tax consequences to Casino when the customer defaults on the debt?

c. What are the tax consequences to Casino when the debt is settled for $1 million?

In formulating your analysis and response, you may want to consider:

- Zarin v. Commissioner, 916 F.2d 110 (3d Cir. 1990), rev'g 92 T.C. 1084 (1989)
- Flamingo Resort, Inc. v. United States, 664 F.2d 1387 (9th Cir. 1982)

4. Sharon owns and operates a small appliance store. All customers who purchase a television are offered a service agreement. For a lump sum amount, her store would provide service and repairs over a fixed amount of time. Sharon does not know the extent of the services she may be required to provide so cannot predict how much profit she will make from any contract. What are the tax consequences to Sharon when a customer enters into a service agreement?

In formulating your analysis and response, you may want to consider:

- Schlude v. Commissioner, 372 U.S. 128 (1963)
- Automobile Club of Michigan v. Commissioner, 353 U.S. 180 (1957)
- Westpac Pacific Food v. Commissioner, 451 F.3d 970 (9th Cir. 2006)

Chapter 34

Restoring Amounts Received under the Claim of Right Doctrine

Methods of Accounting

Cash Basis:	Accrual Basis:	Special Rules:
Income: earlier of— • Actual receipt • Receipt of cash equivalent • Constructive receipt • Economic benefit Payment: considered paid when actual payment made	Income: earlier of— • Actual receipt • All events test Payment: considered accrued when meet the all events test	**Special Rules:** • Installment method • **Restoration of amounts received under a claim of right** • Tax benefit rule • Net operating loss

Read

Code Section 1341(a)

A. Background

In Part II we considered a variety of sources of income that a taxpayer is required to report as gross income. For example, a taxpayer is required to include compensation for services, business profits, profit from the sale of property, interest, rents, royalties, dividends, alimony, and cancellation of debt.[65] Nevertheless, a situation may arise when income that was correctly reported in one year becomes improper in a later year because the taxpayer had to return funds.

Recall *North American Oil Consolidated v. Burnet*[66] discussed in Chapters 32 and 33. There was a dispute between North American Oil and the government about beneficial ownership of land. In 1915 the government filed a lawsuit to oust North American Oil from possession of the land. In 1916 the court appointed a receiver to operate the property and hold the income from the property. In 1917 the district court issued a final decree

---

65. Section 61(a). See also Chapters 2 through 6.
66. 286 U.S. 417 (1932).

dismissing the bill, and the receiver paid the income to North American Oil. The government appealed. In 1920, the appellate court affirmed the trial court and in 1922 an appeal to the Supreme Court was dismissed.

The court held North American Oil had to report the funds in income in the year they were received from the receiver (1917). Inclusion at the time of receipt was required even though there was the possibility North American Oil would have to return the funds if it lost the case on appeal. Section 1341 sets forth the tax treatment if North American Oil had lost the case on appeal and had had to return the funds.

B. Restoring Amount
Received under Claim of Right

For Section 1341 to be applicable, two of the taxpayer's years must be involved. In the earlier year, the taxpayer must have properly included an amount in income. In a later year, the taxpayer must have had to return the funds, making the income inclusion no longer correct.

Example. Scott included a $60,000 bonus from his employer in his income in 2010. The following year his employer told Scott the bonus amount was incorrectly calculated and Scott must return $50,000. He did so.

Because the inclusion of the income in the earlier year was correct, no adjustment is made to that return. Rather, the correction is made in the year the taxpayer discovers the amount of income he reported is no longer correct. In other words, considering both years together, the taxpayer reported too much income and must reduce the amount in the later year.[67] A problem arises when the tax rates applicable in the two years differ.

Example. Scott included a $60,000 bonus from his employer in his income in 2010. If his income were taxed at the marginal rate of 35 percent he would have paid $17,500 in tax on $50,000. The following year his employer told Scott the bonus amount was incorrectly calculated and Scott must return $50,000. He did so. If his income were taxed at the marginal rate of 20 percent, he would be saving $10,000 in tax through use of the $50,000 deduction. Scott's tax savings ($10,000) are less than the tax he previously paid ($17,500) on the $50,000.

Tell Me More

If the taxpayer discovers a mistake on his income tax return, he can file an amended tax return on a Form 1040X to correct the mistake. An amended return is used only to correct errors or admissions on the original return. The determination as to what is properly included on the tax return is based on the facts during that year. Even if events in a subsequent year make the inclusion of an amount improper, because it was proper at the time of filing the return it cannot be addressed by filing an amended return.

---

67. Section 1341(a).

Section 1341 addresses this potential disparity. For taxpayers who come within its provisions, the taxpayer may either:

- Deduct the amount of income previously included; or
- Use the tax previously paid on the amount of income subsequently returned as a credit against the tax liability in the current year.

Section 1341. Computation of Tax Where Taxpayer Restores Substantial Amount Held Under Claim of Right

(a) General Rule. — If —

(1) an item was included in gross income for a prior year (or years) because it appeared that the taxpayer had an unrestricted right to such item;

(2) a deduction is allowable for the taxable year because it was established after the close of such prior taxable year (or years) that the taxpayer did not have an unrestricted right to such item or to a portion of such item; and

(3) the amount of such deduction exceeds $3,000,

then the tax imposed by this chapter for the taxable year shall be the lesser of the following:

(4) the tax for the taxable year computed with such deduction; or

(5) an amount equal to

(A) the tax for the taxable year computed without such deduction, minus

(B) the decrease in tax under this chapter (or the corresponding provisions of prior revenue laws) for the prior taxable year (or years) which would result solely from the exclusion of such item (or portion thereof) from gross income for such prior taxable year (or years).

* * *

To come within Section 1341, and be allowed to select the approach that is most beneficial to the taxpayer, the transaction must meet three criteria. First, the amount at issue must be more than $3,000.[68]

Second, the amount must have been included on the earlier return because it appeared the taxpayer had an unrestricted right to the income.[69] If the taxpayer did not have a right to the income, he does not meet this criterion. For example, if the income at issue is embezzlement income or theft income, the taxpayer does not have the appearance of a right to the income.

Third, in the later year the taxpayer must establish he did not have an unrestricted right to the income.[70] While a good-faith settlement of a dispute can establish the lack of an unrestricted right, a voluntary repayment would not.

The Service has provided guidance as to what it believes constitutes an appearance of an unrestricted right to the income. "Appeared" is a "semblance of an unrestricted right

---

68. Section 1341(a)(3).
69. Section 1341(a)(1).
70. Section 1341(a)(2).

in the year received as distinguished from an unchallengeable right (which is more than an 'apparent' right) and from absolutely no right at all (which is less than an "apparent" right)."[71]

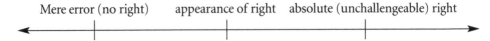

Mere error (no right)   appearance of right   absolute (unchallengeable) right

The courts have not been as rigid as the Service when interpreting whether the taxpayer had the appearance of a right to income. In *Dominion Resources, Inc. v. United States*[72] the corporate taxpayer owned stock of a regulated public utility. It was required to restore $10 million in rate overcharges to it customers. Dominion Resources had included the amounts in income in previous years as they had been received. The rate overcharge resulted from a decrease in the federal corporate income tax rate. Dominion Resources used Section 1341 to correct the previous inclusion.

The Service argued that Section 1341 did not apply because, at the time the amounts were collected, Dominion Resources had more than an appearance of a right—they had the absolute right to amounts received. The change in the law, requiring Dominion Resources to make refunds, did not occur until after the amounts were collected. The Fourth Circuit disagreed with the Service. "Things very often 'appear' to be what they 'actually' are. As a matter of plain meaning, the word "appeared" generally does not, as the IRS urges, imply only false appearance, and generally does not exclude an appearance that happens to be true."[73] The court used the "same circumstances" facts and circumstances rule applied by several other courts. Under this test, the lack of an unrestricted right to an income item permitting the deduction must arise out of the circumstances of the original payment of the item to the taxpayer. The court concluded it did appear Dominion Resources had an unrestricted right to the $10 million in the years the money was received and in a later year it was established it no longer had an unrestricted right to the same income.[74]

Note

If the taxpayer does not meet the criteria of Section 1341, the amount may be deductible under another Code Section, such Section 165(c) (losses) or Section 162 (business expenses).

Summary of Rules — Restoring Amounts Received under Claim of Right Doctrine

If:

- The amount at issue is more than $3,000.
- The amount was included on an earlier return because it appeared the taxpayer had an unrestricted right to the income; and

---

71. Rev. Rul. 68-153, 1968-1 C.B. 371.
72. 219 F.3d 359 (4th Cir. 2000).
73. Dominion Resources, Inc. v. United States, 219 F.3d 359, 364 (4th Cir. 2000).
74. *Dominion Resources*, 219 F.3d at 368.

- In a later year the taxpayer established he did not have an unrestricted right to the income;

Then, the taxpayer can elect to either:

- Deduct the amount of income previously included; or
- Use the tax previously paid on the amount of income subsequently returned as a credit against the tax liability in the current year

---

C. Application of Rules

Example 1. Monique included a $50,000 bonus from her employer in her income. Her income was taxed at the marginal rate of 20 percent, and she paid $10,000 in taxes on the $50,000. The following year her employer told her the bonus was incorrectly paid and Monique had to return the $50,000. She did so and in that year her income was taxed at the marginal rate of 35 percent.

The amount at issue is more than $3,000, Monique included the $50,000 on an earlier return because it appeared she had an unrestricted right to the income, and in the following year she did not have a right to the income. Accordingly, Monique can elect to either deduct the amount previously included or use the tax paid on the returned amount as a credit against her tax liability in the current year.

If she claims a $50,000 deduction, she would save $17,500 in tax through the use of the $50,000 deduction. Or, she could forego the deduction and claim a $10,000 credit against her taxes. Monique would elect to claim the deduction.

Example 2. Patrick included a $30,000 bonus from his employer in his income. His income was taxed at the marginal rate of 35 percent, and he paid $10,500 in taxes on the $30,000. The following year his employer told Patrick the bonus was incorrectly paid and Patrick had to return the $30,000. He did so, and in that year his income was taxed at the marginal rate of 20 percent.

The amount at issue is more than $3,000, Patrick included the $30,000 on an earlier return because it appeared he had an unrestricted right to the income, and in the following year he did not have a right to the income. Accordingly, Patrick can elect to either deduct the amount previously included or use the tax paid on the returned amount as a credit against his tax liability in the current year.

If he claims a $30,000 deduction, he would save $6,000 in tax through use of the $30,000 deduction. Or, he could forego the deduction and claim a $10,500 credit against his taxes. Patrick would elect to use the tax credit.

Example 3. Elaine embezzled $100,000 from her employer. She included the embezzled funds in her gross income. Five years later she was caught and was required to return the $100,000.

The amount at issue is more than $3,000. However, she did not have an unrestricted right to the income in the year she included it. Accordingly, she may not use Section 1341.

Example 4. Elizabeth was paid a salary of $300,000. The following year her employer was audited and a deduction disallowed for the salary paid to her to the extent it exceeded

$200,000. The Service's position was that the additional $100,000 was not an ordinary and necessary expense. Even though Elizabeth believed the $300,000 salary was justified and expert testimony would support her position, she did not want her employer to be subjected to negative publicity due to the audit. She voluntarily agreed to return $100,000 of her salary to her employer.

The amount at issue is more than $3,000. Elizabeth included the $100,000 on an earlier return because it appeared she had an unrestricted right to the income. However, in the following year it was not established she did not have a right to the income. Rather, she voluntarily returned the salary. Accordingly, Elizabeth cannot use Section 1341.

D. Problems

1. Nicole included a $1,000 bonus from her employer in her income. The following year her employer told her the bonus was incorrectly paid and Nicole must return the $1,000. She does so. May Nicole use Section 1341?

2. Ariel included a $20,000 bonus from her employer in her income. Her income was taxed at the marginal rate of 35 percent, and she paid $7,000 in taxes on the $20,000. The following year her employer told her the bonus was incorrectly paid and Ariel must return the $20,000. She does so, and in that year her income is taxed at the marginal rate of 20 percent.

    May Ariel use Section 1341? Is so, which option should she elect?

3. Betsy included a $20,000 bonus from her employer in her income. Her income was taxed at the marginal rate of 20 percent, and she paid $4,000 in taxes on the $20,000. The following year her employer told her the bonus was incorrectly paid and Betsy must return the $20,000. She does so, and in that year her income is taxed at the marginal rate of 35 percent.

    May Betsy use Section 1341? Is so, which option should she elect?

4. Arnold was involved in drug trafficking. He reported $500,000 from his drug trafficking business. Four years later he was arrested and his bank accounts seized. He was required to forfeit all drug-related assets, including the $500,000 in his bank account. May Arnold use Section 1341?

5. Jason was the CEO of YCo. He bought and sold YCo. stock within a 6-month time frame and reported the profit from the sales on his income tax return. The following year a shareholder filed a derivative suit against Jason for a violation of SEC Rule 16(b). The shareholder was successful and Jason was required to return all profits he made from the purchase and sale of YCo. stock. (Under Section 16(b), officers of publicly traded corporations are not entitled to retain profits from sales made within a 6-month time frame.) May Jason use Section 1341?

Chapter 35

Tax Benefit Rule

Methods of Accounting

Cash Basis:	Accrual Basis:	Special Rules:
Income: earlier of— • Actual receipt • Receipt of cash equivalent • Constructive receipt • Economic benefit Payment: considered paid when actual payment made	Income: earlier of— • Actual receipt • All events test Payment: considered accrued when meet the all events test	• Installment method • Restoration of amounts received under a claim of right • **Tax benefit rule** • Net operating loss

Read

Code Section 111(a)

A. Background

In Parts IV, V, and VI we considered a variety of deductions a taxpayer is allowed to claim. For example, a taxpayer is entitled to take a bad debt deduction for those debts he cannot collect.[75] He also may claim a deduction for a charitable contribution (a contribution made to or for the use of a qualified recipient, made with no expectation of a return benefit, actually paid, sufficiently substantiated, and subject to certain limitations.)[76] Nevertheless, a situation may arise when a deduction that was correctly claimed becomes improper in a later year.

---

75. Section 166. See also Chapters 19, 27, and 31.
76. Section 170. See also Chapter 18.

B. Tax Benefit Rule

Under the tax benefit rule, a taxpayer must include in income an amount previously deducted. The tax benefit rule is a judicially-created rule.[77] To be applicable, two of the taxpayer's years must be involved. In the earlier year, the taxpayer properly claimed an allowable deduction. In a later year, the taxpayer determines that the deduction is no longer justified.

Example. Jackson was an accrual basis taxpayer. In 2010 he claimed a bad debt deduction for a $10,000 account receivable from Hillary when Hillary explained she was unable to pay the amount she owed. In 2012 Hillary unexpectedly paid the debt. While the deduction was correct in 2010, it is no longer correct in 2012.

Because the deduction was correct when claimed, no adjustment is made to the earlier return on which the deduction was claimed. Rather, the correction is made in the year the taxpayer discovers the deduction is no longer correct. In other words, the taxpayer received a tax benefit from the deduction in the earlier year and must give back that benefit in the later year.[78]

The amount the taxpayer includes in the later year is the amount he recovers. Unlike Section 1341 (restoring amounts received under the claim of right doctrine), the provision does not take into consideration any difference in tax rate between the year of deduction and the year of inclusion.

In *Alice Phelan Sullivan Corporation v. United States*[79] the taxpayer contributed property to a charity in 1939 and 1940, subject to a condition that the properties be used for a religious or an educational purpose. The taxpayer claimed a charitable contribution deduction in each year. The deductions reduced the corporation's taxable income by $1,877. In 1957 the donee elected to not use the properties and reconveyed them to the corporation. Because of an increase in tax rate, the inclusion of the previously deducted amount resulted in an additional $4,527 of tax. The taxpayer argued it should be required to include no more than the tax benefit of the deduction ($1,877). The court disagreed; the entire amount of the previous deductions was required to be included in income and was subject to tax.

The taxpayer can reduce the amount included in income to the extent he did not receive a tax savings from the deduction in the prior year.[80]

Section 111. Recovery of Tax Benefit Items

(a) Deductions.—Gross income does not include income attributable to the recovery during the taxable year of any amount deducted in any prior taxable year to the extent such amount did not reduce the amount of tax imposed by this chapter.

---

77. Burnet v. Sanford & Brooks Co., 282 U.S. 359 (1931); Alice Phelan Sullivan Corp. v. United States, 381 F.2d 399 (1967).
78. Alice Phelan Sullivan Corp. v. United States, 381 F.2d 399 (1967).
79. 381 F.2d 399 (Ct. Cl. 1967).
80. Section 111(a).

Tax Benefit Rule

Initial year: Taxpayer claims a deduction.

Later year: The deduction is no longer correct.

Result: In the year the deduction is determined to no longer be correct, the taxpayer includes in his income the amount recovered. He can reduce the amount included only to the extent he received no tax benefit from the deduction in the earlier year.

C. Application of Rules

Example 1. Otto, an accrual basis taxpayer, owns and operates a small business. Last year he claimed a $5,000 bad debt deduction when one of his clients was unable to pay his bill. This year his client unexpectedly paid his bill.

Because Otto claimed a deduction and, in a later year, determined the deduction was no longer correct, the tax benefit rule applies. Otto must include $5,000 in his income this year.

Example 2. Larry contributed land to a charitable organization, subject to the restriction that it be used only for a homeless shelter. He claimed a $50,000 charitable contribution deduction. Five years later the organization determined it could not place a homeless shelter on the land; it reconveyed the land to Larry.

Because Larry claimed a deduction and, in a later year, determined the deduction was no longer correct, the tax benefit rule applies. Larry must include $50,000 in his income in the year the land is reconveyed to him.

Example 3. Mabel paid $4,000 in state income tax. For that year the standard deduction was $6,000. Because she claimed other itemized deductions amounting to $3,000, for a total of $7,000 in deductions ($4,000 of state income tax and $3,000 of other deductions), Mabel elected to itemize rather than claim the standard deduction. She earned $50,000 of income, and her net income was $43,000 ($50,000 of gross income, less $7,000 of itemized deductions).

	Itemized deductions
State taxes	$4,000
Misc	3,000
Totals:	$7,000 (compared to $6,000 standard deduction)

In the following year she received a $3,000 refund of the state income tax paid in the prior year. Because Mabel claimed a deduction and, in a later year, determined the deduction was no longer correct, the tax benefit rule applies. Mabel must include $3,000 in income in the year she receives the refund. However, she is only required to include the refund to the extent she received a tax benefit from the deductions. If the amount of state income taxes had been $1,000, her total itemized deductions would have been $4,000 ($1,000 of state income tax and $3,000 of other deductions).

Corrected itemized deductions

State taxes	$1,000
Misc	3,000
Totals:	$4,000 (compared to $6,000 standard deduction)

She would have elected to claim the standard deduction of $6,000. Thus, she is only required to include in income the amount previously deducted to the extent she received a tax benefit, or $1,000 ($7,000 in itemized deductions claimed as compared to the $6,000 standard deduction she should have claimed).

D. Problems

1. Amy is an accrual basis taxpayer who owns and operates a small business. In 2009, she provided $4,000 of services for one of her clients. While she sent him a bill, he did not pay it. In 2010, Amy learned the client was unable to pay the bill. In 2011 the client unexpectedly paid the bill.

    a. What are the tax results to Amy in 2009?

    b. What are the tax results to Amy in 2010?

    b. What are the tax results to Amy in 2011?

2. Beth is a cash basis taxpayer who owns and operates a small business. In 2009, she provided $4,000 of services to one of her clients. While she sent him a bill, he did not pay it. In 2010, Beth learned the client was unable to pay the bill. In 2011 the client unexpectedly paid the bill.

    a. What are the tax results to Beth in 2009?

    b. What are the tax results to Beth in 2010?

    c. What are the tax results to Beth in 2011?

3. Last year Julie paid a $1,000 medical bill; she claimed a $1,000 deduction on her income tax return. This year she was contacted by the doctor's office and told there had been a mistake—the bill should have been only $700. The office refunded $300 to her. Even with the lowered bill, Julie still would have itemized her deductions last year. What are the tax results to Julie in this year?

E. Analysis and Application

1. Five years ago April contributed land to a qualified charitable organization that provided assistance to low income families. The land was subject to the condition that it be used only for operating a food bank. She properly claimed a $100,000 charitable contribution deduction; her marginal tax rate was 35 percent. This year

the organization, unable to use the land to operate a food bank, reconveyed it to April. Her marginal tax rate this year is 35 percent.

    a.   By how much did April reduce her taxes in the year she made the charitable contribution?

    b.   When the land was reconveyed to April this year does the tax benefit rule apply? Why?

    c.   If the tax benefit rule applies, how much will she pay in taxes when she includes the previously deducted amount in her income?

    d.   Has April received any benefit?

2.   Five years ago Marla contributed land to a qualified charitable organization that provided assistance to children in need. The land was subject to the condition that it be used only for a playground for children. She properly claimed a $10,000 charitable contribution deduction; her marginal tax rate was 28 percent. This year the organization, unable to use the land for a playground, reconveyed it to Marla. Her marginal tax rate this year is 35 percent.

    a.   By how much did Marla reduce her taxes in the year she made the charitable contribution?

    b.   When the land was reconveyed to Marla this year does the tax benefit rule apply? Why?

    c.   If the tax benefit rule applies, how much will she pay in taxes when she includes the previously deducted amount in her income?

    d.   Do you have any concerns about this result?

3.   Last year Dennis paid a $5,000 medical bill and claimed a $5,000 deduction on his tax return. This year he was contacted by the doctor's office and told that there had been a mistake — the bill should have been only $1,000. The office refunded $4,000 to him.

In the year he claimed the deduction, with the $5,000 medical bill his itemized deductions totaled $12,000. For that year, the amount of the standard deduction was $10,000. (Ignore any limitations that might apply to the amount of medical expenses Dennis is permitted to deduct.) Under the tax benefit rule and Section 111, how much must Dennis include in his income this year?

4.   Section 1341 allows the taxpayer to take into consideration any difference in tax rates between the two relevant years. This option is not available when the tax benefit rule is applied. As a policy matter, do you agree with this result?

Chapter 36

Net Operating Loss

Methods of Accounting

Cash Basis:	Accrual Basis:	Special Rules:
Income: earlier of— • Actual receipt • Receipt of cash equivalent • Constructive receipt • Economic benefit Payment: considered paid when actual payment made	Income: earlier of— • Actual receipt • All events test Payment: considered accrued when meet the all events test	• Installment method • Restoration of amounts received under a claim of right • Tax benefit rule • **Net operating loss**

Read

Code Section 172(a), (b)(1)(A), (b)(3), (c)

A. Background

One of the overarching objectives of the Code is to impose tax on a taxpayer's accession to wealth. When the taxpayer operates his own business, his taxable increase in wealth is not his gross income. Rather, it is his gross income less the costs he incurred to generate the income.

> Business gross income
> – <u>Costs of operating business for the year</u>
> Taxable income

In some situations, the allowed deductions may exceed the income for the year, resulting in a net loss.

B. Net Operating Loss

If the taxpayer has a net loss in one taxable year, he is able to utilize that loss in another year. The loss is carried back two years and carried forward 20 years until it has been fully utilized.[81] The taxpayer may elect not to carry the loss back and only carry the loss forward.[82]

In general, a net operating loss is the loss from a business to the extent of the excess of the deductions over the gross income.[83] The provision has a number of modifications that must be made when computing the amount of net operating loss.[84] For example, capital losses are not included in the computation,[85] and non-business deductions are allowed only to the extent of non-business income.[86]

C. Application of Rules

Example 1. Mark owns and operates a small business. His taxable income from the business was $30,000 in 2005 and $40,000 in 2006. In 2007 his business deductions exceeded his business income by $40,000 (i.e., he had a $40,000 net operating loss).

The $40,000 net operating loss in 2007 is carried back to 2005. Mark uses $30,000 of the loss in 2005. He will file an amended 2005 return showing zero taxable income. Mark uses the remaining $10,000 net operating loss ($40,000 net operating loss, less $30,000 used in 2005) in 2006. He will file an amended 2006 return showing $30,000 of taxable income.

Example 2. Larry owns and operates a small business. His taxable income from the business was $30,000 in 2005 and $40,000 in 2006. In 2007 his business deductions exceeded his business income by $40,000 (i.e., he had a $40,000 net operating loss). He elected to not carry the loss back two years.

In 2008 his taxable income (before considering the net operating loss carry forward) from the business was $50,000. Larry uses the $40,000 net operating loss to reduce his 2008 taxable income to $10,000 ($50,000 taxable income, less $40,000 net operating loss).

Example 3. Mabel owns and operates a small business. Her taxable income from the business was $20,000 in 2005 and $20,000 in 2006. In 2007 her business deductions exceeded her business income by $50,000 (i.e., she had a $50,000 net operating loss).

The $50,000 net operating loss in 2007 is carried back to 2005. Mabel uses $20,000 of the loss in 2005. She will file an amended 2005 return showing zero taxable income. She also will file an amended 2006 return showing zero taxable income. The remaining $10,000 of loss ($50,000 loss, less $20,000 used in 2005 and $20,000 used in 2006) is carried forward to 2008.

In 2008 her taxable income (before considering the net operating loss carry forward) from the business was $50,000. Mabel uses the $10,000 net operating loss to reduce her taxable income to $40,000 ($50,000 taxable income, less $10,000 net operating loss).

---

81. Section 172(b)(1)(A).
82. Section 172(b)(3).
83. Section 172(c).
84. Section 172(d).
85. Section 172(d)(2).
86. Section 172(d)(4).

D. Problems

1. George owns and operates a small photography studio. His taxable income from the business, before taking into consideration the impact of any net operating loss, was as follows:

Years	Net income/Loss
2006	$30,000
2007	$10,000
2008	$20,000
2009	<$50,000>
2010	$30,000
2011	$40,000

   a. What are the tax consequences from George's 2009 net operating loss?

   b. What are the tax consequences from George's 2009 net operating loss if he elects to not carry the loss back two years?

VIII

Characterization

Ordinary Assets:	Hotchpot Assets:	Capital Assets:
• Inventory or property held for sale to business customers • Accounts receivable • Depreciable property used in a business and held for one year or less • Land used in a business and held for one year or less • Supplies	• Depreciable property used in a business and held for more than one year • Land used in a business and held for more than one year	All assets, except: • Inventory or property held for sale to business customers • Accounts receivable • Depreciable property used in a business • Land used in a business • Supplies

Chapter 37

Capital Assets

Characterization (Determining the Applicable Tax Rate)

Ordinary Assets:	Hotchpot Assets:	Capital Assets:
• Inventory or property held for sale to business customers • Accounts receivable • Depreciable property used in a business and held for one year or less • Land used in a business and held for one year or less • Supplies	• Depreciable property used in a business and held for more than one year • Land used in a business and held for more than one year	All assets, except: • Inventory or property held for sale to business customers • Accounts receivable • Depreciable property used in a business • Land used in a business • Supplies

Read

Code Sections 1(h)(1)-(7); 64; 65; 1211(b); 1212(b)(1); 1221(a)(1), (2), (4), (8); 1222

A. Background

Gross income. Gross income includes income (accessions to wealth) derived from any and all sources.[1] It includes every accession to wealth, unless there is an exception.

Disposition of property. Gross income includes gain derived from dealings in property.[2] The amount of gain is the excess of the amount realized over the adjusted basis.[3] Unless

---

1. Section 61(a).
2. Section 61(a)(3).
3. Section 1001(a).

otherwise provided, the gain realized must be recognized, i.e., reported on the taxpayer's income tax return.[4]

The amount of loss from a disposition of property is the excess of the adjusted basis over the amount realized.[5] The taxpayer can recognize, i.e., report the loss on his tax return, if it was incurred while engaged in a business or in a transaction entered into for profit.[6]

Taxable income. In general, taxable income is the taxpayer's gross income, less all allowable deductions.[7] The taxpayer's liability is based on the amount of the taxpayer's taxable income as the taxpayer multiplies taxable income by the applicable tax rate. The tax rates are graduated, meaning that as the amount of income increases, the tax rate on additional amounts or layers of income increases.[8]

B. Background — Capital Assets

For primarily policy reasons Congress decided to tax gain from certain assets at a lower tax rate. Traditionally, these assets are investment assets that have been held over time. With these assets, the difference between the amount realized and adjusted basis might reflect not only true appreciation in the value of the asset but also inflation. Congress also recognized the unique situation of disposition of property — none of the gain or profit in the property is taxed until the taxpayer disposes of the asset. By bunching all the gain into the year of disposition, the taxpayer's gain may be in a higher tax bracket than it would have been if it had been taxed in increments over the length of time the taxpayer held the property.

In general, the Code identifies capital assets and provides that the gain may be taxed at reduced, or preferential, rates. The actual tax rate applied depends on the how long the taxpayer has held the asset and the type of property sold.[9] If there is a capital loss from the sale, the amount of loss the taxpayer can claim may be limited.[10]

Gain from an asset that is not a capital asset is ordinary gain[11] and is taxed at the taxpayer's regular, non-preferential, rates. If there is an ordinary loss from the sale,[12] if the loss can be recognized,[13] there is no limit on the amount the taxpayer can claim on his tax return.

---

4. Section 1001(c).
5. Section 1001(a).
6. Section 165(c)(1), (2).
7. Section 63(a).
8. Section 1.
9. Id.
10. Section 1211(b).
11. Section 64.
12. Section 65.
13. Section 165(c).

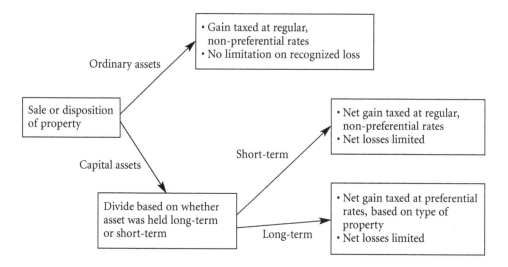

C. Sale or Exchange of a Capital Asset

1. Definition of Capital Asset

The Code defines capital assets by beginning with all property, making it clear that such property is not limited to property used in a taxpayer's business.[14] Thus, capital assets include all assets, whether held for personal purposes, as part of an investment activity, or in a business.

Section 1221. Capital Asset Defined

(a) In general. For purposes of this subtitle, the term "capital asset" means property held by the taxpayer (whether or not connected with his trade or business), but does not include—

(1) stock in trade of the taxpayer or other property of a kind which would properly be included in the inventory of the taxpayer if on hand at the close of the taxable year, or property held by the taxpayer primarily for sale to customers in the ordinary course of his trade or business;

(2) property, used in his trade or business, of a character which is subject to the allowance for depreciation provided in section 167, or real property used in his trade or business;

(3) a copyright, a literary, musical, or artistic composition, a letter or memorandum, or similar property....

(4) accounts or notes receivable acquired in the ordinary course of trade or business for services rendered or from the sale of property described in (1);

---

14. Section 1221(a).

(5) a publication of the United States Government (including the Congressional Record) which is received from the United States Government or any agency thereof, other than by purchase at the price at which it is offered for sale to the public....

(6) any commodities derivative financial instrument held by a commodities derivatives dealer, unless ...

(7) any hedging transaction which is clearly identified as such before the close of the day on which it was acquired, originated, or entered into (or such other time as the Secretary may be regulations prescribe); or

(8) supplies of a type regularly used or consumed by the taxpayer in the ordinary course of a trade or business of the taxpayer.

The Code then excepts assets from this very broad category. The determination of whether an asset meets the definition of a capital asset is made at the time of the asset is sold.[15] Accordingly, if the taxpayer puts the property to a variety of different uses over time, the only relevant use (for tax purposes) is the taxpayer's use of the property at the time it is sold.

2. Assets Excepted from the Definition

The following assets cannot be characterized as capital assets:

Inventory or property held for sale to business customers. Inventory includes property held by the taxpayer for sale to customers. For example, if the taxpayer operates a grocery store, the inventory is the groceries. If the taxpayer operates a car dealership, the inventory is the cars and trucks. If the taxpayer is a housing land developer, the property held for sale to customers is the subdivided lots.

Depreciable property used in a business. Note that only property the taxpayer is using in his business can be depreciated.[16] The taxpayer cannot depreciate inventory or property otherwise held for sale to customers. For example, if the taxpayer operates a book store, the taxpayer can depreciate the cash registers, computers, building, etc. He cannot depreciation the books, which are inventory.

Real property used in a business. Real property used in a business includes land the taxpayer uses in his business. For example, if the taxpayer operates a book store, land includes the land on which the building is built or the parking lot used by the customers.

Accounts or notes receivable. Accounts receivable generally represent the right to be paid for services or for inventory. Both compensation for services and gain from the sale of inventory are characterized as ordinary income and are not eligible for a preferential tax rate (as capital assets). Thus, the sale of the right to receive ordinary income generates ordinary income. Accordingly, accounts receivable and notes receivable are excluded from the definition of capital asset and generate ordinary income.

---

15. Mauldin v. Commissioner, 195 F.2d 714 (10th Cir. 1952); Bynum v. Commissioner, 46 T.C. 295 (1966).

16. Sections 167(a)(1); 168.

Most Commonly Encountered Capital Assets

A capital asset includes all assets, except:

- Inventory or property held primarily for sale to business customers
- Depreciable property used in the taxpayer's business
- Land used in the taxpayer's business
- Accounts receivable acquired in the ordinary course of the taxpayer's business
- Supplies used in the taxpayer's business.

Practice Note

While we often associate the term "capital" with the operation of a business, the definition of capital asset specifically excludes most assets held and used by a taxpayer in his business. Instead, the definition of capital asset mostly includes assets held for investment and personal purposes.

3. Sale or Exchange Requirement

In order to come within the characterization provision, the taxpayer must sell or exchange the asset.[17] This requirement has been interpreted broadly.[18] While including traditional sales, it also includes such events as the abandonment of property subject to a mortgage,[19] a forfeiture,[20] an involuntary foreclosure,[21] and a transfer of land to the mortgagee.[22]

D. Impact of Realizing Capital Gains and Losses

1. Holding Period

The length of time a taxpayer holds a capital asset determines whether the gain or loss on sale is long term or short term. The holding period begins the day after the taxpayer

---

17. Section 1222.
18. See Freeland v. Commissioner, 74 T.C. 980 (1980).
19. Yarbo v. Commissioner, 737 F.2d 479 (5th Cir. 1984).
20. Helvering v. Nebraska Gridge Supply & Lumber Co., 312 U.S. 666 (1941).
21. Helvering v. Hammel, 311 U.S. 504 (1941).
22. Freeland v. Commissioner, 74 T.C. 980 (1980).

acquires the property. Once the taxpayer has held the property for an entire year, any gain or loss on disposition is long-term capital gain or long-term capital loss.[23]

Example. Ted purchased Greenacre on March 5, 2010, for $10,000 and held it for investment purposes. He sold Greenacre for $15,000 on March 6, 2011.

Ted disposed of property. All property is treated as a capital asset unless it comes within the statutory exclusions. Because Ted held Greenacre for investment purposes, it does not come within any of the exclusions; it is a capital asset. Ted has $5,000 of capital gain from the sale.

Ted's holding period began the day after purchase, or March 6, 2010. On the date of sale, March 6, 2011, Ted had held Greenacre for more than one year. The $5,000 gain is long-term capital gain subject to tax at preferential rates.

Tell Me More

The length of time a taxpayer must hold property for it to be considered held "long-term" has varied over the years, ranging from as short as 6 months to as long as two years.

---

2. Preferential Capital Gain Rates for Net Long-Term Capital Gain

The tax rate applicable to net long-term capital gains depends on the nature of the asset sold and the taxpayer's tax bracket. The rate will be one of the following:

- 28 percent;
- 25 percent;
- 15 percent
- zero percent; or
- The tax rate applied to the taxpayer's ordinary income.

Tell Me More

The tax rate applicable to long-term capital gain and the method of taxing long-term capital gain has varied over the years. For example, in 1921 the capital gains tax rate was 12.5 percent. In 1942, only one-half of long-term capital gain and loss was subject to tax and the net gain was taxed at the same rate as the taxpayer's other income. In 1951, the taxpayer was entitled to a deduction equal to one-half of his net long-term capital gains. In 1986, there was no preferential tax rate for capital gains.

---

23. Section 1222.

Collectibles and Section 1202 gain. Collectibles gain is gain from the sale or exchange of any rug, antique, metal, gem, stamp, coin, or other collectible that has been held as a capital asset for more than one year.[24] "Section 1202" gain generally is 50 percent of the gain from the sale or exchange of certain stock described in Section 1202.[25]

If the taxpayer is in a tax bracket higher than 28 percent and the item sold is either "collectibles" or "Section 1202 gain," the maximum tax rate will be 28 percent. If the taxpayer would otherwise be in a lower tax bracket, the taxpayer's lower rate will apply.[26]

Example. Xander, who was in the 35 percent tax bracket, sold an antique rug he had purchased three years earlier for investment purposes. He recognized a long-term capital gain of $30,000. Because the gain was from a collectible and Xander would otherwise have been in a higher tax bracket, the gain from the rug will be taxed at the 28 percent rate. His remaining income will be taxed at the 35 percent rate.

Alternatively, assume Xander had been in the 15 percent tax bracket when he sold the antique rug. He still recognized a long-term capital gain of $30,000. Because he was not in a tax bracket higher than 28 percent, the gain will be taxed at the 15 percent rate, the same as his other income.

Unrecaptured Section 1250 gain. In general, unrecaptured Section 1250 gain is long-term capital gain attributable to depreciation allowed with respect to real estate held for more than one year.[27] If the gain is "unrecaptured Section 1250 gain," it is taxed at a maximum rate of 25 percent.[28]

Example. Bob sold a building that he had used in his business for two years for $100,000. At the time of the sale, the adjusted basis in the building was $75,000 and he had claimed $25,000 of depreciation; he recognized $25,000 of gain. Because the gain from the sale was attributable to the depreciation taken by Bob prior to sale, the gain is characterized as unrecaptured Section 1250 gain and is taxed at a rate not higher than 25 percent.

Adjusted net capital gain. Adjusted net capital gain is the gain remaining after considering the previous two categories of gain, i.e., the net capital gain reduced by the amount of gain from collectibles, Section 1202 gain, and unrecaptured Section 1250 gain.[29] Adjusted net capital gain is taxed at a maximum rate of 15 percent. If the gain would otherwise have been taxed at the 15 percent rate, then the adjusted net capital gain is taxed at a maximum rate of zero percent.[30]

Example. Erin is in the 35 percent tax bracket. She sold stock in GainCo and recognized a long-term capital gain of $20,000. Erin sold no other assets during the year. Because she had no collectibles, Section 1202, or unrecaptured Section 1250 gain, the adjusted net capital gain is $20,000. It will be taxed at the 15 percent rate. All other income will be taxed at the 35 percent rate.

Alternatively, if Erin had been in the 15 percent tax bracket, the gain would otherwise have been taxed at the 15 percent rate. Thus, it will be taxed at the zero percent rate and all other income will be taxed at the 15 percent rate.

---

24. Section 1(h)(5)(A).
25. Section 1(h)(7).
26. Section 1(h)(1)(E).
27. Section 1(h)(6).
28. Section 1(h)(1)(D).
29. Section 1(h)(3).
30. Section 1(h)(1)(B), (C).

Summary of Preferential Tax Rates

Gain From	Highest Tax Rate	Lowest Tax Rate
Collectibles	28 percent	If lower, taxpayer's rate applicable to ordinary income (i.e., taxpayer does not receive a reduced rate).
50 percent of gain from Section 1202 stock	28 percent	If lower, taxpayer's rate applicable to ordinary income (i.e., taxpayer does not receive a reduced rate).
Unrecaptured Section 1250 gain	25 percent	If lower, taxpayer's rate applicable to ordinary income (i.e., taxpayer does not receive a reduced rate).
Remaining long-term capital gain ("adjusted net capital gain")	15 percent	If the gain otherwise would have been taxed at the 15 percent rate, taxed at zero percent.

3. Treatment of Net Capital Losses

To claim a capital loss, the taxpayer must be able to point to authority in the Code that permits recognizing the loss.[31] Only recognized losses are considered. If the taxpayer has a net capital loss, regardless of whether it is long-term or short-term, the maximum he can report on his tax return is $3,000.[32] The remaining net capital loss is carried forward to the following year, retaining its character as long-term or short-term, as applicable.[33]

If the taxpayer has both a net long-term capital loss and a net short-term capital loss, he recognizes the net $3,000 of loss from the short-term loss first.[34] When the entire amount of net short-term loss has been recognized, he begins to recognize his net long-term capital loss. (See further discussion below regarding the netting process.)

Recall

- A taxpayer may recognize a loss from the disposition of property used in a business.[35]

- A taxpayer may recognize a loss from the disposition of property held for investment purposes.[36]

---

31. Section 165(c)(1), (2).
32. Section 1211(b).
33. Section 1212(b).
34. Section 1212(b)(1).
35. Section 165(c)(1).
36. Section 165(c)(2).

Tell Me More

The limitation on the amount of capital loss that can be claimed has varied over the years. For example, in 1921 there was no limitations and gains and loses were not netted. In 1924, capital gains were netted with capital losses and the taxpayer's tax liability could not be reduced by more than 12.5 percent of the "capital net loss" (a term specifically defined in the Code). In 1934, only $2,000 of net capital losses could be claimed and the remainder was carried forward.

In contrast to capital losses, there is no limit on the amount of recognized ordinary loss the taxpayer can claim each year.

Compare and Contrast

- A taxpayer may claim all recognized *ordinary* losses; there is no applicable limitation.

- A taxpayer can claim up to $3,000 of net *capital* losses per year. Any remaining capital loss is carried forward to the following year.

4. Putting It All Together—Determining Net Capital Gain or Loss

If the taxpayer has a net long-term capital gain, the net gain is taxed at the applicable preferential rate. If the taxpayer has a net short-term capital gain, the net gain is taxed at regular rates. If the taxpayer has a net capital loss, whether long-term or short-term, he is allowed to claim a maximum loss of $3,000. Any remaining loss is carried forward to the following year. If the taxpayer has both a net short-term and net long-term capital loss, he uses the net short-term capital loss first.

Summary of Tax Results

	Ordinary	Capital
Gain	Taxed at regular rates	• Net long-term gain—taxed at the applicable preferential rate • Net short-term gain—taxed at regular rates
Loss	No limitation on the amount of recognized loss that can be claimed	• Net capital loss—limited to $3,000 (beginning with net short-term capital loss); any excess loss can be carried forward, retaining its character as long-term or short-term capital loss

To determine the taxpayer's net gain or loss and whether the net amount is long-term or short-term, the long-term gains and losses are netted and short-term gains and losses are netted. If the net amounts from each group are both positive amounts or are both negative amounts, the tax results are determined by considering each category separately. If one net amount is a positive amount and the other is a negative amount, the two amounts are netted together to determine a final amount. The tax result is then applied to that final amount.[37]

Section 1222. Other Terms Relating to Capital Gains and Losses

For purposes of this subtitle—

. . .

(5) Net Short-Term Capital Gain.—The term "net short-term capital loss" means the excess of short-term capital gains for the taxable year over the short-term capital losses for such year.

(6) Net Short-Term Capital Loss.—The term "net short-term capital loss" means the excess of short-term capital losses for the taxable year over the short-term capital gains for such year.

(7) Net Long-Term Capital Gain.—The term "net long-term capital gain" means the excess of long-term capital gains for the taxable year over the long-term capital losses for such year.

(8) Net Long-Term Capital Loss.—The term "net long-term capital loss" means the excess of long-term capital losses for the taxable year over the long-term capital gains for such year.

(9) Capital Gain net Income.—The term "capital gain net income" means the excess of the gains from sales or exchanges of capital assets over the losses from such sales or exchanges.

Steps for Determining Tax Result of Gains and Losses from the Disposition of Capital Assets

Identify all capital assets sold during the taxable year, then:

Step One: Divide gains and losses into two category, one containing long-term gains and losses, the second containing short-term gains and losses.

Step Two: Total the amount in each of the two categories.

Step Three: Are the net amounts from each group both positive amounts or both negative amounts? If yes, continue to Step 4 considering both net amounts separately.

If one net amount is a positive amount and the other is a negative amount, the two amounts are netted together to determine a final amount. Continue to Step 4 with that final amount.

Step Four: Determine the tax result applicable to the net amount(s).

---

37. Section 1222.

Example 1. Tapica sold four capital assets during the taxable year. The gains and losses from the sale of each asset were as follows:

Asset # 1: $50,000 long-term capital gain

Asset # 2: $10,000 short-term capital loss

Asset # 3: $20,000 short-term capital gain

Asset # 4: $60,000 short-term capital gain

Step One: Divide gains and losses into two category, one containing long-term gains and losses, the second containing short-term gains and losses.

Step Two: Total the amount in each of the two categories.

Short-term	Long-term
<$10,000>	$50,000
20,000	
60,000	————
$70,000	$50,000

Step Three: Because the net amount from each group is positive, continue to Step Four with $70,000 of net short-term capital gain and $50,000 of net long-term capital gain.

Step Four. Determine the tax result of the two net amounts.

• $70,000 net short-term capital gain is taxed at regular rates.

• $50,000 net long-term capital gain is taxed at the applicable preferential rate.

Example 2. Unica sold five capital assets during the taxable year. The gains and losses from the sale of each asset were as follows:

Asset # 1: $40,000 long-term capital loss

Asset # 2: $10,000 short-term capital loss

Asset # 3: $10,000 long-term capital gain

Asset # 4: $20,000 short-term capital loss

Asset # 5: $60,000 short-term capital loss

Step One: Divide gains and losses into two category, one containing long-term gains and losses, the second containing short-term gains and losses.

Step Two: Total the amount in each of the two categories.

Short-term	Long-term
<$10,000>	<$40,000>
<20,000>	10,000
<60,000>	————
<$90,000>	<$30,000>

Step Three: Because the net amount from each group is negative, continue to Step Four with $90,000 of net short-term capital loss and $30,000 of net long-term capital loss.

Step Four. Determine the tax result of the two net amounts.

- $3,000 of loss is allowed in the current year (from the $90,000 of net short-term capital loss)
- Carry forward to the next year:
  - $87,000 of net short-term capital loss
  - $30,000 of net long-term capital loss

Example 3. Veronica sold five capital assets during the taxable year. The gains and losses from the sale of each asset were as follows:

Asset # 1:	$60,000 long-term capital loss
Asset # 2:	$10,000 long-term capital loss
Asset # 3:	$10,000 short-term capital loss
Asset # 4:	$50,000 short-term capital gain
Asset # 5:	$10,000 short-term capital loss

Step One: Divide gains and losses into two category, one containing long-term gains and losses, the second containing short-term gains and losses.

Step Two: Total the amount in each of the two categories.

Short-term	Long-term
<$10,000>	<$60,000>
50,000	<10,000>
<10,000>	
$30,000	<$70,000>

Step Three: Because the net short-term is a positive amount and the net long-term is a negative amount, the two amounts are netted together, resulting in a $40,000 net long-term capital loss. Continue to Step Four with $40,000 of net long-term capital loss.

Step Four. Determine the tax result of the net amount.

- $3,000 of net loss[38] is allowed in the current year.
- $37,000 of net long-term capital loss is carried forward to the next year.

Example 4. William sold four capital assets during the taxable year. The gains and losses from the sale of each asset were as follows:

Asset # 1:	$60,000 long-term capital gain
Asset # 2:	$30,000 short-term capital loss
Asset # 3:	$10,000 short-term capital gain

---

38. Note that the total amount of loss the taxpayer was allowed for the year was $20,000 of short-term capital loss and $33,000 of long-term capital loss. The $3,000 net loss referred to is the excess of the net long-term capital loss over the net short-term capital gain, subject to the $3,000 limitation.

Asset # 4: $10,000 long-term capital loss

Step One: Divide gains and losses into two category, one containing long-term gains and losses, the second containing short-term gains and losses.

Step Two: Total the amount in each of the two categories.

Short-term	Long-term
<$30,000>	$60,000
10,000	<10,000>
<$20,000>	$50,000

Step Three: Because the net short-term is a negative amount and the net long-term is a positive amount, the two amounts are netted together, resulting in a $30,000 net long-term capital gain. Continue to Step Four with $30,000 of net long-term capital gain.

Step Four. Determine the tax result of the net amount.

• The $30,000 of net long-term capital gain is taxed at the applicable preferential rate.

Tell Me More

It is possible to have the long-term capital gains from different property each be subject to tax at a different preferential rate. As part of the netting process, capital losses offset capital gains taxed at the highest tax rates first. Thus, any remaining long-term capital gains will be those taxed at the lowest applicable rate.

Review Schedule D below. Locate on the form where the netting of short-term capital gains and losses and long-term capital gains and losses is carried out.

E. Application of Rules

Example 1. Sarah owns a candy store. This year, she sold a stove and three copper pots that she had owned for several years. In addition, throughout the year she sold fudge and lollipops.

The Code defines capital assets by beginning with all property. It then excepts several categories of assets, including depreciable property used in a business and inventory. Accordingly, the stove and copper pots (as depreciable property used in a business) and fudge and lollipops (as inventory) are not capital assets. In sum, none of the items Sarah sold are capital assets.

Example 2. Torrie owns stock in several corporations. This year she sold stock in InvestmentCo and in ProfitCo. She also sold the computer she used exclusively to manage her investments.

Exhibit: Schedule D

SCHEDULE D (Form 1040) Department of the Treasury Internal Revenue Service (99)	Capital Gains and Losses ☒ Attach to Form 1040 or Form 1040NR. ☒ Information about Schedule D and its separate instructions is at www.irs.gov/form1040 . ☒ Use Form 8949 to list your transactions for lines 1, 2, 3, 8, 9, and 10.	OMB No. 1545-0074 **20 12** Attachment Sequence No. 12

Name(s) shown on return	Your social security number

Part I Short-Term Capital Gains and Losses—Assets Held One Year or Less

Complete Form 8949 before completing line 1, 2, or 3. This form may be easier to complete if you round off cents to whole dollars.	(d) Proceeds (sales price) from Form(s) 8949, Part I, line 2, column (d)	(e) Cost or other basis from Form(s) 8949, Part I, line 2, column (e)	(g) Adjustments to gain or loss from Form(s) 8949, Part I, line 2, column (g)	(h) Gain or (loss) Subtract column (e) from column (d) and combine the result with column (g)
1 Short-term totals from all Forms 8949 with box A checked in Part I				
2 Short-term totals from all Forms 8949 with box B checked in Part I				
3 Short-term totals from all Forms 8949 with box C checked in Part I				

4 Short-term gain from Form 6252 and short-term gain or (loss) from Forms 4684, 6781, and 8824 .	4	
5 Net short-term gain or (loss) from partnerships, S corporations, estates, and trusts from Schedule(s) K-1	5	
6 Short-term capital loss carryover. Enter the amount, if any, from line 8 of your Capital Loss Carryover Worksheet in the instructions	6	( )
7 Net short-term capital gain or (loss). Combine lines 1 through 6 in column (h). If you have any long-term capital gains or losses, go to Part II below. Otherwise, go to Part III on the back	7	

Part II Long-Term Capital Gains and Losses—Assets Held More Than One Year

Complete Form 8949 before completing line 8, 9, or 10. This form may be easier to complete if you round off cents to whole dollars.	(d) Proceeds (sales price) from Form(s) 8949, Part II, line 4, column (d)	(e) Cost or other basis from Form(s) 8949, Part II, line 4, column (e)	(g) Adjustments to gain or loss from Form(s) 8949, Part II, line 4, column (g)	(h) Gain or (loss) Subtract column (e) from column (d) and combine the result with column (g)
8 Long-term totals from all Forms 8949 with box A checked in Part II				
9 Long-term totals from all Forms 8949 with box B checked in Part II				
10 Long-term totals from all Forms 8949 with box C checked in Part II				

11 Gain from Form 4797, Part I; long-term gain from Forms 2439 and 6252; and long-term gain or (loss) from Forms 4684, 6781, and 8824	11	
12 Net long-term gain or (loss) from partnerships, S corporations, estates, and trusts from Schedule(s) K-1	12	
13 Capital gain distributions. See the instructions	13	
14 Long-term capital loss carryover. Enter the amount, if any, from line 13 of your Capital Loss Carryover Worksheet in the instructions	14	( )
15 Net long-term capital gain or (loss). Combine lines 8 through 14 in column (h). Then go to Part III on the back	15	

For Paperwork Reduction Act Notice, see your tax return instructions.   Cat. No. 11338H   Schedule D (Form 1040) 2012

Part III	Summary

16 Combine lines 7 and 15 and enter the result . . . . | **16** | |

- If line 16 is a gain, enter the amount from line 16 on Form 1040, line 13, or Form 1040NR, line 14. Then go to line 17 below.
- If line 16 is a loss, skip lines 17 through 20 below. Then go to line 21. Also be sure to complete line 22.
- If line 16 is zero, skip lines 17 through 21 below and enter -0- on Form 1040, line 13, or Form 1040NR, line 14. Then go to line 22.

17 Are lines 15 and 16 both gains?
☐ Yes. Go to line 18.
☐ No. Skip lines 18 through 21, and go to line 22.

18 Enter the amount, if any, from line 7 of the 28% Rate Gain Worksheet in the instructions . . ⊠ | **18** | |

19 Enter the amount, if any, from line 18 of the Unrecaptured Section 1250 Gain Worksheet in the instructions . . . . ⊠ | **19** | |

20 Are lines 18 and 19 both zero or blank?
☐ Yes. Complete the Qualified Dividends and Capital Gain Tax Worksheet in the instructions for Form 1040, line 44 (or in the instructions for Form 1040NR, line 42). Do not complete lines 21 and 22 below.

☐ No. Complete the Schedule D Tax Worksheet in the instructions. Do not complete lines 21 and 22 below.

21 If line 16 is a loss, enter here and on Form 1040, line 13, or Form 1040NR, line 14, the smaller of:

- The loss on line 16 or
- ($3,000), or if married filing separately, ($1,500) } . . . . | **21** | ( ) |

Note. When figuring which amount is smaller, treat both amounts as positive numbers.

22 Do you have qualified dividends on Form 1040, line 9b, or Form 1040NR, line 10b?

☐ Yes. Complete the Qualified Dividends and Capital Gain Tax Worksheet in the instructions for Form 1040, line 44 (or in the instructions for Form 1040NR, line 42).

☐ No. Complete the rest of Form 1040 or Form 1040NR.

The Code defines capital assets by beginning with all property. It then excepts several categories of assets. None of the assets Torrie sold come within those excepted categories. Accordingly, the stock and computer are capital assets.

Example 3. Rick sold five capital assets during the year. The gains and losses from the sale of each asset was as follows:

Asset # 1: $50,000 long-term capital loss

Asset # 2: $10,000 short-term capital loss

Asset # 3: $40,000 short-term capital gain

Asset # 4: $10,000 short-term capital loss

Asset # 5: $10,000 long-term capital loss

Step One: Divide gains and losses into two category, one containing long-term gains and losses, the second containing short-term gains and losses.

Step Two: Total the amount in each of the two categories.

Short-term	Long-term
<$10,000>	<$50,000>
40,000	<10,000>
<10,000>	_____
$20,000	<$60,000>

Step Three: Because the net short-term is a positive amount and the net long-term is a negative amount, the two amounts are netted together, resulting in a $40,000 net long-term capital loss. Continue to Step Four with $40,000 of net long-term capital loss.

Step Four. Determine the tax result of the net amount.

- $3,000 of net loss is allowed in the current year.[39]
- $37,000 of long-term capital loss is carried forward to the next year.

The following year Rick sold two capital assets. The gain from the sales was as follows:

Asset # 1: $30,000 long-term capital gain

Asset # 2: $10,000 short-term capital gain

Step One: Divide gains and losses into two category, one containing long-term gains and losses, the second containing short-term gains and losses. In addition, Rick has $37,000 of long-term capital loss carried forward from the previous year.

Step Two: Total the amount in each of the two categories.

---

39. Note that the total amount of loss the taxpayer was allowed for the year was $20,000 of short-term capital loss and $23,000 of long-term capital loss. The $3,000 net loss referred to is the excess of the net long-term capital loss over the net short-term capital gain, subject to the $3,000 limitation.

Short-term	Long-term
$10,000	$30,000
_____	<37,000>
$10,000	<$7,000>

Step Three: Because the net short-term is a positive amount and the net long-term is a negative amount, the two amounts are netted together, resulting in a $3,000 net short-term capital gain. Continue to Step Four with $3,000 of net short-term capital gain.

Step Four. Determine the tax result of the net amount. The $3,000 of net short-term capital gain is taxed at the taxpayer's regular rates.

Example 4. During the year Sandy had the following sales and income:

- Sold Widget Inc. stock and recognized $2,000 of capital gain. She held the stock for four years prior to sale.

- Sold Loss Co stock and recognized a $10,000 capital loss. She held the stock for three years prior to sale.

- Earned $50,000 from her job as a librarian.

Sandy is in the 25 percent tax bracket.

The Code defines capital assets by beginning with all property. It then excepts several categories of assets. Because the stock sold does not come within any of the exceptions it is a capital asset. In addition, she held the stock long-term. From the sale of the stock:

	Long-term
Widget Co	$2,000
Loss Co	<10,000>
	<$8,000>

Because she has a net long-term capital loss, she can claim $3,000 of the loss and must carry the remaining $5,000 of long-term capital loss forward.

$50,000	income (salary)
<3,000>	long-term capital loss
$47,000	taxable income

In sum, Sandy has $47,000 ordinary income taxed at 25 percent and a $5,000 long-term capital loss carry forward.

Example 5. During the year Ken had the following sales and income:

- Sold Black Co stock and recognized $20,000 of capital gain. He held the stock for four years prior to sale.

- Sold Loss Co stock and recognized an $8,000 capital loss. He held the stock for three years prior to sale.

- Earned $40,000 from his job as a mechanic.

Ken is in the 25 percent tax bracket.

The Code defines capital assets by beginning with all property. It then excepts several categories of assets. Because the stock sold does not come within any of the exceptions it is a capital asset. In addition, she held the stock long-term. From the sale of the stock:

	Long-term
Black Co	$20,000
Loss Co	<u><8,000></u>
	$12,000

He has a net long-term capital gain. The gain is not from collectibles, Section 1202 gain, or unrecaptured Section 1250 gain. It is adjusted net capital gain, taxed at a maximum rate of 20 percent.

In sum, Ken has $40,000 ordinary income taxed at 25 percent and $12,000 of long-term capital gain taxed at 20 percent.

Example 6. During the year Josie had the following sales and income:

- Sold Green Co stock and recognized $20,000 of capital gain. She held the stock for four months prior to sale.

- Sold Loss Co stock and recognized an $8,000 capital loss. She held the stock for three months prior to sale.

- Earned $60,000 from her job as a manager.

Josie is in the 35 percent tax bracket.

The stock is a capital asset and she held it short-term. From the sale of the stock:

	Short-term
Green Co	$20,000
Loss Co	<u><8,000></u>
	$12,000

She has a net short-term capital gain; short-term taxable gain is taxed at the taxpayer's regular rate.

In sum, Josie has $72,000 ($60,000 ordinary salary income and $12,000 short-term capital gain) taxed at 35 percent.

F. Problems

1. Abe owns and operates a novelty store. Which of the following assets are capital assets?

    a. Store inventory

    b. Land on which the store is located

    c. Building in which the store is located

    d. Cash register

    e. Copy machine

    f. Paper for the copy machine.

    g. Cleaning supplies

2. Sam owns a car dealership. This year he sold 1,000 cars. What is the character of the gain from the sales? *ordinary*

3. Teresa sold the following assets during the year:

    *   Her personal ten-speed mountain bike *capital gain*

    *   Her personal residence *capital gain*

    *   Stock in ProfitCo *capital gain*

    *   Several pieces of used furniture (at a garage sale she held) *capital gain*

    Which of the assets she sold are capital assets?

4. This year Zelda sold stock in First Co for a $10,000 profit and stock in Second Co for a $15,000 loss. She had held all of the stock for more than three years.

    a. What is the character of the gain or loss from each sale?

    b. How much net gain or loss must Zelda report?

5. Randy sold the following capital assets during the year:

    Asset # 1: $50,000 long-term capital loss

    Asset # 2: $10,000 long-term capital loss

    Asset # 3: $10,000 short-term capital loss

    Asset # 4: $40,000 short-term capital gain

    Asset # 5: $10,000 short-term capital loss

    What is the net amount Randy can report on his tax return?

6. Nancy sold the following capital assets during the year:

    Asset # 1: $50,000 long-term capital loss

    Asset # 2: $10,000 long-term capital loss
    Asset # 3: $10,000 short-term capital loss

    What is the net amount Nancy can report on her tax return?

7. Paula sold the following capital assets during the year:

    Asset # 1: $60,000 long-term capital gain

    Asset # 2: $10,000 long-term capital loss

Asset # 3: $50,000 short-term capital gain

Asset # 4: $30,000 short-term capital loss

What is the net amount Paula must report on her tax return?

8. Joy sold the following capital assets during the year:

Asset # 1: $20,000 long-term capital gain

Asset # 2: $30,000 long-term capital loss

Asset # 3: $60,000 short-term capital gain

Asset # 4: $10,000 short-term capital loss

What is the net amount Joy must report on her tax return?

9. Sheryl sold InvestCo stock and realized a short-term capital loss of $10,000. She also earned $50,000 from her job as a stylist. What will Sheryl report on her income tax return?

10. Karl sold Black Co stock and recognized $20,000 of long-term capital gain. He also earned $50,000 from his job as a postman. What will Karl report on his income tax return?

11. Carol sold InvestCo stock and realized a long-term capital loss of $20,000. She also earned $50,000 from her job as a real estate agent. The following year, she did not sell any more stock but earned $50,000 from her job as a real estate agent. What are the tax consequences to Carol in each year?

G. Analysis and Application

1. George sold his businesses. As part of the sale agreement, the buyer agreed to pay George $10,000 for a covenant not to compete.

   a. What are the tax consequences to George with respect to the $10,000?

   b. What are the tax consequences to the purchaser with respect to the covenant not to compete?

2. Do you agree that net long-term capital gains should be taxed at a lower rate than ordinary income?

3. Do you agree that net capital losses should be limited to $3,000?

4. Consider a business you might be interested in operating. Identify at least two capital assets you would expect the business to own.

5. How might your understanding of the lower tax rates applicable to capital gains help you when advising a client who is considering selling property?

Chapter 38

Quasi-Capital (Hotchpot) Assets

Characterization (Determining the Applicable Tax Rate)

Ordinary Assets:	Hotchpot Assets:	Capital Assets:
• Inventory or property held for sale to business customers • Accounts receivable • Depreciable property used in a business and held for one year or less • Land used in a business and held for one year or less • Supplies	• **Depreciable property used in a business and held for more than one year** • **Land used in a business and held for more than one year**	All assets, except: • Inventory or property held for sale to business customers • Accounts receivable • Depreciable property used in a business • Land used in a business • Supplies

Read

Code Section 1231(a), (b)(1)

A. Background

Disposition of property. Gross income includes gain derived from dealings in property.[40] The amount of gain is the excess of the amount realized over the adjusted basis.[41] Unless otherwise provided, the gain realized must be recognized, i.e., reported on the taxpayer's income tax return.[42]

The amount of loss from a disposition of property is the excess of the adjusted basis over the amount realized.[43] The taxpayer can recognize, i.e., report the loss on his tax return, if it was incurred while engaged in a business or in a transaction entered into for profit.[44]

---

40. Section 61(a)(3).
41. Section 1001(a).
42. Section 1001(c).
43. Section 1001(a).
44. Section 165(c)(1), (2).

Capital assets. Capital assets are all assets, *except:*[45]

- Inventory or property held for sale to business customers
- Depreciable property used in the taxpayer's business
- Land used in the taxpayer's business
- Accounts receivable acquired in the ordinary course of the taxpayer's business
- Supplies used in the taxpayer's business.

If an asset was excepted from the definition of a capital asset, without any intervening Code provision, the gain or loss would be characterized as an ordinary gain or an ordinary loss.

B. Hotchpot Assets

If an asset has been excluded from the definition of a capital asset, the Code provides an intermediary look at the asset. In some cases, this intermediary look will recharacterize a net gain as long-term capital gain, giving the taxpayer the benefit of the reduced rates applicable to long-term capital gain, even though the asset is not a capital asset. A net loss is not recharacterized but remains an ordinary loss.

The assets that are given this intermediary look are called quasi-capital or hotchpot assets. Hotchpots assets include depreciable property used in a taxpayer's business and held for more than one year and land used in a taxpayer's business and held for more than one year.[46]

Definition — Hotchpot Assets

Include only:

- Depreciable property used in the taxpayer's business and held for more than one year
- Land used in the taxpayer's business and held for more than one year.

---

1. Preliminary Hotchpot

Gain and losses that resulted from an involuntary conversion are given special consideration. Specifically, it includes involuntary conversions arising from fire, storm, shipwreck, or other casualty, or from theft of:[47]

- Property used in a business; or
- Capital assets held for more than one year and held in connection with a business or for investment.

---

45. Section 1221(a).
46. Section 1231(a)(3), (b).
47. Section 1231(a)(3)(A)(ii).

Total all the gains and losses from these involuntary conversions. If the net amount is a loss, the net loss is characterized as an ordinary loss. If the net amount is a gain, the net gain becomes part of the principal hotchpot.[48]

Rules — Preliminary Hotchpot

Step One: Identify all gains and losses from involuntary conversions.

Step Two: Net together such gains and losses.

If a net loss → net loss is characterized as an ordinary loss.

If a net gain → net gain becomes part of the principal hotchpot.

---

2. Principal Hotchpot

The tax result applied to hotchpot assets is based on the net amount of hotchpot gain or loss. Thus, first determine the gains and losses from the disposition of all hotchpot assets. Next, add these amounts together (including any net gain from the preliminary hotchpot). If the net amount is a gain, the hotchpot assets are recharacterized as capital assets (i.e., the net gain is characterized as long-term capital gain).[49] If the net amount is a loss, there is no recharacterization and the assets remain as ordinary assets (i.e., the net loss is characterized as an ordinary loss).[50]

Rules — Principal Hotchpot

Step One: Identify all hotchpot gains and losses (including a net gain from the preliminary hotchpot).

Step Two: Net together such gains and losses.

If a net gain → net gain is characterized as a long-term capital gain.

If a net loss → net loss is characterized as an ordinary loss.

Example. Jenny sold the following assets this year and recognized gain or loss as follows:

Asset	Gain/Loss
Copy machine	<$2,000>
Computer	<500>
Whiteacre	5,000

---

48. Section 1231(a)(4)(C).
49. Section 1231(a)(1).
50. Section 1231(a)(2).

Jenny used each asset in her business and had purchased them more than a year ago.

The Code defines capital assets by beginning with all property. It then excepts several categories of assets, including depreciable property used in a business and land used in a business. Accordingly, the copy machine and computer (as depreciable property used in her business) and land (as land used in her business) are not capital assets.

Hotchpot assets include depreciable property used in the taxpayer's business and held for more than one year and land used in the taxpayer's business and held for more than one year. Because the copy machine and computer are depreciable property used in Jenny's business and held for more than one year, they are both hotchpot assets. Because the land was used in Jenny's business and held for more than one year, it is a hotchpot asset.

The gains and losses from disposition of each of the assets, all hotchpot assets, are netted together.

Asset	Gain/Loss
Copy machine	<$2,000>
Computer	<500>
Whiteacre	5,000
Net gain:	$2,500

Because there is a net gain, the $2,500 gain is characterized as long-term capital gain and netted with the taxpayer's other long-term capital gains and losses.

Tell Me More

Realizing that the composition of gains and losses in the hotchpot can substantially change the tax consequences to the taxpayer, a taxpayer may engage in tax planning. Specifically, the taxpayer may plan to sell depreciated property in one year (generating an ordinary loss) and appreciated property in a subsequent year (generating a long-term capital gain).

Section 1231(c) counters this tax planning. Any time a taxpayer has a net hotchpot gain, he must look back to the preceding five years. To the extent the taxpayer had a net hotchpot loss during that time, he must characterize the current net gain as ordinary income (rather than long-term capital gain). In effect, the result will be the same as what would have occurred if the taxpayer had sold the properties in the same year.

C. Application of Rules

Example 1. Flo owns and operates a bakery. This year the building where the bakery was located burned down. Flo recognized a $10,000 gain on the involuntary conversion. The $10,000 of gain is considered in the preliminary hotchpot. If there are no other items in the preliminary hotchpot, the gain becomes part of the principal hotchpot.

Example 2. Sarah owns a candy store. This year she sold a stove and three copper pots that she had owned for several years. In addition, throughout the year she sold fudge and lollipops.

The Code defines capital assets by beginning with all property. It then excepts several categories of assets, including depreciable property used in a business and inventory. Accordingly, the stove and copper pots (as depreciable property used in a business) and fudge and lollipops (as inventory) are not capital assets.

Hotchpot assets include depreciable property used in the taxpayer's business and held for more than one year. Because the stove and copper pots are depreciable property used in Sarah's business and were held for more than one year, they are both hotchpot assets. The fudge and lollipops do not meet the definition of a hotchpot asset; they are ordinary assets.

Example 3. Marie owns a gas station. This year she sold a cash register she had owned for six months.

The Code defines capital assets by beginning with all property. It then excepts several categories of assets, including depreciable property used in a business. Accordingly, the cash register (as depreciable property used in a business) is not a capital asset.

Hotchpot assets include depreciable property used in the taxpayer's business and held for more than one year. Because the cash register, while depreciable property used in Marie's business, was not held for more than one year, is it not a hotchpot asset; it is an ordinary asset.

Example 4. Maurice sold the following assets this year and recognized gain or loss as follows:

Asset	Gain/Loss
Widget machine	<$3,000>
Equipment	<500>
Whiteacre	5,000

Maurice used each asset in his business and had purchased them more than a year ago.

The widget machine and equipment (as depreciable property used in a business) and Whiteacre (land used in a business) are not capital assets. Because the widget machine and equipment were depreciable property used in Maurice's business and held for more than one year, they are both hotchpot assets. Because Whiteacre was land used in Maurice's business and held for more than one year, it is a hotchpot asset.

The gains and losses from disposition of each of the assets, all hotchpot assets, are netted together.

Hotchpot Asset	Gain/Loss	Capital
Widget machine	<$3,000>	**Long-term**
Equipment	<500>	$1,500
Whiteacre	5,000	
Net gain:	$1,500	

Because there is a net gain, the $1,500 gain is characterized as long-term capital gain and netted with Maurice's other long-term capital gains and losses.

Example 5. Randy earns $70,000 from his business. This year he sold the following assets and recognized gain or loss as follows:

Asset	Gain/Loss
Equipment	<$15,000>
Oven	<3,000>
Greenacre	10,000

Randy used each asset in his business and had purchased them more than a year ago.

None of the assets are capital assets, but each is a hotchpot asset. The gains and losses from disposition of each of the assets, all hotchpot assets, are netted together.

Ordinary	Hotchpot Asset	Gain/Loss
$70,000 Salary	Equipment	<$15,000>
<8,000>	Oven	<3,000>
$62,000	Greenacre	10,000
	Net loss:	<$8,000>

Because there is a net loss, the $8,000 loss continues to be characterized as an ordinary loss. Randy has net ordinary income of $62,000 taxed at regular rates.

Example 6. During the year Ken had the following sales and income:

- Sold Black Co stock and recognized $20,000 of capital gain. He held the stock for four years prior to sale.
- Sold Loss Co stock and recognized an $8,000 capital loss. He held the stock for three years prior to sale.
- Sold Whiteacre, property used in his business and held for more than one year. He recognized a $2,000 gain.
- Earned $40,000 from his job as a mechanic.

The Black Co and Loss Co stock are capital assets, both held long-term. Whiteacre is a hotchpot asset. Because Whiteacre is the only hotchpot asset he sold this year; the net hotchpot gain is $2,000. The net gain is characterized as long-term capital gain.

Ordinary	Hotchpot Assets	Capital Long-term
$40,000 salary	$2,000 Whiteacre	Long-term
	$2,000	$2,000 Hotchpot
		20,000 Black Co
		<8,000> Loss Co
		$14,000

Ken has a $14,000 net long-term capital gain. He also has $40,000 of ordinary income.

Example 7. One of the buildings in which Larry conducts his business burned to the ground when it was struck by lightening, Because Larry had very good insurance on the property, he ended up recognizing a $5,000 gain on the involuntary conversion. In addition, during the year Larry had the following sales:

- Sold equipment used in his business and held for more than one year. He recognized a $3,000 loss

- Sold a computer used in his business and held for more than one year. He recognized a $500 loss.

- Sold Greenacre, property used in his business and held for more than one year. He recognized a $4,000 gain.

The building was subject to an involuntary conversion, and accordingly becomes part of the preliminary hotchpot. Because there is a net gain in the preliminary hotchpot, the net gain becomes part of the principal hotchpot.

Each of the assets Larry sold was a hotchpot asset. The gains and losses from disposition of the assets are netted together.

Hotchpot Asset	Gain/Loss	Capital
Net preliminary hotchpot gain	$5,000	**Long-term**
Equipment	<3,000>	$5,500
Computer	<500>	
Greenacre	4,000	
Net gain:	$5,500	

Because there is a net gain, the $5,500 gain is characterized as long-term capital gain and netted with Larry's other long-term capital gains and losses.

Example 8 — Section 1231(c) lookback rule. In 2005 Sandy sold equipment used in her business that she had held for more than one year, generating a $3,000 hotchpot loss. If the equipment is the only hotchpot asset Sandy sold during the year, there was a net loss in the hotchpot and it was characterized as an ordinary loss.

In 2008 Sandy sold land used in her business that she had held for more than one year, generating a $5,000 hotchpot gain. If the land was the only hotchpot asset Sandy sold during the year, there was a net gain in the hotchpot and initially it was characterized as a long-term capital gain. However, because Sandy had a net loss within the preceding five years, to the extent of the loss, Sandy must recharacterize the gain as ordinary gain. Thus, Sandy has a $3,000 ordinary gain and $2,000 of long-term capital gain.

D. Problems

1. Abe owns and operates a novelty store. Which of the following assets are hotchpot assets? (Except for the inventory, paper for the copy machine, and cleaning supplies, each asset has been held for more than one year.)

    a. Store inventory

    b. Land on which the store is located

    c. Building in which the store is located

    d. Cash register

    e. Copy machine

    f. Paper for the copy machine.

    g. Cleaning supplies

2. Bert sold land next to his business that he had used for a parking lot. He recognized a $5,000 gain from the sale and had held the land for 9 months prior to the sale. What is the character of the gain?

3. Susie owns and operates a hair salon. This year she sold 20 bottles of shampoo and five industrial-strength hair dryers that she had used in her business for the past three years. What is the character of the gain or loss from the sale of the shampoo and the hair dryers?

4. Mary Anne owns and operates a consulting service. This year she sold the following assets, all of which she had held for more than one year:

Asset	Gain or Loss
Copy machine	$2,000 loss
Credit card machine	$1,000 loss

What are the tax consequences to Mary Anne from the sales?

5. Adam owns and operates a movie theatre. This year he sold the following assets, all of which he had held for more than one year:

Asset	Gain or Loss
Popcorn machine	$2,000 loss
Soda pop machine	$1,000 loss
Land used as parking lot	$10,000 gain

He also sold stock he held for investment, recognizing a $10,000 gain. He had held the stock for more than one year.

What are the tax consequences to Adam from the sales?

6. Tom sold XCo stock, recognizing a $20,000 long-term capital gain, and YCo stock, recognizing a $10,000 short-term capital gain.

Tom also owns and operates a business. This year he sold the following assets, all of which he had held for more than one year:

Asset	Gain or Loss
Copy machine	$3,000 loss
Fax machine	$2,000 loss
Land used as parking lot	$10,000 gain

Finally, Tom earned a salary of $70,000. What are the tax consequences to Tom from the above transactions?

E. Analysis and Application

1. Consider a business you might be interested in operating. Identify at least three hotchpot assets you would expect the business to own.

2. Do you agree with the special treatment afforded net hotchpot gains?

3. How might your understanding of how hotchpot assets are treated help you when advising a client who is considering selling property?

Chapter 39

Recapture

Characterization (Determining the Applicable Tax Rate)

Ordinary Assets:	Hotchpot Assets:	Capital Assets:
• Inventory or property held for sale to business customers • Accounts receivable • Depreciable property used in a business and held for one year or less • Land used in a business and held for one year or less • Supplies	• **Depreciable property used in a business and held for more than one year** • Land used in a business and held for more than one year	All assets, except: • Inventory or property held for sale to business customers • Accounts receivable • **Depreciable property used in a business** • Land used in a business • Supplies

Read

Code Sections 179(d)(10); 1245(a)(1), (a)(2)(A), (a)(3)(A)

A. Background

Depreciation. A taxpayer is entitled to depreciate or amortize the cost of an asset if it is purchased by the taxpayer, used in the taxpayer's business or investment activity, has a life of more than one year, and wears out over time. The determination of how much depreciation is allowed each year depends on whether the asset is:[51]

- Tangible personal property
- Real property
- Intangible property
- Another type of property

---

51. Sections 167; 168; 179; 197.

Adjusted basis. The basis of property is the cost of the property at the time it was purchased.[52] As the cost is "recovered" by the taxpayer through depreciation or amortization, the basis is reduced (adjusted).[53]

Disposition of property. Gross income includes gain derived from dealings in property.[54] The amount of gain is the excess of the amount realized over the adjusted basis.[55] Unless otherwise provided, the gain realized must be recognized, i.e., reported on the taxpayer's income tax return.[56]

B. Background —
Depreciation Recapture

A taxpayer engaged in a business or investment activity is permitted to claim depreciation.[57] Any depreciation claimed reduces the taxpayer's income.

Example. Bill owns and operates a music store. In year one he purchased and placed in service a display unit. He paid $25,000 for the unit, and it is five year property. Bill did not elect to claim bonus depreciation. Accordingly, he is entitled to claim $5,000 of deprecation ($25,000 × 20 percent) in the year he placed it into service. Bill earned $60,000 from sales and was in the 25 percent tax bracket. His taxable income would be determined as follows:

$60,000 income
<5,000> depreciation
$55,000 taxable income, taxed at 25 percent

Note that the depreciation reduced his income by $5,000 and that this $5,000 otherwise would have been taxed at the 25 percent tax rate (saving him $1,250 of taxes). Bill's adjusted basis in the display unit is $20,000 ($25,000 basis, less $5,000 of depreciation).

Just over a year later Bill sold display unit for $25,000. For simplicity purposes, ignore any applicable depreciation for year two. Bill had $5,000 gain from the sale:

AR: $25,000
AB: 20,000
Gain: $5,000

Note that even though there is a gain on disposition, the property did not increase in value from the time Bill purchased it. The gain is due solely to the depreciation Bill had claimed.

Because the display unit is depreciable property used in Bill's business and he held it for more than one year, it is a hotchpot asset. As the only hotchpot asset Bill sold during the year, Bill had a net $5,000 hotchpot gain, which was characterized as a long-term capital gain. With no other capital assets sold during the year, Bill had a net $5,000 long-term capital gain, taxed at a preferential rate of 15 percent (resulting in $750 of taxes). The same $5,000 that reduced income taxed at a rate of 25 percent was later included in income, but taxed at a lower, 15-percent rate (resulting in a $500 tax savings).

---

52. Section 1012(a).
53. Section 1016(a).
54. Section 61(a)(3).
55. Section 1001(a).
56. Section 1001(c).
57. See Chapters 25 and 29.

While a taxpayer is entitled to claim depreciation, Congress was dissatisfied with the tax result upon subsequent sale of the property. Congress wanted to tax the gain created by the depreciation deductions at the same rate as the ordinary income it previously had offset. To achieve this result, the gain would have to be recharacterized and taxed as ordinary income. The recapture provision, Section 1245, provides this result.

If property is sold at a loss, the issue described above does not arise and no recharacterization is required.[58] Accordingly, the recapture provision applies only when there is a gain on disposition.

C. Section 1245 Depreciation Recapture

The recapture provision of Section 1245 works to recharacterize gain resulting solely from depreciation deductions as ordinary income.[59] From the example above, the $5,000 gain generated when Bill sold the display unit was due entirely to the depreciation he previously had claimed. Accordingly, the $5,000 is recharacterized as ordinary income. In contrast, any true appreciation in the property will not be recharacterized.

Example. Sue sold equipment she used in her business. She had purchased the equipment three years earlier for $10,000 and had claimed $4,000 in depreciation. She sold the equipment this year for $11,000.

AR:	$11,000
AB:	6,000
Gain:	$5,000

Because the equipment is depreciable property used in her business and held for more than one year, it is a hotchpot asset.

Of the $5,000 gain, $4,000 was due solely to the fact that she claimed depreciation. The remaining $1,000 represents true appreciation in the property (the property increased in value from $10,000 at the time of purchase to $11,000 at the time of sale). Accordingly, $4,000 of the gain must be recharacterized as ordinary income. The remaining $1,000 continues to be characterized as hotchpot gain.

Applicable property. Section 1245 depreciation recapture applies to all depreciable tangible personal property and depreciable intangible property. It does not apply to depreciable real property (buildings).[60]

Rule — Section 1245 Depreciation Recapture

On the sale of any depreciable or amortizable property except buildings, depreciation recapture recharacterizes the lesser of:

- the gain on disposition; or
- depreciation claimed

as ordinary income.

---

58. Treas. Reg. § 1.1245-1(d).
59. Section 1245(a)(1).
60. Section 1245(a)(3)(A), (b)(8); Treas. Reg. § 1.1245-3(b).

The reason why there is a "lesser of rule" is to take into consideration the fact that the property may have actually decreased in value. For example, Kaylie sold equipment she used in her business. She had purchased the equipment three years earlier for $10,000 and had claimed $4,000 in depreciation. She sold the equipment this year for $9,000.

AR:	$9,000
AB:	6,000
Gain:	$3,000

Because the equipment is depreciable property used in her business and held for more than one year, it is a hotchpot asset.

All the $3,000 gain is due solely to the fact that she claimed depreciation. Note that, of the total $4,000 depreciation taken, $1,000 of decrease in value actually occurred. The remaining $3,000 of depreciation was tax depreciation only. The "lesser of" rule takes into consideration this true $1,000 decrease in value and requires the taxpayer to recapture only the $3,000 of tax depreciation.

Tell Me More

The Code provides a more complicated computation for determining the amount of gain to be recharacterized as ordinary income. It recharacterizes as ordinary income the difference between the taxpayer's adjusted basis and the lesser of two amounts. The first amount is the recomputed basis and the second amount is the amount realized. Recomputed basis is the adjusted basis plus the depreciation or amortization taken with respect to the property (considering both regular and bonus depreciation).[61] The first amount will be less than the second amount when the property is sold for more than its original purchase price.

D. Section 1250 Depreciation Recapture

The same issue can arise when dealing with depreciation claimed on depreciable real property (buildings). However, the recapture provision applicable to buildings requires the taxpayer to recharacterize only the depreciation claimed in excess of straight-line depreciation ("additional depreciation") as ordinary income.[62] Under MACRS, the taxpayer is entitled to claim only straight-line depreciation. Accordingly, there is no amount in excess of straight-line depreciation (there is no "additional depreciation") and nothing is required to be recharacterized. In pre-1986 versions of the Code, some real estate was subject to accelerated depreciation; this real estate still would be subject to recapture under Section 1250.

---

61. Section 1245(a)(2)(A). The depreciation recapture rule achieves the same result with fewer calculations.

62. Section 1250(a)(1), (b)(1). If the real property is not held for more than one year the claimed depreciation is considered additional depreciation and is subject to the recapture rules.

E. Application of Rules

Example 1. Alex sold equipment he used in his business. He had purchased the equipment three years earlier for $50,000 and had claimed $10,000 in depreciation. He sold the equipment for $55,000.

AR:	$55,000
AB:	40,000
Gain:	$15,000

The equipment is a hotchpot asset. Of the $15,000 gain, $10,000 is due solely to the fact that he claimed depreciation and is recharacterized as ordinary. (Depreciation recapture recharacterizes the lesser of gain on disposition ($15,000) or depreciation ($10,000) as ordinary income, or in this case recharacterizes $10,000 as ordinary income.) The remaining $5,000 continues to be characterized as hotchpot gain.

$15,000 gain $\Big\}$ $10,000 ordinary income
$5,000 hotchpot gain

Example 2. Jerry sold equipment he used in his investment activity. He had purchased the equipment four years earlier for $10,000 and had claimed $3,000 in depreciation. He sold the equipment for $9,000.

AR:	$9,000
AB:	7,000
Gain:	$2,000

The equipment is a capital asset. All the $2,000 gain is due solely to the fact that he claimed depreciation and is recharacterized as ordinary. (Depreciation recapture recharacterizes the lesser of gain on disposition ($2,000) or depreciation ($3,000) as ordinary income, or in this case recharacterizes $2,000 as ordinary income.) Even though the equipment is a capital asset, all the gain is characterized as ordinary income.

Example 3. Janice sold equipment she used in her business. She had purchased the equipment three years earlier for $60,000 and had claimed $10,000 in depreciation. She sold the equipment for $45,000.

AR:	$45,000
AB:	50,000
Loss:	<$5,000>

The equipment is a hotchpot asset. There is a loss from the sale. Depreciation recapture does not apply to losses. Accordingly, the loss continues to be characterized as a hotchpot loss. If it is the only hotchpot asset she sold this year, because she has a net hotchpot loss, the $5,000 loss is characterized as an ordinary loss.

Example 4. Paul sold land used in his business. He held the land for two years and recognized a $10,000 gain from the sale. He also sold equipment he used in his business. He had purchased the equipment three years earlier for $50,000 and had claimed $10,000 in depreciation. He sold the equipment for $55,000.

Equipment

AR: $55,000
AB: <u>40,000</u>
Gain: $15,000

Both the land and equipment are hotchpot assets.

Hotchpot

Land $10,000
Equipment $15,000

However, of the $15,000 gain from the equipment, $10,000 is due solely to the fact that he claimed depreciation and is recharacterized as ordinary. (Depreciation recapture recharacterizes the lesser of gain on disposition ($15,000) or depreciation ($10,000) as ordinary income, or in this case recharacterizes $10,000 as ordinary income.) The remaining $5,000 continues to be characterized as hotchpot gain.

	Ordinary	Hotchpot	Capital
Land	—	$10,000	Long-term
Equipment	<u>$10,000</u>	<u>5,000</u>	$15,000
	$10,000	$15,000 ⟶	

Because the hotchpot has a net gain, the net gain is characterized as long-term capital gain and considered with Paul's other capital gains and losses.

Example 5. Jeff sold a building he used in his business. He had purchased the building five years earlier for $100,000 and had claimed $30,000 in depreciation pursuant to MACRS. He sold the equipment for $85,000.

AR: $85,000
AB: <u>70,000</u>
Gain: $15,000

The building is a hotchpot asset. Even though all the $15,000 of gain is due solely to the fact he claimed depreciation, he did not claim any depreciation in excess of that allowed under the MACRS system (i.e., claimed no depreciation in excess of straight-line). None of the gain is recharacterized and it continues to be hotchpot gain.

F. Problems

1. Will sold equipment used in his business at a loss of $2,000. He had held the equipment for four years and had previously claimed $5,000 in depreciation. What is the character of the loss?

2. Harry sold equipment he had used in his business for $40,000. He had purchased the equipment two years earlier for $30,000 and had claimed $10,000 in depreciation. What is the character of the gain?

3. Kate sold equipment she had used in her business for $40,000. She had purchased the equipment three years earlier for $50,000 and had claimed $20,000 in depreciation. What is the character of the gain?

4. Pippa sold equipment she used in her business for $50,000. She had purchased the equipment three years earlier for $40,000 and had claimed $20,000 in depreciation. She also sold XCo stock, recognizing a $10,000 long-term capital gain. What are the tax consequences to Pippa?

5. Charles sold equipment he used in his business for $50,000. He had purchased the equipment three years earlier for $40,000 and had claimed $20,000 in depreciation. He also sold land that he used in his business for $60,000. He had purchased the land two years earlier for $70,000. What are the tax consequences to Charles?

6. Camilla sold a building she had used in her business for $160,000. She had purchased the building five years earlier for $150,000 and had claimed $50,000 in depreciation. What are the tax consequences to Camilla?

G. Analysis and Application

1. Could you explain to a client how the recapture provision works?

2. Elizabeth owned and operated an art gallery. This year she sold the gallery to Phillip for $410,000. Phillip is not related to her. The adjusted basis and fair market value for each asset she sold is as follows:

Asset	Adjusted basis	Fair market value
Inventory – *ordinary*	$40,000	$100,000
Equipment – *Hotchpot*	80,000	220,000
Furniture	20,000	10,000
Goodwill	-0-	80,000

    Elizabeth held all the assets for more than one year. She had claimed $120,000 of depreciation on the equipment and $80,000 of depreciation on the furniture. Because the goodwill was self-generated, Elizabeth was not entitled to claim any amortization. What are the tax consequences to Elizabeth in the year of sale?

3. In May of 2010 Keith purchased a business. One of the assets he purchased was the goodwill, for which he paid $54,000. In January of 2012 he sold the business. As part of the sale he sold the goodwill for $64,000. What are the tax consequences to Keith from the sale of the goodwill?

Chapter 40

Installment Method

Methods of Accounting

Cash Basis:	Accrual Basis:	Special Rules:
Income: earlier of— • Actual receipt • Receipt of cash equivalent • Constructive receipt • Economic benefit Payment: considered paid when actual payment made	Income: earlier of— • Actual receipt • All events test Payment: considered accrued when meet the all events test	• **Installment method** • Restoration of amounts received under a claim of right • Tax benefit rule • Net operating loss

Read

Code Section 453(a), (b)(1), (c), (d), (i)

A. Background

Disposition of property. When a taxpayer disposes of property, unless a non-recognition provision applies, he must recognize the gain.[63]

Cash basis taxpayer. A taxpayer who reports his income under the cash basis includes the accession to wealth in his gross income when he has actual receipt, receives a cash equivalent, or is in constructive receipt.

Accrual basis taxpayer. A taxpayer who reports his income under the accrual basis includes the accession to wealth in his gross income at the earlier of actual receipt or when he meets the all events test. He meets the all events test when the right to the income is fixed and the amount can be determined with reasonable accuracy.

---

63. Section 61(a)(3).

B. Gain from Disposition of Property

When a taxpayer disposes of appreciated property, he must recognize (report) the gain. The situation becomes more complicated if the taxpayer sells the property and receives the payments over time (on an installment basis).

Example. Dick sells Whiteacre for $100,000. He had previously purchased the property for $20,000. He agreed to accept a $20,000 down payment and a promissory note from the buyer for the remaining $80,000. The note required the buyer to pay Dick $20,000 a year for four years, begin the year following the sale. Dick has disposed of property and recognized a gain of $80,000 ($100,000 amount realized, less $20,000 basis). Even though Dick will receive payment for the property over five years, he must report the gain in the year of disposition.

In some situations the amount of the down payment will be less than the amount of tax liability due on the gain recognized. (In other words, the taxpayer will be required to find another source of cash to pay the tax.) Congress addressed this disparity between receipt of sales proceeds and payment of tax under certain circumstances by allowing the taxpayer to report the gain over time. The amount of the gain the taxpayer reports is tied to the amount of sales proceeds received each year.

C. Installment Sales

If the sale qualifies as an installment sale, the taxpayer can report eligible gain as he receives payments from the buyer.[64] Note that, if the taxpayer disposes of the property at a loss, he may not use the installment method to report the loss. The entire loss is reported in the taxable year of sale.

Installment sales. A sale comes under the installment sale provisions if at least one payment is received in a year subsequent to the year of disposition.[65] It does not matter how much of the payment is received in the subsequent year, as long as some portion is received in a subsequent year.

Eligible gain. Not all gain from the disposition of property is eligible to be reported using the installment method. Gains from the disposition of inventory and recapture (Section 1245) gain cannot be reported using the installment method.[66]

Tell Me More

When the taxpayer agrees to receive payments over time the terms of payment must include interest. If the agreement does not include interest the Code requires that interest be imputed. This means that, while the total payments made by the purchaser will remain the same, the sales price will be reduced and a portion of

---

64. Section 453(a), (c).
65. Section 453(b)(1).
66. Section 453(i).

each payment treated as interest. The re-determined purchase price plus the deemed interest payments will equal the total amount paid by the purchaser. The deemed interest payment must be included in the taxpayer's income each year.[67]

Election out. The default rule is that if the taxpayer sells property that is eligible to be reported using the installment method, the taxpayer reports gain as the payments are made. However, the taxpayer can elect out of using the installment method.[68] If the taxpayer makes the election, all of the gain is reported in the year of sale.

If the taxpayer elects out of reporting the gain under the installment method, the gain must be reported based on the taxpayer's accounting method, with some special rules applied. If the taxpayer is a cash basis method taxpayer, he must treat the fair market value of the obligation as having been realized in the year of sale. The fair market of the value of the obligation cannot be less than the fair market value of the property sold. If the taxpayer is an accrual basis method taxpayer, the total amount payable on the obligation is treated as realized in the year of sale (without considering any interest to be a part of the amount payable).[69]

Reporting installment sale gain. The amount of gain reported each year is determined by applying the following formula:[70]

$$\frac{\text{eligible gain}}{(\text{selling price} - \text{mortgage})} \quad \text{x yearly payment} = \text{gain reported for the year}$$

The fraction is called the gross profit percentage. Note that, once determined, the gross profit percentage remains the same for the duration of the payments. Thus, the amount of gain that must be reported each year is the gross profit percentage multiplied by the yearly payment.

In the denominator of the fraction, the mortgage refers to any mortgage the purchaser assumes or takes the property subject to. When the purchaser assumes the mortgage, the yearly payment includes only the cash payments made by the purchaser, and the mortgage relief is treated as a tax-free return of basis.

When the property is subject to a mortgage that the purchaser assumes or takes the property subject to, it is possible that the amount of the mortgage will be greater than the property's basis. There may be instances were, after taking into consideration the mortgage,

Tell Me More

When the property is subject to a mortgage that the purchaser assumes or takes the property subject to, it is possible that the cash payments will be less than the amount of the taxpayer's gain. In these situations, total cash payments will equal the actual cash payments plus the amount by which the debt exceeds the basis.[71]

---

67. See Sections 483; 7872.
68. Section 453(d).
69. Treas. Reg. § 15A.453-1(d)(2)(ii)(A).
70. Section 453(c).
71. Treas. Reg. § 15A.453-1(b)(3)(i).

In determining the gross profit percentage, for the denominator the selling price is reduced only by the mortgage to the extent of basis.

Example: Rex sells Pinkacre to Buzz for $200,000. Rex previously purchased the property for $80,000. The property was subject to a $100,000 mortgage that Buzz agreed to assume. Buzz also agreed to pay Rex $25,000 a year for four years.

Rex has $120,000 of gain realized and will receive $100,000 in cash payments. Note that if he recognized gain to the extent of all the cash payments, he would recognize only $100,000 of gain. Thus, when calculating the gross profit percentage, the mortgage cannot exceed the property's basis. The percentage is as follows:

$$\frac{\$120,000}{(\$200,000 - \$80,000)} = 100 \text{ percent}$$

The total gain Rex will realize is the deemed cash payment of the amount by which the debt exceeds the basis, $20,000, and a total of $100,000 when the installment payments are received ($25,000 × 4), for a total gain recognized of $120,000.

Character of gain. The gain reported in all years depends on the gain of the property disposed of. For example, if the taxpayer sold a capital asset, the gain reported in each year will be capital gain.

Summary — Installment Sales

Installment sale: At least one payment is made in a year subsequent to the year of disposition.

Eligible gain: All gain, except gain from the sale of inventory or recapture (Section 1245) gain.

Amount of gain reported per year: gross profit percentage × yearly payment

Gross profit percentage: $\dfrac{\text{eligible gain}}{(\text{selling price} - \text{mortgage})}$

Contingent payment sales. If the amount the purchaser is required to pay is contingent, therefore unknown, the selling price is unknown. Accordingly, it is not possible to compute the gross profit percentage.

If there is a stated maximum sales price, for purposes of computing the gross profit percentage, the maximum sales price is treated as the selling price.[72] If there is no maximum sales price, but there is a fixed time frame for completion of the payments the taxpayer's basis is allocated evenly over that time frame.[73] If the payment for the year exceeds the taxpayer's allocated basis, he must report the excess of the payments over the basis. If the payment is less than his basis, the amount of the excess basis (the amount by which the basis exceeds the payment) is carried forward to the next year and added to the year's allocable share of basis.[74]

---

72. Treas. Reg. § 15A.453-1(c)(2)(i).
73. Treas. Reg. § 15A.453-1(c)(3)(i).
74. Id.

D. Application of Rules

Example 1. Andy buys and sells used cars. Last month he sold a 2010 Prius for $15,000. He had purchased the car for $10,000. The buyer paid $5,000 down and agreed to pay $2,000 a year for the next five years.

Andy has disposed of property and realized $5,000 of gain ($15,000 amount realized, less $10,000 basis). Because Andy will receive a payment in a year subsequent to the year of disposition, the sale is an installment sale. However, because the gain is from the sale of inventory, Andy cannot report it using the installment method. All $5,000 of ordinary gain must be reported in the year of sale.

Example 2. Carrie sold Blackacre for $100,000. She had purchased the land five years earlier for $120,000 and held it as investment property. The buyer paid $20,000 down and agreed to pay $20,000 a year for the next four years.

Carrie has disposed of property and realized $20,000 of loss ($100,000 amount realized, less $120,000 basis). Because Carrie will receive a payment in a year subsequent to the year of disposition, the sale is an installment sale. However, because she realized a loss, Carrie cannot report it using the installment sale. Carrie has $20,000 of long-term capital loss in the year of sale.

Example 3. Frank sold Whiteacre for $150,000. He had purchased the land five years earlier for $100,000. The buyer paid $50,000 down and agreed to pay $20,000 a year for the next five years. Frank elected out of reporting using the installment method.

Frank has disposed of property and realized a $50,000 gain ($150,000 amount realized, less $100,000 basis). Because Frank will receive a payment in a year subsequent to the year of disposition, the sale is an installment sale. However, because he elected out of installment method reporting, he reports the $50,000 gain in the year of sale.

Example 4. Beth sold Yellowacre for $150,000. She had purchased the land five years earlier for $100,000. The buyer made no down payment, but agreed to pay the full purchase price the following year.

Beth has disposed of property and realized a $50,000 gain ($150,000 amount realized, less $100,000 basis). Because Beth will receive a payment in a year subsequent to the year of disposition, the sale is an installment sale. Because she received all payments in the year subsequent to the sale, she will report all the gain in that year.

Example 5. Whitney sold Greenacre for $180,000. She had purchased the land five years earlier for $100,000 and held it as investment property. The buyer paid $55,000 down and agreed to pay $25,000 a year for the next five years.

Whitney has disposed of property and realized a $80,000 gain ($180,000 amount realized, less $100,000 basis). Because Whitney will receive a payment in a year subsequent to the year of disposition, the sale is an installment sale. The amount of long-term capital gain she must report each year is determined by applying the following formula:

$$\frac{\text{eligible gain}}{(\text{selling price} - \text{mortgage})} \times \text{yearly payment} = \text{gain reported for the year}$$

All the long-term capital gain is eligible gain and there is no mortgage. Thus, the gross profit percentage is $80,000/$180,000, or 44.44 percent. The amount of gain she reports each year is as follows:

Year	Payment	Gain Recognized
1	$55,000	44% × $55,000 = $24,442
2	25,000	44% × 25,000 = 11,111
3	25,000	44% × 25,000 = 11,111
4	25,000	44% × 25,000 = 11,111
5	25,000	44% × 25,000 = 11,111
6	25,000	44% × 25,000 = 11,111
Totals:	$180,000	$80,000

Example 6. Phyllis sold equipment used in her business for $100,000. She had purchased the equipment two years earlier for $80,000 and had claimed $10,000 of depreciation, making her adjusted basis $70,000. The buyer paid $20,000 down and agreed to pay $20,000 a year for the next four years.

Phyllis has disposed of property and realized a $30,000 gain ($100,000 amount realized, less $70,000 basis). The $30,000 gain is composed of $10,000 of recapture income and $20,000 of hotchpot gain. Because Phyllis will receive a payment in a year subsequent to the year of disposition, the sale is an installment sale. The $10,000 of recapture gain is not eligible for reporting using the installment sale. The amount of hotchpot gain she must report each year is determined by applying the following formula:

$$\frac{\text{eligible gain}}{(\text{selling price} - \text{mortgage})} \times \text{yearly payment} = \text{gain reported for the year}$$

Phyllis has $20,000 of eligible gain and there is no mortgage. Thus, the gross profit percentage is $20,000/$100,000, or 20 percent. The amount of gain she reports each year is as follows:

Year	Payment	Gain Recognized
1	$20,000	20% × $20,000 = $4,000
2	20,000	20% of 20,000 = 4,000
3	20,000	20% × 20,000 = 4,000
4	20,000	20% × 20,000 = 4,000
5	20,000	20% × 20,000 = 4,000
Totals:	$100,000	$20,000

Note that in the first year Phyllis will report $10,000 of ordinary (recapture) gain and $4,000 of hotchpot gain. And, when considering the $10,000 of recapture gain reported in the first year and the $20,000 of hotchpot gain reported over the five years, she will have reported a total gain of $30,000.

Example 7. Flo sold Pinkacre for $250,000. She had purchased the land five years earlier for $150,000 and it was subject to a $50,000 mortgage. She held the property as investment property. The buyer agreed to assume the mortgage, pay $50,000 down, and pay $50,000 a year for the next three years.

Flo has disposed of property and realized a $100,000 gain ($250,000 amount realized, less $150,000 basis). Because Flo will receive a payment in a year subsequent to the year of disposition, the sale is an installment sale. The amount of long-term capital gain she must report each year is determined by applying the following formula:

$$\frac{\text{eligible gain}}{(\text{selling price} - \text{mortgage})} \times \text{yearly payment} = \text{gain reported for the year}$$

All the long-term capital gain is eligible gain and there is a $50,000 mortgage. Thus, the gross profit percentage is $100,000/($250,000 − $50,000) or $100,000/$200,000, or 50 percent. The amount of gain she reports each year is as follows:

Year	Payment	Gain Recognized
1	$50,000	50% × $50,000 = $25,000
2	50,000	50% × 50,000 = 25,000
3	50,000	50% × 50,000 = 25,000
4	50,000	50% × 50,000 = 25,000
Totals:	$200,000	$100,000

E. Problems

1. Russ owns and operates a rare book store. He sold a first edition of Canterbury Tales for $20,000. He had purchased it five years early for $15,000. The buyer paid $5,000 down and agreed to pay $5,000 a year for the next three years. What are the tax consequences to Russ?

2. Paula sold Redacre for $500,000. She had purchased it four years earlier for $300,000 and held it as investment property. The buyer paid $100,000 down and agreed to pay $100,000 a year for the next four years. What are the tax consequences to Paula?

3. Bella sold Greenacre for $500,000. She had purchased the land three years earlier for $200,000 and held it as investment property. The property was subject to a $100,000 mortgage. The buyer assumed the mortgage, paid $100,000 down, and agreed to pay $100,000 a year for the next three years. What are the tax consequences to Bella?

4. Amy sold Whiteacre for $200,000. She had purchased the land two years earlier for $250,000 and held it as investment property. The buyer paid $50,000 down and agreed to pay $50,000 a year for the next three years. What are the tax consequences to Amy?

5. Alfonse sold equipment used in his business for $200,000. He had purchased the equipment two years earlier for $170,000 and had claimed $20,000 of depreciation, making his adjusted basis $150,000. The buyer paid $50,000 down and agreed to pay $50,000 a year for the next three years. What are the tax consequences to Alfonse?

6. Jerry sold Wideacre for $500,000. He had purchased it four years earlier for $300,000 and held it as investment property. The buyer paid $100,000 down and agreed to pay $100,000 a year for the next four years. Jerry is a cash basis taxpayer and has elected out of the installment method. What are the tax consequences to Jerry?

7. Pam sold Shortacre for $500,000. She had purchased it four years earlier for $300,000 and held it as investment property. The buyer paid $100,000 down and agreed to pay $100,000 a year for the next four years. Pam is an accrual basis taxpayer and has elected out of the installment method. What are the tax consequences to Pam?

F. Analysis and Application

Can you think of a situation where it would be to the taxpayer's advantage to elect out of the installment method of reporting gain?

Chapter 41

Application of Characterization

Characterization (Determining the Applicable Tax Rate)

Ordinary Assets:	Hotchpot Assets:	Capital Assets:
• Inventory • Accounts receivable • Depreciable property used in a business and held for one year or less • Land used in a business and held for one year or less • Supplies	• Depreciable property used in a business and held for more than one year • Land used in a business and held for more than one year	All assets, except: • Inventory • Accounts receivable • Depreciable property used in a business • Land used in a business • Supplies

A. Background

When a taxpayer disposes of multiple pieces of property, any of the following rules may be relevant:

Disposition of property:

• Gross income includes gain derived from dealings in property. The amount of gain is the excess of the amount realized over the adjusted basis. Unless otherwise provided, the gain realized must be recognized, i.e., reported on the taxpayer's income tax return.

• The amount of loss from a disposition of property is the excess of the adjusted basis over the amount realized.

   ○ A taxpayer may recognize a loss from the disposition of property used in a business.

   ○ A taxpayer may recognize a loss from the disposition of property held for investment purposes.

Capital assets:

• Includes all assets, except:

   ○ Inventory or property held primarily for sale to business customers

   ○ Depreciable property used in the taxpayer's business

   ○ Land used in the taxpayer's business

   ○ Accounts receivable acquired in the ordinary course of the taxpayer's business

- ○ Supplies used in the taxpayer's business.
- Net long-term capital gains are taxed at preferential rates; net short-term capital gains are taxed at regular rates.
- A taxpayer may claim all recognized *ordinary* losses; there is no applicable limitation.
- A taxpayer can claim up to $3,000 of net *capital* losses per year. Any remaining net capital loss is carried forward to the following year.

Hotchpot assets:

- Includes
  - ○ Depreciable property used in the taxpayer's business and held for more than one year.
  - ○ Land used in the taxpayer's business and held for more than one year.

Ordinary income property:

- Includes all property that is not a capital asset or a hotchpot asset.

Section 1245 depreciation recapture:

- Applies to the sale of any depreciable or amortizable property except buildings.
- Recharacterizes the lesser of the gain on disposition or depreciation claimed as ordinary income.

Installment Sales:

- A sale is an installment sale when at least one payment is made in a year subsequent to the year of disposition.
- Eligible gain is all gain, except gain from the sale of inventory and recapture Section 1245) gain.
- The amount of gain to report each year from an installment sale is the gross profit percentage, multiplied by the yearly payment.
- The gross profit percentage is eligible gain/(selling price – mortgage).

B. Application

To better understand the interaction of the rules related to capital assets, hotchpot assets, depreciation recapture, and the installment method of reporting, it is helpful follow a particular order of application.

Step One: Divide into sales/disposition of property and other sources of income (i.e., wages, bonuses, prizes, etc.). For other sources of income — ordinary income, regular tax rates will apply.[75] With respect to sales or other dispositions of property, continue.

Step Two: Calculate the gain or loss realized from each disposition. Is the gain or loss recognized? For all gain or loss that is recognized, continue.

Step Three: Divide the gains and losses into three categories based on the character of the property: capital assets, hotchpot property, ordinary property.

---

75. Note that dividends are taxed at preferential rates, but are not subject to the netting applicable to the sale of capital assets. Section 1(h)(11).

Step Four: If applicable, apply Section 1245 depreciation recapture.

Step Five: If the property has been sold on the installment method, determine the amount of gain reported this year. Going forward, consider only the amount of gain reported during the applicable year.

Step Six: Net the amount in the hotchpot. If the net amount is a loss, the net amount becomes an ordinary loss. If the net amount is a gain, the net amount becomes a long-term capital gain, included in the capital gains and losses netting process.

Step Seven: Divide into long term capital gains and losses and short term capital gains and losses. Determine the net amount in each group. If one is a loss and the other is a gain, add the net amounts together. If both net amounts are losses or both are gains, do not add the net amounts.

Step Eight: Determine the net amount of ordinary gain or loss.

Step Nine: Determine the tax consequences of the ordinary and capital net gains or losses based on the character.

Ordinary	Capital
gain – taxed at regular rates	**gain** – long term – taxed at reduced rate – short term – taxed at regular rates
loss – no limitation on loss deduction	**loss** – long and short term – limited to $3,000 – use short-term first – carry forward excess, retaining character

C. Example

Mona owned and operated an art gallery. This year, she sold the gallery to Don for $410,000. Don is not related to her.

The adjusted basis and fair market value for each asset she sold is as follows:

Asset	Adjusted Basis	Fair Market Value
Inventory	$40,000	$100,000
Equipment	80,000	220,000
Furniture	20,000	10,000
Goodwill	-0-	80,000

Mona has held all the assets for more than one year.

She had claimed $120,000 of depreciation on the equipment. In addition, the equipment is subject to a mortgage in the amount of $20,000, which Don agreed to assume.

She had claimed $80,000 of depreciation on the furniture. Because the goodwill was self-generated, Mona was not entitled to claim any amortization.

Don will pay 25 percent of the cash selling price of each asset to Mona in the year of sale. He signed a promissory note agreeing to pay the remainder of the selling price of each asset in equal installments over the next three years (i.e., Don will pay 25 percent of the cash selling price of each asset to Mona each year for the next three years). While the promissory note also requires Don to pay interest, for purposes of this problem this interest will be ignored.

In considering the selling price of the equipment, the promissory note takes into consideration only the cash payment Don is required to make. Because the sales price is $220,000 and Don is assuming the $20,000 mortgage, he will be making cash payments totaling $200,000.

Mona makes no elections for the year.

In the year of sale, the tax consequences to Mona are determined as follows:

Step One: Divide into sales/disposition of property and other sources of income (i.e., wages, bonuses, prizes, etc.). All are sales from dispositions of property.

Step Two: Calculate the gain or loss realized. Is the gain or loss recognized? All the gains and losses are recognized.

Asset	Adjusted Basis	Amount Realized	Gain or Loss
Inventory	$40,000	$100,000	$60,000
Equipment	80,000	220,000	140,000
Furniture	20,000	10,000	<10,000>
Goodwill	-0-	80,000	80,000

Step Three: Divide the gains and losses into three categories based on the character of the property: capital assets, hotchpot property, ordinary property.

Ordinary	Hotchpot	Capital
Inventory $60,000	Equipment $140,000	Goodwill $80,000
	Furniture <10,000>	

Step Four: If applicable, apply Section 1245 depreciation recapture.

Only the equipment is subject to the recapture provision. Of the gain, $120,000 is recharacterized as ordinary, leaving $20,000 of the gain in hotchpot.

Ordinary	Hotchpot	Capital
Inventory $60,000	Equipment $20,000	Goodwill $80,000
Equipment 120,000	Furniture <10,000>	

Step Five: If the property has been sold on the installment method, determine the amount of gain reported this year. Going forward, consider only the amount of gain reported during the applicable year.

All the property was sold on the installment method. However, the gain from the inventory, the recapture gain from the equipment, and the loss from the furniture are not eligible to be reported using the installment method. The hotchpot gain from the sale of the equipment and the gain from the goodwill can be reported using the installment method.

Equipment: There is 20,000 of eligible gain. The selling price is $220,000 and the property is subject to a $20,000 mortgage. Taking into consideration the mortgage, Don will be making a total cash payment to Mona of $200,000 ($220,000 selling price, less the mortgage Don is assuming). Paying 25 percent of the cash payment each year, Don will pay Mona $50,000 each year.

The gain to be reported this year is: $20,000/($220,000 − $20,000) × $50,000 = $5,000.

Goodwill: There is $80,000 of eligible gain. The selling price is $80,000 and the property is not subject to a mortgage. The entire purchase price is being paid in cash. Paying 25 percent of the cash payment each year, Don will pay Mona $20,000 each year.

The gain to be reported this year is: $80,000/$80,000 × $20,000 = $20,000

Only the gain reported during the year is taken into consideration.

Ordinary	Hotchpot	Capital
Inventory $60,000	Equipment $5,000	Goodwill $20,000
Equipment 120,000	Furniture <10,000>	

Step Six: Net the amount in the hotchpot. If the net amount is a loss, the net amount becomes an ordinary loss. If the net amount is a gain, the net amount becomes a long-term capital gain, included in the capital gains and losses netting process.

Ordinary	Hotchpot	Capital
Inventory $60,000	Equipment $5,000	Goodwill $20,000
Equipment 120,000	Furniture <10,000>	
Hotchpot <5,000> ⟵——————— <5,000>		

Step Seven: Divide into long term capital gains and losses and short term capital gains and losses. Determine the net amount in each group. If one is a loss and the other is a gain, add the net amounts together. If both net amounts are losses or both are gains, do not all the net amounts.

There is one capital asset, the goodwill. All the gain is long-term capital gain.

Step Eight: Determine the net amount of ordinary gain or loss.

Ordinary	
Inventory	$60,000
Equipment	120,000
Hotchpot	<5,000>
Total:	$175,000

Step Nine: Determine the tax consequences of the ordinary and capital net gains or losses based on the character.

In the year of sale, Mona will report $175,000 or ordinary income, taxed at her regular rates, and $20,000 of long-term capital gain, taxed at preferential rates.

D. Problem

Sue owned and operated a bookstore. This year, she sold the store to Jeff for $548,000. Jeff is not related to her.

The adjusted basis and fair market value for each asset she sold is as follows:

Asset	Adjusted Basis	Fair Market Value
Inventory	$5,000	$10,000
Equipment	100,000	400,000
Building	20,000	10,000
Parking lot	18,000	28,000
Goodwill	0	100,000

Sue has held all the assets for more than one year.

She had claimed $100,000 of depreciation on the equipment. In addition, the equipment is subject to a mortgage in the amount of $200,000, which Jeff agreed to assume.

She had claimed $40,000 of depreciation on the building. Because the goodwill was self-generated, Sue was not entitled to claim any amortization.

Jeff will pay 10 percent of the cash selling price of each asset to Sue in the year of sale. He signed a promissory note agreeing to pay the remainder of the selling price of each asset in equal installments over the next nine years (i.e., Jeff will pay 10 percent of the cash selling price of each asset to Sue each year for the next nine years). While the promissory note also requires Jeff to pay interest, for purposes of this problem this interest will be ignored.

In considering the selling price of the equipment, the promissory note takes into consideration only the cash payment Jeff is required to make. Because the sales price is $400,000 and Jeff is assuming the $200,000 mortgage, he will be making cash payments totaling $200,000.

Sue makes no elections for the year.

a. What are the tax consequences in the year of sale?

b. What are the tax consequences in the year following the year of sale?

c. What are the tax consequences in the year of sale if Sue also had $50,000 of compensation for services income and had sold Blackacre for $50,000. Before selling, she had held Blackacre for six months for investment purposes. She had paid $60,000 for the property.

E. Analysis and Application

Mr. Greig invests in real property. He has several parcels he has held for investment purposes that he is considering selling. In January of next year (Year 2), he plans to sell the Shortstreet parcel for $30,000. He bought the parcel in November for $20,000. He also intends to sell the Longstreet parcel for $20,000. He bought the parcel five years ago for $10,000.

Summary of sales for next year (Year 2):

Property	AB	Fair Market Value
Shortstreet	$20,000	$30,000
Longstreet	10,000	20,000

His plans for next year (Year 2) are fixed.

What he has come to you for advice about is which parcel to sell this year (Year 1). He could either sell Greenacre for $20,000 or Blueacre for $20,000. He bought both Greenacre and Blueacre for $33,000 each, but he bought Greenacre five years ago and Blueacre two months ago. He holds both parcels for investment purposes. Whichever property he chooses to sell, it would be the only property he sells this year.

Summary of potential sales for this year (Year 1):

Property	AB	AR/fmv
Greenacre	$33,000	$20,000
- OR -		
Blueacre	33,000	20,000

Which one do you advise Mr. Greig to sell this year (Year 1)? Why?

IX

Non-Recognition Provisions

Exclusion of Gain:	Deferral of Gain:
• Disposition of principal residence	• Like kind exchange • Involuntary conversion • Transfer between spouses or ex-spouses Deferral of Loss: • Like kind exchange • Transfer between spouses or ex-spouses

Chapter 42

Disposition of Principal Residence

Deferral or Exclusion of Gain or Loss

Exclusion of Gain:	Deferral of Gain:
• Disposition of principal residence	• Like kind exchange • Involuntary conversion • Transfer between spouses or ex-spouses Deferral of Loss: • Like kind exchange • Transfer between spouses or ex-spouses

Read

Code Section 121

Treas. Reg. §§ 1.121-1(a), (b)(1), (2), (3)(i), (c)(1), (2); 1.121-2(a)(1), (2)

A. Background

Gross income. Gross income includes income (accessions to wealth) derived from any and all sources.[1] It includes every accession to wealth, unless there is an exception, including gains from dealings in property.[2]

Gain realized and recognized. The difference between the amount realized and the adjusted basis of the property sold or otherwise disposed of by the taxpayer is the gain realized.[3] This formula permits the taxpayer to recover the amount he paid for the property tax free. This recovery is sometimes called a return of capital.

> Amount realized
> – <u>Adjusted basis</u>
> Gain realized

---

1. Section 61(a).
2. Section 61(a)(3).
3. Section 1001(a).

Unless the Code provides otherwise, any gain realized must be recognized.[4] To recognize gain means to report it on the taxpayer's income tax return.

B. Exclusion of Gain

There are many policy reasons for allowing a taxpayer to exclude gain from the sale of a principal residence from gross income. Primarily, the exclusion encourages home ownership. (Recall that Congress also encourages home ownership through the interest mortgage deduction.[5]) It also facilitates the transition from one home to another, such as when the taxpayer is moving into a smaller home, moving to a different part of the country, or moving into a retirement community. Congress chose to assist the taxpayer by allowing him to make the transition with the benefit of all the proceeds of sale, undiminished by a tax liability.

Note

Because a residence is used for personal purposes, if the taxpayer sold the property at a loss, he would not be able to recognize the loss realized. In contrast, if he sold the residence at a gain, he must recognize the gain realized unless a non-recognition provision applies.

If the taxpayer meets the requirements of Section 121 (whether married or single), he may exclude up to $250,000 of gain on the sale of his principal residence.[6] He can take advantage of the exclusion once every two years.[7] If the taxpayer files a joint return, the exclusion allowed the husband and wife can be combined, and, if the requirements are met, the taxpayers may exclude up to $500,000 of gain.[8]

Tell Me More

Over the years Congress has enacted a variety of provisions dealing with a taxpayer's sale of his residence. Prior to 1997 the Code provided:

Old Section 121: A taxpayer who was age 55 or older could exclude up to $125,000 of gain from the sale of his residence. The gain was excluded (not deferred). A taxpayer could take advantage of the provision once.

Old Section 1034: A taxpayer could defer reporting gain from the sale of his residence to the extent he reinvested the sale proceeds in a new home within two years. The deferred gain was preserved in the basis of the new home. A taxpayer could take advantage of the provision every two years.

---

4. Section 1001(c).
5. See Chapter 15.
6. Section 121(a), (b)(1).
7. Section 121(b)(3)(A).
8. Section 121(b)(2).

C. Statutory Requirements

To come within Section 121, during the five years prior to sale the taxpayer must have:[9]

- owned the property for periods aggregating two or more years; and
- used the property as his principal residence for periods aggregating two or more years.

Section 121. Exclusion of Gain from Sale of Principal Residence

(a) Exclusion. — Gross income shall not include gain from the sale or exchange of property if, during the 5-year period ending on the date of the sale or exchange, such property has been owned and used by the taxpayer as the taxpayer's principal residence for periods aggregating 2 years or more.

The ownership and use requirements do not have to be concurrent. Short temporary absences do not impact the use requirement.[10] Moreover, the taxpayer is not required to be using the property as his principal residence at the time of sale.[11] The taxpayer can use the exclusion once every two years.[12]

A married taxpayer who meets the statutory requirements may file a return separate from the spouse and exclude up to $250,000 of gain. Married taxpayers may file a joint return and exclude up to $500,000 of gain. When a joint return is filed, only one of the spouses need satisfy the ownership requirement and neither spouse must have taken advantage of the exclusion within the previous two years. Both spouses must always satisfy the use requirement.[13]

A husband and wife may separately qualify for the exclusion. For example, assume husband and wife each owned a home they separately used as their principal residence and both sold their respective homes just after they married. Each spouse is entitled to exclude up to $250,000 of gain. Note that if one spouse cannot use the entire exclusion, the unused portion cannot be used by the other spouse. For example, if the gain on the wife's house was $200,000, the remaining $50,000 of exclusion cannot be used by her husband on the sale of his principal residence.

Practice Note

If any of the gain realized is due to depreciation deductions previously claimed by the taxpayer, to that extent the exclusion does not apply.[14] A taxpayer might have claimed depreciation if he had rented out a portion of his house or used it as a home office.

---

9. Section 121(a).
10. Treas. Reg. § 1.121-1(c)(2)(i).
11. Treas. Reg. § 1.121-1(c)(1), (2).
12. Section 121(b)(3).
13. Section 121(c).
14. Section 121(d)(6).

Principal residence. The taxpayer must have used the home as his principal residence for periods aggregating two or more years. If the taxpayer uses more than one home, he will need to determine which home is the principal residence. In general, the residence he uses the majority of the time during the year is his principal residence.[15] The regulations set forth other, non-exclusive, factors to consider, including:[16]

- The taxpayer's place of employment;
- Where the family members live;
- The address used for the taxpayer's federal income tax return, state tax return, driver's license, automobile registration, voter registration card;
- Mailing address used for bills and correspondence;
- Location of the taxpayer's bank; and
- Location of the taxpayer's religious organizations and recreational clubs.

1. Special Rules Regarding Ownership

Section 121 has several special rules addressing ownership issues for unique situations, including:

- If an unmarried individual sells the home after the death of his spouse, the use and ownership periods include the period the deceased spouse owned and used the home.[17]
- If an individual received the property from his spouse or ex-spouse (such that Section 1041 applies[18]), the ownership period includes the period the spouse or ex-spouse owned the home.[19]
- If an individual owns a home but the individual's spouse or ex-spouse has the right to use the residence under a divorce or separation agreement, the use period includes the period the spouse or ex-spouse has use of the home.[20]

2. Change in Employment, Health-Related Issues, and Unforeseen Circumstances

If the taxpayer sells his home because he has had a change in place of employment, has had a health related issue, or because of unforeseen circumstances and he cannot meet the use or ownership requirements, a portion of the gain might still be able to be excluded.[21] The exclusion will be a portion of the available $250,000, with the portion dependent on the length of use and ownership of the property prior to sale.[22]

---

15. Treas. Reg. § 1.121-1(a)(2).
16. Treas. Reg. § 1.121-1(a)(2).
17. Section 121(d)(2).
18. Section 1041 is discussed in Chapter 47.
19. Section 121(d)(3)(B).
20. Section 121(d)(3)(B).
21. Section 121(c).
22. Section 121(c).

pick up here

The reduced exclusion amount is $250,000 multiplied by a fraction. The numerator is the shortest of the following time periods (measured in days or months):

- Period the taxpayer owned the property during the five-year period;
- Period the taxpayer used the property as his principal residence; or
- Period between the date of a prior sale or exchange or property for which the taxpayer excluded gain under Section 121 and the date of the current sale or exchange.

The denominator is 730 days or 24 months.[23]

The regulations provide safe harbors. A sale is deemed to be by reason of a change in place of employment if:[24]

- the change in place of employment occurs during the period of the taxpayer's ownership and use of the property as the taxpayer's residence; and
- the qualified individual's new place of employment is at least 50 miles farther from the residence sold or, if there was no former place of employment, the distance between the qualified individual's new place of employment and the residence sold is at least 50 miles.

A sale is deemed to be by reason of health if a physician recommends a change of residence for reasons of health.[25]

A sale is deemed to be by reason of unforeseen circumstances if any of the following events occur during the period of the taxpayer's ownership and use of the residence as his principal residence:[26]

- involuntary conversion of the residence;
- natural or man-made disasters or acts of war or terrorism resulting in casualty to the residence; or
- The taxpayer or his spouse dies, becomes unemployed and is eligible for unemployment compensation; changes his employment status and the change results in the taxpayer's inability to pay housing costs and reasonable basic living expenses for the taxpayer's household; divorce or legal separation; or multiple births from the same pregnancy.

D. Application of Rules

Example 1. Charles owned a house in Fort Wayne. He purchased it in November of last year for $300,000 and had always used it as his principal residence. He sold the home in March of this year for $400,000. Charles has $100,000 of gain realized ($400,000 amount realized, less $300,000 basis).

To come within Section 121, during the five years prior to sale Charles must have owned the property for two or more years and used the property as his principal residence for periods aggregating two or more years. Because he cannot satisfy the requirements, Charles must recognize $100,000 of gain.

---

23. Section 121(c)(1); Treas. Reg. § 1.121-3(g)(1).
24. Treas. Reg. § 1.121-3(c)(2).
25. Treas. Reg. § 1.121-3(d)(2).
26. Treas. Reg. § 1.121-3(e)(2).

Example 2. Don owned a house in Orlando. He purchased it three years ago for $300,000 and had always used it as his principal residence. He sold the home this year for $400,000. Don has $100,000 of gain realized ($400,000 amount realized, less $300,000 basis).

During the five years prior to sale Don owned the property for two or more years and used the property as his principal residence for two or more years. He can exclude the $100,000 of gain.

Example 3. Amy and Darren owned a house in Tampa. They purchased it six years ago for $300,000 and had always used it as their principal residence. They sold the home this year for $900,000. They have $600,000 of gain realized ($900,000 amount realized, less $300,000 basis).

During the five years prior to sale they owned the property for two or more years and used the property as their principal residence for two or more years. If they file a joint return they can exclude $500,000 of gain and must recognize the remaining $100,000 of gain.

Example 4. Mabel owned a house in Reno. She purchased it five years ago for $250,000 and used it as her principal residence until last year, when she moved to Las Vegas. She sold the home this year for $450,000. Mabel has $200,000 of gain realized ($450,000 amount realized, less $250,000 basis).

During the five years prior to sale Mabel owned the property for two or more years and used the property as her principal residence for two or more years. It does not matter that she did not use the home as her principal residence at the time of sale. She can exclude the $200,000 of gain.

E. Problems

1. Bob owns a house in Phoenix. He purchased it four years ago for $300,000 and has always used it as his principal residence. What are the tax consequences to Bob if he sells it this year for $800,000?

2. Nancy and Mike are married and live in Portland. Nancy purchased the house six years earlier for $300,000. While it is held in Nancy's name, both Nancy and Mike have always used it as their principal residence. What are the tax consequences to Nancy and Mike if Nancy sells the home this year for $800,000?

3. Beth owns a house in Tucson. She purchased it four years ago for $300,000 and used it as her principal residence until last year, when she moved to San Diego. What are the tax consequences to Beth if she sells the Tucson home this year for $800,000?

4. Andy owns a house in Lansing. He purchased it four years ago for $300,000 and had always used it as his principal residence. What are the tax consequences to Andy if he sells this year for $200,000?

5. In January Bernard bought a house in Phoenix for $200,000 and used it as his principal residence. Because he developed respiratory issues he sold the house in December for $250,000 and moved to Orlando. What are the tax consequences to Bernard?

6. Alex owns a house in Seattle. He purchased it last year for $400,000. He had always used it as his principal residence. This year, after having lived in the home for a year, his employer transferred him to the St. Louis office. Alex sold his house for $425,000. What are the tax consequences to Alex?

F. Analysis and Application

1. Mary Jean owns a home in Atlanta. She purchased it five years ago for $300,000 and has always used it as her principal residence. It is currently worth $800,000.

    a. What are the tax results to Mary Jean if she sells the home for $800,000?

    b. Alternatively, what are the tax results to Mary Jean is she gives the home to her niece? What are the tax results to her niece?

    c. Alternatively, what are the tax results to Mary Jean is she leaves the home to her niece in her will? What are the tax results to her niece?

2. Meredith lives and works in Boston. She has a summer home located on a lake 90 miles outside of Boston. The summer home has appreciated substantially during the ten years Meredith has owned it. She would like to sell it and pay the least amount of taxes as possible. What would you advise Meredith to do? Before you can prepare a plan, do you need any information from her? If so, what information?

3. Can you explain to your client when the gain from the sale of a principal residence may be excluded from income?

4. Research project: Research opinions addressing what constitutes a "short temporary absence." Prepare a presentation.

Chapter 43

Like Kind Exchange

Deferral or Exclusion of Gain or Loss

Exclusion of Gain:	Deferral of Gain:
• Disposition of principal residence	• **Like kind exchange**
	• Involuntary conversion
	• Transfer between spouses or ex-spouses
	Deferral of Loss:
	• **Like kind exchange**
	• Transfer between spouses or ex-spouses

Read

Code Section 1031(a)-(d)

Treas. Reg. §§ 1.1031(a)-1(a)-(c); 1.1031(b)-1(a); 1.1031(c)-1

A. Background

Gross income. Gross income includes income (accessions to wealth) derived from any and all sources.[27] It includes every accession to wealth, unless there is an exception, including gains from dealings in property.[28]

Adjusted basis. The basis of property is the amount the taxpayer originally paid for the property.[29] In general, a taxpayer will purchase an item for its fair market value. The adjusted basis reflects an increase for any subsequent capital expenditures and a decrease for depreciation.[30]

Amount realized. The amount realized is the amount the taxpayer sold the property for.[31] In general, a taxpayer will sell an item for its fair market value. What types of assets the taxpayer receives as payment for the item he is selling is irrelevant; what is important

---

27. Section 61(a).
28. Section 61(a)(3).
29. Section 1012(a).
30. Section 1016(a).
31. Section 1001(b).

is that the total value of all assets received is equal to the value of the property the taxpayer is selling. Most often the taxpayer will be paid in cash, property, services, debt relief, or a combination of those items.

Gain realized and recognized. When the property has appreciated, the difference between the amount realized and the adjusted basis of the property sold or otherwise disposed of by the taxpayer is the gain realized.[32] This formula permits the taxpayer to recover the amount he paid for the property tax free. This process is sometimes called a return of capital.

> Amount realized
> − Adjusted basis
> Gain realized

Unless the code provides otherwise, any gain realized must be recognized, or reported, on the taxpayer's income tax return as an accession to wealth.[33]

Loss realized and recognized. When the property has depreciated, the difference between the amount realized and the adjusted basis of the property sold or otherwise disposed of by the taxpayer is the loss realized.[34]

> Amount realized
> − Adjusted basis
> <Loss realized>

Unless the taxpayer can provide authority, no loss realized may be recognized, or reported, on the taxpayer's income tax return as a loss.[35]

Personal losses. In general, the taxpayer may not recognize any loss from the disposition of property used for personal purposes.[36]

B. Policy

When a taxpayer disposes of property and receives property in exchange, there is an argument that the taxpayer has continued his investment in property. Because of this continuity of investment, it may not be the appropriate time to impose tax on the disposition. In addition, in a property-for-property exchange, the taxpayer does not have cash with which to pay any tax due from the disposition. While Congress is not always concerned with these policy or practical considerations, in the area of like kind exchanges it has taken these facts into consideration.

Tell Me More

The Code has several sections that defer the recognition of gain or loss when the taxpayer has continued his investment in the property. For example, even though the taxpayer has disposed of property when he transfers it to a corporation in exchange for stock, the gain or loss on the transfer may be deferred.[37] Similarly,

---

32. Section 1001(a).
33. Section 1001(c).
34. Section 1001(a).
35. Section 165(c)(1), (2).
36. Section 165(c)(3).
37. See Section 351.

> even though the taxpayer has disposed of property when he transfers it to a partnership in exchange for a partnership interest (or to a limited liability company in exchange for a member interest), the gain or loss on the transfer is deferred.[38]
>
> Note that the exchanges described above (property exchanged for an interest in an entity) are different from exchanging the actual ownership interest in the entity (i.e., stock exchanged for other stock or a partnership interest exchanged for a different partnership interest).

While the like kind exchange rules are beneficial to most taxpayers, in some situations a taxpayer would rather not have the deferral. Nevertheless, the statutory provision is mandatory; if a taxpayer comes within its provisions, the deferral is required.

C. Qualifying for Like Kind Exchange Treatment

In a like kind exchange, two taxpayers (and occasionally more than two) are disposing of property. Whether the exchange qualifies as a like kind exchange is made on a taxpayer-by-taxpayer basis. For example, Windsor transfers Whiteacre to Rife and Rife transfers Blackacre to Windsor. The like kind exchange analysis must be considered with respect to Windsor. Then, the like kind exchange analysis must be considered with respect to Rife. It is possible for the transaction to be a like kind exchange for Windsor but not Rife and vice versa.

Sale or exchange. The like kind exchange rules apply when there is an exchange of properties, as opposed to a sale of property for cash (or non-qualifying property) and a separate purchase of other property. In general, if property is sold and the property received in exchange is not like kind to the property sold, the deferral provisions do not apply.[39] However, the substance of the transaction will control. Thus, even if the transaction is structured as a sale of property for cash followed by a purchase of other property, if the substance of the transaction is an exchange, the transaction will be recast as an exchange and the like kind exchange provisions will apply.[40]

Like Kind Requirement. For the transaction to qualify, the property received must be "like" the property given up.[41] When considering real estate (meaning building or land with or without improvements), all real estate is considered to be like all other real estate.[42] Accordingly, a parking lot can be exchanged for investment property. Investment property can be exchanged for an apartment building. An apartment building can be exchanged for a shopping mall. As long as it is an interest in real property, it will qualify.

---

38. See Section 721.

39. See, e.g., Bell Lines, Inc. v. United States, 480 F.2d 710 (4th Cir. 1973).

40. See, for example, Redwing Carriers, Inc. v. Tomlinson, 399 F.2d 652 (5th Cir. 1968) (where the taxpayer sold old trucks to a parent corporation and purchased new trucks from its subsidiary, the transactions were treated as an exchange and not a sale and purchase); Rev. Rul. 61-119, 1961-1 C.B. 395 (where the taxpayer sold used business equipment and, in a separate transaction, purchased new business equipment from the same dealer, the transactions were treated as an exchange and not a sale and purchase).

41. Section 1031(a)(1).

42. Treas. Reg. § 1.1031(a)-1(b), (c).

Examples of Exchanges of Real Estate That Qualify

- Remainder interest in farm land for remainder interest in other farm land[43]
- Tenancy in common interest in land for undivided ownership interest in smaller portion of same parcel[44]
- Leasehold in a building for a sublease in another part of the building[45]
- Golf club property for property subject to 99-year condominium leases[46]

When considering tangible personal property, it is more difficult for the exchange to qualify. Tangible personal property can be considered "like" other tangible property in three general ways. First, property is like kind if both are assigned to the same class life, or "General Asset Class," for depreciation purposes.[47] Second, property is like kind if within the same "Product Class." Product Classes are created by the North American Industry Classification System.[48] Finally, if the property is not depreciable tangible property, is intangible property, or otherwise does not have a class life or a product class, the taxpayer must establish that the properties are like kind.[49]

Use of the property. The property disposed of must be used in the taxpayer's business or be held for investment. The property received in the transaction must be used in the taxpayer's business or held for investment. Property used for personal purposes does not qualify.[50]

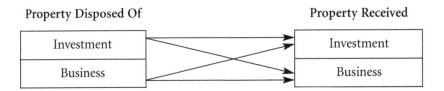

Neither the Code nor the regulations state a minimum holding period for the property prior to the exchange or for the property received in the exchange; it only requires that the property be held for a qualifying puposes.[51]

Ineligible property. The Code specifically identifies property that does not qualify for like kind exchange treatment. Included in the list are stocks and bonds and partnership interests.[52]

---

43. Rev. Rul. 78-4, 1978-1 C.B. 256.
44. Rev. Rul. 73-476, 1973-2 C.B. 300.
45. Rev. Rul. 75-515, 1975-2 C.B. 466.
46. Koch v. Commissioner, 71 T.C. 54 (1978).
47. Treas. Reg. § 1.1031(a)-2(b)(1), (2).
48. Treas. Reg. § 1.1031(a)-2(b)(1), (3).
49. See, e.g., Treas. Reg. § 1.1031(a)-2(c)(1).
50. Section 1031(a)(1).
51. There is one exception. For property transferred to a related person, there is a two-year holding period applicable to both the property transferred and the property received. Section 1031(f), (g). If the taxpayer fails to meet the holding period, the deferred gain or loss is recognized in the year the disqualifying transfer occurs. Section 1031(f)(1).
52. Section 1031(a)(2).

Checklist for Like Kind Exchange

❏ There must be an exchange.

❏ The property received must be "like" the property given up.

❏ The property given up must have been used in the taxpayer's business or held for investment purposes.

❏ The property received must be used by the taxpayer in his business or held for investment purposes.

❏ Neither property is disqualified from like kind exchange treatment.

D. Computations

1. Determining Amount of Boot, Gain Recognized, and Deferral

Property can be exchanged solely for like kind property. In this situation, the tax result is the same regardless of whether the like kind property disposed of has a gain realized or loss realized. All gain or loss is deferred.[53] When determining if the transaction is solely in exchange for like kind property, the focus is on what the taxpayer is receiving in the transaction. Whether the taxpayer is also disposing of non-like kind property is not relevant to this portion of the analysis.

Boot. It is unusual for two properties to have the same value. Accordingly, the taxpayer may receive property in addition to the like kind property. This non-like kind property is called "boot." (As with transactions that are solely of like kind property, whether the taxpayer is also disposing of non-like kind property is not relevant to this portion of the analysis.) In this situation, the tax result depends on whether the like kind property disposed of has a gain realized or a loss realized. If there is a loss realized, all the loss is deferred.[54] If there is a gain realized, the taxpayer must recognize gain to the extent of the lesser of boot received or the gain realized.[55] Note that the assumption of a mortgage is treated as boot.[56]

	Receive only like kind property	Receive like kind property and "boot"
Gain	Defer all gain realized.	Recognize gain to the extent of the lesser: • boot; or • gain realized.
Loss	Defer all loss realized.	Defer all loss realized.

---

53. Section 1031(a).
54. Section 1031(c).
55. Section 1031(b).
56. Section 1031(d).

Practice Note — Boot

Boot is any property the taxpayer *receives* in the transaction that is not like kind property. Boot may include such items as cash, stock, a car, a boat, debt relief, etc.

Because boot reflects the amount by which the taxpayer has not continued his investment in the property, gain recognition is appropriate. However, to the extent the amount of boot exceeds the amount of gain realized, it represents a recovery of the taxpayer's investment in the like kind property, which he is able to recover tax free. Thus, the taxpayer recognizes gain to the extent of the lesser of boot or gain realized.

Practice Note

In some situations, in order to have the value of the two sides of the transaction equal, the taxpayer may have to dispose of property or cash in addition to the like kind property. Unless this additional property also qualifies under the like kind exchange rules, the taxpayer must recognize any gain realized or may recognize any loss realized if authorized by the code with respect to this property.

Example. Fred transferred Whiteacre to Derris in exchange for Blackacre. Whiteacre was worth $80,000 and Blackacre was worth $100,000. Accordingly, for Derris to be willing to enter into the transaction, Fred had to transfer additional property valued at $20,000 to Derris. Fred agreed to transfer $20,000 of stock.

Fred is giving up		Fred is receiving	
Whiteacre	$80,000	Blackacre	$100,000
Stock	20,000		———
Total:	$100,000		$100,000

The transfer of Whiteace in exchange for Blackacre will qualifies as a like kind exchange. The disposition of the stock does not qualify as a like kind exchange. If Fred's basis in the stock is $15,000, Fred must recognize $5,000 of gain on the disposition of the stock. Alternatively, if his basis in the stock is $25,000, Fred has a $5,000 loss on the disposition of the stock and he may recognize the loss under Section 165(c)(2).

Example

It is easy to identify whether a taxpayer is receiving boot in a transaction. Make a list of all the items that constitute the amount realized. Eliminate the like kind property. Any remaining payment constitutes boot.

Example. Geoffrey transferred Redacre to Hoover. Redacre was worth $100,000 and was subject to a $15,000 mortgage. Hoover took the property subject to the mortgage. In exchange Hoover transferred Greenacre, worth $80,000, and $5,000 to Geoffrey.

Geoffrey:

Geoffrey is giving up		Geoffrey is receiving	
Redacre	$100,000	Cash	$5,000
		~~Greenacre~~	~~80,000~~
	_____	Debt relief	15,000
Total:	$100,000		$100,000

The transfer of Redacre in exchange for Greenacre qualifies as a like kind exchange. Geoffrey has received $20,000 of boot ($5,000 of cash and $15,000 of debt relief).

Hoover:

Hoover is giving up		Hoover is receiving	
Cash	$5,000	~~Redacre~~	~~$85,000*~~
Greenacre	80,000		_____
Total:	$85,000		$85,000

* With respect to Redacre, the amount received is the fair market value of the property, $100,000, less the liability the property was taken subject to, $15,000.

The transfer of Greenacre qualifies as a like kind exchange. Because he has only received like kind property, Hoover has not received any boot.

2. Determining Gain or Loss Realized

If the taxpayer is disposing of more than one asset, the total of all the assets received is the amount realized. This total amount realized must be allocated among all the items disposed of. Once the amount realized for each asset is determined, the adjusted basis is subtracted to determine the gain or loss realized.

Example *(continuation of previous example)*

Geoffrey's basis in Redacre was $70,000. Hoover's basis in Greenacre was $60,000.

Geoffrey:

Geoffrey is giving up		Geoffrey is receiving	
Redacre	$100,000	Cash	$5,000
		Greenacre	80,000
	————	Debt relief	15,000
Total:	$100,000		$100,000

Geoffrey gain realized is computed as follows:

Amount realized	$100,000
Adjusted basis	70,000
Gain realized	$30,000

Because he received $20,000 of boot, Geoffrey must recognize $20,000 of gain. The remaining $10,000 of gain realized is deferred.

Hoover:

Hoover is giving up		Hoover is receiving	
Cash	$5,000	Redacre	$85,000
Greenacre	80,000		————
Total:	$85,000		$85,000

Hoover's amount realized, $85,000, must be allocated between the two items he disposed of, or $80,000 to Greenacre and $5,000 to the cash. His gain realized on the two items is computed as follows:

Greenacre		Cash	
Amount realized	$80,000	Amount realized	$5,000
Adjusted basis	60,000	Adjusted basis	5,000
Gain realized	$20,000		-0-

Because he received no boot, all of the gain realized from Redacre can be deferred.

---

3. Determining Basis in Property Received

The gain or loss that is deferred must be captured and preserved. The Code does so by building the deferred amount into the basis of the like kind property at the time of the transaction. If there is a deferred gain, it is subtracted from the fair market value of the like kind property received in the transaction. If there is a deferred loss, the amount of the loss (ignoring the minus sign) is added to the fair market value of the like kind property received in the transaction.[57]

If the taxpayer also received non-like kind property, the regular basis rules apply. The basis of the property is equal to what the taxpayer paid for the property.[58]

Example *(continuation of previous example)*

Geoffrey:

Geoffrey was able to defer $10,000 of the gain realized from the disposition of Redacre. Accordingly, his basis in Greenacre is its fair market value ($80,000), less the deferred gain ($10,000), or $70,000.

Note that this makes sense. If Geoffrey sold the property tomorrow for $80,000, he would have $10,000 of gain realized (amount realized of $80,000, less $70,000 adjusted basis) that he would now have to recognize — the exact amount of gain previously deferred.

Hoover:

Hoover was able to defer $20,000 of the gain realized from the disposition of Greenacre. Accordingly, his basis in Redacre is its fair market value ($100,000), less the deferred gain ($20,000), or $80,000.

Note that this makes sense. If Hoover sold the property tomorrow for $100,000, he would have $20,000 of gain realized (amount realized of $100,000, less $80,000 adjusted basis) that he would now have to recognize — the exact amount of gain previously deferred.

Summary — Basis Rules

For *gain* that has been deferred, the basis of the like kind property is:

> Fair market value of the like kind property received in the transaction
> – Deferred gain
> Basis in the like kind property received

For *loss* that has been deferred, the basis of the like kind property is:

> Fair market value of the like kind property received in the transaction
> + The amount of loss deferred
> Basis in the like kind property received

For property received that is not like kind property, the basis is equal to the cost of the property.

---

57. Section 1031(d).
58. Section 1012(a).

Tell Me More

The basis rules set forth in the Code and regulations are much more complicated than those set forth above. Under Section 1031(d) and the accompanying regulations, the basis of like kind property received is determined as follows. The adjusted basis of all like kind and non-like kind property disposed of is determined. To that amount is added any gain recognized, liability taken on, or cash paid. From that amount is subtracted any loss recognized, liability shed, or cash received. The result is allocated first to non-like kind property received to the extent of its fair market value. The remaining amount is the basis of the like kind property.

The basis rules set forth above reach the same result as the Code, but more simply.

Steps for Analyzing a Like Kind Exchange

Step One: Was there a disposition of property? If yes, continue.

Step Two: Calculate the gain or loss realized for *each* piece of property disposed of.

Step Three: Considering each property the taxpayer is disposing, is the property the taxpayer is giving up "like" the property the taxpayer is receiving?

• If no, the taxpayer must recognize any gain or may recognize a loss if allowed.

• If yes, continue.

Step Four: Was the property the taxpayer is giving up used in his business or held for investment and is the property his is getting going to be used in his business or held for investment?

• If no, the taxpayer must recognize any gain and may recognize a loss if allowed.

• If yes, continue.

Step Five: • If the property has a loss realized, no loss can be recognized. All the loss is deferred. Skip to step 7.

• If the property has a gain realized, the gain is recognized to the extent of the lesser of boot received or the gain realized.

Step Six: Any gain realized that is not recognized is unrecognized (deferred) gain.

> realized gain
> – <u>recognized gain</u>
> unrecognized (deferred) gain

Step Seven: Determine the basis in the property received in the transaction.

• If gain was deferred:

> Fair market value of the like kind property received
> – <u>Deferred gain</u>
> Basis in the like kind property received

• If loss was deferred:

Fair market value of the like kind property received
+ <u>The amount of loss deferred</u>
Basis in the like kind property received

• Property received that is not like kind property:

Basis = cost

Tell Me More

It is often difficult to find two taxpayers who are interested in exchanging the exact properties they each own. The Code offers some flexibility. First, it allows for "round robin" exchanges, where property is transferred between three or more taxpayers. Tom could transfer his property to Sally. Sally could transfer her property to Harry. Harry could transfer his property to Tom. The like kind exchange rules could apply to each of the three transfers.

Second, it allows for exchanges that are not simultaneous. Harry would like to enter into a like kind exchange with respect to a ranch he owns. Ray wants to acquire the ranch, but Harry is not interested in acquiring any property Ray owns. Harry transfers his ranch to Ray and Ray is obligated to purchase property identified by Harry and transfer that property to Harry.

In *Starker v. United States*[59] the taxpayer was entitled to like kind exchange treatment on just such an arrangement. However, he had reserved the right to locate the replacement property at any time during the next five years. Unhappy with the length of time the taxpayer in *Starker* had to complete the transaction, Congress amended Section 1031. The Code now requires the taxpayer to identify replacement property within 45 days of the transfer of the property being disposed of and receive the replacement property no later than 180 days after the transfer or the due date of the taxpayer's return for the year of transfer.[60]

Third, the regulations provide several "safe harbor" transactions, including those facilitated by a qualified intermediary. Nancy would like to exchange her apartment building for a shopping mall. She transfers the apartment building to a qualified intermediary. The intermediary sells the apartment building, uses the proceeds to purchase a shopping mall identified by Nancy, and transfers the mall to Nancy.

E. Application of Rules

Example 1. Holly agreed to transfer an apartment building to Inez in exchange for Inez's farm (which she operated as a soy bean farm). Holly will use the farm to operate a corn products business. With respect to Holly, the transaction qualifies as a like kind exchange. With respect to Inez, the transaction qualifies as a like kind exchange.

---

59. 602 F.2d 1341 (9th Cir. 1979).
60. Section 1031(a)(3).

Example 2. Ray agreed to transfer a parking lot to Rihanna in exchange for Rihanna's commercial building. With respect to Ray, the transaction qualifies as a like kind exchange. If Rihanna uses the parking lot in her business or holds it for investment, with respect to her the transaction qualifies as a like kind exchange.

Example 3. Bruno agreed to transfer investment property to Katy in exchange for Katy's house. Bruno will use the house as a rental property. With respect to Bruno, the transaction qualifies as a like kind exchange. With respect to Katy, because she used the property she disposed of for personal purposes, the transaction does not qualify as a like kind exchange.

Example 4. Mark agrees to transfer InvestCo stock to Lorrie in exchange for Lorrie's investment property. Because stock is not property that qualifies for like kind exchange treatment, the transaction does not qualify as a like kind exchange for either Mark or Lorrie.

Example 5. Terry sells Blackacre to Gerald for $100,000. Terry then purchases Blueacre from Gerald for $120,000. Even though the transaction was structured as a sale followed by a separate purchase, the substance of the transaction appears to be a like kind exchange. The like kind exchange provisions will likely determine the tax consequences of the exchange.

Example 6. Martha transferred Blackacre to Jackson. The land had a fair market value of $710,000 and was subject to a $160,000 mortgage. Her basis in the land was $400,000.

Jackson took the land subject to the mortgage. Jackson also transferred the following assets to Martha:

- Building that had a fair market value of $500,000 and adjusted basis of $400,000
- InvestCo stock that had a fair market value of $50,000 and adjusted basis of $70,000

Martha had held Blackacre for investment purposes and will use the building she receives from Jackson in her business. Jackson used the building he transferred to Martha in his business and will hold Blackacre for investment purposes.

Martha:

Martha is giving up		Martha is receiving	
Blackacre	$710,000	Building	$500,000
		Stock	50,000
	_____	Debt relief	160,000
Total:	$710,000		$710,000

Martha has disposed of one piece of property. Her gain realized is computed as follows:

Amount realized	$710,000
Adjusted basis	400,000
Gain realized	$310,000

Blackacre is "like" the building. Furthermore, she held Blackacre for investment purposes and will use the building in her business. Thus, the transfer qualifies as a like kind exchange.

Martha has received $210,000 of boot ($50,000 of stock and $160,000 of debt relief. She must recognize gain to the extent of the lesser of boot ($210,000) or gain realized ($310,000). Martha must recognize $210,000 of gain. The remainder of the gain realized, $100,000 ($310,000, less $210,000) is deferred.

Martha's basis in the building, the like kind property, is its fair market value, less the deferred gain, or $400,000 ($500,000, less $100,000). Her basis in the stock is its cost, or $50,000.

In summary:

Martha must recognize $210,000 of gain. She must defer $100,000 of gain.

Her basis in the building is $400,000.

Her basis in the stock is $50,000.

Jackson:

Jackson is giving up		Jackson is receiving	
Building	$500,000	Blackacre	$550,000*
Stock	50,000		————
Total:	$550,000		$550,000

* With respect to Blackacre, the amount received is the fair market value of the property, $710,000, less the liability the property was taken subject to, $160,000.

Jackson has disposed of two pieces of property. His gain or loss realized is computed for each piece of property as follows:

Building:		Stock:	
Amount realized	$500,000	Amount realized	$50,000
Adjusted basis	400,000	Adjusted basis	70,000
Gain realized	$100,000	Loss realized	<$20,000>

Because the stock is not "like" Blackacre it does not qualify as a like kind exchange. Jackson can recognize the loss if a Code provision provides authority. He can claim the loss under Section 165(c)(2).

The building is "like" Blackacre. Furthermore, he used the building in his business and will hold Blackacre for investment purposes. Thus, the transfer of the building qualifies as a like kind exchange.

Because Jackson did not receive any boot, all of the gain from the building ($100,000) is deferred.

Jackson's basis in Blackacre, like kind property, is its fair market value, less the deferred gain, or $610,000 ($710,000, less $100,000).

In summary:

Jackson must defer $100,000 of gain.

His basis in Blackacre is $610,000.

Example 7. Jason transferred Greenacre to Lauren. The land had a fair market value of $1,200,000 and was subject to a $200,000 mortgage. His basis in the land was $800,000.

Lauren took the land subject to the mortgage. Lauren also transferred the following assets to Jason:

- Farmland that had a fair market value of $600,000 and adjusted basis of $800,000
- Boat used for personal purposes that had a fair market value of $200,000 and adjusted basis of $300,000
- $200,000 cash

Jason had held Greenacre for investment purposes and will use the farmland in a farming business. Lauren used the farmland in her business and will hold Greenacre for investment purposes.

Jason:

Jason is giving up		Jason is receiving	
Greenacre	$1,200,000	Cash	$200,000
		Boat	200,000
		Farmland	600,000
		Debt relief	200,000
Total:	$1,200,000		$1,200,000

Jason has disposed of one piece of property. His gain realized is computed as follows:

Amount realized	$1,200,000
Adjusted basis	800,000
Gain realized	$400,000

Greenacre is "like" the farmland. Furthermore, he held Greenacre for investment purposes and will use the farmland in his business. Thus, the transfer qualifies as a like kind exchange.

Jason has received $600,000 of boot ($200,000 of cash, a $200,000 boat, and $200,000 of debt relief). He must recognize gain to the extent of the lesser of boot ($600,000) or gain realized ($400,000). Jason must recognize $400,000 of gain. Because all of the gain realized ($400,000) was recognized, no gain is deferred.

Jason's basis in the farmland, the like kind property, is its fair market value, less the deferred gain, or $600,000 ($600,000, less $0). His basis in the boat is its cost, or $200,000.

In summary:

Jason must recognize $400,000 of gain. No gain is deferred.

His basis in the farmland is $600,000.

His basis in the boat is $200,000.

Lauren:

Lauren is giving up		Lauren is receiving	
Cash	$200,000	Greenacre	$1,000,000*
Boat	200,000		
Farmland	600,000		
Total:	$1,000,000		$1,000,000

* With respect to Greenacre, the amount received is the fair market value of the property, $1,200,000, less the liability the property was taken subject to, $200,000.

Lauren has disposed of three pieces of property. Her gain or loss realized is computed for each piece of property as follows:

	Farmland	Cash	Boat
Amount realized	$600,000	$200,000	$200,000
Adjusted basis	800,000	200,000	300,000
Gain/loss realized	<$200,000>	-0-	<$100,000>

Because the boat is not "like" Greenacre it does not qualify as a like kind exchange. If the boat was used for personal purposes Lauren may not recognize the $100,000 loss.

The farmland is "like" Greenacre. Furthermore, she used the farmland in her business and will hold Greenacre for investment purposes. Thus, the transfer of the farmland qualifies as a like kind exchange.

Because there was a loss realized in the farmland, the entire loss ($200,000) is deferred.

Lauren's basis in Greenacre, the like kind property, is its fair market value, plus the amount of loss deferred, or $1,400,000 ($1,200,000, plus $200,000).

In summary:

Lauren must defer $200,000 of loss.

Her basis in Greenacre is $1,400,000.

She cannot recognize the personal loss from the boat.

F. Problems

1. Justin transferred vacant city land to Maxwell. The land had a fair market value of $1,000,000 and was subject to a $300,000 mortgage. His basis in the land was $400,000.

    Maxwell took the land subject to the mortgage. Maxwell also transferred the following assets to Justin:

    • Building that had a fair market value of $500,000 and adjusted basis of $400,000

- InvestCo stock that had a fair market value of $200,000 and adjusted basis of $50,000.

Justin held the vacant city land for investment purposes and will use the building he receives from Maxwell in his business. Maxwell used the building he transferred to Justin in his business and will hold the vacant city land for investment.

With respect to Justin:

a. What are the tax consequences from the disposition of the city land?

b. What is his basis in the building?

c. What is his basis in the stock?

With respect to Maxwell:

d. What are the tax consequences from the disposition of the building?

e. What are the tax consequences from the disposition of the stock?

f. What is his basis in the city land?

2. Mary transferred Whiteacre to Cindy. The land had a fair market value of $1,000,000 and Mary's basis in the land was $1,200,000.

Cindy transferred the following assets to Mary:

- Greenacre, which had a fair market value of $500,000 and adjusted basis of $400,000

- InvestCo stock that had a fair market value of $200,000 and adjusted basis of $300,000

- $300,000 cash.

Mary held Whiteacre for investment purposes and will hold Greenacre for investment purposes. Cindy held Greenacre for investment purposes and will hold Whiteacre for investment purposes.

With respect to Mary:

a. What are the tax consequences from the disposition of Whiteacre?

b. What is her basis in Greenacre?

c. What is her basis in the stock?

With respect to Cindy:

d. What are the tax consequences from the disposition of Greenacre?

e. What are the tax consequences from the disposition of the stock?

f. What is her basis in Whiteacre?

G. Analysis and Application

1. Can you explain the rationale behind each step of the Steps for Analyzing a Like Kind Exchange?

2. Can you explain what boot in excess of gain represents?

3. Nadia owns Yellowacre. It has a fair market value of $100,000 and an adjusted basis of $900,000.

    a.   If Nadia transfers Yellowacre to Howard in exchange for Purpleacre and she held Yellowacre for investment purposes and will hold Purpleacre for investment purposes, will the transaction qualify as a like kind exchange?

    b.   Is there a reason why Nadia would prefer it not qualify as a like kind exchange?

    c.   Can Nadia elect out of the like exchange provisions?

    d.   How might you recommend Nadia structure the transaction?

4.   Betty wants to acquire Cathy's farmland. Because the fair market value of the farmland is $2 million and her adjusted basis is $500,000, Cathy is interested only in disposing of the farmland (which she uses in a farming business) through a like kind exchange. Moreover, Cathy will only enter into a transaction in which she receives a shopping mall in exchange. Accordingly, Betty acquires a shopping mall for $2 million and then Betty transfers the shopping mall to Cathy and Cathy transfers the farmland to Betty.

    a.   With respect to Cathy, does the transaction qualify as a like kind exchange?

    b.   With respect to Betty, does the transaction qualify as a like kind exchange? How worried is Betty about your answer? Why?

5.   Jeff wants to sell his used semi-truck and acquire a new semi-truck. He enters into an agreement with Used Trucks Inc. in which Used Trucks Inc. agrees to buy his old semi-truck for $1,000,000. Jeff's basis in the old semi-truck was $100,000. Jeff also enters into an agreement with New Trucks, Inc. for the purchase of a new semi-truck for $1,000,000. The old semi-truck and the new semi-truck have the same class life (are like kind assets). New Trucks Inc. is a subsidiary of Used Trucks Inc.

    a.   Will the transaction qualify as a like kind exchange?

    b.   If so, what are the tax consequences to Jeff from the transaction?

    c.   Why might Jeff *not* want the transaction to qualify as a like kind exchange?

6.   Suri wants to sell her ranch (which she uses in a ranching business) and acquire Jennifer's farm. Because there is a lot of appreciation in the ranch, Suri wants the transaction to qualify as a like kind exchange. Unfortunately, while Jennifer is interested in disposing of her farm in a tax-free transaction, she is not interested in acquiring Suri's ranch. Jezabell wants to buy Suri's ranch.

Can you structure the transaction in such a way that each party receives the property she is interested in, with the tax consequences she wants? Can you prepare more than one proposal?

Chapter 44

Involuntary Conversion

Deferral or Exclusion of Gain or Loss

Exclusion of Gain:	Deferral of Gain:
• Disposition of principal residence	• Like kind exchange • Involuntary conversion • Transfer between spouses or ex-spouses
	Deferral of Loss: • Like kind exchange • Transfer between spouses or ex-spouses

Read

Code Section 1033(a)(1), (a)(2)(A), (a)(2)(B), (a)(2)(E)(ii), (b)(1), (2)

Treas. Reg. §§ 1.1033(a)-1(a); 1.1033(a)-2(b), (b), (c)(1)

A. Background

Gross income. Gross income includes income (accessions to wealth) derived from any and all sources.[61] It includes every accession to wealth, unless there is an exception, including gains from dealings in property.[62]

Adjusted basis. The basis of property is the amount the taxpayer originally paid for the property.[63] In general, a taxpayer will purchase an item for its fair market value. The adjusted basis reflects an increase for any subsequent capital expenditures and a decrease for depreciation.[64]

Amount realized. The amount realized is the amount the taxpayer sold the property for.[65] In general, a taxpayer will sell an item for its fair market value. What types of assets

---

61. Section 61(a).
62. Section 61(a)(3).
63. Section 1012(a).
64. Section 1016(a).
65. Section 1001(b).

the taxpayer receives as payment for the item he is selling is irrelevant; what is important is that the total value of all assets received is equal to the value of the property the taxpayer is selling. Most often the taxpayer will be paid in cash, property, services, debt relief, or a combination of those items.

Gain realized and recognized. When the property has appreciated, the difference between the amount realized and the adjusted basis of the property sold or otherwise disposed of by the taxpayer is the gain realized.[66] This formula permits the taxpayer to recover the amount he paid for the property tax free. This process is sometimes called a return of capital.

> Amount realized
> – <u>Adjusted basis</u>
> Gain realized

Unless the code provides otherwise, any gain realized must be recognized, or reported, on the taxpayer's income tax return as an accession to wealth.[67]

B. Qualifying for Involuntary Conversion Gain Deferral

Throughout many of the previous chapters, the primary focus has been on voluntary dispositions of property and the resulting tax consequences. What happens when the taxpayer does not intend to dispose of the property, but he is forced to convert it or it is otherwise involuntarily converted?

When the taxpayer replaces the converted property, as with like kind exchanges, there is an argument that the taxpayer has continued his investment in property. Because of this continuity of investment, it may not be the appropriate time to impose tax on the disposition. Congress agreed; the Code offers some relief to those taxpayers who have a gain realized on such conversions. If the taxpayer reinvests in qualifying property, the gain realized can be deferred.

Involuntary conversion events. Property can be involuntarily converted through a seizure, requisition, or condemnation.[68] "Seizure" usually refers to an uncompensated taking of property by the government, such as property taken from taxpayers involved in the drug trade. A "requisition" or "condemnation" usually refers to a compensated taking of property by the government, such as when property is taken for a public use.

The property can also be destroyed by fire, storm, shipwreck, or theft. Destruction by fire, storm, shipwreck, or theft is language found in Section 165(c)(3) dealing with casualty losses. While a casualty loss must be from a destruction that is sudden, unusual, and unexpected, an involuntary conversion event is not required to be sudden.[69]

---

66. Section 1001(a).
67. Section 1001(c).
68. Section 1033(a), (a)(2)(E)(ii).
69. Rev. Rul. 59-102, 1959-1 C.B. 200.

Clarification

- When property suffers a casualty or is stolen and the taxpayer has a *loss* realized on the disposition, any loss would be allowed under Section 165(c).

- When property suffers a casualty, is stolen, or suffers an involuntary conversion event and the taxpayer has a *gain* realized on the disposition, the gain is addressed under Section 1033.

Qualified replacement property. There are two different methods by which the taxpayer can obtain replacement property. Under the first method, the property is involuntarily converted directly into qualified replacement property. For example, the county takes the taxpayer's farmland and in return provides him with other farmland located in a different part of the county. This type of conversion is rare.

Under the second method, the property is involuntarily converted into cash (or nonqualified property) and the cash (or nonqualified property) is invested by the taxpayer in qualified replacement property. For example, the property is destroyed by fire. The taxpayer receives insurance proceeds and invests the funds in qualified replacement property.

Under either method, the replacement property must be qualified replacement property. To determine if the replacement property is qualified property, the focus is on the taxpayer's use of the property. The type of property, such as investment, business, or personal, is not determinative.

Comparison — Types of Property That May Qualify

Like kind exchange	Involuntary Conversion
√ Business property	√ Business property
√ Investment property	√ Investment property
	√ Property held for personal purposes

The replacement property must be "similar or related in service or use to the property so converted."[70] In *Liant Record, Inc. v. Commissioner*[71] the taxpayer owned an office building that was 25 stories and had been rented to 82 commercial tenants. New York City condemned the building, acquired title, and paid the taxpayer for the property. The taxpayer used all of the condemnation proceeds to purchase three apartment buildings. The first building was nine stories and contained 77 apartments and six commercial tenants. The second building was six stories and contained 47 apartments and four stores. The third building was 11 stories and contained 40 apartments and 6 commercial tenants.

---

70. Section 1033(a)(2)(A).
71. 303 F.2d 326 (2d Cir. 1962).

The only issue before the court was whether the replacement property was "similar or related in service or use."

The court considered the actual, physical use of the original property as compared to the replacement property. It noted that the taxpayer could be the end user of the property or hold the property for lease or rent to others.

> [I]t is the service or use which the properties have to the taxpayer-owner that is relevant. Thus when the taxpayer-owner himself uses the converted property, the Tax Court is correct in comparing the actual physical service or use which the end user makes of the converted and the replacement properties. However, if the taxpayer-owner is an investor rather than a user, it is not the lessees' actual physical use but the nature of the lessor's relation to the land which must be examined.
>
> * * *
>
> There is, therefore, a single test to be applied to both users and investors, i.e., a comparison of the services or uses of the original and replacement properties to the taxpayer-owner. In applying such a test to a lessor, a court must compare, inter alia, the extent and type of the lessor's management activity, the amount and kind of services rendered by him to the tenants, and the nature of his business risks connected with the properties.[72]

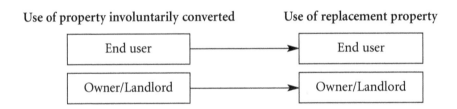

Use of property involuntarily converted   Use of replacement property

End user → End user

Owner/Landlord → Owner/Landlord

Regulatory Examples of Property Not Similar or Related in Service or Use to the Property Converted[73]

- Proceeds of unimproved real estate invested in improved real estate.
- Proceeds from conversion of real property used to reduce the indebtedness previously incurred in the purchase of a leasehold.
- Proceeds from requisitioned tugs invested in barges.

Timing. When the taxpayer's property is compulsorily or involuntarily converted into cash (or nonqualified property), he has two years following the conversion to invest in

---

72. Liant Record, Inc v. Commissioner, 303 F.2d 326, 328-29 (2d Cir. 1962).
73. Treas. Reg. § 1.1033(a)-2(c)(9).

qualified replacement property.[74] The Code has no minimum holding period for the qualified replacement property.

Checklist for Involuntary Conversions

❏ The property suffered an involuntary conversion (including thefts and casualties regardless of whether they are sudden) or was compulsorily converted.

❏ There is a gain realized on the disposition.

❏ The taxpayer reinvests in qualified replacement property (property that is similar or related in service or use) or the property was converted directly into qualified replacement property.

❏ The qualified replacement property is obtained within two years of the conversion.

C. Computations

1. Deferral of Gain

To come within the involuntary conversion provisions, there must be a gain upon disposition of the property. If the property is compulsorily or involuntarily converted directly into qualified replacement property and there is a gain realized, the taxpayer is required to defer the gain.[75]

If the property is involuntarily converted into cash (or nonqualified property) and the cash (or nonqualified property) is timely invested by the taxpayer in qualified replacement property, the taxpayer can defer the gain. The deferral applies only to the extent the taxpayer has continued his investment. Conversely, to the extent he has not continued his investment, he must recognize gain. Thus, the taxpayer must recognize gain equal to the lesser of the gain realized or the extent the amount realized from the conversion exceeds the cost of the replacement property. Alternatively, the taxpayer can elect to recognize the gain.[76]

Example. Wes used a car in his trade or business. Last year, the car was destroyed in a storm. His adjusted basis in the car as of the time of the storm was $10,000. He received insurance proceeds of $15,000. The following year he purchased a similar car to replace the car that had been destroyed. The new car cost him $12,000.

Wes's car was involuntarily converted. His gain realized on the conversion was $5,000 ($15,000 amount realized from conversion, less $10,000 adjusted basis). Wes invested in

---

74. Section 1033(a)(2)(B). There are some exceptions to the two-year replacement period. See Section 1033(g) dealing with condemnation of real property used for business or investment and Section 1033(h) dealing with personal residences and contents damaged in Presidentially declared disasters.

75. Section 1033(a)(1).

76. Section 1033(a)(2).

qualified replacement property, a new car (property similar or related in service or use), within two years of the conversion of his old car.

Wes must $3,000 of recognized gain ($15,000 amount realized from the conversion, less the $12,000 cost of the replacement property) and $2,000 of gain is deferred (gain realized of 5,000, less $3,000 gain recognized).

2. Determining Basis in Replacement Property

The gain that is deferred must be captured and preserved. The Code does so by building the deferred gain into the basis of the replacement property at the time of purchase. Accordingly, to determine the basis in the replacement property, the deferred gain is subtracted from the fair market value of the replacement property.[77]

Continuation of Example. Wes's basis in the new car is $10,000 ($12,000 cost of the replacement car, less $2,000 deferred gain).

Steps for Analyzing an Involuntary Conversion

Step One: Was the property compulsorily or involuntary converted?

If yes, continue.

Step Two: Calculate the gain or loss realized.

amount realized from the conversion
– <u>adjusted basis</u>
gain or loss realized

• If there is a gain realized, continue.

• If there is a loss realized, continue analysis under Section 165(c).

Step Three: Did the taxpayer invest in qualified replacement property (property similar or related in service or use) within the appropriate time frame (generally, within 2 years from date of conversion)?

Or was the property converted directly into qualified replacement property?

• If yes, continue.

• If no, the taxpayer must recognize the gain realized.

Step Four: The taxpayer must recognize gain to the extent he has not continued his investment in the replacement property.

amount realized from the conversion
– <u>cost of replacement property</u>
gain recognized

Step Five: Any gain realized that is not recognized is unrecognized (deferred) gain.

---

77. Section 1033(b).

realized gain
– <u>recognized gain</u>
unrecognized (deferred) gain

Step Six: Determine the basis in the replacement property.

Cost of replacement property
– <u>unrecognized gain</u>
Basis in replacement property

D. Application of Rules

Example 1. Harris owns an apartment building with a fair market value of $50,000 and adjusted basis of $80,000. Earlier in the year the building was destroyed by fire. Harris filed a claim with his insurance company and received $60,000.

Harris has a $20,000 loss ($60,000 amount realized, less $80,000 adjusted basis). Because there is a loss on disposition, the involuntary conversion provision is not applicable. He could recognize the loss under Section 165(c)(2).

Example 2. Yancy owned an apartment building with a fair market value of $1,000,000 and adjusted basis of $800,000. Earlier in the year the building was destroyed fire. Yancy filed a claim with his insurance company and received $950,000. A few months later he purchased a new apartment building for $900,000.

Yancy's apartment building was involuntarily converted. His gain realized on the conversion is $150,000 ($950,000 amount realized from conversion, less $800,000 adjusted basis). Yancy invested in qualified replacement property (property similar or related in service or use) within two years of conversion of the old apartment building.

Yancy has $50,000 of recognized gain ($950,000 amount realized from the conversion, less the $900,000 cost of the replacement property). Of the $150,000 gain realized, $100,000 is deferred ($150,000 of gain realized, less $50,000 gain recognized).

Yancy's basis in the new apartment building is $800,000 ($900,000 cost of the new apartment building, less $100,000 deferred gain).

Example 3. Caroline owned a summer vacation home along the coast. It had a fair market value of $500,000 and adjusted basis of $200,000. Earlier in the year the home was destroyed by a hurricane. Caroline filed a claim with her insurance company and received $500,000. A few months later Caroline purchased a new summer vacation home for $550,000.

Caroline's summer home was involuntarily converted. Her gain realized on the conversion is $300,000 ($500,000 amount realized from conversion, less $200,000 adjusted basis). Caroline invested in qualified replacement property (property similar or related in service or use) within two years of conversion of the old summer home.

Caroline does not have to recognize any of the gain (she invested all of the proceeds into a replacement property). All of the $300,000 gain is deferred.

Caroline's basis in the new summer vacation home is $250,000 ($550,000 cost of the new summer vacation home, less $300,000 deferred gain).

Example 4. Dirk owns an apartment building with a fair market value of $100,000 and adjusted basis of $80,000. Earlier in the year the city carried out a taking of the property. In exchange, the city gave Dirk a comparable apartment building on the other side of town. The fair market value of the new apartment building was $100,000.

Dirk's apartment building was compulsorily converted. Because the property was converted directly into qualified replacement property, Dirk must defer the $20,000 of gain realized from the disposition of his apartment building. His basis in the new apartment building is $80,000 ($100,000 fair market value of the new apartment building, less $200,000 deferred gain).

E. Problems

1. Joe owned a shopping center with a fair market value of $1,000,000 and adjusted basis of $800,000. Earlier in the year the shopping center was destroyed by a tornado. Joe filed a claim with his insurance company and received $850,000. A few months later he purchased a new shopping center for $900,000.

    a. What are the tax consequences to Joe from disposition of the shopping center?

    b. What is Joe's basis in the new shopping center?

2. Willis owned an apartment building with a fair market value of $900,000 and adjusted basis of $800,000. Earlier in the year the building was destroyed by a fire. Willis filed a claim with his insurance company and received $950,000. A few months later, he purchased a new apartment building for $900,000.

    a. What are the tax consequences to Willis from disposition of the apartment building?

    b. What is Willis's basis in the new apartment building?

3. Heather owned a summer vacation home along the coast. It had a fair market value of $600,000 and adjusted basis of $400,000. Earlier in the year the home was destroyed by a hurricane. Heather filed a claim with her insurance company and received $600,000. A few months later Heather purchased a new summer vacation home for $650,000.

    a. What are the tax consequences to Heather from disposition of the summer vacation home?

    b. What is Heather's basis in the new summer vacation home?

4. Mark owned an office building with a fair market value of $700,000 and adjusted basis of $800,000. Earlier in the year the building was destroyed fire. Mark filed a claim with his insurance company and received $700,000. A few months later Mark purchased a new office building for $700,000.

    a. What are the tax consequences to Mark from disposition of the office building?

    b. What is Mark's basis in the new office building?

5. Katerina owned a building out of which she operated her business. It had a fair market value of $100,000 and adjusted basis of $80,000. Earlier in the year the building was destroyed by a fire. Katerina filed a claim with her insurance company and received $100,000. A few months later Katerina purchased an office building for $100,000 and rented out the office space.

a. What are the tax consequences to Katrina from disposition of the building?

b. What is Katerina's basis in the office building?

F. Analysis and Application

1. Can you explain the rationale behind each step of the Steps for Analyzing an Involuntary Conversion?

2. William owned a commercial building out of which he operated his business. It had a fair market value of $300,000 and adjusted basis of $200,000. Earlier in the year the building was destroyed by a fire. William filed a claim with his insurance company and received $300,000. He used the money to purchase a different commercial building for $300,000 and now operates his business out of the new building.

    a. Does the transaction qualify for the involuntary conversion provision?

    b. How much gain can William defer?

    c. Can you imagine a scenario in which William would want to elect out of the deferral provision? What is it?

3. Can you explain to a client the difference between what types of property the like kind exchange provision applies to and what types of property the involuntary conversion provision applies to?

4. Research project: Research the variety of casualties and other events that have qualified as involuntary conversion events. Prepare a presentation.

5. Prepare a concept map to explain the relationship between exclusion of gain on sale of principal residence (Section 121), like kind exchanges (Section 1031), and involuntary conversions (Section 1033).

X

Assignment of Income

Kiddie Tax	• Assignment of compensation • Assignment of income from property • Assignment of gain from disposition of property

Chapter 45

Kiddie Tax

Assignment of Income

Kiddie Tax	• Assignment of compensation • Assignment of income from property • Assignment of gain from disposition of property

Read

Code Section 1(g)

A. Background

Gross income. Gross income includes income (accessions to wealth) derived from any and all sources.[1] It includes every accession to wealth, unless there is an exception.

Taxable income. In general, taxable income is the taxpayer's gross income, less all allowable deductions.[2] The taxpayer's liability is based on the amount of the taxpayer's taxable income.[3]

B. Kiddie Tax

Each taxpayer files his own tax return and the information included on that tax return is based on the individual's accession to wealth. This approach ignores the fact that individuals may be part of a larger economic unit, specifically a family unit. Because tax rates are graduated, if taxable income can be spread out evenly among all family members, the family as a unit will pay the least amount of tax possible. With this in mind, some taxpayers transferred income-producing assets to their young child and had the child file

---

1. Section 61(a).
2. Section 63(a).
3. Section 1.

an income tax return. While the income was taxed at the child's (lower) rate, the parent retained effective control over the property.

Example. Peter has a CD that generates $50,000 of income. Peter reports the interest income on his income tax return. If he is taxed at a 35 percent marginal rate, Peter would pay $17,500 in taxes. If, instead, Peter transferred the CD to his 10-year-old child, the child reports the income on his income tax return. If the child was taxed at a 10 percent marginal rate, the child would pay $5,000 in taxes. By transferring the CD to the child, the family unit saved $12,500 in taxes.

Congress ended a family unit's ability to save taxes through these types of transfers by enacting what is referred to as the kiddie tax. For income that is subject to the kiddie tax, the child continues to report the income but pays tax at his parent's rate.

Kids to which the kiddie tax applies. For the kiddie tax to apply, the child must be under 18 years of age.[4] It also applies to two other groups: a child who turned 18 during the year and whose earned income does not exceed one-half of the amount of the child's support; and a child who is a full-time student, under 24 years old, and whose earned income does not exceed one-half of the amount of the child's support.[5] The kiddie tax does not apply if the child's parents are deceased or if the child is married and files a joint return.[6]

Earned income and unearned income. Earned income generally is personal service income. Unearned income includes everything else, such as interest income and dividends, even if the income is earned on assets purchased with the child's earned income.[7]

Computation of tax. In general, if another individual is permitted to claim the child's dependency deduction, the child may not claim a personal exemption.[8] A child's standard deduction may not exceed the greater of $500[9] or the total of $250 and the child's earned income.[10]

The tax the child pays is the greater of two amounts. The first amount is the tax the child would pay based on his own marginal tax rate. This amount will be the greater amount if the child has a higher marginal tax rate than his parents.

The second amount is the amount of tax the child would pay on his total taxable income reduced by his net unearned income (in effect, his earned income), taxed at his own marginal rate, plus the amount of tax the child would pay on the net unearned income based on his parent's rate.[11]

For purposes of this computation, net unearned income is unearned income less two amounts. The first is a limited standard deduction. The second is a standard deduction or allowable itemized deductions, whichever is greater.[12]

---

4. Section 1(g)(2)(A)(i).
5. Section 1(g)(2)(A)(ii).
6. Section 1(g)(2)(B), (C).
7. Section 1(g)(4)(A).
8. Section 151(d)(2).
9. This amount is adjusted for inflation. Section 63(c)(4).
10. Section 63(c)(5).
11. If the parents are not married or are married but file separate returns, Section 1(g)(5) provides rules for determining which parent's taxable income is taken into account.
12. Section 1(g)(4)(A). Because it is unusual for the child's itemized deductions to exceed the amount of the limited standard deduction, the child usually will deduct twice the limited standard deduction amount.

If the child's gross income is from only interest and dividends and is more than the limited standard deduction but less than ten times the limited standard deduction, the parents may just elect to include the child's unearned income on their return.[13]

C. Application of Rule

Example 1. Drew is 14 years old. He has a paper route for which he is paid $10,000 each year. The income Drew earns is earned income, not subject to the kiddie tax. He reports the income on his income tax return and pays tax based on his own rate.

Example 2. Drew is 14 years old. He has a paper route for which he is paid $10,000 each year. He always deposits each paycheck in his savings account. This year he earned $5,000 of interest. The interest income Drew earns is unearned income, subject to the kiddie tax. He reports the income on his income tax return and pays tax on the net unearned income at his parent's rate.

Example 3. Cynthia gave her 10-year old niece, Regina, 100 shares of InvestCo stock. This year, the corporation paid Regina $10,000 in dividends. The dividends are unearned income, subject to the kiddie tax. Regina reports the dividends on her income tax return and pays tax on the net unearned income at her parent's rate.

Example 4. Gregg is 12 years old and receives $5,000 of dividends. The dividends are unearned income, subject to the kiddie tax. The limited standard deduction is $900 and he has no allowable itemized deductions. His net unearned income is:

Unearned income	$5,000
Standard deduction[14]	− 900
Standard deduction[15]	− 900
Net unearned income	$3,200

If his parent's marginal tax rate is higher than his marginal rate, the $3,200 of net unearned income is taxed at his parent's rate.

D. Problem

Mary-Kate, at 12 years of age, is a well-known child actor, earning $1 million for each movie in which she stars. She has a financial advisor who invests 80 percent of each paycheck in stock and bonds. This year she earned $2 million for appearing in two movies and $500,000 in dividends and interest from her investments.

a. Will the amount she is paid for appearing in movies be subject to the kiddie tax?

b. Will her investment income be subject to the kiddie tax? If so, what tax rate is applicable, her rate or her parents' rate?

---

13. Section 1(g)(7).
14. Section 1(g)(4)(A)(ii)(I).
15. Section 1(g)(4)(A)(ii)(II).

Chapter 46

Assignment of Income

Assignment of Income

Kiddie Tax	• Assignment of compensation • Assignment of income from property • Assignment of gain from disposition of property

Read

Code Section 64(a); 102

A. Background

Gross income. Gross income includes income (accessions to wealth) derived from any and all sources.[16] It includes every accession to wealth, unless there is an exception.

Taxable income. In general, taxable income is the taxpayer's gross income, less all allowable deductions.[17] The taxpayer's liability is based on the amount of the taxpayer's taxable income.[18]

Gifts. Property received as a gift can be excluded from gross income.[19] A gift proceeds from a detached and disinterested generosity, out of affection, respect, admiration, charity or like impulses. The most critical consideration is the transferor's intent and the transferor's intent is determined based on the facts and circumstances.[20]

Neither income generated from property received as a gift nor a gift of income are excludable from gross income.[21]

---

16. Section 61(a).
17. Section 63(a).
18. Section 1.
19. Section 102(a).
20. Commissioner v. Duberstein, 363 U.S. 278 (1960).
21. Section 102(b).

B. Assignment of Income

Each taxpayer files his own tax return and the information included on that tax return is based on the individual's accession to wealth. This approach ignores the fact that individuals may be part of a larger economic unit, specifically a family unit. Because tax rates are graduated, if taxable income can be spread among all family members, the family as a unit will pay the least amount of tax possible. With this in mind, a taxpayer might attempt to assign compensation income or income from property to a family member with a lower marginal tax rate.

1. Assignment of Compensation Income

In *Lucas v. Earl*[22] Mr. Earl assigned one-half of his salary to his wife. The issue before the court was whether Mr. Earl had to report all of his salary or just the one-half he received. (At the time Mr. Earl entered into the agreement with his wife, the Code did not have a provision allowing a husband and wife to file a joint income tax return.) The Supreme Court held that Mr. Earl had to report his entire salary, not just the portion he received. The assignment of one-half of the salary to his wife was not relevant to the tax result. The Court concluded the opinion with memorable language—

> That seems to us the import of the statute before us and we think that no distinction can be taken according to the motives leading to the arrangement by which the fruits are attributed to a different tree from that on which they grew.[23]

Tell Me More

If the taxpayer is married and resides in a community property state, community property rules provide that earnings are property of the husband-wife community and not just the spouse providing the services. Each spouse must report one-half of the income.[24]

The taxpayer is not required to report any compensation income if he agrees to work for free. To do so, the taxpayer cannot control what his employer otherwise does with his salary, and he must have agreed to work for free before any amounts were earned.[25]

If the taxpayer is acting as an agent for another, such that the compensation does not belong to the taxpayer, he is not required to report any of the income.[26]

---

22. 281 U.S. 111 (1930).
23. Lucas v. Earl, 281 U.S. 111, 115 (1930).
24. Poe v. Seaborn, 282 U.S. 101 (1930).
25. Commissioner v. Giannini, 129 F.2d 638 (9th Cir. 1942).
26. Fogarty v. Commissioner, 780 F.2d 1005 (Fed. Cir. 1986) (Jesuit priest employed by the University of Virginia was not an agent of the Jesuit order and was required to include the income); Rev. Rul. 84-13, 1984-1 C.B. 21 (psychologist who had taken a vow of poverty as a member of a religious order was not an agent of the order and was required to include the income); Rev. Rul. 74-581, 1974-2 C.B. 25 (faculty members who participated in a clinical program were agents of the law school and were not required to report the income).

2. Assignment of Income from Property

In *Helvering v. Horst*[27] Mr. Horst owned a coupon bond.[28] Before an interest coupon had matured, he detached the coupon and gave it to his son. When the coupon matured, his son collected the interest payment. The issue before the court was whether Mr. Horst or his son had to report the interest. The Supreme Court noted that Mr. Horst, by assigning the coupon to his son, had controlled the disposition of the income. Because he could control the underlying property, Mr. Horst had to include the income from the property. The Court concluded the opinion with memorable language, reflective of *Lucas v. Earl*—

> [H]e has enjoyed the economic benefits of the income in the same manner and to the same extent as though the transfer were of earnings, and in both cases the import of the statute is that the fruit is not to be attributed to a different tree from that on which it grew.[29]

Helvering v. Eubank[30] was decided at the same time as *Helving v. Horst*. Mr. Eubank had been a life insurance agent. When he left his employment, he assigned to a third party the renewal commissions for two insurance contracts. The issue before the court was who had to include the commissions, Mr. Eubank or the third party. Citing *Horst*, the Supreme Court held that Mr. Eubank had to include the commissions in his income.

In some situations, a taxpayer's services can create property. If the property is transferred and then sold, it may be difficult to determine if the amount received in the sale represents compensation for services or gain from the sale of property. For example, an author writes a novel and transfers the copyright on the novel to her daughter. The daughter sells the novel to a publishing company. In this situation, the property interest in the novel was transferred via the copyright to the author's daughter. The daughter reports the amount received from the sale of the copyright. The amount received does not represent compensation of the author's services, but rather gain from the daughter's sale of property.[31]

3. Gain from the Disposition of Property — Substance Over Form

The same type of issue has arisen with respect to the gain from the disposition of an asset. As with the other types of assignment of income, taxpayers want to distribute gain among members of a family in such a way that the family as a unit will pay the less cumulative tax than if one of the members reported the entire gain. With this objective in mind, a taxpayer might attempt to transfer ownership of an asset to family members just prior to sale. The Service and the Court will closely scrutinize such transfers to determine the substance of the transaction and who effectively owned the property at the time of sale.

---

27. 311 U.S. 112 (1940).

28. A bond is a type of loan. The borrower has agreed to repay the bondholder the amount of the bond. At the time this case was decided, interest was paid through coupons attached to the bond. When a coupon matured (interest became due and payable), the bondholder would detach the coupon and present it for payment).

29. Helvering v. Hort, 311 U.S. 112, 120 (1940).

30. 311 U.S. 122 (1940).

31. Rev. Rul. 54-599, 1954-2 C.B. 52.

In *Salvatore v. Commissioner*[32] the taxpayer owned a gas station. On July 24, 1963, she entered into an agreement to sell the property to Texaco. On August 28, 1963, she transferred ownership of one-half of the property to her children. The taxpayer and her children then completed the sale to Texaco. The issue before the court was who had to report the gain from the sale, the taxpayer or the taxpayer and her children? While the form of the transaction was a sale by the taxpayer and her children, the court concluded the substance of the transaction was a sale by the taxpayer alone. The taxpayer was required to include all the gain from the sale of the gas station in her gross income.

Summary of Rules — Assignment of Income

- **Compensation:** Compensation for services must be included in the income of the taxpayer who earned it.

- **Income from property:** Income from property must be included in the income of the taxpayer who controls the property and/or the income.

- **Gain from disposition of property:** Gain from the disposition of property must be included in the income of the taxpayer who owned the property. Which taxpayer owned the property is based on the substance of the transaction, not the form.

C. Application of Rules

Example 1. David's marginal tax rate is 35 percent. He instructs his employer to pay his salary to David's son, who is in the 15 percent tax bracket. Because David earned the compensation, he must include it in his income.

Example 2. Ray owns an apartment building. He assigns all rental payments to his daughter. Because Ray controls the property and the rental income, he must include the rental payments in his income.

D. Problems

1. On July 1 Melissa transferred a savings account to her adult son Jeb. During the year the savings account earned $5,000 in interest. Who must report the interest income?

2. In June, Alex, feeling philanthropic, decided that he should work for free. He instructed his employer to pay all his remaining salary for the year to the Red Cross. Beginning with the July payment, the employer did so. Is Alex required to include in his income the salary payments for July through December?

---

32. T.C. Memo. 1970-30.

3. Patrick owned a pizzeria. His son was in medical school. To help his son financially, Patrick agreed to transfer one-half of the profits from the pizzeria to his son. Who must report the profits from the pizzeria?

4. Tina owned stock in InvestCo. On January 1st she notified InvestCo that all future dividends were to be paid to her son. InvestCo paid $5,000 in dividends during the year. Who must include the dividends in income?

E. Analysis and Application

1. Lisa's marginal tax rate is 35 percent. She owned an apartment building and collected $200,000 in rent each year. Her sister, Allison, had a marginal tax rate of 10 percent.

   a. If Lisa reports all the rental income, how much tax will she pay?

   b. If Lisa reports one-half of the rental income and Allison reports one-half of the rental income, how much total tax will they pay?

   c. If Allison reports all of the rental income, how much tax will she pay?

   d. What is the tax result to Lisa if she assigns the rental income to Allison?

2. Lynn owned stock in ProfitCo. She notified ProftCo that all future dividends were to be paid to her son. She then transferred the stock to her daughter. ProfitCo paid $5,000 in dividends during the year. Who must include the dividends in income?

3. Andy owned a coupon bond. Before interest on any of the coupons had matured, he detached them all and gave them to his son. When each coupon matured, his son collected the interest payment.

   a. In what way are the above facts different from those in *Helvering v. Horst*?

   b. Who must report the interest income?

4. Corban was a successful screenwriter. He entered into a contract with a production company to write the script for a sci-fi thriller. When he had completed the script, he transferred it to his niece. His niece transferred the script to the production company and the production company paid her the amount due under the contract. Who must report the amount paid by the production company?

5. Paula owns a warehouse that has substantially increased in value. When she retires, she plans to sell the warehouse, invest one-half of the proceeds in an annuity for herself, and transfer the remainder of the proceeds to her two sons. Paula is in the highest marginal tax bracket and her sons are in the lowest marginal tax bracket.

   a. How might you recommend Paula structure the transaction? Why?

   b. What concerns do you have and how would you address them?

XI

Select Tax Topics

Chapter 47

Tax Consequences of Divorce

Tax Consequences of Divorce

Child Support:	Transfer of Property:	Alimony:
• not income to recipient • no deduction to payor	• not income to recipient • no gain or loss on disposition • carryover basis	• income to recipient • deductible by the payor

Read

Code Sections 71(a)-(d); 215(a), (b); 1041(a), (b), (c)

Treas. Reg. §§ 1.71-1T(a) Q&A 1, 2, -1T(b) Q&A 5, -1T(c) Q&A 15, 16, 17, 18; 1.1041-1T Q&A 1, -1T(a) Q&A 2, 4, -1T(b) Q&A 6, 7, -1T(c) Q&A 9, -1T(d) Q&A 10, 11

A. Background

Gross income. Gross income includes income (accessions to wealth) derived from any and all sources.[1] It includes every accession to wealth, unless there is an exception, including gains from dealings in property.[2]

Gain realized and recognized. When property has appreciated, the difference between the amount realized and the adjusted basis of the property sold or otherwise disposed of by the taxpayer is the gain realized.[3] This formula permits the taxpayer to recover the amount he paid for the property tax free. This process is sometimes called a return of capital.

> Amount realized
> – <u>Adjusted basis</u>
> Gain realized

---

1. Section 61(a).
2. Section 61(a)(3).
3. Section 1001(a).

Unless the code provides otherwise, any gain realized must be recognized, or reported, on the taxpayer's income tax return as an accession to wealth.[4]

Loss realized and recognized. When property has depreciated, the difference between the amount realized and the adjusted basis of the property sold or otherwise disposed of by the taxpayer is the loss realized.[5]

Amount realized
– Adjusted basis
<Loss realized>

Unless the taxpayer can provide authority, no loss realized may be recognized, or reported, on the taxpayer's income tax return as a loss.[6]

Personal expenditures. In general, personal expenses are not deductible. Congress does not consider a personal expense an item that should offset the taxpayer's gross income.[7] In other words, it is not considered part of the cost of earning or generating gross income. Any deduction permitted for a personal expense is an exception to this broad-based rule. Accordingly, if the taxpayer wants to claim a deduction on his income tax return for a personal expense, he must establish that Congress specifically provided an exception to this general rule.

B. Tax Consequences of Divorce

The tax consequences of a divorce can be understood by considering three separate aspects. While each of these aspects could have been addressed in other places in this text, because they usually occur together as part of the divorce process it makes more sense to address them together.

1. Child Support

There are no tax consequences when one spouse[8] pays the other spouse child support. It is not income to the recipient spouse and the payor spouse is not entitled to claim a deduction.[9]

Any payment that constitutes child support cannot qualify as alimony. Moreover, if the payment is clearly associated with a contingency related to a child, it will be treated as child support regardless of the label given to the payment.[10] For example, if a payment is reduced within six months of the child turning 18, 21, or the local age of majority, the payment will be presumed to be child support. This presumption is a rebuttable presumption.

---

4. Section 1001(c).
5. Section 1001(a).
6. Section 165(c)(1), (2).
7. Section 262.
8. References in this chapter to "spouse" includes ex-spouses.
9. Section 71(c).
10. Temp. Reg. § 1.71-1T(c), Q&A-18.

2. Alimony

There are tax consequences when one spouse pays the other spouse alimony. The recipient spouse must include the payment in income[11] and the payor spouse is entitled to claim a deduction.[12]

The Code sets forth specific criteria that must be met for a payment to constitute alimony. The payment must be:[13]

- Cash;
- to or for the benefit of the spouse;
- pursuant to a divorce or separation agreement;
- not designated as not alimony;
- not members of same household if legally separated or divorced;
- no liability after the death of the payee; and
- not for child support.

The payment must be made in cash. Payments made with services or property do not qualify. If the payment had been made with property, the transaction would be covered by the non-recognition provision for property transferred between spouses.

The payments must be made pursuant to a written agreement. Both parties must agree to a payment of alimony; one of the parties cannot unilaterally decide to begin making alimony payments.

If the spouses are legally separated under a divorce decree or separate maintenance agreement they cannot be members of the same household. If the parties are not legally separated, the parties can be members of the same household.

Consistent with the purpose of alimony payments, the obligation of the payor spouse must terminate upon the death of the recipient spouse. Some states have statutes that provide alimony terminates upon the death of the recipient spouse. These statutes can be used to satisfy this element.

The Code allows the parties to elect out of alimony treatment.[14] If they make the election, the recipient spouse is not required to include the payment in income and the payor spouse is not entitled to a deduction for the payment.

If a payment is not sufficient to cover both child support payments and alimony payments, it is allocated first to child support.

---

11. Section 71(a).

12. Section 215.

13. Section 71(b). If the parties "front load" the alimony payments, to the extent of "excess alimony payments" the tax consequences are reversed. The payor must include the amounts paid in income and the recipient spouse is allowed a deduction. See Section 71(f).

14. Section 71(b)(1)(B).

Section 71. Alimony and Separate Maintenance Payments

(a) General Rule. — Gross income includes amounts received as alimony or separate maintenance payments.

(b) Alimony or Separate Maintenance Payments Defined. — For purposes of this section—

  (1) In general. — The term "alimony or separate maintenance payment" means any payment in cash if—

    (A) such payment is received by (or on behalf of) a spouse under a divorce or separation instrument,

    (B) the divorce or separation instrument does not designate such payment as a payment which is not includible in gross income under this section and not allowable as a deduction under section 215,

    (C) in the case of an individual legally separated from his spouse under a decree of divorce or of separate maintenance, the payee spouse and the payor spouse are not members of the same household at the time such payment is made, and

    (D) there is no liability to make any such payment for any period after the death of the payee spouse and there is no liability to make any payments (in cash or property) as a substitute for such payments after the death of the payee spouse.

* * *

(c) Payments to Support Children. —

  (1) In General. — Subsection (a) shall not apply to that part of any payment which the terms of the divorce or separation instrument fix (in terms of any amount of money or a part of the payment) as a sum which is payable for the support of children of the payor spouse.

  (2) Treatment of Certain Reductions Related to Contingencies Involving Children. — For purposes of paragraph (1), if any amount specified in the instrument will be reduced—

    (A) on the happening of a contingency specified in the instrument relating to a child (such as attaining a specified age, marrying, dying, leaving school, or a similar contingency), or

    (B) at a time which can clearly be associated with a contingency of a kind specified in subparagraph (A),

an amount equal to the amount of such reduction will be treated as an amount fixed as payable for the support of children of the payor spouse.

Section 215. Alimony, Etc., Payments

(a) General Rule. — In the case of an individual, there shall be allowed as a deduction an amount equal to the alimony or separate maintenance payments paid during such individual's taxable year.

(b) Alimony or Separate Maintenance Payments Defined. — For purposes of this section, the term "alimony or separate maintenance payment" means any alimony or separate maintenance payment (as defined in section 71(b)) which is includible in the gross income of the recipient under section 71.

* * *

Tell Me More

Because alimony payments are deductible by the payor spouse, Congress was concerned the payor spouse would accelerate payments into the initial years after divorce or separation to accelerate his deductions. Congress was also concerned that a division of property could be disguised as alimony, again allowing a tax benefit to the payor spouse. The front-loading rules of Section 71(f) attempt to identify such payments and reverse the tax treatment, with the identified amount required to be included in the income of the payor spouse and deducted by the recipient spouse.

---

3. Transfer of Property

When spouses transfer property between themselves, the transaction is governed by the non-recognition provision of Section 1041. Regardless of whether the property was transferred while they are married or is incident to a divorce, no gain or loss is recognized.[15] The non-recognition treatment is mandatory; the spouses cannot agree to have the provision not apply. The recipient spouse takes the transferor spouse's basis in the property.[16]

The property is transferred incident to a divorce if it is transferred within one year after the day the marriage ends or is related to the cessation of the marriage.[17] The regulations provide a presumption that a transfer occurring more than six years after cessation of the marriage is not incident to the divorce. However, the presumption is a rebuttable presumption.[18]

A transfer of property can come within the non-recognition provision when it is paid to a third party on behalf of the payor spouse. The transfer to the third party must be required by the divorce or separation instrument or be made pursuant to the written request of the non-transferring spouse.[19] The property is treated as first being transferred from the transferring spouse to the recipient spouse in a transaction covered by the non-recognition provision. Next, the recipient spouse is treated as transferring the property to the third party in a transaction not covered by the non-recognition provision.

---

15. Section 1041(a).
16. Section 1041(b).
17. Section 1041(c).
18. Temp. Reg. § 1.1041-1T(a), Q&A-7.
19. Temp. Reg. § 1.1041-1T(c), Q&A-9.

Section 1041. Transfers of Property Between Spouses or Incident to Divorce

(a) General Rule. — No gain or loss shall be recognized on a transfer of property from an individual to (or in trust for the benefit of) —

(1) a spouse; or

(2) a former spouse, but only if the transfer is incident to the divorce.

(b) Transfer Treated as Gift; Transferee Has Transferor's Bases. — In the case of any transfer of property described in subsection (a) —

(1) for purposes of this subtitle, the property shall be treated as acquired by the transferee by gift; and

(2) the basis of the transferee in the property shall be the adjusted basis of the transferor.

(c) Incident to Divorce. — For purposes of subsection (a)(2), a transfer of property is incident to the divorce if such transfer —

(1) occurs within 1 year after the date on which the marriage ceases; or

(2) is related to the cessation of the marriage.

* * *

Summary of Rules — Tax Consequences of a Divorce

Child Support: Not included in the income of the recipient spouse and not deductible by the payor spouse.

Alimony: Included in the income of the recipient spouse and deductible by the payor spouse.

Transfer of property: No gain or loss is recognized; recipient spouse takes transferor spouse's basis.

C. Miscellaneous Issues

A few other issues may arise related to a divorce.

Dependency Exemption. A parent is entitled to claim a dependency exemption for a qualifying child. If the parents are divorced, generally the custodial parent will be entitled to claim the exemption.[20] Which parent provides more support for the child is not relevant. Generally, the non-custodial parent is entitled to the dependency exemption only if, among other requirements, the custodial parent has released his right to the exemption in writing.[21]

---

20. Section 152(a)(1), (c)(1)(B), (c)(4)(B).
21. Section 152(e)(2).

Filing status. A parent who has custody of the child can file as head of household. This status does not change if the parent has released the dependency exemption to the non-custodial spouse.

Legal fees. As part of the divorce process the parties may have obtained legal counsel. Whether the fees paid to the respective attorneys are deductible is determined based on the "origin of the claim." Because a divorce falls into the "personal" category, generally such legal fees are not deductible. However, fees related to obtaining alimony are deductible.[22]

D. Application of Rules

Example 1. Sandy and Tom are divorced. Under the divorce decree Tom is required to pay Sandy $5,000 each year in child support. Sandy is not required to include the $5,000 in income and Tom is not entitled to a deduction.

Example 2. Monique and David are divorced. Under the divorce decree Monique is required to pay David $10,000 in alimony payments each year until their child turns 18. Because the payments are clearly associated with a contingency related to a child, the payment is presumed to be child support irrespective of the fact the parties called the payment alimony. Unless the presumption can be rebutted, David is not required to include the $10,000 in income and Monique is not entitled to a deduction for the payment.

Example 3. Brett and Meg are divorced. Under the divorce decree Brett is required to pay Meg $5,000 each year in alimony. Brett is entitled to a $5,000 deduction and Meg must include $5,000 in her income.

Example 4. Susan and Jeff are married. Jeff transfers InvestCo stock to Susan. His basis in the stock is $10,000 and it is worth $50,000. Because the property is transferred between spouses, the non-recognition provision applies. Jeff does not recognize any gain on disposition of the stock, and Susan's basis in the stock is $10,000.

Example 5. Randy and Julie are divorced. As part of the property settlement Julie transfers InvestCo stock to Randy. Her basis in the stock is $20,000 and it is worth $5,000. Because the property is transferred incident to a divorce, the non-recognition provision applies. Julie does not recognize any loss on disposition of the stock, and Randy's basis in the stock is $20,000.

E. Problems

1. Kevin and Kim are divorced. Under the divorce decree Kevin is required to pay Kim $5,000 each year in child support. What are the tax consequences to Kevin and Kim from the payment of child support?

2. Verne and Brittney are divorced. Would the payment under the following facts be considered alimony?

---

22. Treas. Reg. § 1.262-1(b)(7). Such fees are for the production of income and are subject to the 2 percent floor rule of Section 67.

a.   Verne began making $1,000 monthly payments to Brittney. He mailed them to her each month with a note that she was to treat them as alimony.

b.   Verne and Brittney were talking by phone and agreed that Brittney would pay Verne $1,000 per month as alimony.

c.   Verne's attorney sent a letter to Brittney's attorney proposing alimony payments from Verne to Brittney of $1,000 per month. Brittney's attorney sent a letter agreeing to the arrangement.

3.   Martha and Mike entered into a written agreement providing that Martha would pay Mike $5,000 each year in alimony. This year, because she did not have any cash, she transferred a painting valued at $5,000 to Mike. What are the tax consequences to Martha and Mike?

4.   Hillary and Tom have one child, Kitty. Hillary and Tom entered into a written agreement providing that Tom would pay Hillary $5,000 each year in alimony and $10,000 each year in child support. All payments will stop when Kitty turns 18. What are the tax consequences to Hillary and Tom?

5.   Doug and Annette are getting divorced. Doug agreed to transfer Blueacre to Annette as long as Annette agreed to treat the transfer as a sale by Doug. Doug's basis in Blueacre was $10,000 and its fair market value was $2,000.

a.   What are the tax consequences to Doug?

b.   What are the tax consequences to Annette?

6.   Pursuant to the divorce agreement Amy was required to transfer Blackacre to Harrison. Amy's basis in Blackarce was $2,000 and its fair market value was $10,000. Before Amy could complete the transfer she received a written request from Harrison to transfer the property to Rick. Rick is not related to Amy or Harrison. What are the tax consequences to Amy, Harrison, and Rick?

7.   Jason and Lauren went through a bitter divorce. Both Jason and Lauren hired an attorney and incurred substantial legal fees. Lauren argued that she was entitled to stock owned by Jason and to alimony payments. Jason disagreed. The parties eventually agreed that Jason would keep the stock, but pay Lauren $10,000 a year in alimony.

a.   Can Jason deduct the legal fees he incurred?

b.   Can Lauren deduct the legal fees she incurred?

F. Analysis and Application

1.   Do you agree that legal fees related to obtaining alimony should be deductible while other legal fees related to the divorce are not?

2.   Kirk and Dayna are getting divorced. They are in negotiations for the amount of alimony and child support payments Dayna will be required to pay to Kirk. Dayna believes she will pay Kirk a total of $10,000 of each year. How would she want the payments allocated between child support and alimony? Do you need any additional information to make the decision? If so, what information?

3.   Stacey and Don are getting divorced. Don will be required to pay Stacey $10,000 each year in alimony.

a. If they elect to have the payment not be treated as alimony, what are the tax consequences?

b. Under what circumstances might the parties elect out of alimony treatment?

4. Max and Marlene are getting divorced. They own the following assets and have agreed they each will receive half the value of the assets. If you represent Marlene, which assets would you recommend she receive? Why?

Asset	Adjusted basis	Fair market value
Cash	$10,000	$10,000
Stock	1,000	20,000
Investment property	18,000	20,000

5. Diana and Charles are getting divorced. They own the following assets and have agreed they each will receive half the value of the assets. If you represent Diana, which assets would you recommend she receive? Why?

Asset	Adjusted basis	Fair market value
Car	$10,000	$3,000
Boat	50,000	47,000
Cash	50,000	50,000
Stock	50,000	70,000
Investment property	100,000	120,000
Apartment building	100,000	200,000

Chapter 48

Hobbies

Deductions

Personal:	Investment:	Business:
• Interest	• Expenses	• Start up expenses
• Taxes	• Depreciation and	• Expenses
• Medical expenses	amortization	• Depreciation and
• Education expenses	• Loss from the	amortization
• Moving expenses	disposition of property	• Losses from the
• Child care expenses	• Non-business bad debts	disposition of property
• Charitable contributions		• Business bad debts
• Casualty loses		
• Non-business bad debts		
• Alimony		

Read

Code Section 183(a)-(d)

Treas. Reg. §§ 1.183-1(a), (b)(1), (b)(2), (d)(1), (d)(2), (e); 1.183-2

A. Background

Gross income. Gross income includes income (accessions to wealth) derived from any and all sources.[23] It includes every accession to wealth, unless there is an exception, including gains from dealings in property.[24]

Business. Neither the Code nor the regulations provides a definition of business. The Supreme Court held that, to be engaged in a business, the taxpayer had to be involved in the activity with continuity and regularity; the taxpayer's primary purpose for engaging in the activity must be for income or profit. A sporadic activity, a hobby, or an amusement diversion does not qualify. The determination is based on an examination of the facts.[25]

---

23. Section 61(a).
24. Section 61(a)(3).
25. Commissioner v. Groetzinger, 480 U.S. 23 (1987).

Personal expenditures. In general, personal expenses are not deductible. Congress does not consider a personal expense an item that should offset the taxpayer's gross income.[26] In other words, it is not considered part of the cost of earning or generating gross income. Any deduction permitted for a personal expense is an exception to this broad-based rule. Accordingly, if the taxpayer wants to claim a deduction on his income tax return for a personal expense, he must establish that Congress specifically provided an exception to this general rule.

B. Expenditures Arising from Hobbies — General Rules

The taxpayer may enter into an activity that has both personal and business characteristics. In some situations, the personal aspects outweigh the business aspects. Such activities are often referred to as hobbies. Congress did not want taxpayers to be able to use the cost of their hobbies to offset their income from other sources. While it is actually a deduction-allowing provision, Section 183 provides this limitation.

If the taxpayer's activity is engaged in for profit, any deductions would be allowed under the relevant Code section, such as Section 212 for investment activities or Section 162 for business activities. If the activity is not engaged in for profit, Section 183 allows a taxpayer to claim deductions up to the amount of the income earned from the activity. Because the relevant applicable Code section depends on whether the activity is engaged in for profit, it is important to determine if the taxpayer meets this criteria. The regulations provide nine factors that can be used to make this determination:[27]

- Manner in which the taxpayer carries on the activity;
- Expertise of the taxpayer or his advisors;
- Time and effort expended by the taxpayer in carrying on the activity;
- Expectation that assets used in the activity may appreciate in value;
- Success of the taxpayer in carrying on other similar or dissimilar activities;
- Taxpayer's history of income or losses with respect to the activity;
- Amount of occasional profits;
- Financial status of the taxpayer; and
- Elements of personal pleasure or recreation.

No one factor is determinative nor is the evaluation of the activity limited to the nine factors. All relevant facts and circumstances are taken into consideration.[28] Less weight is given to the taxpayer's statement of his intent than to objective facts.[29] However, the fact that a taxpayer enjoys an activity does not, based on that alone, make the activity a hobby.[30]

---

26. Section 262.
27. Treas. Reg. § 1.183-2(b).
28. Treas. Reg. § 1.183-2(b).
29. Treas. Reg. § 1.183-2(a).
30. Treas. Reg. § 1.183-2(b)(9).

One of the leading cases in the area of hobby losses is *Dreicer v. Commissioner*.[31] The taxpayer wrote a book on tourism and dining, but the book was not a success. He planned to write a second book which would be a compilation of his opinions on travel and fine restaurants. For 20 years he traveled around the world, staying in fine hotels and eating at fine restaurants. He used the information he had gathered to lecture before travel organizations and make public appearances. Eventually, he prepared a draft of the second book but could not find a publisher. On his 1972 and 1973 income tax return he claimed losses of $21,796 and $28,022 related to his travel and other related expenses.

In determining whether the expenses were deductible the test, as established by the Court of Appeals for the District of Columbia, was whether the evidence established the activity was engaged in for profit. It was not relevant whether there was a reasonable expectation of profit. On remand, the Tax Court noted that the taxpayer's stated motive was not controlling. Rather, the determination was to be made based on the facts and circumstances.

The taxpayer argued he was dedicated, continuing his activities even though he had not been successful in the hopes of one day making a large profit. The Tax Court noted the substantial losses incurred each year for many years, that there was no realistic possibility profits could offset the losses, and the fact the taxpayer could cover the expenses from his personal resources. It concluded that the taxpayer did not enter into the activity with an intent to make a profit. Accordingly, Section 183 was applicable, allowing him to claim deductions only to the extent of income from the activity.

Presumption. There is a rebuttable presumption that the taxpayer was engaged in the activity for profit during the year if the activity was profitable for three years in the five-year period ending with the year being considered. If the activity is breeding, training, showing, or racing horses, the rebuttable presumption arises if the taxpayer was profitable for two years in the seven-year period ending with the year being considered.[32] If the presumption does not apply, the taxpayer can still establish the activity was for-profit under the facts and circumstances test.[33]

Application of Section 183. If the activity is not engaged in for profit, the taxpayer can claim deductions only as allowed by Section 183.

Note

If the activity was a business, the taxpayer could deduct any expenses as allowed by Section 162 (and Section 183 would not be applicable).

If the activity was an investment, the taxpayer could deduct any expenses as allowed by Section 212 (and Section 183 would not be applicable).

Section 183 divides expenses into three groups. The first group consists of expenses the taxpayer could deduct irrespective of whether the activity was engaged in for profit.[34] Examples of expenses that would fall into this category are home mortgage interest and

---

31. 78 T.C. 642 (1982).
32. Section 183(d).
33. Treas. Reg. § 1.183-1(c)(1).
34. Section 183(b)(1); Treas. Reg. § 1.183-1(b)(1)(i).

state and local taxes. The taxpayer can deduct these expenses regardless of the amount of income the activity generates.

Expenses in the second and third groups can be deducted only to the extent of any net income after taking into consideration the deductions allowed from the first group. The second group of deductions includes those that do not result in an adjustment to basis and that would be allowed if the activity were engaged in for profit.[35] This group includes expenses that traditionally would fall within Section 162 and 212 if the activity were engaged in for profit.

Expenses in the third group can be deducted only to the extent of any net income after taking into consideration the deductions allowed from the first and second groups. The third group of deductions includes those that result in an adjustment to basis and would be allowed if the activity were engaged in for profit.[36] This group includes items such as depreciation and amortization.

General Rules — Hobby Activities

Determine all activities that are hobbies (i.e., an activity not engaged in for profit). For each hobby activity, deductions are allowed to the extent of income as follows:

First: Expenses the taxpayer could deduct irrespective of whether the activity was engaged in for profit.

Second: To the extent of any remaining income, expenses.

Third: To the extent of any remaining income, depreciation.

Any remaining income must be reported.

C. Application of Rules

Example 1. Scott operated a farm that abutted a residential area. The farm had been in his family for many years and during that time it had never generated a profit. Scott is employed as a banker and earns a substantial income. While Scott lived on the farm property, a farm manager operated the farm. Scott does not engage in the farming activity for profit.

Example 2. Angus is an independent oil and gas operator. He often searched for oil on undeveloped and unexplored land that was not near proven fields. He used the same exploration methods as others who engaged in the same activity. Based on the nature of the industry, it was unlikely Angus would find a commercially-profitable oil deposit. However, if a well were discovered, he would earn a sizable return. Angus is engaged in the activity of oil drilling for profit.

---

35. Section 183(b)(2); Treas. Reg. § 1.183-1(b)(1)(ii).
36. Section 183(b)(2); Treas. Reg. § 1.183-1(b)(1)(iii).

D. Problems

1. Irwin intended to be a fiction writer. In support of his craft he would write for five hours every day. In addition, he kept a journal of his everyday experiences so that he could draw upon them as needed in his writing. Based on his writing activity and use of his everyday experiences in his writing, Irwin deducted his living expenses, including the cost of a hot tub, his daughter's college board expense, and travel to a funeral. He had not yet been published. Is Irwin engaged in the writing activity for profit?

2. Trish owned a golden retriever, Striker, who had won many confirmation competitions. After he had won champion at the local competition, she began a dog breeding operation. Given the vet costs, showing costs, food costs, etc., to date she has not earned a profit. Is she engaged in the dog breeding activity for profit? Do you need any additional information?

3. Nora had owned horses growing up and had always wanted to work with horses as an adult. Five years ago, she purchased seven Arabians and began a breeding operation. While she had a full time job, when she wasn't working at her job, she trained, rode, and showed the horses. During the past five years, she sold only two horses, and sold them for half the asking price. She and her daughter won many awards when showing the horses and participated in nationally competitive horse shows. She advertised her sale horses on a website. Each year since she began the operation she had a net loss. Is Nora engaged in the horse breeding activity for profit?

Chapter 49

Dual-Use Property

Deductions

Personal:	Investment:	Business:
• Interest • Taxes • Medical expenses • Education expenses • Moving expenses • Child care expenses • Charitable contributions • Casualty loses • Non-business bad debts • Alimony	• Expenses • Depreciation and amortization • Loss from the disposition of property • Non-business bad debts	• Start up expenses • Expenses • Depreciation and amortization • Losses from the disposition of property • Business bad debts

Read

Code Sections 280A(a), (b), (c)(1), (c)(5), (d)(1), (d)(2), (e)

A. Background

Gross income. Gross income includes income (accessions to wealth) derived from any and all sources.[37] It includes every accession to wealth, unless there is an exception, including gains from dealings in property.[38]

Business. Neither the Code nor the regulations provides a definition of business. The Supreme Court held that, to be engaged in a business, the taxpayer had to be involved in the activity with continuity and regularity; the taxpayer's primary purpose for engaging in the activity must be for income or profit. A sporadic activity, a hobby, or an amusement diversion does not qualify. The determination is based on an examination of the facts.[39]

Personal expenditures. In general, personal expenses are not deductible. Congress does not consider a personal expense an item that should offset the taxpayer's gross income.[40]

---

37. Section 61(a).
38. Section 61(a)(3).
39. Commissioner v. Groetzinger, 480 U.S. 23 (1987).
40. Section 262.

In other words, it is not considered part of the cost of earning or generating gross income. Any deduction permitted for a personal expense is an exception to this broad-based rule. Accordingly, if the taxpayer wants to claim a deduction on his income tax return for a personal expense, he must establish that Congress specifically provided an exception to this general rule.

B. Deductions Related to a Home Office

When a taxpayer uses space in his home for an office, there is a blurring of the lines between business use and personal use. Moreover, it provides an opportunity for a taxpayer to convert personal expenses into deductible expenses. Accordingly, the Service has carefully scrutinized claims for deductions based on a business use of a portion of the home.

The general rule is that a taxpayer is not entitled to a deduction for use of a dwelling unit during the year as a residence.[41] The Code provides an exception with respect to the portion of the home used as a home office if the taxpayer can show the space is exclusively used on a regular basis and is:[42]

- The business's principal place of business;
- A place of business used by patients, clients, or customers in meeting or dealing with the taxpayer in the normal course of business; or
- In the case of a separate structure not attached to the home, used in connection with the taxpayer's business.

If the taxpayer is an employee, the deduction is allowed if the taxpayer can establish one of the above uses and the exclusive use is for the convenience of his employer.[43]

Principal place of business. A home office can be a principal place of business if used for administrative or management activities and there is no other fixed location for the business where the taxpayer conducts substantial administrative or management activities.[44]

Convenience of the employer. If the taxpayer is an employee, he must establish the use was for the convenience of his employer. The taxpayer can satisfy this criteria if he can establish the office was necessary as a practical matter to carry out his employment duties. In *Weissman v. Commissioner*,[45] the taxpayer was a college professor. As a condition of his

---

41. Section 280A(a). Deductions otherwise permitted are still allowed, such as deductions for home mortgage interest, taxes, and casualty losses. Section 280A(b).

42. Section 280A(c)(1).

43. Section 280A(c), flush language.

44. Section 280A(c), flush language. Before being amended by Congress, the place of business element was considered by the Supreme Court. In *Soliman v. Commissioner*, 113 S. Ct. 701 (1993), the taxpayer was a self-employed anesthesiologist who worked at three hospitals. His most significant services were provided at the hospitals. Accordingly, even though his home office was essential to carrying on his medical practice, it was not his principal place of business. The Supreme Court held that the principal place of business was the most important or significant place for the business, which in turn was based on "the relative importance of the activities performed at each business location and the time spent at each place." Because the activities performed at home were the least important, he was not entitled to the home office deduction.

45. 751 F.2d 512 (2d Cir. 1984).

employment, he was required to engage in scholarly research and writing. Because his employer provided him only with office space shared with several other professors, he used a room in his home as an office. He spent 80 percent of his work hours in his home office. The court held that use of a home office was not the taxpayer's personal preference. In addition, because it spared the employer the cost of providing private office space, it was for the convenience of the employer.

Limitation on amount of deductions. If the taxpayer meets the criteria of Section 280A(c)(1), there is a limit on the amount he can deduct.[46] A deduction for certain expenses cannot exceed the amount of income derived from the use of the residence for business purposes, reduced by two amounts.[47] The first amount is amounts the taxpayer could deduct irrespective of whether the home office was used for business purposes.[48] Examples of expenses that would fall into this category are home mortgage interest and real estate taxes allocable to the home office. The second amount is deductions attributable to the business activity but not allocable to the home office itself.[49] Examples of expenses that would fall into this category are business telephone, secretarial expense, and internet access.

C. Deductions Related to a Vacation Home

When a taxpayer rents out a vacation home, there is a blurring of the lines between investment use and personal use. Moreover, it provides an opportunity for a taxpayer to convert personal expenses into deductible expenses. Accordingly, the Service has carefully scrutinized claims for deductions based on an investment use of a vacation home.

The general rule is that a taxpayer is not entitled to a deduction for use of a dwelling unit during the year as a residence.[50] The limitation does not apply to costs related to the rental of a dwelling unit. The Code provides that a taxpayer uses a dwelling unit as a residence if he uses the unit for personal purposes for a number of days that exceeds the greater of:[51]

- 14 days; or

- 10 percent of the number of days during the year for which the vacation home is rented at fair market value.

Limitation on amount of deductions. If the taxpayer meets the criteria of Section 280A(d)(1), there is a limit on the amount he can deduct.[52] The deductions cannot exceed the amount of rental income, reduced by two amounts.[53] The first amount is amounts

---

46. Section 280A(c)(5).

47. Section 280A(c)(5). For the deductions that are not allowed, Section 280A provides a limited carryover to the following year. Section 280A(c)(5), flush language.

48. Section 280A(c)(B)(i).

49. Section 280A(c)(B)(ii).

50. Section 280A(a). Deductions otherwise permitted are still allowed, such as deductions for home mortgage interest, taxes, and casualty losses. Section 280A(b).

51. Section 280A(d)(1). Any day the property is used for personal purposes, it cannot be considered as being rented for fair value.

52. Section 280A(c)(5).

53. Section 280A(c)(3), (c)(5). For the deductions that are not allowed, Section 280A provides a limited carryover to the following year. Section 280A(c)(5), flush language.

the taxpayer could deduct irrespective of whether the property was rented.[54] Examples of expenses that would fall into this category are home mortgage interest and real estate taxes allocable to the property.

The second amount is deductions attributable to the rental activity but not allocable to the rental property itself.[55] Examples of expenses that would fall into this category are house cleaning, garbage pick-up, and internet access. In general, the expenses should be allocated on a ratable basis to each day of the tax year, regardless of the use of the unit on any given day.[56] The portion of expenses allocable to rental activities is limited to an amount based on the ratio of time the home is rented to the total time the vacation home is used for all purposes, including rental.[57]

D. Application of Rules

Example 1. Stan is a self-employed computer consultant. He uses a home office on a regular basis as a place of business for meeting with clients. He does not use the office for other reasons and has no other office from which he works. He has a business phone line and occasionally employs a secretary. Stan determined that 10 percent of the expenses associated with the residence are allocable to the home office.

Stan can show the home office is exclusively used on a regular basis and is his business's principal place of business. Stan has established a home office and can deduct the expenses associated with the office (subject to the limitation of Section 280A(c)(5)).

Example 2. Paulette is a buyer for a department store. Her employer provides her an office on its business premises. Because some of the suppliers are in different time zones, Paulette often finds it convenient to call suppliers from her home office.

Paulette cannot establish that the home office is the business's principal place of business or a place of business used by patients, clients, or customers in meeting or dealing with the taxpayer in the normal course of business. Nor can she establish that use of the home office is for the convenience of her employer. Paulette is not entitled to any deductions based on her use of the home office.

Example 3. Nicole owns and operates a hotel which is used exclusively by paying customers on a short-term basis. Nicole's hotel operation is a business and her deductions are not limited by Section 280A.

Example 4. Meg owns a condo on Kauai. While Meg lives in Wisconsin, she stays in the condo during the entire month of January and February. During the remainder of the year she offers the condo for rent. Because she uses the condo as a dwelling unit (she uses it for personal purposes for greater than 10 days or 10 percent of the days it is offered for rent), she can claim deductions attributable to the rental, as limited by Section 280A.

---

54. Section 280A(c)(B)(i).
55. Section 280A(c)(B)(ii).
56. Bolton v. Commissioner, 694 F.2d 556 (9th Cir. 1982).
57. Section 280A(e)(1).

E. Problems

1. Kevin is a high school science teacher. While he has been assigned a home room, he does not have an office at the school. During the school year Kevin assigns many experiments. He likes to go through each experiment before he assigns it. Given the flow of students through the classroom during the day, it is not possible for Kevin to run them at the school. Accordingly, he uses a spare room in his house to carry out the experiments.

    Is Kevin entitled to a home office deduction for the use of the spare room in his house?

2. Martha is a self-employed therapist. She has an office where she meets with clients. However, she prefers to complete her administrative responsibilities from her home office. Accordingly, she uses a room in her home to bill clients, update file notes, and schedule appointments. She does not use the space in her home for other purposes.

    Is Martha entitled to a home office deduction for the use of the room in her home?

3. Katie is a traveling large animal vet, traveling to her clients' residences to treat their horses. She stores all of her equipment and medicines in the truck she uses for her veterinary business. She uses a room in her home to bill clients, order supplies, schedule appointments, and make follow-up calls to clients. Occasionally clients will pick up medicine from her at her home. Katie does not use the room in her home for other purposes.

    Is Katie entitled to a home office deduction for the use of the room in her home?

4. Bob owns a townhouse in Vail, Colorado. He uses the townhouse during one weekend each year. The remainder of the year he lives and works in Tampa, Florida, and rents out the townhouse.

    a. Are the expenses attributable to the townhouse deductible?

    b. If so, is the amount he can deduct limited by Section 280A?

5. Melissa owns a cabin in Tahoe City. Each year she spend one week at the cabin. The remainder of the year she lives and works in Seattle and rents out the cabin.

    a. Are the expenses attributable to the cabin deductible?

    b. If so, is the amount she can deduct limited by Section 280A?

XII

Miscellaneous

Chapter 50

Tax Litigation

A. U.S. Constitution

The authority of Congress to impose tax is found in the Constitution of the United States. Specifically, the Constitution gives Congress the authority "to lay and collect Taxes, Duties, Imposts and Excises."[1] This provision has been interpreted as giving Congress a very broad power of taxation.

The uniformity clause provides that "all Duties, Imposts and Excises shall be uniform throughout the United States."[2] This clause has been interpreted as requiring that the same tax regime apply regardless of the locale of the taxpayer. In other words, the tax code that applies to the residents of Alaska must be the same tax code that applies to the residents of Florida.

If the tax constitutes a "direct tax," the Constitution imposes the additional requirement that it "be apportioned among the several States"[3] and that "[n]o capitation, or other direct, Tax shall be laid, unless in Proportion to the Census or Enumeration herein before directed to be taken."[4] The courts have interpreted these provisions as requiring that any direct tax be apportioned among the states based on their respective populations. The Sixteenth Amendment removed the apportionment requirement. Since this amendment was ratified the courts have found all income tax codes to be constitutional.

B. Determination of a Deficiency in Taxpayer's Income Tax

If the Internal Revenue Service (IRS) proposes changes to the taxpayer's income tax return that would increase the taxpayer's tax liability and the taxpayer does not agree with the proposed changes, there are three possible trial courts to which the taxpayer can go to have his case heard—the Tax Court, the Court of Federal Claims, or federal district court. Procedurally, a case pursued in the Tax Court is at a different stage in the administrative process than a case pursued in the Court of Federal Claims or district

---

1. Article I, section 8.
2. Article I, section 8, clause 1
3. Article I, section 2, clause 3.
4. Article I, section 9, clause 4.

court. Nonetheless, because the taxpayer is the party who initiates the lawsuit, which court hears the dispute is determined largely by the taxpayer.

Practice Note

With a few limited exceptions, in tax litigation the taxpayer is always the party bringing the suit — the petitioner or complainant.

To bring an action in the Tax Court, the taxpayer must file a petition generally within 90 days from the date a statutory notice of deficiency was mailed to him.[5] No tax has been assessed (an assessment is a bookkeeping entry noting the liability of the taxpayer), and the taxpayer does not pay the tax prior to filing suit.

To bring an action in the Court of Federal Claims or district court, all tax liabilities must be assessed and paid.[6] Next, the taxpayer must file a claim for refund with the IRS for the amount he believes he overpaid.[7] If the IRS denies the refund claim, he can file suit in the Court of Federal Claims or district court.

The court in which the taxpayer decides to bring his suit will depend in part on the characteristics of the trial courts and in part on the taxpayer's individual circumstances. Once the taxpayer has made his decision and the trial-level proceedings are concluded, the losing party can appeal the decision to the applicable circuit court of appeals.[8] From the circuit court of appeals, the next level of judicial review is the United States Supreme Court.[9]

Relationship of the Courts

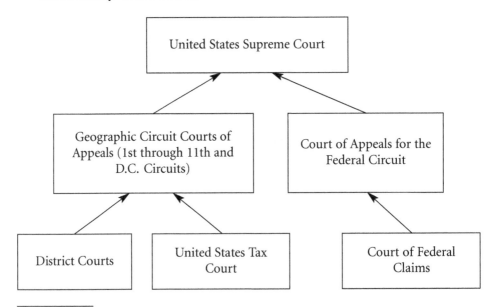

---

5. Sections 6212; 6213.
6. Flora v. United States, 362 U.S. 145 (1960).
7. Section 7422.
8. Section 7482; 28 U.S.C. § 1291.
9. 28 U.S.C. § 1291.

C. Trial Courts

Tax Court. The United States Tax Court is a specialized court established under Article I of the United States Constitution.[10] It hears only tax cases.[11] As a regular judicial court, it has the same powers regarding contempt and the carrying out of writs and orders as other federal courts. Its jurisdiction extends to hearing tax disputes concerning notices of deficiency, notices of transferee liability, certain types of declaratory judgment, readjustment and adjustment of partnership items, review of the failure to abate interest, administrative costs, worker classification, relief from joint and several liability on a joint return, and review of certain collection actions.

Because the Tax Court hears only tax cases, the judges are specialists in tax law. The Tax Court is located in Washington, D.C., but the judges travel to locations throughout the country. Hearings and trials are held before a single judge, and no jury trial is available.[12] The IRS is represented in the Tax Court by the Office of Chief Counsel.

Practice Note

To practice before the United States Tax Court, the representative need not be an attorney. However, he must be admitted to the Tax Court Bar and enter an appearance in the Tax Court case.

Court of Federal Claims. The U.S. Court of Federal Claims began as the U.S. Court of Claims in 1855. In 1982, the Court of Claims was abolished and replaced by the U.S. Claims Court. In 1992, the court was renamed the U.S. Court of Federal Claims.

Years	Name
1855–1982	U.S. Court of Claims
1982–1992	Claims Court
1992–present	U.S. Court of Federal Claims

The court has jurisdiction over all monetary claims against the Federal government, one of which is tax refunds.[13] The judges are not specialists in technical tax law. Like the Tax Court, the Court of Federal Claims is a national court located in Washington, D.C., and the judges travel to locations throughout the country.[14] Hearings and trials are held before a single judge, and no jury trial is available.[15] The IRS is represented in the Court of Federal Claims by the Department of Justice.

---

10. Section 7441.
11. See Section 6213.
12. Section 7445.
13. 28 U.S.C. §§ 1346(a)(1); 1491.
14. 28 U.S.C. §§ 173; 795.
15. 28 U.S.C. § 2402.

District Court. United States district courts are trial courts located throughout the United States that hear legal issues on any matter that could arise under the United States Code, including tax issues.[16] Therefore, the judges are not tax specialists.

The district court where the taxpayer would file his claim depends on the location in which he lives or conducts business. Either the taxpayer or the government can request a jury trial.[17] The IRS is represented in district court by the Department of Justice.

D. The Internal Revenue Service and the Office of Chief Counsel

Internal Revenue Service. The Internal Revenue Service is responsible for the collection of taxes and enforcement of the Internal Revenue Code. It is overseen by the Commissioner. The IRS is organized into units that serve groups of taxpayers with similar needs, or operating divisions based on the type of taxpayer served:

- Wage and Investment Division. It serves individuals earning wages who do not file a Schedule C, E, F, or Form 2106.

- Small Business/Self-Employed Division. It serves individuals filing Schedules C, E, F and Form 2106, corporations and partnerships having assets of less $10 million, estate and gift taxpayers, fiduciary returns, and individuals with international returns.

- Large Business and International Division. It serves C corporations, S corporations, and partnerships with assets equal to or greater than $10 million. It also includes an International unit.

- Tax-Exempt and Government Entities Division. It serves the customer segments of Employee Plans, Exempt Organizations, and Government Entities (including Indian Tribal Governments, Federal, State and Local Governments, and Tax Exempt Bond Issuances).

There is a Criminal Investigation Division that provides the law enforcement arm of the IRS. Its agents participate in many types of criminal cases, including money laundering and illegal source income.

Office of Chief Counsel. The Office of Chief Counsel is the legal arm for the IRS. It is overseen by the Chief Counsel. Within the Office of Chief Counsel are Offices of Associate Chief Counsel. These Offices make up what is generally referred to as the National Office. Each Office has jurisdiction over specific Code sections or issues and is responsible for addressing issues and/or preparing guidance involving the Code sections or issues over which it has jurisdiction.

The Office of Chief Counsel has a field component, or the Division Counsel Offices. Each Office is responsible for representing the Commissioner in litigation before the Tax Court and related matters. While the Headquarters of each Division is located in Washington, D.C., there are many local, or field, offices throughout the United States. The Divisions mirror those of the IRS, being organized by the taxpayer served.

---

16. 28 U.S.C. §§ 132; 1331; 1340
17. 28 U.S.C. §§ 2402; 1346(a)(1).

Comparison of Trial Courts

	United States Tax Court	District court	Court of Federal Claims
Must the taxpayer prepay the tax in dispute?	No.	Yes.	Yes.
Is a jury trial available?	No.	Yes.	No.
Which circuit court law is precedential?	Precedent from the circuit court of appeals of the circuit in which the case is brought (generally the circuit in which the taxpayer resided or where the corporation's principal place of business was when the litigation began).	Precedent from the circuit court of appeals of the circuit in which the case is brought (generally the circuit in which the taxpayer resided or where the corporation's principal place of business was when the litigation began).	Precedent from the Court of Appeals for the Federal Circuit.
Expertise of the judge?	Tax expert.	Not a tax expert.	Not a tax expert.
Location of the court?	Various; the court is located in Washington, D.C., but circuit rides.	Various districts.	Various; the court is located in Washington, D.C., but circuit rides.
Who represents the government?	Attorneys from the IRS's Office of Chief Counsel.	Attorneys from the Department of Justice.	Attorneys from the Department of Justice.
Who is the defendant?	Commissioner.	United States.	United States.
Who has the burden of proof?	Generally, the taxpayer.	Generally, the taxpayer.	Generally, the taxpayer.

Chapter 51

Tax Research

A. Court Opinions

The Tax Court issues three types of opinions. It publishes only those opinions it considers as containing legal principles useful as precedent. Such cases are referred to as regular opinions and, of all the Tax Court opinions, are the most authoritative. The government publishes the regular opinions of the Tax Court in the Reports of the United States Tax Court. Or, they can be found on the Tax Court website, www.ustaxcourt.gov.

The bulk of the remainder of the opinions, memorandum opinions, are not officially published by the Tax Court. Such opinions do not set forth any new law but are helpful in illustrating particular factual situations or demonstrating how the court applies a particular rule of law. They are published by commercial publishers. The last category of opinions, summary opinions, are issued under the small case procedures and have no precedential value.

While district court, Court of Federal Claims, circuit courts of appeals, and Supreme Court opinions can be found in traditional sources (Federal Reporters and Federal Supplements), commercial publishers have compiled opinions that address tax issues from all of these courts into one series. CCH publishes United States Tax Cases (USTC) and RIA publishes American Federal Tax Reports (AFTR). Note that neither of these publications contains any Tax Court opinions, whether regular or memorandum.

B. Regulations

Regulations are issued to assist the public in interpreting and understanding the Code. Section 7805 gives the Secretary of the Treasury Department general authority to issue such regulations.

Proposed regulations. A regulation is first issued in proposed form, followed by a notice and comment period. Because a proposed regulation is nothing more than a proposed interpretation of a Code section advocated by the IRS, courts do not give it any judicial deference. However, as a practical matter, if the proposed regulation closely follows the legislative history of the section and the IRS's interpretation has been consistent over a number of years, a court will generally use it as a guide in interpreting the section.

Final regulations. After the public has been given an opportunity to provide input, the regulation can be issued in its final form. Generally, before issuing the final regulation, the IRS will make minor changes it deems necessary to the proposed regulation based on comments received from the public.

Temporary Regulations. By statute, temporary regulations are a hybrid form of regulation.[18] They are treated the same as a final regulation that has been through the notice and comment period even though they are in fact issued without a notice and comment period.[19] However, at the same time it issues the temporary regulation, the IRS must issue the regulation as a proposed regulation and follow the same notice and comment procedures, just as it would with any other proposed regulation.[20]

The IRS issues a temporary regulation when it wants to provide immediate guidance to the public without waiting for a notice and comment period. Temporary regulations are issued most often when Congress has passed new legislation and the public needs immediate guidance on implementing the legislation. For temporary regulations issued after November 20, 1988, the IRS has three years from issuance of the temporary regulation to process it from its proposed form into a final regulation. If it fails to do so, the temporary regulation will expire and no longer be given the same effect as a final regulation.[21] If the temporary regulation was issued on or before November 20, 1988, it remains effective, even if it never becomes a final regulation.

Numbering system. Each regulation is given a number. The number before the period reflects the "part" of the Code of Federal Regulations (CFR) in which the regulation is contained and indicates the type of regulation, such as income tax, estate and gift tax, or excise tax. The number after the period indicates the section to which the regulation relates. The number after the dash indicates the sequential order of the regulation issued under that section. A "T" following the number indicates the regulation is a temporary regulation. There is no correlation between the number after the dash and the subsection or other subdivision of the section it is interpreting.

Guide to Common Types of Tax Regulations

1. income tax
20. estate tax
25. gift tax
26. generation-skipping transfer tax
31. employment taxes
54. pension excise taxes
301. procedure and administration
601. procedural rules

---

18. See Section 7805(e).
19. Robinson v. Commissioner, 119 T.C. 44, 68 (2002); Peterson Marital Trust v. Commissioner, 102 T.C 790, 797 (1994), aff'd, 78 F.3d 795 (2d Cir. 1996).
20. Section 7805(e)(1).
21. Section 7805(e)(2).

C. Guidance Issued by the Government

The Office of Chief Counsel can issue a variety of types of guidance, all aimed at giving the public additional information about how the IRS interprets and intends to apply the Code and, therefore, how it expects the public to interpret and apply the Code. The specific purpose the guidance is to serve will dictate the form in which it is issued, e.g., Revenue Ruling, Revenue Procedure, or Publication. Because such guidance addresses an issue set forth in a non-taxpayer specific format, it is intended to be relied upon by all taxpayers to whom it might apply.

Revenue Rulings. A revenue ruling gives guidance on how the IRS will treat a particular transaction by applying the Code, regulations, and any related statutes or tax treaties to a specific factual situation. The rulings generally follow one basic format. First, the ruling sets forth the issues to be analyzed. Next, it sets forth a brief statement of non-taxpayer specific facts. It follows with a short analysis of the issue presented, primarily by setting forth the applicable Code sections and regulations. It ends with a conclusion for each issue presented.

Revenue rulings do not have the force and effect of regulations, but may be relied upon by a taxpayer if his facts and circumstances are substantially the same. A ruling is merely the position of the IRS on a particular issue. It may be helpful in interpreting a statute, but is not binding on the court; it will be given no special deference by the courts and is only as persuasive as the reasoning and precedents upon which it relies.[22] To the extent the IRS's position is favorable to the taxpayer, but inconsistent with legal precedent, it will be considered a concession by the IRS.[23]

A revenue ruling is identified by two numbers. The first number is the year in which the revenue ruling was issued. The second number represents, sequentially, the order in which the revenue rulings were issued that year. Revenue rulings can be found first in the Internal Revenue Bulletin and then in the Cumulative Bulletin.

Example. Rev. Rul. 79-24 was issued in 1979 and was the 24th revenue ruling issued that year.

Revenue Procedures. A revenue procedure is a statement of procedure that affects the rights or duties of taxpayers; it is published to announce practices and procedures for public guidance. A revenue procedure does not have the force and effect of a regulation, but may be relied upon by a taxpayer if his facts and circumstances are substantially the same.[24]

Revenue procedures are identified by two numbers. The first number is the year in which the revenue procedure was issued. The second number represents, sequentially, the order in which the revenue procedures were issued that year. As with revenue rulings, revenue procedures can be found first in the Internal Revenue Bulletin and then in the Cumulative Bulletin.

Example. Rev. Proc. 2010-1 was issued in 2010 and was the first revenue procedure issued that year.

---

22. See, e.g., Halliburton Company v. Commissioner, 100 T.C. 216, 231–32, 234 (1993), aff'd, 25 F.3d 1043 (5th Cir. 1994).
23. See Rauenhorst v. Commissioner, 119 T.C. 157, 169–73 (2002).
24. See, e.g., Security Bank of Minnesota v. Commissioner, 98 T.C. 33, 43 (1992).

Publications. The IRS has prepared a large number of pamphlets called publications covering a broad range of issues. They are prepared to assist taxpayers in understanding the Code. The publications rarely contain citations to the Code or regulations, but rather explain the Code in simple, layperson terms. They are intended for guidance purposes only and do not have the force and effect of law.

Practice Note

Publications can be found on the IRS website at www.irs.gov.

Examples

Publication 1, *Your Rights as a Taxpayer.*

Publication 17, *Your Federal Income Tax.*

Publication 587, *Business Use of Your Home.*

Publication 1542, *Per Diem Rates.*

Internal Revenue Bulletin and Cumulative Bulletin. The Internal Revenue Bulletin (IRB) is published weekly. It is the authoritative instrument for the publication of official rulings and procedures issued by the IRS as well as other tax documents of interest to taxpayers and tax practitioners.

Twice a year, the IRS compiles the weekly IRB into the Cumulative Bulletin. Volume 1 contains the IRB from week 1 through the IRB from week 26. Volume 2 contains the IRB from week 27 through the IRB from week 52. Public laws are published in Volume 3.

D. Treatises

Various commercial publishers have prepared treatises that contain a substantial amount of information about the Code and how it has been interpreted. Depending on the service, a researcher might find the Code, regulations, legislative history, and references to case law and various documents published by the government within the treatise.

Research through treatises organized by Code section. Commerce Clearing House (CCH) and the Research Institute of America (RIA) offer treatises that are organized by Code section. Quite simply, to begin researching in CCH or RIA, the researcher could turn to the Code section of interest.

CCH publishes the Standard Federal Tax Reporter series. Most tax research will begin in the relevant volume of the Compilations. The spine of each volume indicates which Code section and CCH paragraph reference numbers are contained in the volume. Thus, the researcher could simply turn to the Code section of interest. However, if the researcher is unsure which Code section to consider, he could use the topical index to locate paragraph references to places in the Compilations that discuss the matter of interest.

The Research Institute of America (RIA) publishes the United States Tax Reporter. Within its volumes the Code is arranged in numerical order. First, the Code section is presented, followed by portions of relevant Committee Reports, applicable regulations, RIA's explanation of the Code provision, and annotations of decisions and rulings. The spine of each volume indicates which Code section and RIA paragraph reference numbers and keyword topics are contained in the volume. The researcher could simply turn to the Code section of interest. However, if the researcher is unsure which Code section to consider, he could use the main topical index to locate paragraph references to places in the compilation volumes that discuss the matter of interest.

Research through treatises organized by topic. RIA and the Bureau of National Research (BNA) offer treatises that are organized by topic. To begin researching in RIA or BNA, the researcher could simply locate the volume that contains the topic of interest.

RIA publishes the RIA Tax Coordinator 2d. Each chapter discusses a particular subject matter or transaction. The analysis may include a discussion of the Code, regulations, legislative history, or important cases. If there has been a change in the law, the analysis will discuss the law prior to and after the change. To begin research, the researcher could simply locate the volume that contains the topic of interest. The spine of each volume indicates the topics covered in the volume.

BNA has prepared over 300 portfolios, authored by prominent attorneys or accountants, covering a myriad of topics. Each portfolio is divided into three sections. The first section, Detailed Analysis, offers a detailed analysis of the topic and might include any of the following: planning opportunities, alternative approaches, probable IRS positions, pertinent Code provisions, IRS rulings and procedures, tax cases on point and conflicting cases, and pitfalls to avoid. The second section, Working Papers, includes relevant forms, documents, and other background tools. The Working Papers might include any of the following: procedural checklists, IRS forms and documents, suggested resolutions and documents, forms for state and local use, sample plans and clauses, and related IRS information. The last section, the Bibliography and Reference section, includes a comprehensive list of documents useful to practitioners in conducting research.

Practice Note

BNA Portfolios are often a favored research source of practitioners due to the substantial number of Working Papers included in each portfolio.

Index